THE ROUGH GUIDE TO

HONOLULU

Forthcoming titles include

The Algarve • The Bahamas • Cambodia
The Caribbean • Costa Brava
New York Restaurants • South America • Zanzibar

Forthcoming reference guides include

Children's Books • Online Travel • Videogaming
Weather

Rough Guides online

www.roughguides.com

Rough Guide Credits

Text editors: Mary Callahan and Don Young
Series editor: Mark Ellingham
Production: Rachel Holmes
Cartography: Melissa Baker
Proofreading: Russell Walton

Publishing Information

This second edition published November 2001
by Rough Guides Ltd,
62–70 Shorts Gardens, London WC2H 9AH

Distributed by the Penguin Group:

Penguin Books Ltd, 80 Strand, London WC2R ORL
Penguin Putnam, Inc., 375 Hudson Street, New York 10014, USA
Penguin Books Australia Ltd, 487 Maroondah Highway,
PO Box 257, Ringwood, Victoria 3134, Australia
Penguin Books Canada Ltd, 10 Alcorn Avenue,
Toronto, Ontario, Canada M4V 1E4
Penguin Books (NZ) Ltd,
182–190 Wairau Road, Auckland 10, New Zealand

Typeset in Bembo and Helvetica to an original design by Henry Iles.
Printed in Spain by Graphy Cems.

THE ROUGH GUIDE TO

HONOLULU

by Greg Ward

ROUGH GUIDES

We set out to do something different when the first Rough Guide was published in 1982. Mark Ellingham, just out of university, was traveling in Greece. He brought along the popular guides of the day, but found they were all lacking in some way. They were either strong on ruins and museums but went on for pages without mentioning a beach or taverna. Or they were so conscious of the need to save money that they lost sight of Greece's cultural and historical significance. Also, none of the books told him anything about Greece's contemporary life – its politics, its culture, its people, and how they lived.

So with no job in prospect, Mark decided to write his own guidebook, one which aimed to provide practical information that was second to none, detailing the best beaches and the hottest clubs and restaurants, while also giving hard-hitting accounts of every sight, both famous and obscure, and providing up-to-the-minute information on contemporary culture. It was a guide that encouraged independent travelers to find the best of Greece, and was a great success, getting shortlisted for the Thomas Cook travel guide award, and encouraging Mark, along with three friends, to expand the series.

The Rough Guide list grew rapidly and the letters flooded in, indicating a much broader readership than had been anticipated, but one which uniformly appreciated the Rough Guide mix of practical detail and humor, irreverence and enthusiasm. Things haven't changed. The same four friends who began the series are still the caretakers of the Rough Guide mission today: to provide the most reliable, up-to-date and entertaining information to independent-minded travelers of all ages, on all budgets.

We now publish more than 200 titles and have offices in London and New York. The travel guides are written and researched by a dedicated team of more than 100 authors, based in Britain, Europe, the USA and Australia. We have also created a unique series of phrasebooks to accompany the travel series, along with an acclaimed series of music guides, and a best-selling pocket guide to the Internet and World Wide Web. We also publish comprehensive travel information on our website: **www.roughguides.com**

Help us update

We've gone to a lot of trouble to ensure that this Rough Guide is as up to date and accurate as possible. However, things do change, and all suggestions, comments and corrections are much appreciated, and we'll send a copy of the next edition (or any other Rough Guide if you prefer) for the best letters.

Please mark letters **"Rough Guide Honolulu Update"** and send to:

Rough Guides, 62–70 Shorts Gardens, London WC2H 9AH, or Rough Guides, 4th Floor, 345 Hudson St, New York, NY 10014.

Or send email to: mail@roughguides.co.uk
Online updates about this book can be found on Rough Guides' website (see opposite)

The author

Greg Ward has worked for Rough Guides since 1985, in which time he has also written Rough Guides to Hawaii, Maui, the Big Island of Hawaii, Southwest USA, Las Vegas, Essential Blues CDs, and Brittany and Normandy, as well as co-authored the *Rough Guide to the USA* and the *Rough Guide to Online Travel*. He has edited andcontributed to numerous other Rough Guides, and worked on travel guides for Fodors and Dorling Kindersley as well.

Acknowledgments

Thanks once again to Samantha Cook for her encouragement, support and patience, and for all the fun too. At Rough Guides, thanks to Mary Callahan for her thorough and conscientious editing, Don Young for additional editorial assistance, and to Andrew Rosenberg, Rachel Holmes, Melissa Baker, Audra Epstein and Sharon Martins for their hard work. For their generous assistance with my research for this new edition, I'd also like to thank Ron and Donna Katz, Gale Mejia, Marty Milan, Gail Morris,

Alexandra Pangas, Shae Page, Carole Sheehan, Sandi Yara and everyone who sent emails via the Rough Guides' website.

Readers' letters

Paul Norfolk, Gustavo Woltmann, John McDaniel, Phil Foley, Jan Bishop, Colette Engel, Charlie Holmes, all the many business operators who wrote in, and those whose email addresses or signatures were totally inscrutable or just plain missing.

CONTENTS

MAP LIST

MAP SYMBOLS

═══	Major road	∴	Ancient site
──	Minor road	♟	Museum
-----	Trail	🕆	Public gardens
──	Waterway	⚜	Viewpoint
✈	Airport	▲	Peak
▣	Accommodation	ℓ	Waterfall
◉	Places to eat and drink	⚓	Shipwreck
⚠	Campsite	♦	General point of interest
⚑	Church (regional maps)	✚	Church (town maps)
⊠	Post office	▨	Park
ⓘ	Information office	▨	National Park
⛩	Chinese temple	▨	Lava flow

Introduction

Although **Oahu** is only the third largest of the Hawaiian islands — its six hundred square miles are dwarfed by the four thousand square miles of the aptly-named Big Island -- it's home to almost 900,000 people, or roughly three-quarters of the state's population. Half of those in turn live along a narrow strip of Oahu's southeast coast, in the city of **Honolulu**, while the powerhouse that keeps the whole Hawaiian economy going is even smaller and more crowded still — the tiny, surreal enclave of **Waikīkī**, three miles east of downtown.

After a century of mass tourism to Hawaii, the very name of Waikīkī continues to epitomize beauty, sophistication and glamour. Of course, squeezing enough tower blocks to hold 100,000 hotel beds into a mere two square miles leaves little room for unspoiled tropical scenery. The legendary **beach**, however, remains irresistible, and Waikīkī offers a full-on resort experience to match any in the world. Around five million visitors per year spend their days on the sands of Waikīkī, and their nights in its hotels, restaurants and bars; for many of them, barring the odd expedition to the nearby Ala Moana shopping mall, the rest of Honolulu might just as well not exist.

All of which suits the average citizen of Honolulu, for whom Waikīkī is a small and seldom-visited suburb, just fine.

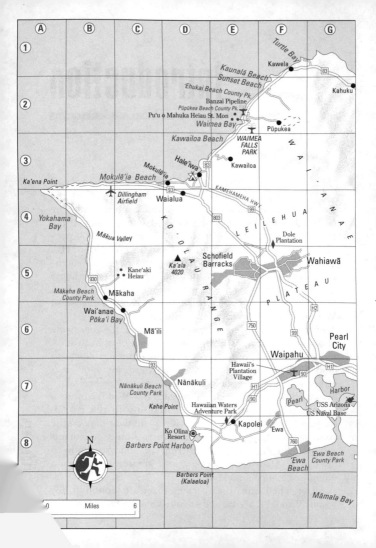

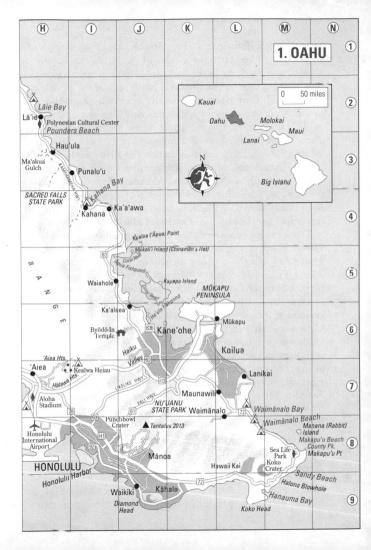

Honolulu is a distinctive and remarkably attractive city in its own right. The setting is gorgeous, right on the Pacific Ocean, and reaching back into a succession of spectacularly lush valleys cut into the dramatic *pali* (cliffs) of the Ko'olau Mountains. **Downtown Honolulu**, centered around a group of administrative buildings that date from the final days of the Hawaiian monarchy, nestles at the foot of the extinct **Punchbowl** volcano, now a military cemetery. As well as boasting top-quality museums such as the **Bishop Museum** and the **Academy of Arts**, it also offers superb **rainforest hikes**, especially in **Makiki** and **Mānoa** valleys, just a mile or so away. Immediately to the west of downtown stands lively **Chinatown**, while five miles further is the **airport**, just before the sheltered inlet of **Pearl Harbor**.

Thanks to massive immigration, the **population** of modern Hawaii is among the most ethnically diverse in the world, and Honolulu's status as a major international crossroads makes it an extraordinarily cosmopolitan city to visit. Only perhaps 2 percent of its inhabitants are pure Hawaiians, while another 20 percent claim at least some Hawaiian blood. The rest of the population includes the 26 percent who identify themselves as Caucasian, 16 percent Japanese, and 15 percent Filipino, though as over half of all marriages are classified as inter-racial such statistics grow ever more meaningless. In addition, almost as many tourists these days travel eastward to reach Hawaii, especially from Japan and Korea, as travel west from North America. Once there, you'll find that almost everyone speaks English. As a rule the Hawaiian language is only encountered in the few words – such as *aloha* ("love"), the all-purpose island greeting – that have passed into general local usage.

Around the island

All the Hawaiian islands are the summits of a chain of sub-marine volcanoes, poking from the Pacific more than two thousand miles off the west coast of America. Each has continued to grow for as long as it remained poised above a stationary "hot spot" in the earth's crust, and then, as it has drifted away to the northwest and lost its steady supply of fresh lava, has begun to erode back beneath the ocean.

Oahu is what's known as a "volcanic doublet", in that it consists of two separate but overlapping volcanoes. Roughly speaking, the island is shaped like a butterfly, with its wings formed by the volcanoes of the **Wai'anae Range** in the west – which first emerged from the waves around six million years ago – and the wetter, higher **Ko'olau Range** in the east. In between lies the narrow, flat **Leilehua Plateau**, with the triple lagoon of **Pearl Harbor** at its southern end. The symmetrical outline of Oahu is only spoiled by the more recent eruptions that elongated its southeast coastline, producing craters such as **Punchbowl**, **Diamond Head** and **Koko Head**, and thrusting the island out towards Molokai and Maui. Geologists see the fact that volcanic activity was taking place on Oahu as little as ten thousand years ago as suggesting that further eruptions may still be possible.

Just across the Ko'olaus from Honolulu, the green cliffs of the **windward coast** are magnificent, lined with safe, secluded beaches and indented with remote time-forgotten valleys. Towns such as **Kailua**, **Kāne'ohe** and **Lā'ie** may be far from exciting, but you're unlikely to tire of the sheer beauty of the shoreline drive – so long as you time your forays to miss the peak-hour traffic jams.

Mere mortals can only marvel at the winter waves that make the **North Shore** the world's premier **surfing** destination; for anyone other than experts, entering the water at that time is almost suicidal. However, **Waimea**, **Sunset** and **'Ehukai** beaches are compelling spectacles, little **Hale'iwa** makes a refreshing contrast to Waikīkī, and in summer you may manage to find a safe spot for a swim.

Although the **west** or **leeward** coast of Oahu also holds some fine beaches – including the prime surf spot of **Mākaha** – it remains very much off the beaten track. There's just one route in and out of this side of the island, and the locals are happy to keep it that way.

As you travel around, keep in mind that no one owns any stretch of beach in Hawaii. Every beach in the state – defined as the area below the vegetation line – is regarded as public property. That doesn't mean that you're entitled to stroll across any intervening land between the ocean and the nearest highway; always use the clearly signposted "public right of way" footpaths. Whatever impression the large oceanfront hotels may attempt to convey, they can't stop you using "their" beaches; they can only restrict, but not refuse to supply, parking places for non-guests.

Climate and when to go

Of all the major US cities, Honolulu is said to have both the lowest average maximum temperature and the highest minimum, at 85°F and 60°F respectively. Neither fluctuates more than a few degrees between summer and winter. Waikīkī remains a balmy tropical year-round resort, and the only seasonal variation likely to make much difference to travelers is the state of the **surf** on the North Shore. For surfers, the time to come is from October to April, when mighty winter waves scour the sand off many beaches and come curling in at heights of twenty feet or more. In summer, the surf-bums head off home, and some North Shore beaches are even safe for family swimming.

As for room rates, **peak season** in Waikīkī runs from December to March, and many mid-range hotels lower their prices by anything from ten to thirty dollars at other times. Waikīkī is pretty crowded all year, though, and there are few savings to be made by coming in summer.

BASICS

Getting there from the US and Canada

The vast majority of flights to Hawaii from North America land at Honolulu Airport (HNL). Virtually every large US airline flies to the city, with United being the major player; in addition, the state's own Hawaiian Airlines runs services to and from the western states.

The **journey time** from LA or San Francisco to Honolulu is roughly five and a half hours.

FARES AND CUTTING COSTS

There is no high or low season for flights to Hawaii, and fares remain relatively consistent year-round. However, at **peak periods** – June to August, and around Christmas, the New Year and Thanksgiving – services tend to be booked long in advance, and you might have to pay a slight premium. Flying on a weekday rather than a weekend saves anything from $50 to $200 on a round trip.

The simplest way to save money is to buy a **package** deal including both flight and accommodation. If you buy a flight only, through a **specialist flight agent**, aim to pay around \$400 for a round-trip to Honolulu from the West Coast, more like \$700 from New York.

AIRLINES AND FLIGHT AGENTS IN NORTH AMERICA

Airlines

Air Canada ☏ 1-888/247-2262; ⓦ www.aircanada.ca
Aloha ☏ 1-800/367-5250; ⓦ www.alohaairlines.com
American Airlines ☏ 1-800/433-7300; ⓦ www.aa.com
American Trans Air ☏ 1-800/435-9282; ⓦ www.ata.com
Continental ☏ 1-800/523-3273; ⓦ www.continental.com

Delta ☏ 1-800/221-1212; ⓦ www.delta.com
Hawaiian ☏ 1-800/367-5320; ⓦ www.hawaiianair.com
Northwest ☏ 1-800/225-2525; ⓦ www.nwa.com
TWA ☏ 1-800/221-2000; ⓦ www.twa.com
United ☏ 1-800/241-6522; ⓦ www.ual.com

Flight agents

Airhitch ☏ 1-800/326-2009; ⓦ www.airhitch.org
Cheap Tickets ☏ 1-888/922-8849; ⓦ www.cheaptickets.com
Council Travel ☏ 1-800/226-8624; ⓦ www.counciltravel.com
Expedia ⓦ www.expedia.com
High Adventure Travel ⓦ www.airtreks.com
Hotwire ⓦ www.hotwire.com
Orbitz ⓦ www.orbitz.com

Priceline ⓦ www.priceline.com
Qixo ⓦ www.qixo.com
STA Travel ☏ 1-800/777-0112; ⓦ www.sta-travel.com
TicketPlanet ⓦ www.ticketplanet.com
Travelocity ⓦ www.travelocity.com
Travelscape ⓦ www.travelscape.com

NORTH AMERICAN TOUR OPERATORS

- -

American Airlines Vacations
Ⓣ 1-800/321-2121;
Ⓦ www.aa.com

Continental Airlines Vacations
Ⓣ 1-800/634-5555;
Ⓦ www.coolvacations.com

Delta Certified Vacations
Ⓣ 1-800/654-6559;
Ⓦ www.deltavacations.com.

Earthwatch Ⓣ 617/926-8200;
Ⓦ www.earthwatch.org

Elderhostel Ⓣ 1-877/426 8056;
Ⓦ www.elderhostel.org

Globus and Cosmos
Ⓦ www.globusandcosmos.com

Pacific Quest, Hale'iwa, HI
96712 Ⓣ 1-800/776-2518

Pleasant Hawaiian Holidays,
Westlake Village, CA
Ⓣ 1-800/7HAWAII;
Ⓦ www.2hawaii.com

**Questers Worldwide Nature
Tours**, New York, NY
Ⓣ 212/251-0444 or
1-800/468-8668;
Ⓦ www.questers.com

Sierra Club, San Francisco, CA
Ⓣ 415/977-5522;
Ⓦ www.sierraclub.org

Tauck Tours, Westport, CT
Ⓣ 1-800/788-7885;
Ⓦ www.tauck.com

TWA Getaway Vacations
Ⓣ 1-800/GETAWAY;
Ⓦ www.twa.com

United Vacations
Ⓣ 1-800/328-6877;
Ⓦ www.unitedvacations.com

World of Vacations, Etobicoke,
ON Ⓣ 416/620-8050;
Ⓦ www.macktravel.ca

FLIGHTS FROM THE WEST COAST

All the airlines quote round-trip fares **from the West Coast to Honolulu** at $350 to $550. **Los Angeles** is generally the cheapest departure point, and is served by six carriers: Hawaiian, United, American, Continental, Northwest, and Delta.

Hawaiian Airlines flies from six mainland US cities to Honolulu. Daily flights leave from **Las Vegas** at 10.10am; **Los Angeles** at 8.55am, 12.30pm and 5.25pm; **Portland** at 9.10am; **San Diego** at 9.15am; **San**

Francisco at 8.40am and 10.15am; and **Seattle** at 8.50am (with an additional later flight on five days of the week).

United flies to Honolulu from **San Francisco** at 9.05am, 1.40pm, 4.30pm and 7.25pm daily, and from **Los Angeles** at 8am, 1.45pm, 5.20pm and 7.15pm.

Of the **other operators** who fly to Honolulu from the West Coast, Delta offers four daily flights from LA and one daily from San Francisco; American has two daily flights from LA, one from San Francisco, and one from San Jose; Northwest has two services from LA and two from Seattle; and Continental flies once from LA.

FLIGHTS FROM THE EAST COAST

There are no scheduled nonstop flights from the **East Coast** to Hawaii (although charter service American Trans Air has in recent years offered once-weekly nonstop flights during the busiest parts of the year between New York's JFK airport and Honolulu). Most visitors fly via California, though American flies direct to Honolulu **from Chicago** and **Dallas**, as do Northwest **from Minneapolis**, Continental **from Houston**, Delta **from Atlanta**, and TWA **from St Louis**; all take 8–10 hours.

FLIGHTS FROM CANADA

Getting to Honolulu from any **Canadian** city apart from Vancouver will almost certainly require you to change planes on the US mainland. United flies from **Toronto** via San Francisco for around CDN$1250, or from **Vancouver** for CDN$700–850; better from Vancouver is Northwest, with fares starting at CDN$650, via Seattle. Flying from either **Toronto** or **Montréal**, you can go via Chicago or Dallas with American (CDN$1300); via Detroit or

Minneapolis on Northwest (CDN$1250); or via Atlanta on Delta (CDN$1350).

Air Canada flies daily to Honolulu from **Toronto** (CDN$1200) via **Vancouver** (CDN$700). Canadian has daily nonstop flights to Honolulu from **Vancouver**, with fares around CDN$700, and flights three times weekly (Tues, Wed & Fri) from **Toronto** starting around CDN$1000. Through trips from **Montréal**, via Vancouver, start at around CDN$1050.

Canadians flying to Hawaii need passports, but not visas.

INSURANCE

Your existing insurance may offer full cover when you're away from home. Some homeowners' policies are valid on vacation, and credit cards such as American Express often include medical or other insurance, while most Canadians are covered for medical mishaps overseas by their health plans. If you're not already covered, either contact a specialist travel insurance company, or consider Rough Guides' own travel insurance, customized for our readers and available for anyone, of any nationality, traveling anywhere in the world.

There are two main plans: Essential, for basic, no-frills cover, and Premier, which offers more generous benefits. You can also take out annual multi trip insurance, which covers you for any number of trips (maximum sixty days each) throughout the year. If you intend to be away for the whole year, the Adventurer policy will cover you for 365 days. Each plan can be supplemented with a "Hazardous Activities Premium" if you plan to indulge in sports considered dangerous, such as scuba diving.

For a policy quote, call the Rough Guide Insurance Line on US toll-free ☎1-866/220-5588, UK toll-free ☎0800/

015 0906, or, if you're calling from elsewhere Ⓣ +44 1243/621046. Alternatively, get an online quote at ⓦ www.roughguides.com/insurance.

Getting there from Australia and New Zealand

There's no shortage of flights from Australia and New Zealand to **Honolulu**, and very little price difference between airlines. Five airlines operate daily services, with journey times of around nine hours.

Fares vary seasonally by around AUS/NZ$200–300. **Low** season counts as mid-January through February, and all of October and November; **high** season runs from mid-May to August and December to mid-January; and **shoulder** season is the rest of the year.

From Australia, most flights to Honolulu are out of **Sydney**, with daily nonstop services on Qantas, American Airlines and Air Canada for around AUS$1500 in low season or AUS$1750 in high season. For around the same price, United fly via Auckland.

From New Zealand, the best deals to Honolulu are on varying combinations of the United/Air New Zealand partnership out of Auckland, costing from NZ$1599 in low season up to NZ$1899 in high season, whether you fly nonstop, or via Fiji, Tonga or Papeete. Air Canada also flies nonstop, while Qantas can take you via either Sydney or Western Samoa.

AIRLINES AND AGENTS IN AUSTRALIA AND NEW ZEALAND

Airlines
Air New Zealand ☎132476 (Aus); ☎0800/737 000 (NZ); ⓦwww.airnz.com
Air Pacific ☎1800/230 150 (Aus); ☎09/379 2404 (NZ); ⓦwww.airpacific.com
Cathay Pacific ☎131747 (Aus); ☎09/379 0861 (NZ); ⓦwww.cathaypacific.com
Qantas ☎131313 (Aus); ☎0800/808 767 (NZ); ⓦwww.qantas.com.au
Singapore Airlines ☎131011 (Aus); ☎0800/808 909 (NZ); ⓦwww.singaporeair.com

Flight agents
Anywhere Travel, Sydney ☎02/9663 0411; ⓔanywhere@ozemail.com.au
Budget Travel, Auckland ☎09/366 0061
Destinations Unlimited, Auckland ☎09/373 4033
Flight Centre, Sydney ☎02/9235 3522; Auckland ☎09/358 4310; ⓦwww.flightcentre.com.au

Northern Gateway, Darwin
ⓣ 08/8941 1394;
ⓔ oztravel@norgate.com.au

STA Travel ⓣ 1300/360 960
(Aus); ⓣ 09/366 6673 (NZ);
ⓦ www.statravel.com.au

Specialist agents

Creative Holidays, Sydney
ⓣ 02/9386 2111; ⓦ www
.creativeholidays.com.au
Hawaiian Island Golf Tours,
Sydney ⓣ 02/968 1778
Padi Travel Network, Sydney
ⓣ 02/9417 2800;
ⓦ www.padi.com.au

Surf Travel Co, Sydney
ⓣ 02/9527 4522;
ⓦ www.surftravel.com.au
**Sydney International Travel
Centre**, Sydney ⓣ 02/9299
8000; ⓦ www.sydneytravel
.com.au

ENTRY REQUIREMENTS

Under the visa waiver scheme, Australian and New Zealand passport holders who stay less than ninety days in the US **do not require visas**, so long as they have an onward or return ticket.

For longer stays, a twelve-month US tourist or business visa costs AUS\$85.50/NZ\$108. You'll need an application form – available from the US visa information service (ⓣ 1-902/262-682) – one signed passport photo and your passport. For details, contact the US Embassy (Aus: 21 Moonah Place, Canberra ⓣ 02/6214 5600; NZ: 29 Fitzherbert Terrace, Thorndon, Wellington). In both countries, you can apply and pay for US visas at all post offices.

INSURANCE

Travel insurance, including medical cover, is essential in view of the high costs of health care in the US. For details of Rough Guides' own policies, see p.7.

Getting there from Britain and Ireland

Much the quickest and cheapest route from the UK or Ireland to Hawaii is via the mainland United States or Canada, so your options are more or less the same as they are for North Americans.

With a ten-hour flight across the Atlantic to the West Coast, and a five-hour flight over the Pacific, that makes for a very long journey. On the other hand, it is possible to get to Honolulu on the same day you set off, thanks to the ten- or eleven-hour time difference (see p.235).

Four airlines can get you all the way **from London** to Honolulu in a single day: United via Los Angeles and San Francisco (taking the 9am flight to San Francisco enables you to touch down in Honolulu at 3.55pm), Delta via Atlanta, Air Canada via Toronto, and British Airways, in conjunction with Air New Zealand, via Vancouver.

From Ireland, Delta provide same-day connections from Dublin to Honolulu via Atlanta and Los Angeles, and Shannon to Honolulu via New York and Los Angeles. Aer Lingus and American also offer daily services to Los Angeles, where you join other carriers for the onward leg to Honolulu.

As for **fares**, a typical round-trip ticket from London to Honolulu costs from around £450 from January to March (peak season in Hawaii), up to as much as £800 in July and August.

AIRLINES AND FLIGHT AGENTS

Airlines

Aer Lingus ℡ 020/8899 4747;
℡ 01/705 3333 (Dublin);
Ⓦ www.aerlingus.ie
Air Canada ℡ 0870/524 7226;
Ⓦ www.aircanada.ca
Air New Zealand ℡ 020/8741
2299; Ⓦ www.airnz.co.uk
American Airlines ℡ 0845/778
9789; Ⓦ www.aa.com
British Airways ℡ 0845/
773 3377;
Ⓦ www.britishairways.com
Continental ℡ 0800/776464;
Ⓦ www.flycontinental.com

Delta ℡ 0800/414767;
℡ 1800/414767 (Dublin);
Ⓦ www.delta.com
Hawaiian Airlines
℡ 01753/664406;
Ⓦ www.hawaiianair.com
KLM/Northwest ℡ 0870/507
4074; Ⓦ www.klmuk.com
United Airlines ℡ 0845/844
4777; Ⓦ www.ual.com
Virgin Atlantic
℡ 01293/747747;
Ⓦ www.virgin-atlantic.com

Flight agents

a2btravel
Ⓦ www.a2btravel.com
The Airline Network
Ⓦ www.netflights.com
Bridge The World ℡ 020/7911
0900; Ⓦ www.bridgetheworld
.com
Ebookers
Ⓦ www.ebookers.com

1stnetflights
Ⓦ www.1stnetflights.com
Flynow http://flynow.com
Seaforths Travel
Ⓦ www.telme.com
STA Travel ℡ 0870/160 6070;
Ⓦ www.statravel.co.uk
Trailfinders ℡ 020/7628 7628;
Ⓦ www.trailfinders.com

Travel Bag ⓣ0870/900 1350;   ⓦwww.usitcampus.co.uk
ⓦwww.travelbag.co.uk   **usit NOW** Dublin ⓣ01/602
usit CAMPUS ⓣ0870/240 1010;   1777; ⓦwww.usitnow.ie

ENTRY REQUIREMENTS

Passport-holders from **Britain**, **Ireland** and most European countries do not require visas for trips to the United States of less than ninety days. Instead you simply fill in the **visa waiver form** handed out on incoming planes. Immigration control takes place at your point of arrival on US soil, which, if you're flying from Britain, will not be in Hawaii. For further details, contact the **US embassy** in Britain (24 Grosvenor Square, London W1A 1AE; ⓣ020/7499 9000; premium-rate visa hotline ⓣ0906/820 0290) or Ireland (42 Elgin Rd, Ballsbridge, Dublin; ⓣ01/668 8777).

There is no British or Irish **consulate** in Hawaii.

TOUR OPERATORS IN BRITAIN AND IRELAND

Bon Voyage ⓣ0800/316 3012;
ⓦwww.bon-voyage.co.uk
Contiki Tours ⓣ1-
888/CONTIKI;
ⓦwww.contiki.com
Destination Pacific
ⓣ020/7400 7003

The Hawaiian Dream
ⓣ020/8552 1201
Hawaiian Travel Centre
ⓣ020/7706 4142
North America Travel Service
ⓣ0845/766 0209
Page & Moy ⓣ0870/010 6250;
ⓦwww.page-moy.co.uk

INSURANCE

Travel insurance, including medical cover, is essential in view of the high cost of health care in the US. For details of Rough Guides' own policies, see p.7.

Arriving in Honolulu

T he runways of Honolulu's **International Airport**, roughly five miles west of the downtown area, extend out to sea on a coral reef. The main Overseas Terminal is connected to the Inter-Island and Commuter terminals by the free Wikiwiki shuttle service. All the terminals are on a loop road, which is constantly circled by a wide array of hotel and rental-car pick-up vans, taxis and minibuses.

Virtually every arriving tourist heads straight to Waikīkī; if you don't have a **hotel reservation** use the courtesy phones in the baggage claim area, where you'll also find boards advertising room rates. Several competing **shuttle buses**, such as the Waikīkī Airport Express (☏566-7333) and Reliable Shuttle (☏591-1493), pick up regularly outside the terminals, and will carry passengers to any Waikīkī hotel ($8 one-way, $13 round-trip). A **taxi** from the airport to Waikīkī will cost around $20, and a stretch limo as little as $25.

In addition, **TheBus** #19 and #20 run to Waikīkī from the airport, leaving from outside the departure lounge of the

Overseas Terminal. The ride costs $1.50 one-way, but you must travel light: TheBus won't carry large bags, cases or backpacks. There are **lockers** at the airport for large items.

The nine-mile – not at all scenic – **drive** from the airport to Waikīkī can take anything from 25 to 75 minutes; the quickest route is to follow H-1 as far as possible, running inland of downtown Honolulu, and then take the Waikīkī exit.

Transport and tours

Although Oahu boasts "TheBus," an exemplary and very comprehensive bus service, it's much easier to explore the island at your own pace with a **rental car**. However, with limited parking and heavy traffic, a car is a liability in Waikīkī itself, so think carefully before renting one for your entire stay.

THEBUS

A network of more than sixty **bus** routes, officially named **TheBus** and radiating out from downtown Honolulu and the Ala Moana Shopping Center, covers the whole of Oahu (contact ☎848-5555 or ⊛www.thebus.org for route information). All journeys cost $1.50 (ages 6–19 75¢), with free transfers to any connecting route if you ask as you board. One of the best sightseeing routes is TheBus #52 or #55, which circles the whole of the Ko'olau Range, including the North Shore and the Windward Coast, still for just $1.50. The only disadvantage is that passengers may not carry large bags or bulky items, which rules out using TheBus to get to or from the airport.

The **Oahu Discovery Passport**, available from ABC stores in Waikīkī (and deliberately under publicized, following complaints from commercial tour operators), offers four days of unlimited travel on TheBus for $15, while **monthly passes**, obtainable at 7–11, Star Market and Foodland stores, as well as at Satellite City Halls, cost $27. Senior citizens (aged over 65) can buy a pass valid for two years for a mere $25.

OTHER BUS COMPANIES

Rival companies operate a number of alternative bus services from Waikīkī. The open-sided and overpriced **Waikīkī Trolley** (☎596-2199) tours a circuit of Honolulu's main attractions – 'Iolani Palace, the Bishop Museum, Ala Moana, and so on – at half-hourly intervals, with the first departure from Waikīkī's Royal Hawaiian Shopping Center at 8am daily, and the last at 4.30pm. You can get on and off as often as you choose for a daily rate of $18 ($8 for under-12s). Four-day passes cost $30, $10 for under-12s.

The similar **Rainbow Trolley** (daily 8.30am–11pm; ☎539-9495) loops between the main Waikīkī hotels and

THEBUS ROUTES

The following is a selection of TheBus routes most useful for tourists. For a complete list, pick up brochures from the satellite city hall at the Ala Moana Center, or call TheBus information line (daily 5.30am–10pm ☎ 848-5555; ⓦ www.thebus.org), which can tell you not only which bus to take but when the next one will arrive.

Express B	Waikīkī to Kalihi via downtown Honolulu.
#2	Waikīkī to downtown Honolulu and Bishop Museum.
#8	Waikīkī to Ala Moana.
#19	Waikīkī to Honolulu Airport via downtown.
#20	Waikīkī to Pearl Harbor via downtown and Honolulu Airport.
#22	Waikīkī to Hanauma Bay and Sea Life Park.
#40	Honolulu to Mākaha and Leeward Coast.
#52	"Circle Isle" clockwise; Ala Moana to Hale'iwa and the North Shore.
#55	"Circle Isle" counterclockwise; Ala Moana to Kāne'ohe and the Windward Shore.
#58	Ala Moana to Waikīkī and Sea Life Park.

Honolulu's Aloha Tower Marketplace, passing by way of the Ala Moana Center, Hilo Hattie's and Chinatown, but not the Bishop Museum, charging adults $10 for one day, $18 for two days, or $30 for four days, while the **Aloha Tower Express** (daily 9am–9pm; ☎ 566-2337) runs direct from Waikīkī to the Aloha Tower Marketplace, for a much more reasonable $1 one-way fare.

TRANSPORT AND TOURS

CAR RENTAL

Officially, Honolulu ranks as having the lowest **car rental** rates of the hundred largest cities in the US, at an average of $41 per day. All the major rental chains have outlets at the airport, and many have offices in Waikīkī as well. Reservations can be made using the national toll-free numbers listed below, but check first to see if you can get a better room-and-car deal through your hotel. With so much competition, it's hard to quote specific prices, but a target rate for the cheapest economy car with unlimited mileage should be around $35 per day or $175 per week. No companies rent cars to anyone under 21.

While renting a car enables you to explore Oahu in much greater depth than would otherwise be possible, **driving** in Honolulu itself is not a pleasant experience. The **traffic** on major roads, such as H-1 along the northern flanks of the city, and Likelike Highway and the Pali Highway across the mountains, can be horrendous, and **parking** is always a problem. Waikīkī hotels charge guests around $7–12 per night to **park**. There are meters on the back streets of Waikīkī, near the Ala Wai Canal; downtown, the largest metered parking lot is on the edge of Chinatown at Smith and Beretania streets.

CAR RENTAL CHAINS

Alamo ⊤ 1-800/327-9633 (US, Can & HI); 0870/606 0100 (UK); ⓦ www.alamo.com.

Avis ⊤ 1-800/331-1212 (US & Can); 1-800/831-8000 (HI); 020/8848 8733 (UK); 1800/ 225 533 (Aus); 0800/655 111 (NZ); ⓦ www.avis.com.

Budget ⊤ 1-800/527-0700 (US, Can & HI); 0800/181181 (UK); 1300/362 848 (Aus); 0800/ 652 227 (NZ); ⓦ www.budgetrentacar.com.

Dollar ⊤ 1-800/800-4000 (US & Can); 1-800/367-7006 (HI); 01895/233300 (UK);

TRANSPORT AND TOURS

1800/358 008 (Aus);
Ⓦ www.dollar.com.
Hertz ⓣ 1-800/654-3001 (US &
HI); 1-800/263-0600 (Can);
0870/844 8844 (UK); 1800/
550 067 (Aus); 0800/655 955

(NZ); Ⓦ www.hertz.com.
National ⓣ 1-800/227-7368
(US, Can & HI); 0870/536
5365 (UK); 09/537 2582 (NZ);
Ⓦ www.nationalcar.com.

BIKE AND MOPED RENTAL AND TOURS

Honolulu is a great city to cycle around, so long as you stay off the very largest roads. Lots of Waikīkī-based companies – such as Aloha Funway (ⓣ 942-9696), which has seven locations; Island Scooters (ⓣ 924-6743), which has six; and Adventure Rentals, which adjoins the *Island Hostel* at 1946 Ala Moana Blvd (ⓣ 944-3131) – rent out **mopeds** and **bicycles**. Typical rates for bikes are $15 per day (8am–6pm) or $20 for 24 hours; mopeds cost a couple of dollars extra.

'Ohana Adventure Tours (ⓣ 734-4214; Ⓦ www.bike-hawaii.com) offers a half-day's mountain biking excursion in Ka'a'awa Valley on the Windward Coast (adults $85, under-14s $68), or a combination of a five-mile downhill bike ride and a two-mile hike to a waterfall in the Ko'olau mountains (adults $65, under-14s $52).

TAXIS AND LIMOUSINES

Honolulu **taxi** firms include Charley's (ⓣ 531-2333), Sida's (ⓣ 836-0011) and TheCab (ⓣ 422-2222). Alternatively, you could rent a **limousine** with tinted windows – for $45 per hour, or $30 for a one-way airport ride – from Continental (ⓣ 226-4466). Accessible Vans of Hawaii (ⓣ 879-5521; Ⓦ www.accessiblevans.com) provides transportation for **disabled visitors**.

BUS TOURS

Countless operators in Waikīkī, such as Polynesian Adventure Tours (☏ 833-3000; ⓦ www.polyad.com), E Noa Tours (☏ 591-2561; ⓦ www.enoa.com), and Roberts (☏ 539-9400; ⓦ www.roberts-hawaii.com), advertise **bus tours** of Honolulu and Oahu. The standard choice is between a half-day city tour, including Pearl Harbor, for around $14–20, and a full-day island tour starting at $24 (not including Waimea Valley Park; see p.130), or up to $60 including the park and a picnic. Most companies also offer tours to other attractions on Oahu, such as the Polynesian Cultural Center and Sea Life Park. Low-priced **ticket agencies** include Magnum Tickets & Tours, 2134 Kalākaua Ave (☏ 923-7825) and Aloha Express, at the *Waikīkī Circle* Hotel, 2464 Kalākaua Ave (☏ 924-4030).

Hawaii Film and Celebrity Tours (☏ 926-3456; ⓦ www.hawaiifilmtours.com) run daily five-hour $45 narrated bus tours of Oahu movie locations, visiting sites familiar from the likes of *Pearl Harbor*, *Blue Hawaii* and, of course, *Hawaii Five-O*.

WALKING TOURS

Both Waikīkī and downtown Honolulu are compact enough to explore on foot on your own, but you can get a great sense of their histories and hidden byways by joining an expert-led **walking tour**.

Honolulu Time Walks runs a regular program of entertaining and informative tours on subjects such as Haunted Honolulu, Old Waikīkī, Mark Twain's Honolulu, and Scandals and Sinners ($7–8; ☏ 943-0371). Note that all *Sheraton* hotel guests can join a free Time Walks tour of Waikīkī each Wednesday at 9am.

Similar tours on topics including Hawaiian royalty,

ROUGH GUIDE FAVORITES: HIKING

Descriptions of Oahu's most enjoyable **hiking trails** can be found on the following pages:

plantation life, and the history of Chinatown, are conducted by Kapi'olani Community College ($5–10; reserve at ☎734-9245). Other Chinatown tours are arranged by the Chinese Chamber of Commerce (Tues 9.30am; $5; ☎533-3181), and the Hawaii Heritage Center (Fri 9.30am; $5, ☎521-2749).

The American Legion organizes one-hour walking tours of the National Cemetery of the Pacific in Punchbowl Crater (adults $15, under-10s free; includes Waikīkī hotel pick up; ☎946-6383).

For more energetic **hiking**, the Hawaii chapter of the Sierra Club sponsors treks and similar activities on weekends (☎538-6616; ⓦwww.hi.sierraclub.org), while the Hawaii Nature Center arranges hikes most weekends ☎955-0100). Likehike (☎455-8193; http://gayhawaii.com/likehike/index.html) is a gay **hiking** club that runs group hikes on alternate Sundays.

On Saturdays, the Clean Air Team (☎948-3299) runs a **Diamond Head walk**, meeting at 9am in front of the Honolulu Zoo; adults pay $5, kids go free.

As for **commercial tours**, Oahu Nature Tours (☎924-2473 or 1-800/861-6018; ⓦwww.oahunaturetours.com) runs hiking and birding excursions ranging from a sunrise walk up Diamond Head (daily 6.30–8am; $24) to a four-hour hike in the Ko'olau rainforest (daily 2–6pm; $40).

TRANSPORT AND TOURS

Mauka Makai Excursions (☎593-3525; ⓦwww.oahu-eco-tours.com) offers a choice of full-day or half-day hikes in the remoter parts of the island.

GLIDER FLIGHTS

Finally, if you want to see Oahu from the **air**, take a **glider** flight from Dillingham Airfield on the North Shore with Skysurfing Glider Rides (from $35 per person; daily 10am–5.30pm ☎256-0438).

Information and maps

Vast quantities of written information are available about Hawaii. Tourism is big business, and plenty of people and organizations are eager to tell you what's available. For information before you arrive, contact the head office of the **Hawaii Visitors Bureau (HVB)**, Waikīkī Business Plaza, Suite 801, 2270 Kalākaua Ave, Honolulu, HI 96815 (☎923-1811 or 1-800/GO-HAWAII, ⓕ924-0290; ⓦwww.gohawaii.com), or the **Oahu Visitors Bureau**, 733 Bishop St, #1872, Honolulu, HI 96813 (☎1-877/525-OAHU or 524-0722, ⓕ521-1620; ⓦwww.visit-oahu.com).

The HVB also runs a **visitor center** (Mon–Fri 8am–4.30pm) in Waikīkī, on the fourth floor of the Royal Hawaiian Shopping Center, on the Lewers Street end of Kalākaua Avenue. However, you need not visit it; the center has fewer free-listings magazines and leaflets than the racks in either the Arrivals hall at the airport or virtually all the Waikīkī hotels. Most hotels have information desks as well, for advice (albeit hard-sell) on island activities.

An ever-increasing amount of information is also available on the **internet** and World Wide Web. The official HVB site, ⓦwww.gohawaii.com, has links to dozens of accommodation options, activity operators, and the like. The best sites for current news and listings are run by the city's two daily newspapers, the *Honolulu Star Bulletin* (ⓦwww.starbulletin.com) and the *Honolulu Advertiser* (ⓦwww.honoluluadvertiser.com), and also the weekly *Honolulu Weekly* (ⓦwww.honoluluweekly.com).

HAWAII VISITORS BUREAUS OVERSEAS

Australia ☎02/9955 2619, ⓕ9955 2171

Canada ☎604/669-6691, ⓕ683-9114

New Zealand ☎09/379 3708, ⓕ309 0725

United Kingdom ☎020/8941 4009, ⓕ0941 4011

MAPS

Much the best **maps** of Oahu are the three separate sheets published by James Bier: *Honolulu and Oahu South Shore* ($4.50), *Central Oahu and the Windward Coast* ($4.50), and *North Shore and Leeward Coast* ($2.95). Decent free maps also abound – you'll get a map booklet with your rental car, for example. These can be useful for pinpointing specific hotels and restaurants, but only the James Bier maps are at all reliable for minor roads.

For extreme detail, TMK Maps publishes a full-color gazetteer of street maps that covers Honolulu and all of Oahu, available in all the city's major bookstores for $9.95.

Costs, money and banks

Although it's possible to have an inexpensive vacation in Honolulu, prices in Hawaii are consistently higher than in the rest of the US. With 85 percent of the state's food and 92 percent of its fuel having to be shipped in, the cost of living is around forty percent above the US average.

How much you spend per day is, up to you, but it's hard to get any sort of breakfast for under $6, a cheap lunch easily comes to $12, and an evening meal in a restaurant, with drinks, is likely to be $25–30. Even the cheapest hotel is likely to charge well over $60 for a double room, and a rental car with gas won't cost less than $25 per day. It's easy to spend $75 per person per day before you do anything; pay for a snorkel cruise, let alone a helicopter ride, and you've cleared $100.

The state **sales tax** of four percent on all transactions is almost never included in the prices displayed. Hotels impose an additional 7.25 percent tax, adding a total premium of more than eleven percent to accommodation bills.

MONEY AND BANKS

US dollar **travelers' checks** are the best way to carry significant quantities of money, for both American and foreign visitors, as they offer the security of knowing that lost or stolen checks will be replaced. Foreign currency, whether cash or travelers' checks, can be hard to exchange, so foreign travelers should change some of their money into dollars at home. However, Honolulu is absolutely bursting with **ATM machines**, which accept most cards issued by domestic and foreign banks. Call your bank before you leave home if you're in any doubt.

For many services, it's taken for granted that you'll be paying with a **credit card**. Hotels and car-rental companies routinely require an imprint whether or not you intend to use it to pay. The two major **banks** are the Bank of Hawaii, whose main Waikīkī branch is at 2220 Kalākaua Ave, and the First Hawaiian Bank, which is nearby at 2181 Kalākaua Ave.

Telephones

Telephone connections on and between the Hawaiian Islands and to the rest of the US are generally efficient and reliable. The **area code** for the entire state of Hawaii is ☎808. Calls from anywhere on Oahu to anywhere else on the island count as local; you don't need to dial the area code and it costs a flat-rate 25¢ on pay phones. Calling any of the other islands, you must prefix ☎1-808 before the number. For **directory assistance** for any Oahu number, call ☎1-411; for the rest of Hawaii call ☎1-808/555-1212.

Hotels impose huge surcharges, so it's best to use a **phone card** for long-distance and international calls. In preference to the ones issued by the major phone companies, you'll find it simpler and cheaper to choose from the various **prepaid** cards sold in almost all groceries and general stores. In general, in Waikīkī, the cards on sale in small stores along Kūhiō Avenue and in the King's Village mall are much better value than those available in the ABC chain or in the hotels' own stores

---

To make an international call to Hawaii, dial your country's international access code, then 1 for the US, then 808 for Hawaii. To place an international call from Hawaii, dial 011 then the relevant country code (Britain is 44, Ireland is 353, Canada is 1, Australia is 61 and New Zealand is 64).

TELEPHONES

Mail services

M ail services from Hawaii can be slow; allow a week for anywhere in the US, two weeks or more for the rest of the world.

Honolulu's main **post office**, facing the inter-island terminal at the airport at 3600 Aolele St, Honolulu, HI 96820 (Mon–Fri 7.30am–8.30pm, Sat 8am–2.30pm, is the only one in the city that accepts **general delivery** (poste restante) mail. There are other post offices at 330 Saratoga Rd in Waikīkī (Mon, Tues, Thurs & Fri 8am–4.30pm, Wed 8am–6pm, Sat 9am–noon); at the Ala Moana shopping mall (Mon–Fri 8.30am–5pm, Sat 8.30am–4.15pm); and downtown in the Old Federal Building at 335 Merchant St (Mon, Tues, Thurs & Fri 8am–4.30pm, Wed 8am–6pm). Call ☎423-3990 for all information concerning post offices and mail service on Oahu.

THE GUIDE

Waikīkī

O n any one day, half of all the tourists in the state of Hawaii are crammed into the tiny, surreal enclave of **WAIKĪKĪ**, three miles east of downtown Honolulu. Effectively, it's an island in its own right, a two-mile-long, quarter-mile-wide strip sealed off from the rest of the city by the Ala Wai Canal and almost completely surrounded by water. Its incredible profusion of skyscrapers, jostling for position along the shoreline, hold enough hotel rooms to accommodate more than 100,000 guests. There are also hundreds of restaurants, and stores providing anything the visitor could possibly want.

Long before Kamehameha the Great built a thatched hut here at the start of the nineteenth century, Waikīkī – the name means "spouting water" – was a favored residence of the chiefs of Oahu. They coveted not only its waterfront coconut groves and well-stocked fishponds, but also the mosquito-free swamps and wetlands that lay immediately behind them. Such terrain was then a rare and valuable resource, being ideal for growing *taro*, which is cultivated like rice in semi-submerged fields, and whose roots are pounded to create the Hawaiian staple food, *poi*. By the end of the century, however, with Hawaii annexed by the United States, the wetlands were considered all but useless.

31

Waikīkī's value lay instead in its being the best beach within easy reach of Honolulu. When the *Moana* hotel went up in 1901, signaling the start of the tourist boom, a handful of inns were already dotted among the luxurious homes of elite missionary and merchant families.

Waikīkī, however, only began to regain a significant population during the 1920s, when a vast program of land reclamation was instigated. The Ala Wai Canal was dug to divert the mountain streams, and the central area was filled in with chunks of coral sawed from the reef that then ran the full length of the shoreline. Since then, Waikīkī has mushroomed beyond belief. By looking beyond the towerblocks to Diamond Head or the mysterious valleys that recede into the mountains, you can remind yourself that this is a Pacific island. In Waikīkī itself, however, there's precious little left of the real Hawaii.

So long as you're prepared to enter into a spirit of rampant commercialism, you'll have a great time in Waikīkī. You could survive with little money by buying snacks from the omnipresent ABC convenience stores, but if saving money is your main priority there's no point staying long in Waikīkī – there's very little to see, and the only alternative to swimming and sunbathing is to shop until you drop.

WAIKĪKĪ BEACH

Viewed objectively, **Waikīkī Beach** would rank pretty low on a list of Hawaii's best beaches. Elsewhere on Oahu, it's not hard to find a stretch of deserted, palm-fringed, tropical shoreline – a tranquil contrast to Waikīkī, where you can hardly see the sand for the sunbathers, and the traffic on Kalākaua Avenue outroars the surf. Somehow, however, the ruckus barely seems to matter. Waikīkī Beach may be crowded, but it's crowded with enthusiastic holiday-makers, wringing every last ounce of pleasure from being on one of the world's most famous beaches.

Glance at the ocean, and you'll be caught up in the ever-changing action. At the water's edge, families splash about while oblivious honeymoon couples gaze hand-in-hand at the horizon; beyond them, circling surfers await the next wave; and, out in the deep-water channel, cruise liners, merchant ships and aircraft carriers make their stately way toward the docks of Honolulu and Pearl Harbor.

Meanwhile, the beach itself plays host to a constant parade of characters; undiscovered starlets in impenetrable sunshades sashay around in the latest swimsuits; local beach boys busy themselves making new friends and renting out the occasional surfboard; over-excited children dart between the sedate seniors with their fancy deckchairs and bulging coolers; and determined European backpackers pick their way through the throng on their dogged search for the perfect plot of sand. On the sidewalk behind, jet-lagged new arrivals wonder how they'll ever get through the crush to dabble their toes in the Pacific for the first time.

Waikīkī's natural setting is just as beguiling as its melee of activity. Off to the east, the sharp profile of Diamond Head spears into the ocean, while straight back inland the lush green Ko'olau Mountains soar between the skyscrapers. In the early evening especially, as the sun sinks far out to sea and the silhouettes of the palm trees grow ever starker, the overall effect is magical.

Few visitors, however, realize that Waikīkī Beach is almost entirely **artificial**. The landscaping that created Waikīkī changed the ocean currents so that its natural beaches were swept away; ever since, the hotels have had a considerable stake in importing sand. So much was shipped in – much of it from Pāpōhaku Beach on Molokai – that the contours of the sea bottom have been permanently altered. As a result, the **surfing** conditions at what is generally acknowledged to be the birthplace of the sport are no longer all that spectacular – which is why the experts head straight up to Oahu's North Shore, covered on p.126.

Public access is guaranteed on every single beach in Hawaii; whatever it may look like, no hotel ever owns the beach adjacent to it.

Central Waikīkī Beach

Although Waikīkī Beach officially stretches the full length of the Waikīkī shoreline, from the Ala Wai Harbor in the west to within a couple of hundred yards of Diamond Head, each of its many distinct sections has its own name. The **center** of the beach – the segment that everyone still calls Waikīkī Beach – is the point near Duke Kahanamoku's statue (see p.40), where the buildings on the ocean side of Kalākaua Avenue come to a halt and the sidewalk turns into a beachfront promenade. This is the main area for surfing lessons and rentals, but swimmers too enjoy the conditions, with softly shelving sands, and waters that are generally calm.

Surfboards can be rented at several beach stands in central Waikīkī, for $8–10 per hour or $30 per day (no deposit required); surf lessons cost around $40 in a group, or $60 one-to-one.

Royal-Moana Beach

To the **west**, central Waikīkī Beach merges with **Royal-Moana Beach**, which fronts the *Sheraton Moana, Outrigger*

Waikīkī, and *Royal Hawaiian* hotels. It can sometimes be a struggle to walk along this narrow, busy strip because of the crowds, but the swimming is, again, excellent. It's also another good spot for **novice surfers**: head slightly to the right as you enter the water to reach the easy break known as Canoes' Surf (so called because these gentle waves were all the heavy old *koa* canoes could ride). The waves are slightly stronger further left, at the Queen's Surf break.

Giving directions, Honolulu residents often say "'Ewa" rather than "west;" 'Ewa is a small town west of Pearl Harbor.

Halekūlani (Gray's) Beach

West of the *Royal Hawaiian*, a raised walkway curves around in front of the *Sheraton Waikīkī*, where the sea comes right over the sand. After a tiny little "pocket beach," where the swimming is again fine but to find any shade you have to crouch beneath some very low branches, a long arrow-straight walkway squeezes between the waves and the grand *Halekūlani Hotel*. At the far end comes a slightly larger stretch of beach, extending from the *Halekūlani* as far as the groin in front of the *Outrigger Reef on the Beach*. This is generally known as **Halekūlani Beach**, or, in memory of a small inn that previously stood here, **Gray's Beach**, but to the ancient Hawaiians it was renowned as Kawehewehe, a place where the waters were said to have special healing properties. There's still plenty of sand on the seabed, so it's another popular swimming spot. Inconspicuous footpaths squeeze through to the beach from Kālia Road on either side of the *Halekūlani*.

Fort DeRussy and Kahanamoku beaches

Beyond Gray's Beach, the sands sloping down to the sea
grow progressively broader as you pass in front of the military base. The going can be a bit slow if you choose to
trudge along **Fort DeRussy Beach** itself, but it's backed
by some pleasant lawns and an open pavilion naturally sheltered by interlaced trees. As the ocean floor at this point is
sharp and rocky, few people swim here, which makes it all
the more appealing for windsurfers. The westernmost section of the Waikīkī shorefront, **Kahanamoku Beach**,
flanks the *Hilton Hawaiian Village* (reviewed on p.158).
Duke Kahanamoku's grandfather was granted most of the
twenty-acre plot on which the *Hilton* now stands in the
Great Mahele of 1848. Thanks to its carefully sculptured
shelf of sand, the beach where Duke was raised is ideal for
family bathing, but it somehow lacks the concentrated
glamor or excitement of central Waikīkī.

Kūhiō Beach

Large segments of the long beach that runs **east** of central
Waikīkī did not even exist until well after World War II.
Until 1922, the shoreline at what's now broad **Kūhiō
Beach** was dominated by the oceanfront home of Prince
Kūhiō (see p.41). When he donated the land to the city
after his death, it held only sporadic patches of sand, and
several structures stood *makai* (on the ocean side) of
Kalākaua Avenue as recently as 1970.

Now, however, Kūhiō Beach is one of Waikīkī's busiest
areas. In the past few years, the protective walls and breakwaters that jut out into the ocean here have been extended
to create two separate very sheltered lagoons in which
swimming is both safe and comfortable. The easternmost
wall, the **Kapahulu Groin**, projects from the end of

Kapahulu Avenue, following the line of the vanished Kuʻekaunahi Stream. Standing well above the waterline, it makes a good vantage point for photos of the Waikīkī panorama. On the other hand, the long **Slippery Wall**, parallel to the beach roughly fifty yards out, is washed over by every wave in turn. Its top is covered with seaweed, and the water to either side is shallow, so diving off is not recommended. Daredevil locals boogie-board just outside the wall, but the currents are so strong that you should only join them if you really know what you're doing. Similarly, don't try to swim to the east of the Groin; it's all too easy to blunder into deep spots where the former riverbed has been exposed by underwater drifts.

Kapiʻolani Park Beach

Immediately east of the Kapahulu Groin, at the end of the built-up section of Waikīkī, the point where the sand first reappears is not suitable for bathing. Not far beyond, however, to either side of the **Waikīkī Aquarium** (described on p.46), **Kapiʻolani Park Beach** is the favorite beach of many local families and fitness freaks, and is also known for having a strong gay presence. Banyans and coconut palms offer plenty of free shade and its lawns make a perfect picnic spot. Waikīkī's only substantial stretch of reasonably unspoiled coral reef runs a short distance offshore, shielding a pleasant, gentle swimming area. The most-used segment of the beach, nearest to Waikīkī, is **Queen's Surf Beach Park**.

Not far past the Aquarium stands the solemn concrete facade of the **War Memorial Natatorium**. This curious combination of World War I memorial and swimming pool, with seating for 2500 spectators, was opened with a 100-meter swim by Duke Kahanamoku (see p.40) on August 24, 1927 – his 37th birthday. During its inaugural championships, Johnny "Tarzan" Weissmuller set world records in the 100-, 400- and 800-meter races.

Ironically, the Natatorium has never really recovered from being taken over for training purposes by the US Navy during World War II, and for many years it was in a very sorry state indeed. Bit by bit, it's now being restored, in face of vociferous opposition from those who argue that the last thing this relatively quiet section of Waikīkī needs is a major tourist attraction.

Sans Souci Beach

East of the Natatorium, palm-fringed **Sans Souci Beach** commemorates one of Waikīkī's earliest guesthouses, built in 1884 and twice stayed in by Robert Louis Stevenson. In addition to being sheltered enough for young children, the beach also offers decent snorkeling – which is unusual for Waikīkī, where most of the reef has been suffocated by dumped sand.

The *New Otani Kaimana Beach* hotel (see p.156), now occupying the site of the *Sans Souci*, marks the return of buildings to the shoreline and is as far as most visitors would consider strolling along Waikīkī Beach. However, beyond it lies the **Outrigger Canoe Club Beach**, which was leased in 1908 by the Outrigger Canoe Club on the condition that its waters be set aside for surfing, canoeing and ocean sports. The club headquarters were later replaced by the first of the *Outrigger* chain of hotels, but the ocean remains the preserve of surfers and snorkelers.

Kaluahole Beach

As Kalākaua Avenue heads out of Waikīkī past the Outrigger Canoe Club Beach, curving away from the shoreline to join Diamond Head Road and skirt the base of the volcano, it passes a little scrap of sandy beach known as **Kaluahole Beach** or **Diamond Head Beach**. Though too small for anyone to want to spend much time on the beach itself, it does offer some quite good swimming, and makes a good launching-point for windsurfers.

Diamond Head Beach Park

The coast immediately to the east of Kaluahole Beach, officially **Diamond Head Beach Park**, is much too rocky and exposed for ordinary swimmers. It is, however, noteworthy as the site of the 55-foot **Diamond Head Lighthouse**, built in 1899 and still in use. The area also has a reputation as a nudist hangout, especially popular with gay men.

A short distance further on, the highway, by now raised well above sea level, rounds the point of Diamond Head; the island of Molokai to the east is visible across the water on clear days. Little scraps of sand cling here and there to the shoreline, but the great majority of those who pick their way down to the ocean from the three roadside lookouts that constitute **Kuilei Cliffs Beach Park** are keen surfers.

Ka'alāwai Beach

Opposite the intersection where Diamond Head Road loops back inland and Kāhala Avenue continues beside the ocean, **Ka'alāwai Beach**, at the end of short Kulumanu Place, is a narrow patch of white sand popular with snorkelers and surfers. It is brought to a halt by Black Point, where lava flowing from Diamond Head into the sea created Oahu's southernmost point.

WAIKĪKĪ ON FOOT

Most of the **walking** you do in Waikīkī is likely to be by necessity rather than choice; it's not an exciting place to explore on foot, and offers little in the way of conventional sightseeing. Its roads may once have been picturesque lanes that meandered between the coconut groves and *taro* fields, but they're now lined by dull concrete malls and hotels, and a building erected before 1970 is a rare sight. In addition, the daytime **heat** can make walking more than a few blocks uncomfortable.

However, vestiges of the old Waikīkī are still scattered here and there, as pointed out by the helpful surfboard-shaped placards of the waterfront **Waikīkī Historical Trail**. There are also a couple of museums illustrating aspects of Hawaiian history, and the lawns of Kapiʻolani Park to the east make a welcome break from the bustle of the resort area. It may come as a surprise that for some people Waikīkī still counts as home; you may well see groups of seniors practicing their ukuleles or playing chess in the oceanfront pavilions.

West from the Duke Kahanamoku statue

The logical place to start a walking tour of Waikīkī is right in the middle, on seafront **Kalākaua Avenue**. The central stretch of Waikīkī Beach here is marked by a statue of **Duke Kahanamoku** (1890–1968), which is always wreathed in *leis*. The archetypal "Beach Boy," Duke represented the US in three Olympics, winning swimming golds in both 1912 and 1920. His subsequent exposition tours popularized the Hawaiian art of surfing all over the world, and as Sheriff of Honolulu he continued to welcome celebrity visitors to Hawaii until his death in 1968. He

STREET NAMES OF WAIKĪKĪ

Waikīkī's unfamiliar street names may seem easier to remember if you know the stories that lie behind them:

Helumoa Road: Literally "chicken scratch"; the road crosses the site of a *heiau* used for human sacrifices, where chickens scratched for maggots amid the corpses.

Kā'iulani Avenue: The young Princess Victoria Ka'iulani (1875–99) was immortalized in a poem by Robert Louis Stevenson.

Kalaimoku Street: Kamehameha the Great's Prime Minister, Kalaimoku, who died in 1827, also called himself "William Pitt" in honor of his British equivalent.

Kalākaua Avenue: Originally named Waikīkī Road, it was renamed in honor of David Kalākaua, the "Merrie Monarch" (1836–91; see p.247), in 1905.

Kālia Road: Kālia was a fishing village that stood between Waikīkī and what's now downtown Honolulu.

Kūhiō Avenue: Prince Jonah Kūhiō Kalaniana'ole (1871–1922), or "Prince Cupid," bequeathed much of the eastern end of Waikīkī to the city after his death.

Lili'uokalani Avenue: Queen Lili'uokalani was the last monarch to rule over Hawaii (1838–1917; see p.248).

Nāhua Street: Chiefess Nāhua once owned an oceanfront estate in Waikīkī.

'Olohana Street: The captured English sailor, John Young (1745–1835), was known as 'Olohana to the Hawaiians after his naval cry of "All hands on deck."

Tusitala Street: Named after author Robert Louis Stevenson, whose Hawaiian name was taken from the Samoan word for "storyteller."

Uluniu Avenue: Literally "coconut grove," it marks the site of a cottage owned by King David Kalākaua.

owed his unusual Christian name to his father, who was also called "Duke" because he had been born on the day that Queen Victoria's second son, the Duke of Edinburgh, visited Honolulu in 1869. Sadly, Duke's back is to the ocean, a pose he seldom adopted in life; otherwise he'd be gazing at the spot where in 1917 he rode a single 35-foot wave a record total of one and a quarter miles.

Slightly west of the statue, on the beach side next to a small police station and snack shop, a railed enclosure holds four large boulders known as the **sacred stones of Ulukou**. Standing on a raised stone platform, these are said to embody the healing and spiritual powers of four magician-priests from Tahiti, who set them in place before returning to their home island of Raiatea in the fourteenth century.

Still further west, the wedge of the **Sheraton Moana Surfrider** forces Kalākaua Avenue away from the ocean. Though not Waikīkī's first hotel, the *Moana* is the oldest left standing, and since 1983 it has been transformed back to a close approximation of its original 1901 appearance. Like all Waikīkī hotels, the *Moana* is happy to allow nonguests in for a peek; the luxurious settees of its long Beaux Arts lobby make an ideal spot to catch up with the newspapers.

Follow Kalākaua Avenue west from here, and you'll come to the **Royal Hawaiian Shopping Center**, Waikīkī's most upmarket mall (though not a patch on Honolulu's Ala Moana Center; see p.216), and across from that the tackier open-air **International Marketplace**, which has a bargain food court (see p.173). Once the site of an ancient *heiau*, and later of the ten-thousand-strong royal Helumoa coconut grove – of which a few palms still survive – the beachfront here is today dominated by the **Royal Hawaiian Hotel**, also known as the "Pink Palace." Its Spanish-Moorish architecture was all the rage when it opened in 1927, with a room rate of $14 per night, but its grandeur is now somewhat swamped by a towering new wing.

Fort DeRussy and the US Army Museum

Map 3, A7. US Army Museum Tues–Sun 10am–4.30pm; free.

On the map, the military base of **Fort DeRussy** looks like a welcome expanse of green at the western edge of the main built-up area of Waikīkī. In fact, it's largely taken up by parking lots and tennis courts, and is not a place to stroll for pleasure. At its oceanfront side, however, the **US Army Museum** is situated in a low concrete structure that, as **Battery Randolph**, housed massive artillery pieces directed by observers stationed atop Diamond Head during World War II. Displays here trace the history of warfare in Hawaii back to the time of Kamehameha the Great, with the bulk of the collection consisting of the various guns and cannons that have defended Honolulu since the US Army first arrived, four days after annexation in 1898. One photo shows a young, giggling Shirley Temple perched astride a gun barrel during the 1930s, but the mood swiftly changes with a detailed chronicling of the pivotal role played by Hawaii during the Pacific campaign against Japan.

The museum stands on the original site of the villa of Chun Afong, celebrated as the "merchant prince of the Sandalwood Mountains." Hawaii's first Chinese millionaire, he lived here from 1855 onward.

East from the Duke Kahanamoku statue

The first thing you come to as you head **east** from the Duke Kahanamoku statue is a magnificent well-groomed Indian banyan tree, supported by two "trunks" that on close inspection turn out to be tangled masses of aerial roots. White doves have made their nests in the hollow recesses where the tree has been repeatedly cut back. This area has been attractively landscaped, and the site now includes appealing little lagoons and waterfalls as well as shaded pavilions and lots of open-air benches.

Across the street, the central atrium of the *Hyatt Regency Waikīkī* hotel holds a much larger waterfall, surrounded by palm trees. A couple of blocks along, the gimmick at the *Pacific Beach Hotel* is its Oceanarium, a multistory fish tank that reaches from the lobby up through the upstairs restaurants (see p.176).

The Damien Museum

Map 3, I6. 130 Ohua Ave; Mon–Fri 9am–3pm; free; ☎ 923-2690.

Father Damien, the nineteenth-century Belgian priest who ranks with Hawaii's greatest heroes, is commemorated in the simple **Damien Museum**, one block east of the *Pacific Beach Hotel*. This unobtrusive shrine sits beneath a schoolroom behind the angular, modern Catholic church of **St Augustine**, which is itself tucked in behind an ABC store.

Although he established churches all over Hawaii, Damien's fame derives principally from his final sojourn in the leper colony at **Kalaupapa** on the island of Molokai. When he arrived there in 1873, Kalaupapa was by all accounts a place of misery and despair. For eight years, real or suspected sufferers of what's now known as Hansen's Disease had been shipped there against their will, and abandoned to fend for themselves. Damien gave them their first medical and pastoral care, irrespective of religious background, but eventually succumbed to the disease himself on April 15, 1889, at the age of 49. The museum evokes his life and work with an assortment of mundane trivia, such as receipts for cases of soda and barrels of flour, and his prayerbooks and vestments. Its most powerful punch is saved until last: a series of harrowing photos of Damien on his deathbed, ravaged by disease.

KAPI'OLANI PARK

Beyond the eastern limit of central Waikīkī, as defined by Kapuhulu Avenue, lies Hawaii's first-ever public park, **Kapiʻolani Park**. This much-needed breathing space was established in 1877 by King David Kalākaua, and named for his queen. It originally held a number of ponds, until the completion of the Ala Wai Canal in 1928 cut off its supply of fresh water. Now locals flock to its open green lawns, with joggers pounding the footpaths, and practitioners of t'ai chi weaving slow-motion spells beneath the banyans.

Tourists pour in from 9am on Tuesdays, Wednesdays and Thursdays, for the free **Pleasant Hawaiian Hula Show**, which starts at 10am. This kitsch relic of bygone days, sponsored for many years by Kodak, but now run under the auspices of the Pleasant Hawaiian tour group, culminates with grass-skirted *hula* "maidens" (some of whom have participated since it began in 1937) holding up letters to spell out A-L-O-H-A H-A-W-A-I-I. The adjoining **Waikīkī Shell** hosts large concerts, especially in summer, while the Royal Hawaiian Band performs on the park's **bandstand** on Sundays at 2pm.

Honolulu Zoo

Map 4, I4. Daily 8.30am–5.30pm, last admission 4.30pm; closed Christmas and New Year's Day; adults $6, ages 6–12 $1. Additional night walks take place two nights either side of each full moon; adults $7, ages 6–12 $5; call ☎ 971-7171 for schedules.

The **Honolulu Zoo** occupies a verdant wedge on the fringes of Kapiʻolani Park. With its main entrance barely a minute's walk from the bustle of Waikīkī, the zoo's luxuriant tropical undergrowth and blossoming trees, set against the backdrop of Diamond Head, are as much of an attraction as the animals, which range from wallowing hippos and gray kangaroos to some unfortunate monkeys trapped on tiny islands in a crocodile-infested lagoon. The zoo's pride and joy, the African Savanna exhibit, is a reasonably successful attempt to re-create the swamps and grasslands of Africa. In this world of reddish mud live "black" rhinos, which are, in fact, the color of their surroundings.

Waikīkī Aquarium

Map 4, I5. Daily 9am–5pm, closed Christmas Day; adults $7, seniors and students $5, ages 13–17 $3.50, under-12s free.

A few minutes walk east of the zoo, along the Kapi'olani Park waterfront, stands the slick, but disappointingly small, **Waikīkī Aquarium**. Windows in its indoor galleries offer views into the turquoise world of Hawaiian reef fish, among them the lurid red frogfish – an ugly brute that squats splay-footed on the rock waiting to eat unwary passersby – and a teeming mass of small sharks. The highlight is the "leafy sea dragon," a truly bizarre Australian relative of the by-comparison very normal seahorse; there's also a whole tank devoted to Hanauma Bay (see p.102). Outside, the mocked-up "edge of the reef," complete with artificial tide pools, feels a bit pointless with the real thing just a few feet away. Nearby is a long tank of Hawaiian monk seals, dog-like not only in appearance but also in their willingness to perform tawdry tricks for snacks. As well as a description of traditional fish-farming, there's a display of the modern equivalent, in which *mahimahi* fish grow from transparent eggs to glistening six-footers in what appear to be lava lamps.

DIAMOND HEAD

Map 2, H7. Diamond Head State Monument daily 6am–6pm; $1.

The craggy 762-foot pinnacle of **Diamond Head**, immediately southeast along the coast from Waikīkī, is

Honolulu's most famous landmark. It's among the youngest of the chain of volcanic cones – others include Punchbowl (see p.73) and Koko Head (p.104) – that stretch across southeast Oahu. All were created by brief, spectacular blasts of the Ko'olau vent, which reawakened a few hundred thousand years ago after slumbering for more than two million years. The most recent of the series date back less than ten thousand years, so geologists consider further eruptions possible. Diamond Head itself was formed in a matter of a few days or even hours: the southwestern side is so much higher than the others because the trade winds were blowing from the northeast at the time.

Ancient Hawaiians knew Diamond Head as either Lei'ahi ("wreath of fire," a reference to beacons lit on the summit to guide canoes) or Lae'ahi ("brow of the yellow-fin tuna"). They built several *heiaus* in and around it, slid down its walls to Waikīkī on *hōlua* land-sleds as sport, and threw convicted criminals from the rim. Its modern name derives from the mistake of a party of English sailors early in the nineteenth century, who stumbled across what they thought were diamonds on its slopes and rushed back to town with their pockets bulging with glittering but worthless calcite crystals.

As a remarkable natural fortress, Diamond Head has long been prized by the military. Its lower outer slopes, on the oceanward side especially, are now fringed with luxury homes, but its rim still bristles with spear-like antennae. For most of the twentieth century, the interior was sealed off by the US armed forces, who based long-range artillery here during World War I, and after Pearl Harbor used the bunkers to triangulate the guns of Waikīkī's Fort DeRussy. In the 1960s it was reopened as the Diamond Head State Monument public park.

Access to the crater is via a short road tunnel that drills through the surrounding walls from its *mauka* side. The entrance is about two miles by road from Waikīkī; it's not a particularly pleasant walk, so most people either drive or take the bus. Buses #22 and #58 from Waikīkī climb up Monsarrat Avenue past the zoo to join Diamond Head Road, and stop not far from the tunnel; if you're driving, you can also follow the shoreline highway below the mountain and climb the same road from the bottom.

Because the floor of the crater stands well above sea level – it's gradually filling in as the walls erode – Diamond Head is not quite so dramatic from the inside. In fact, the lawns of the crater interior are oddly bland, almost suburban. Often parched, but a vivid green after rain, they're still dotted with little-used military installations, some of which remain restricted. There have been suggestions that these should be replaced by tennis and golf facilities, but the prevailing wisdom is to allow the place to return to nature in due course.

For details of guided Diamond Head guided hikes, see p.21.

The hike to the rim

Most people come to Diamond Head to **hike** the hot half-hour trail up to the rim, for a superb panorama of the whole southern coast of Oahu. The climb is more demanding than you may be led to expect, so wear suitable footwear and bring a flashlight.

The paved footpath climbs slowly across the crater floor from the fee station beside the central parking lot, then meanders up the inside walls. Many of the holes visible but out of reach on the hillside are ancient burial caves. Before long, you're obliged to enter the vast network of military bunkers and passageways that riddle the crater. Immediately after passing through the first long, dark tunnel – watch out for the bolts poking from the ceiling – a tall, narrow flight of yellow-painted stairs leads up between two high walls to the right. It's also possible to head left here to join a path along the outside – a reasonably safe option as long as you follow the contours, and bear in mind that several people have fallen while attempting to scramble straight up.

If you continue up the steps instead, you soon come to another tunnel, then climb a dark spiral staircase through four or so cramped tiers of fortifications, equipped with eye-slit windows and camouflaged from above. Beyond that, a final outdoor staircase leads to the summit, where you get your first sweeping views of Waikīkī and Honolulu. In theory an official geodetic plate marks the highest point; however often it's replaced, it soon gets stolen again.

On days when a *kona* (southwest) wind is blowing, planes landing at Honolulu Airport approach from the east, passing low enough over Diamond Head for you to see the passengers inside.

Taxis wait in the parking lot back on the crater floor, ready to ferry weary hikers who can't face the walk back to Waikīkī.

Downtown Honolulu

Downtown Honolulu, the administrative heart of first the kingdom, and now the state, of Hawaii, stands a few blocks west of the original city center. Most of the compact grid of streets where the port grew up is now taken up by Chinatown – as covered in Chapter Three – while downtown generally focuses on the cluster of buildings that surround 'Iolani Palace, home to Hawaii's last monarchs. This is certainly a presentable district, with several well-preserved historic buildings, but it's not a very lively one. At lunchtime on weekdays, office workers scurry through the streets, but the rest of the time the contrast with the frenzy of Waikīkī is striking. With few shops, bars or restaurants to lure outsiders, the whole place is usually empty by 8pm.

'IOLANI PALACE

Map 5, H5. Call ☏ 522-0832 to join a reservation-only tour; Tues–Sat every 15min 9am–2.15pm; adults $15, ages 5–12 $5, under-5s not admitted.

'**Iolani Palace** was the official home of the last two monarchs of Hawaii. It was built for **King David Kalākaua** in

1882, near the site of a previous palace that had been destroyed by termites, and he lived here until his death in 1891. For his sister and successor, **Queen Lili'uokalani**, it served first as a palace, and then, after her overthrow in 1893 (see p.249), a prison. Until 1968, by which time the termites had pretty much eaten up this palace too, it was the Hawaiian state capitol building. Since the new Capitol was completed in 1969, it has been preserved as a museum.

Although the palace has become a symbol for the Hawaiian sovereignty movement and is occasionally the scene of large pro-independence demonstrations, the official **tours** are firmly apolitical. Guides revel in the lost romance of the Hawaiian monarchy without quite acknowledging that it was illegally overthrown by the United States. The fact that visitors have to shuffle around in cotton booties to protect the hardwood floors adds to the air of unreality.

Apart from its *koa*-wood floors and staircase, the palace contains little that is distinctively Hawaiian. In the largest of its **downstairs** rooms, the **Throne Room**, Kalākaua held formal balls to celebrate his coronation and fiftieth birthday, and Lili'uokalani was tried for treason for allegedly supporting moves for her own restoration. The *kapu* stick that separates the thrones of Kalākaua and his wife Kapi'olani was made from a narwhal tusk given to Kalākaua by a sea captain. Other reception rooms lead off from the grand central hall, with all available wall space taken up by formal portraits of Hawaiian and other monarchs. Though the plush **upstairs** bedrooms feel similarly stately and impersonal, there's one touching exhibit – the glass case in the front room containing a quilt made by Queen Lili'uokalani during her eight months under house arrest.

A grass-covered mound in the garden marks the original resting place of King Kamehameha II and Queen Kamamalu. Their remains, brought here by George Byron

'IOLANI PALACE

(the cousin of the poet) after they died of measles in England in 1824, were later moved to the royal mausoleum in Nu'uanu (see p.83).

The palace's **ticket office** is housed in the castellated 'Iolani Barracks, an odd structure that predates the palace by about fifteen years. It now stands on the west side of the grounds, having been moved to this spot in 1965 to make room for construction of the new capitol. Before becoming king – the monarch was by this time an elective rather than a hereditary position – Kalākaua is said to have encouraged its soldiers in a mutiny to embarrass his predecessor King Lunalilo, whom he regarded as too pro-Western. If you arrive without a reservation and can't get on the next tour, you can watch a video about the palace here instead.

QUEEN LILI'UOKALANI STATUE

Map 5, H4.

Beyond the impressive banyan tree at the foot of the palace steps, a walkway separates the grounds of 'Iolani Palace from the State Capitol to the north. In its center, a statue of **Queen Lili'uokalani** looks haughtily toward the state's present-day legislators. Festooned with *leis* and plumeria blossoms, she's depicted holding copies of her mournful song *Aloha 'Oe*, the Hawaiian creation chant known as the *Kumulipo*, and her draft Constitution of 1893, which precipitated the coup d'état against her.

THE STATE CAPITOL

Map 5, H4.

Hawaii's **State Capitol** is a confused child of the 1960s. It's a bizarre edifice, propped up on pillars above its own little lake, and with each of its two legislative chambers shaped like a volcano. As a deliberate democratic gesture, the layout ensures that legislators can't move between their offices and the meeting chambers without passing in view of the open spaces where demonstrators might gather.

It took little more than twenty years for the flaws in the capitol's design to force its closure for extensive and very expensive rebuilding. That work has now been completed, though public tours have yet to recommence. In front of the main entrance, there's a peculiar cubic statue of Father Damien (see p.44) wearing a black cloak; the black, metal sculpture was created by Marisol Escobar in 1968. Well-tended memorials to Hawaiians who died in Korea and Vietnam stand in the grounds to the west.

HONOLULU HALE

Map 5, J5.

The seat of Honolulu's city government – **Honolulu Hale**, opposite the eastern end of the 'Iolani Palace walkway – is a more successful architectural experiment than the State Capitol. An airy 1920s melding of Italianate and Spanish Mission styles, with whitewashed walls, ornate patterned ceilings, and red-tiled roofs, it boasts a grand central atrium packed with colorful murals and sculptural flourishes. Various anterooms often host temporary exhibitions of local art or history; even when there's nothing on, visitors are free to stroll through.

WASHINGTON PLACE

Map 5, H3.

Though **Punchbowl Crater** looms large as you look north from the Capitol, and you may be able to spot visitors on the rim, it's a long way away by road; for a full account, see p.73. Much closer at hand, across Beretania Street, is the white-columned, Colonial-style mansion known as

Washington Place. During the 1860s, Queen Lili'uokalani resided here as plain Mrs Dominis, wife to the governor of Hawaii under King Kamehameha V. After her dethronement she returned to live here as a private citizen once more, and died at the mansion in 1917. Five years later it became, as it remains, the official residence of the governor of Hawaii and is not open to the public.

ST ANDREW'S CATHEDRAL

Map 5, G3. Mon–Fri 8am–4pm; free.

Behind Washington Place and a short distance to the east rises the central tower of **St Andrew's Cathedral**. Work began on this Gothic-influenced Episcopal church in 1867, in realization of plans formed ten years previously by King Kamehameha IV, who wanted to encourage Anglican missionaries to come to Hawaii to counterbalance the prevailing Puritanism of their American counterparts. Kamehameha IV had become a staunch Anglophile during an extended visit to Europe. After he died (on St Andrew's Day 1863 – hence the name of the cathedral), his widow Queen Emma (see p.83) kept up the connection. Construction work ended in 1958, with the completion of the Great West Window, a stained-glass rendition of the story of Hawaiian Christianity.

THE KAMEHAMEHA STATUE

Map 5, H6.

The flower-bedecked gilt figure of **Kamehameha the Great** (1758–1819), the first man to rule all the islands of Hawaii, stares northward across King Street toward 'Iolani Palace from outside Ali'iōlani Hale. Kamehameha is depicted wearing the *'ahu'ula* (royal cloak), *malo* (loincloth), *kā'ei* (sash), and *mahiole* (feather helmet), and clutching a spear.

The work of Thomas R. Gould, an American sculptor based in Florence, the statue was commissioned by the Hawaiian legislature in 1878 to celebrate the centenary of the arrival of Captain Cook. On its way to Hawaii, however, it was lost when the ship that was carrying it caught fire off the Falkland Islands, so a second copy was cast and dispatched. That arrived in 1880 and was unveiled by King Kalākaua at his coronation in 1883; surplus insurance money from the lost statue paid for the sequence of four panels depicting scenes from Kamehameha's life around its base. Meanwhile, a whaling captain bought the original statue from a curio shop in Port Stanley, and brought it over to Hawaii in return for an $875 reward. It was packed off to Kamehameha's birthplace on the Big Island.

Ceremonies are held at King Kamehameha's statue on June 11 each year, to mark Kamehameha Day, a state holiday.

ALI'IŌLANI HALE

Map 5, H6. Judiciary History Center Mon–Fri 10am–4pm; free.

Erected in 1874, **Ali'iōlani Hale** – "House of the Heavenly King" in Hawaiian – was Hawaii's first library and national museum. It was also the first building taken over by the conspirators who overthrew the monarchy in 1893. Throughout its history, however, its main function has been as the home of the state's Supreme Court. The first floor houses the fascinating **Judiciary History Center**, which outlines the history of Hawaiian law from the days of the ancient *kapu* (see p.257) onward and chronicles the role played by the Supreme Court in replacing the tradition under which all land was held in common with the concept of private ownership. There's also an intriguing scale model of Honolulu in 1850.

KAWAIAHA'O CHURCH

Map 5, J5. Mon–Sat 8am–4pm, plus church service Sun 10.30am; free.

Although **Kawaiaha'o Church**, just east of 'Iolani Palace near the junction of Punchbowl and King streets, was erected less than twenty years after the first Christian missionaries came to Hawaii, it was the fifth church to stand on this site. According to its Protestant minister, Rev Hiram Bingham, each of the four predecessors was a thatched "cage in a haymow." This one, by contrast, was built with thousand-pound chunks of living coral, hacked from the reef. It's not especially huge, but the columned portico is grand enough, topped by a four-square clock tower.

Inside, broad balconies run down both sides of the nave, lined with royal portraits. Below, plaques on the walls honor early figures of Hawaiian Christianity. The plushest pews – at the back of the church, upholstered in velvet and marked off by *kahili* standards – were reserved for royalty.

In the gardens on the *mauka* side of the church, a fountain commemorates the site of a spring formerly known as *Ka wai a Ha'o*, "the water of Ha'o." A rare treasure in this barren region, it was used exclusively by *ali'i nui*, or high chiefs, such as chiefess Ha'o.

The small mausoleum in the grounds fronting the church holds the remains of **King Lunalilo**, who ruled for less than two years after his election in 1872. Feeling slighted that his mother's body had not been removed from the churchyard to the royal mausoleum (see p.83), he chose to be buried here instead. The rest of the graves in the **cemetery** around the back serve as a brief history of Hawaii's nineteenth-century missionary elite, with an abundance of Castles and Cookes, Alexanders and Baldwins, and the only president of the Republic, Sanford B. Dole.

THE MISSION HOUSES

Map 5, K5. 553 S King St; Tues–Sat 9am–4pm; adults $6, under-19s $3; ⓣ 531-0481.

Hawaii's first Christian missionaries are recalled by the partly reconstructed **Mission Houses** behind Kawaiahaʻo Church. Standing cheek by jowl on South King Street, these three nineteenth-century buildings commemorate the pioneers of the Sandwich Islands Mission, who arrived from Boston in 1820.

The oldest edifice, the two-story **Frame House**, was shipped in whole from New England in 1821. Reluctant to let outsiders build permanent structures, the king only allowed it to go up with the words "when you go away, take everything with you." Local fears that its cellar held weapons for use in a planned takeover of the islands were allayed when Kamehameha's principal adviser, Kalanimoku, built a house with a larger cellar across the street. The house, whose tiny windows were entirely unsuited to the heat of Honolulu, was home to four missionary families. A kitchen had to be added because cooking outdoors attracted too much attention from the islanders, as it was *kapu* (forbidden) for women to prepare food.

One of the missionaries' first acts, in 1823, was to set up the **Print House**, which produced the first Hawaiian-language Bible – *Ka Palapala Hemolele*. The current building – not the original, but its 1841 replacement – holds a replica of its imported Ramage printing press, whose limitations were among the reasons that to this day the Hawaiian alphabet only has twelve letters.

The largest of the three buildings, the **Chamberlain House**, started life in 1831 as the mission storehouse. As the missionary families became increasingly embroiled in the economy of the islands, it was turned into the com-

THE MISSION HOUSES

mercial headquarters of Castle and Cooke, one of the original "Big Five" sugar companies (see p.246).

HONOLULU ACADEMY OF ARTS

Map 5, N1. 900 S Beretania St; Tues–Sat 10am–4.30pm, Sun 1–5pm; tours Tues–Sat 11am, Sun 1.15pm; free first Wed of month, otherwise $7, under-13s free; ⊤ 532-8700. TheBus #2 from Waikīkī stops outside.

Honolulu residents take great pride in the stunning fine art on display at the **Academy of Arts**. Few tourists find their way here – half a mile east of the Capitol – but two or three hours wandering the galleries of this elegant former private home, with its open courtyards and fountains, is time well spent.

The bulk of the Academy's superb collection of **paintings** adorns the galleries that surround the **Mediterranean Court**, to the right of the entrance. Highlights include Van Gogh's *Wheat Field*, Gauguin's *Two Nudes on a Tahitian Beach* and one of Monet's *Water Lilies*. Other pieces date from the Italian Renaissance, with two separate *Apostles* by Carlo Crivelli, as well as engravings by Rembrandt and Dürer; more recent canvases include lesser works by Picasso, Léger, Braque, Matisse and Tanguy.

A separate gallery within the complex has been set aside to house some fascinating **depictions of Hawaii** by visiting artists. Most of these works, including an 1838 pencil sketch of Waikīkī, have more historic value than artistic merit. The much-reproduced portrait of *Kamehameha in Red Vest*, painted by the Russian Louis Choris in 1816, shows the redoubtable monarch in his later years, and there are several dramatic renditions of the changing face of the volcano at Kīlauea. John Webber, who accompanied Cook to Hawaii in 1779, contributes a pen and watercolor sketch of the village of "Kowrooa" (Ka'awaloa), nestling beneath the palms of Kealakekua Bay, where Cook died.

Contemporary European images of Cook's death reveal the extent to which both Cook and the islands themselves soon became romanticized and idealized.

The Academy's **Modern and Contemporary** collection ranges from a Francis Bacon triptych and a Nam June Paik video installation to Yan Pei-Ming's 1997 portrait of the singer Israel Kamakawiwoʻole (see p.201) in slathered black and grey oils. Tucked away in a side corridor are Georgia O'Keeffe's vivid, stylized studies of Maui's ʻĪao Valley and Hāna coast.

The Academy's courtyard café serves lunch Tues–Sat 11.30am–2pm (reservations on ☏ 532-8734), and tea Tues–Sun 2–4pm.

To the left of the entrance, the centerpiece of the **Asian Court** is a collection of 2000 pieces of ancient **Chinese** art, a 1993 bequest. Among these magnificent artifacts are beautiful ceramics, four-thousand-year-old jade blades, green Zhou bronzes, and a column from a two-thousand-year-old Han tomb that looks like an Easter Island statue. There then follows a cornucopia of works from all over the world: Buddhist and Shinto deities, plus miniature *netsuke* (buckles) from Japan; Tibetan *thangkas* (religious images), Indian carvings ranging from Rajasthani sandstone screens to a stone Chola statue of Krishna; Mayan effigies and Indonesian stick figures; Melanesian masks incorporating such elements as boars' tusks and cobwebs; Egyptian, Roman and Assyrian friezes and reliefs, and pottery from the *pueblos* of Arizona and New Mexico. There are also a few ancient Hawaiian artifacts, though better ones are on display at the Bishop Museum (see p.87).

HONOLULU ACADEMY OF ARTS

Chinatown

Barely five-minutes' walk west of 'Iolani Palace, a pair of matching stone dragons flank either side of Hotel Street, marking the transition between downtown Honolulu and the oldest part of the city, **Chinatown**. For well over a century, this was renowned as the city's red-light district. Though most of the pool halls, massage parlors and tawdry bars that formerly lined the narrow streets leading down to the Nu'uanu Stream have now gone, the fading green-clapboard storefronts and bustling market ambience still make Chinatown seem like another world. Cosmopolitan, atmospheric and historic in equal proportions, it's the one local neighborhood that's genuinely fun to explore on your own. It's also changing fast, blending futuristic elements in with its relics of the past to create a hybrid of old and new, East and West.

TheBus #2 and #20 run from Waikīkī to
North Hotel Street, on the edge of Chinatown.

EXPLORING CHINATOWN

Of Chinatown's two main axes, North Hotel and Maunakea streets, **Hotel Street** best lives up to the area's low-life reputation, with drunken sailors lurching to and from the *Club Hubba Hubba Topless-Bottomless* and assorted sawdust-floored bars.

The actual intersection of Hotel and Maunakea is dominated by the ornate facade of **Wo Fat's**, topped by a pagoda-style green-tiled roof. A hundred years old, *Wo Fat's* is Chinatown's – indeed, Hawaii's – longest-standing restaurant. Its main rival as the leading local landmark is the Art Deco **Hawaii Theatre**, further east at 1130 Bethel St, which reopened after extensive restoration in 1996. Guided tours of the theater ($5) take place on every Tuesday at 11am, but a far better way to appreciate the gorgeous interior is by attending one of its varied programs of (mostly one-time) performances; contact ☎528-0506 or ⓦwww.hawaiitheatre.com for more details.

Many of Chinatown's old walled courtyards have been converted into open malls, but the businesses within remain much the same. Apothecaries and herbalists weigh out dried leaves in front of endless arrays of bottles, shelves and wooden cabinets, while groups of deft-fingered women gather around tables to thread *leis*. Every hole-in-the-wall store holds a fridge bursting with colorful blooms, while appetizing food smells waft from backstreet bakeries.

To join an organized walking tour of Chinatown, call either the Chinese Chamber of Commerce (Tues 9.30am; $5; ☎533-3181), or the Hawaii Heritage Center (Fri 9.30am; $5; ☎521-2749).

Chinatown's markets

If you get hungry, call in at *Char Hung Sut*, 64 North Pauahi at Smith (Mon & Wed–Sat 5.30am–2pm, Sun 5.30am–1pm) for freshly made dim sum, or browse through

THE CHINESE IN HAWAII

Strangely enough, there was a Hawaiian in China before there were any Chinese in Hawaii – Kai'ana, a chief from Kauai, was briefly abandoned in Canton in 1787 by a British fur-trader he had thought was taking him to Europe. Within three years, however, Chinese seamen were starting to jump ship to seek their fortunes in the land they knew as Tan Hueng Shan, "the Sandalwood Mountains." Trading vessels regularly crossed the Pacific between China and Hawaii, and Cantonese merchants and entrepreneurs became a familiar sight in Honolulu. Even the granite that paved the streets of what became Chinatown was brought over from China as ballast in ships.

Some of Hawaii's earliest Chinese settlers were sugar boilers, and the islands' first sugar mill was set up by a Chinese immigrant on Lanai in 1802. American capital proved itself more than a match for any individual Chinese endeavor, however, and the Chinese only began to arrive in Hawaii in sizeable numbers when the sugar plantations commenced importing laborers in 1852. Workers were usually indentured for five years, so by 1857 Chinese laborers were leaving the plantations and using their small savings to finance their own businesses. At first, the majority were on Kauai, where they began to turn neglected Hawaiian farmlands into rice paddies, even using water buffalo shipped over from China.

In time, however, the Chinese settled increasingly in Honolulu, where "friendly societies" would help new arrivals find their feet. Inevitably, many of these were renegades and outlaws, ranging from gang members to political dissidents. **Sun Yat-sen**, for example, who became the first President of the Republic of China when the Manchu Dynasty was overthrown in 1911, was educated at 'Iolani School.

By the 1860s there were more Chinese than white residents in Hawaii. With the native Hawaiian population shrinking, the pro-American establishment in Honolulu felt threatened. In response, they maneuvered to ensure that white residents could vote for the national legislature while Asians could not. They also induced the plantations to switch their recruiting policies and focus on other parts of the globe.

At the end of the nineteenth century, Chinatown was at its zenith. Its crowded lanes held more than 7000 people, including Japanese and Hawaiians as well as Chinese. When bubonic plague was detected in December 1899, however, city authorities decided to prevent its spread by systematic burning. The first few controlled burns were effective, but on January 20, 1900, a small fire started at Beretania and Nu'uanu rapidly turned into a major conflagration. The flames destroyed Kaumakapili Church as well as a 38-acre swath that reached to within a few yards of the waterfront. Police cordons prevented the quarantined residents from leaving during the fire, while any already outside were unable to return to salvage possessions. White-owned newspapers were soon rhapsodizing about the opportunity to expand downtown Honolulu, convincing the Chinese community, which never received adequate compensation, that the destruction was at the very least welcome and at worst deliberate.

Nonetheless, Chinatown was rebuilt, and the fact that almost all its surviving structures date from that rebuilding gives it an appealing architectural harmony. Chinatown has since 1974 been declared a preservation district, and it still remains Honolulu's liveliest, most characterful quarter, albeit much more commercial than it is residential. Most local Chinese, like the rest of the city's inhabitants, live in outlying suburbs.

THE CHINESE IN HAWAII

the Oriental food specialities at **Oahu Market**, on North King and Kekaulike. This traditional market was scheduled for demolition in 1988, but the traders banded together to buy it. The fastest-selling item seems to be *ahi* (yellow-fin tuna), used for making sashimi or *poke*, but this is also the place to go if you're looking for a pig's snout or a salmon's head.

The best selection of fast food in Chinatown is at the newer **Maunakea Marketplace**, a couple of blocks north and entered via either Hotel or Maunakea streets. Once you enter the main building, beneath the watchful gaze of the statue of Confucius in its central plaza, the temperature is likely to be sweltering, but the choice of cuisines is amazing, and it's all available at the lowest prices in Honolulu. Here once again, fresh ingredients are also on sale. The plaza itself is surrounded by a wide assortment of souvenir and trinket stores, with Chinese calendar scrolls and miniature statuettes among the specialties.

Some of the best Chinatown restaurants are listed on p.185.

Nu'uanu Stream and beyond

Chinatown is bordered to the west by the **Nu'uanu Stream**, flowing down to Honolulu Harbor. **River Street**, which runs alongside, becomes an attractive, restaurant-filled pedestrian mall between Beretania and Kukui streets. At the port end stands a *lei*-swaddled statue of **Sun Yat-sen**, while over Kukui Street at the opposite end is the tiny Lum Hai So Tong **Taoist temple**. Most of the interior of the block next to the mall is occupied by the **Chinatown Cultural Plaza**, filled with slightly tacky souvenir stores and conventional businesses that cater to the Chinese community.

Across the stream, a block south beyond the Izumo Taisha **Shinto shrine**, erected by local Japanese citizens in 1923, retired citizens of Chinatown unwind in **'A'Ala Triangle Park**. The **railroad station** here was used by the Oahu Railway until it went broke in 1947; it's now owned by the Hawaii Railway Society (see p.137).

Foster Botanic Garden

Map 5, B–C1. 180 N Vineyard Blvd. Daily 9am–4pm; adults $5, under-13s $1; guided tours, no extra charge, Mon–Fri 1pm.
At the top end of River Street, and entered via a short driveway that leads off North Vineyard Boulevard beside the Kuan Yin **Buddhist temple**, is the twenty-acre **Foster Botanic Garden**. Established in the middle of the nineteenth century as a sanctuary for Hawaiian plants and a testing ground for foreign imports, it has become one of Honolulu's best-loved city parks. Different sections cover spices such as vanilla and pepper, herbs, flowering orchids and tropical trees from around the world. As well as sausage trees from Mozambique, the latter collection includes a *bo* (or *peepal*) tree supposedly descended from the *bo* tree at Bodh Gaya in North India where the Buddha achieved enlightenment.

FOSTER BOTANIC GARDEN

Waterfront Honolulu

t's all too easy to lose sight of the fact that central Honolulu stands just a few yards up from the turquoise waters of the Pacific, which even in the heart of the city is clean enough to support conspicuous populations of bright tropical fish. Sadly, pedestrians exploring both Chinatown and downtown have to brave the fearsome traffic of Nimitz Highway in order to reach the ocean. That effort is rewarded by a short but enjoyable stroll along the segment of the **waterfront** that stretches for a couple of hundred yards east of the venerable Aloha Tower. Until 1857, this area was covered by the waves; then the city fort, which had previously stood at Fort and Queen streets, was torn down, and the rubble used to fill in a fifteen-acre expanse of the sea floor. Now in addition to watching the comings and goings of Honolulu Harbor, you can join a sunset dinner cruise or similar expedition from the piers nearby or learn something of the port's history in the Hawaii Maritime Center.

Long and surprisingly quiet **beaches** fringe the shoreline a little further to the east, especially in the vicinity of **Ala**

Moana, which is home to the city's largest beach park as well as a huge shopping mall.

ALOHA TOWER

Map 5, E9. Observation deck April–Sept daily 9am–7.30pm, Oct–March daily 9am–7pm; free.

The **Aloha Tower**, on Pier 9 of Honolulu Harbor, was built in 1926 to serve as a control center for the port's traffic and a landmark for arriving cruise passengers. At 184ft high, it was then the tallest building in Honolulu; with its four giant clock-faces, each surmounted by the word "ALOHA," it was also the most photographed. Seventy years of skyscraper construction made it seem progressively smaller and smaller, but the tower has since the late 1990s returned to prominence as the centerpiece of the **Aloha Tower Marketplace** shopping mall.

- -
Both TheBus #2 and the Aloha Tower Express
run from Waikīkī to Aloha Tower; see p.17.
- -

The stores and restaurants tend to be expensive and predictable (see p.217 and 187), and with much fewer parking spaces available here than at the major malls they're heavily dependent on day-trippers from Waikīkī as opposed to local residents. As for the tower itself, it feels a little stranded and incongruous; as the placard at its base puts it, "Aloha Tower now stands alone for the first time in its history." However, with the mall walkways ending right at the dockside, and several of the restaurants and bars upstairs offering large open-air terraces, this is an unexpectedly enjoyable place to get a sense of the ongoing life of the port. Cargo vessels from all over the world tie up alongside, and there's always something going on out in the water.

Taking a free trip up to the tenth-floor **Observation**

ALOHA TOWER

Deck of the Aloha Tower is also worthwhile. Balconies on each of its four sides, originally used as lookouts by harbor pilots, offer views that are just short of ugly – freeways, airport runways and grimy harbor installations – but provide an excellent orientation to the city. As you look toward Diamond Head – which may well be obscured by haze, the twin pink-trimmed "stereo speakers" of the Waterfront Towers condominiums loom above the black glass of Restaurant Row (see p.187); meanwhile, Pearl Harbor sprawls to the west, and the green mountains soar inland.

HAWAII MARITIME CENTER

Map 5, F9. Daily 8.30am–5pm; adults $7.50, under-18s $4.50; ⓣ 536-6373.

A short walk east of the Aloha Marketplace, the **Hawaii Maritime Center**, at Pier 7, illustrates Hawaii's seafaring past in riveting detail.

You may prefer to explore the modern museum building – known as the King Kalākaua Boathouse – at your own pace, rather than follow the audiocassette tour, but in any case, begin on the second floor. Displays here trace the voyages of **Captain Cook**, who sailed the world in small flat-bottomed boats originally designed for trips along the English coast, and named "Whitby Cats" after his home port. A crude copper plaque left by an English ship at the site of Cook's death – and seen there by Mark Twain in 1866, as noted in his book, *Roughing It* – stands alongside a cannonball found nearby.

The **whaling** industry is then recalled by exhibits such as huge iron try-pots, scrimshaw carved by nineteenth-century seamen on ivory smoothed with sharkskin "sandpaper" and a large painting of whalers at anchor at Lahaina. In the center of the gallery hangs the skeleton of a humpback whale beached on the uninhabited island of Kahoolawe in 1986.

Posters, timetables, menus and reconstructed interiors cover the growth of **tourism** and the heyday of cruise ships and passenger ferries – Hawaii's last inter-island steamer, the *Humu'ula*, ceased regular runs in 1952. Having examined plans and photos showing the development of Honolulu Harbor, you can see the whole thing yourself by climbing the 81 steps up the museum's observation tower.

On the first floor, the emphasis is on the **Polynesians**. A full-sized, double-hulled canoe has been cut in half and framed in cross-section behind clear plastic to show the equipment and cargo carried by the first voyagers. There's also a wall of huge historic **surfboards** – and some smaller *paipus*, the ancient equivalent of today's boogie boards – together with a brief history of the sport. Its modern popularity stems from the international successes during the early 1900s of Olympic champion Duke Kahanamoku, who appears prominently in photos of Waikīkī's first surfing clubs.

For many, however, the **chief attractions** of the Maritime Center are the two distinguished vessels moored on the adjacent dock. The **Falls of Clyde**, floating to the right of the entrance, is the only four-masted, full-rigged sailing ship left in the world. Built of wrought iron in Glasgow in 1876, it's also the world's only sail-powered oil tanker; after years of ferrying sugar and passengers between California and Hawaii, it was converted to carry petroleum in 1907.

When it's not sailing to Tahiti, New Zealand or the far reaches of the South Pacific, the replica Polynesian sailing canoe **Hōkūle'a** is moored at the end of the pier. Its long-distance voyages, designed to rediscover the routes and methods used by Hawaii's first human inhabitants, have inspired a huge revival of interest in traditional methods of navigation, and parties of eager schoolchildren flock here for close-up inspections. During its frequent absences, visitors content themselves with "navigating" an enjoyable computer simulation of the *Hōkūle'a*.

HAWAII MARITIME CENTER

THE WESTERN WATERFRONT: SAND ISLAND

Honolulu Harbor, inaccessible to casual viewing west of the Aloha Tower, is a relatively narrow deep-water channel shielded from the open ocean by the bulk of **Sand Island**. The seaward side of the island is a state park, where the plentiful supply of restrooms, showers and pavilions does little to alleviate the impression of being trapped in an industrial wasteland. There's a certain amount of sandy beach, and locals come to hang out and fish, but it's hard to see why any tourist would drive five miles to get here. If you insist on doing so, follow Nimitz Highway almost as far as the airport, and then loop back along Sand Island Access Road.

EAST TO WAIKĪKĪ: ALA MOANA

East of Aloha Tower and the Maritime Center, **Ala Moana Boulevard** runs along the shoreline toward Waikīkī. Along the way it passes a few more of Honolulu's main **shopping malls** – the Ward Warehouse, the Ward Centre and the pick of the bunch, the Ala Moana Center. Year after year, the stores here seem to increase both in quality and quantity, and for an ever-greater proportion of visitors to Waikīkī, the Ala Moana district constitutes their only foray into Honolulu proper. The openness of its upper levels to the sea breezes makes the Ala Moana Center the nicest place to hang out. For more details on Honolulu shopping, see the "Shopping" chapter, on p.212 onward.

The first spot where you can enter the ocean in this stretch is the appropriately named **Point Panic**, in **Kakaʻako Waterfront State Park**. Serious board- and body-surfers swear by its powerful waves, but a lack of sand, an abundance of sharks, and the fact that the surf hammers straight into a stone wall combine to ensure that few visitors are tempted to join them.

Next up, across from the Ward Warehouse, **Kewalo Basin Park** occupies the thin oceanfront groin that shelters the Kewalo Basin harbor, used by several small-boat operators. Though the setting is attractive, the park is a hangout for local transients which makes it a no-go area for outsiders.

ALA MOANA BEACH COUNTY PARK

Though tourists tend not to realize it, the long green lawns across Ala Moana Boulevard from the malls flank a superb **beach** – the long white-sand strand preserved as the **Ala Moana Beach County Park**. Honolulu city-dwellers come here, in preference to Waikīkī, to enjoy excellent facilities and, especially during working hours, a relative absence of crowds. Artificial like most Waikīkī beaches, it was constructed during the 1930s on the site of a garbage dump. The name "Ala Moana," meaning "path to the sea," is a postwar coinage. Inshore swimming is generally safe and good, and there's some potential for snorkeling around the reef. Watch out for the steep drop-off, only a few yards out at low tide, that marks the former course of a boat channel.

At its eastern end, Ala Moana Beach curves out and around a long promontory. Known as **Magic Island** or **'Aina Moana**, this too is artificial. It was one of the most ambitious elements of the state's plans to expand tourism in the early 1960s, the idea being to reclaim an "island" of shallow coral reef, connect it to the mainland and build luxury hotels on it. The hotels never materialized, so the vast sums of money involved have instead resulted in the creation of a tranquil park ideal for sunset strolls. A five-minute walk leads from the parking lot to the lovely little crescent lagoon at its tip, just far enough to ensure that it feels like a haven of peace away from the city. Joggers, ta'i-chi practitioners and picnickers enjoy the roomy lawns, while surfers and swimmers congregate around the gently sloping beach.

Tantalus, Makiki Heights and Mānoa Valley

The more time you spend in Honolulu, the more your eyes are likely to stray toward the mysterious mountains that soar just a short distance inland, and the valleys that lie between them. Many former wilderness areas have been colonized by residential developments over the years, but there are still plenty of stretches of pristine rainforest within easy reach of downtown, waiting to be explored along a comprehensive network of spectacular hiking trails. In addition, the few roads that wind through the hills also hold some notable city landmarks, including Punchbowl cemetery and the Contemporary Museum.

Tantalus and Makiki Valley

For a quick escape into Honolulu's hilly hinterland, there's no better choice of route than **Tantalus** and **Round Top** drives. They're actually a single eight-mile road that climbs up one flanking ridge of **Makiki Valley** and then wriggles back down the other, changing its name from Tantalus Drive in the west to Round Top Drive in the east. Along the way are plenty of views of Honolulu and Waikīkī, but the real attraction is the dense rainforest that cloaks the hillside, with greenery often meeting overhead to turn the road into a tunnel. It's a slow drive, which in places narrows to just a single lane of traffic, but a spellbinding one.

To join Tantalus Drive from downtown, follow signs for the **Punchbowl cemetery** until you reach the right turn onto Pūowaina Drive, and head straight on instead. Coming from Waikīkī, take Makiki Street up from Wilder Avenue, which runs parallel to and just north of H-1 west of the university. It's also possible to skip the bulk of the circuit by taking **Makiki Heights Drive**, which passes the stimulating **Contemporary Museum** as well as trailheads for some superb mountain **hikes**.

PUNCHBOWL: NATIONAL MEMORIAL CEMETERY

Map 2, F3. March–Sept daily 8am–6.30pm, Oct–Feb daily 8am–5.30pm; TheBus #15 from downtown Honolulu.

The extinct volcanic caldera known as Punchbowl, perched above downtown Honolulu, makes an evocative setting for the **National Memorial Cemetery of the Pacific**. To ancient Hawaiians, this was Pūowaina, the hill of human sacrifices; somewhere within its high encircling walls stood a sacrificial temple. It's now possible to drive right into the crater – having first spiraled around the base of the cone to meet up with Pūowaina Drive from the back – and park in one of the many small bays dotted around the perimeter road.

Beneath the lawns that carpet the bowl-shaped interior, far removed from the noise of the city, well over 25,000 victims of US Pacific wars, including Vietnam, now lie buried. Famous names include the Hawaiian astronaut Ellison Onizuka, killed when the *Challenger* shuttle exploded, but no graves are singled out for special attention. Instead, each gravestone, marked perhaps with a bouquet of ginger and heliconia, is recessed into the grass, with space left for their families or still-living veterans to join those laid to rest.

At the opposite end to the entrance rises the imposing marble staircase of the **Honolulu Memorial**, where ten "Courts of the Missing" commemorate 28,778 service personnel listed as missing in action. It culminates in a thirty-foot marble relief of the prow of a naval ship, bearing the words sent by President Lincoln to Mrs Bixby, whose five sons were killed in the Civil War: "The solemn pride that must be yours to have laid so costly a sacrifice upon the altar of freedom." As with all such US memorials, a "graphic record" of the conflicts is provided, so colored maps of the war in the Pacific cover the walls to either side.

Only when you climb the footpath to the top of the crater rim and find yourself looking straight down Punchbowl Street to the Capitol do you appreciate how close this all is to downtown Honolulu. During World War II, before the creation of the cemetery, this ridge held heavy artillery trained out to sea.

CONTEMPORARY MUSEUM

Map 7, A7. 2411 Makiki Heights Drive; Tues–Sat 10am–4pm, Sun noon–4pm; $5, free on the first Thurs of every month, under-13s free; ☎ 526-1322. TheBus #15 from downtown Honolulu.

Just above Makiki Heights Drive and a short distance east of its intersection with Mott-Smith Drive, a grand 1920s country estate houses the lovely **Contemporary Museum**. Tastefully landscaped with ornamental Oriental gardens that offer a superb overview of Honolulu – and are packed with playful sculptures – the museum hosts changing exhibitions of up-to-the-minute fine art. Few last more than eight weeks, but each is installed with lavish attention to detail, and the effect is consistently magnificent.

A separate pavilion houses a permanent display of the sets created by David Hockney for the Metropolitan Opera's production of Ravel's *L'Enfant et les Sortilèges*; a recording of the work plays constantly. Excellent lunches, with daily specials priced at $10–12, are available at the on-site *Contemporary Café* (Tues–Sat 11am–3pm, Sun noon–3pm; ☎ 523-3362), and there's also a very good gift store.

MAKIKI VALLEY TRAILS

Honolulu's finest **hiking trails** wind their way across and around the slopes of **Makiki Valley**. The network is most easily accessed via a short spur road that leads inland from a hairpin bend in Makiki Heights Drive, roughly half a mile east of the Contemporary Museum, or half a mile west of the intersection with Makiki Street. Follow the dead-end road to park just beyond the ramshackle green trailers of the **Hawaii Nature Center** (a volunteer educational group that works mainly with schoolchildren). If you haven't already picked up trail maps from the state office downtown (see p.166), they may have some at the center.

The best loop trip from this point begins by following the **Maunalaha Trail**, which starts across the Kanealole Stream beyond the center's restrooms. From the banana grove here, you swiftly switchback onto the ridge for a long straight climb, often stepping from one exposed tree root to the next. Despite being in the shade most of the way, it's a grueling haul. Looking back through the deep-green woods, you'll glimpse the towers of downtown Honolulu and then of Waikīkī. At first you can see the valleys to either side of the ridge, but before long only Mānoa Valley to the east is visible. After roughly three-quarters of a mile, you come to a **four-way intersection** at the top of the hill.

The Hawaii Nature Center organizes guided hikes,
open to all, on weekends – call ☏ 955-0100 for details.

Continuing straight ahead from here for around three miles connects you via the Moleka and Mānoa Cliff trails to the Nu'uanu Valley Lookout, described on p.78; turn left and you're on the Makiki Valley Trail, detailed below. Turning right onto the **'Ualaka'a Trail**, however, adds an enjoyable if muddy half-mile to the loop trip (making it a total of three miles in all). Plunging into the forest, the level path soon passes some extraordinary banyans, perched on the steep slopes with their many trunks, that have engulfed older trees. Having rounded the ridge, where a magnificent avenue of Cook pines marches along the crest in parallel rows, an arm-span apart, you curve back to cross Round Top Drive twice. In between the two crossings, take the short spur trail that leads left and up to the highest point on the hike. A clearing here perfectly frames Diamond Head against the ocean, with Waikīkī to the right and the gleaming silver dome of the sports stadium at the University of Hawaii straight below. Once you rejoin the main trail on the far side of Round Top Drive – it starts fifty yards to the right – a brief woodland walk returns you to the four-way junction.

The next stretch, on the **Makiki Valley Trail**, is the most gorgeous of the lot. A gentle descent along the steep valley wall, it heads inland to cross Moleka Stream at Herring Springs, amid a profusion of tiny bright flowers. Climbing again you're treated to further ravishing views of the high valley, bursting with bright gingers and fruit trees. Birds sing all around, and dangling lianas festoon the path. Take **Kanealole Trail**, which cuts away to the left shortly before this trail meets Tantalus Drive, and you'll drop back down through endless guava trees to your starting point at the Nature Center.

TANTALUS TRAILS

Tantalus Drive is at its highest just below the 2013-foot pinnacle of **Tantalus** itself, near the point, halfway between the two intersections with Makiki Heights Drive, where it changes its name to Round Top Drive. Two roadside parking lots here stand close to the trailhead for the three-quarter-mile **Pu'u 'Ōhi'a Trail**. The initial climb up through the eucalyptus trees to the summit is steep enough to require the aid of a wooden staircase, which comes out after a few hundred yards onto a little-used paved track. Follow this to the right until you reach a fenced-off electrical substation, then cut down the footpath to the left, which leads through a dense grove of bamboo before veering right to join the **Mānoa Cliff Trail**. By now you'll have seen the vastness of Nu'uanu Valley extending away to your left; heading left brings you, in a couple hundred yards, to the **Pauoa Flats Trail**. As that in turn heads for three-quarters of a mile into the valley, it's met first by the Nu'uanu Trail from the west, and then by the Aihualama Trail from Mānoa Falls (see p.80) from the east.

The Pauoa Flats Trail officially ends at a vantage point poised high above Nu'uanu Valley, though for even more dramatic views you can double back slightly and climb the knife-edge ridge to your left. It's obvious from here how Nu'uanu Valley cuts right through the heart of Oahu, but you can't quite see the abrupt *pali* at its eastern end that traditionally made reaching the windward shore so perilous (see p.82). Down below the lookout, the **Nu'uanu Reservoir** is an artificial lake that's kept stocked with crayfish and catfish; fishing is only permitted on three weekends in the year.

PU'U 'UALAKA'A PARK

Map 7, C7.

The single best view along Round Top Drive comes at **Pu'u 'Ualaka'a Park**, on the western flank of Mānoa Valley. There's not much of a park here, though there's a sheltered hilltop picnic pavilion at the first of its two parking lots. Continue to the second lot, however, where a paved walkway leads to a railed-off viewing area right at the end of the ridge, and you'll be rewarded with a panorama of the entire southern coast of Oahu. The twin craters of Diamond Head to the left and Punchbowl to the right most readily draw the eye, but looking away to the west you can see beyond the airport and Pearl Harbor and all the way to Barber's Point. Pools of glittering glass in the parking lot attest to the many break-ins up here, so don't spend too long away from your vehicle.

The small summit that separates the two lots is Round Top itself. The Hawaiians called it *'Ualaka'a*, ("rolling sweet potato"), because Kamehameha the Great decreed the planting of sweet potatoes here, which when dug up rolled down the hillside.

Mānoa Valley

Mānoa Valley may lie just a couple of miles from Waikīkī – directly inland, to the north – but it's light-years away from the commercial hustle of the city. Behind the **University of Hawaii** – a mecca for students from around the Pacific, but of no great appeal for casual visitors – lies a quiet residential suburb that peters out as it narrows into the mountains, to culminate in a spectacular tropical **waterfall**.

UNIVERSITY OF HAWAII

Map 2, H4.

The main campus of the **University of Hawaii** sprawls along University Avenue in Mānoa, bounded on its southern side by H-1, Honolulu's major east–west freeway. The university has recently undergone massive budget cuts and has found itself forced to choose between providing a full spectrum of courses or concentrating on its specialties of geology, marine studies, astronomy and other Pacific-related fields. As only a tiny proportion of students live on campus, there are fewer stores, restaurants and clubs in the vicinity than you might expect. The **Campus Center**, set a little way back from University Avenue, has general information and orientation. **Hemenway Hall** alongside holds the inexpensive *Mānoa Garden* café, as well as a movie theater, and its bulletin boards carry details of short-term courses open to visitors.

LYON ARBORETUM

Map 7, G4. Mon–Sat 9am–3pm; $1 donation. TheBus #5 from Ala Moana.

To drive to the uppermost reaches of Mānoa Valley, continue along University Avenue beyond the campus, cross East

Mānoa Road onto Oahu Avenue, and then turn right onto Mānoa Road itself. Immediately you'll see the silver stream of Mānoa Falls amid the trees at the head of the valley. Mānoa Road comes to a halt just beyond the **Lyon Arboretum**, which belongs to the University and preserves Hawaiian and imported trees in a reasonable approximation of their native environment. Several short trails crisscross beneath the canopy.

MĀNOA FALLS

Map 7, G2.

The half-hour trail to **Mānoa Falls** follows straight on from the point where it becomes impossible for Mānoa Road to squeeze any further back into the valley. Parking at the end of the road should be no problem, though, as ever, it's unwise to leave valuables in your car – and be sure not to set off without mosquito repellent. Having passed over a footbridge and through a soggy meadow, the trail soon starts to climb beside one of the two main tributaries of Mānoa Stream. After scrambling from root to protruding root, over intertwined banyans and bamboos, you come out at the soaring high falls, where the flat, mossy cliff face is at enough of an angle that the water flows rather than falls into the small pool at its base.

Many hikers cool off in the pool before attempting the more demanding **Aihualama Trail**, which switchbacks away west of the falls. After something over a mile, it comes out on top of the ridge, amid a thick cluster of bamboo, to connect with the Makiki network of trails half a mile short of the Nu'uanu Lookout (see p.78).

The Pali and Likelike highways

In ancient times, the Ko'olau Mountains constituted an impassable obstacle between the Honolulu area and windward Oahu. Early tourists to Hawaii would make a point of riding up to the 3000-foot ridge at the top of the Nu'uanu Valley, but there was no way to get down the far side – as was grimly attested by the skeletons strewn at the bottom, the remains of warriors driven over the cliffs in a mighty battle in 1795.

These days, three separate roads cross the mountains, the long suffering **Pali** and **Likelike Highways** having been joined in 1997 by the **Hwy-3** freeway. Thirty-seven years in the making, thanks to an interminable series of disputes over its environmental and archeological impact, Hwy-3 was originally intended for military use, as a direct link between Pearl Harbor and the Marine Corps base at Kāne'ohe. With the end of the Cold War, that role ceased to be a high priority, and critics charged that Hwy-3 was a fast-track route "from nowhere to nowhere." In the last four decades, however, windward communities such as **Kailua** and **Kāne'ohe** (see p.110 and p.111) have become home to an ever-higher proportion of Honolulu's work-force, and Hwy-3 has considerably eased the strain for local commuters.

The Hawaiian word *pali* simply means "cliff"; Likelike, which is pronounced *leek-e-leek-e*, is named after the younger sister of Queen Lili'uokalani.

The opening of Hwy-3 has little significance for tourists, on the other hand, as the Pali and Likelike highways hold far more potential for sightseeing. Both can still get hideously congested at peak times, but the Pali Highway in particular is an exhilarating drive, whether you head straight for the clifftop **Nu'uanu Pali Lookout**, or stop at the various **royal sites** on the way up.

The Pali Highway

Christian missionaries hacked a crude footpath into the sheer windward cliffs beyond Nu'uanu Valley during the first half of the nineteenth century, but not until 1898 did the first proper trans-Koolau road open to traffic. Its original route, which included sections poised above the abyss on wooden trestles, was finally superseded with the completion of a tunnel through the mountains in 1961. High-speed traffic thunders along the **Pali Highway** day and night, but it remains an attractive drive nonetheless, and at several points along the way it's possible to detour onto delightfully peaceful stretches of its former route, now known as **Nu'uanu Pali Drive**.

To reach the Pali Highway from downtown Honolulu, either drive straight up **Bishop Street**, which becomes Pali

Highway as soon as it cross the H-1 freeway, or take **Nu'uanu Avenue**, which connects with the highway a mile or so further up.

ROYAL MAUSOLEUM

Map 2, F2. Mon–Fri 8am–4.30pm; free.

The Gothic-influenced **Royal Mausoleum** is very near the top of Nu'uanu Avenue, shortly before it joins the Pali Highway. It would be easy to miss – there's no sign, so watch out on the right as soon as you've passed the Japanese cemetery – and frankly it's not worth losing any sleep if you do.

The drab, gray mausoleum itself, built in 1865 to replace the overcrowded Kamehameha family tomb at 'Iolani Palace, stands at the end of a short oval driveway ringed with lumpy palm trees. It's now simply a chapel, as the bodies it held for its first forty years or so were later moved to various sarcophagi dotted around the lawns. Kamehameha the Great was buried in secret on the Big Island, but most of his closest family, as Christians, now lie here. His widow Ka'ahumanu, along with Kamehameha II to V are in the pink-granite tomb to the left, while members of the separate Kalākaua dynasty were reinterred in the gilded vault beneath the central black column. Incidentally, this spot is said to be the precise site where the Nu'uanu Valley battle began in 1795.

QUEEN EMMA SUMMER PALACE

Map 2, F1. Daily 9am–4pm; adults $5, under-12s $1; ℡595-3167.

A couple of miles up the Pali Highway, just over half a mile after its intersection with Nu'uanu Avenue, a former royal retreat stands on the brow of a small hill to the right of the road. The **Queen Emma Summer Palace** made a welcome escape from the heat of Honolulu for the former

Emma Rooke, who married King Kamehameha IV in 1856, was queen consort until 1863, and lived here until her death in 1885. It's now run as a somewhat cloying shrine to Emma by the Daughters of Hawaii, a group composed of descendants of missionary families.

Behind its entrance stairway, framed with six Doric pillars, the single-story, white frame house is surprisingly small. Guided tours proceed at a snail's pace through rooms lined with royal souvenirs; only the splendidly grumpy Princess Ruth relieves the monotony of the official portraits. Among touching memorabilia of the young Prince Albert Edward – Queen Emma's only child, who died at the age of four – are his beautiful *koa*-wood crib, carved to resemble a canoe rocked by the waves, and a fireman's outfit he once wore in a parade. Gifts from Queen Victoria – after whose husband the boy was named – make up a large proportion of the items on display. Both Victoria and Emma were widowed – Emma was still only 27 when her husband died a year after their son – and the two women continued to exchange presents until Emma died.

NU'UANU PALI DRIVE

Half a mile up the Pali Highway beyond Queen Emma's palace, an inconspicuous right turn leads onto **Nu'uanu Pali Drive**. Other than having to drive slower, you lose nothing by taking this detour into succulent rainforest, which curves back to meet the highway two miles up. There are no specific stops en route, but the density of the overhanging tropical canopy, lit with flashes of color, is irresistible.

THE BATTLE OF NU'UANU VALLEY

For early foreign visitors, the ride to the top of Nu'uanu Pali was an essential part of a Hawaiian itinerary. As their horses struggled up, native guides would recount tales of the epic Battle of Nu'uanu Valley in 1795, in which Kamehameha the Great (from the Big Island) defeated Kalanikūpule and conquered the island of Oahu.

No two versions completely agree, but according to James Macrae, who accompanied Lord Byron to Hawaii in 1825 (soon enough after the battle to meet some of the participants), Kamehameha's army landed at Honolulu to find Kalanikūpule waiting for them in Nu'uanu Valley. Kamehameha sent men along the tops of the ridges to either side, and advanced toward Kalanikūpule in the center. By this time, his entourage included Europeans and, crucially, a few European guns. Isaac Davis, who five years previously had been the sole survivor of a Hawaiian raid on a small boat at Kawaihae on the Big Island, positioned himself at the front of the attack.

Before the usual ritual of challenges and counter-challenges could even begin, Davis killed Kalanikūpule's leading general with a single lucky shot. The soldiers of Oahu turned and ran, pursued all the way to the head of the valley. When they reached the top, where the thousand-foot Nu'uanu Pali precipice drops away on the far side, they had no choice and hurled themselves to their deaths.

NU'UANU PALI STATE PARK

Map 1, K7. Daily 4am–8pm; free.

Back on the highway, it's now just a mile until the next right turn – confusingly, it too is Nu'uanu Pali Drive – which leads in a few hundred yards to **Nu'uanu Pali State Park**. Miss this, and you'll miss a staggering overview of the cliffs of windward Oahu; the highway goes into a tunnel at this point, and emerges much lower down the hillside. At the edge of a small parking lot – which is the most notorious spot in the state for car **break-ins**, so leave no valuables in your vehicle – the railed viewing area of the **Nu'uanu Pali Lookout** is perched near the top of a magnificent pleated curtain of green velvet, plunging more than a thousand feet. Straight ahead lie the sprawling coastal communities of **Kailua** and **Kāne'ohe**, separated by the Mōkapu Peninsula, but your eye is likely to be drawn north, where the mighty *pali* seems to stretch away forever, with a waterfall in every fold.

It was over this fearsome drop that the defeated warriors of Oahu were driven in 1795 (see box, overleaf); placards at the overlook explain the course of the battle and point out assorted landmarks. Notches higher up the ridge are said to have been cut to provide fortified positions for the defenders, an estimated four hundred of whose skulls were found down below when the Pali Highway was built a century later. The stairs that lead down to the right enable you to join the highway's original route (abandoned when it was upgraded to take automobiles) as it edges its way above the precipice. It's blocked off about a mile along, but walking to the end makes a good, if windy, mountain hike.

If you're heading across the island, you would naturally expect to turn right as you leave the parking lot. In fact you must drive back down to rejoin the highway where you left it. To the right, Nu'uanu Pali Drive crosses over the tunnel and meets the highway's other carriageway on the far side, to drop back into Honolulu.

Likelike Highway

You're most likely to use the Pali Highway to get to wind-ward Oahu from Honolulu, but the **Likelike Highway**, which was completed in 1961, provides a less spectacular alternative. Starting roughly two miles to the west, it runs through residential Kalihi Valley and then passes through its own tunnel to emerge just above Kāne'ohe. There's no great reason to cross the island this way – the traffic is unlikely to be any easier – but you must drive a short stretch of Likelike Highway to visit Honolulu's best mus-eum, the **Bishop Museum**.

BISHOP MUSEUM

Map 2, E1. 1525 Bernice St; daily 9am–5pm; adults $14.95, ages 4–12 and seniors $11.95; prices include the planetarium.
Planetarium shows take place daily at 11am & 2pm, plus Fri & Sat at 7pm; admission to those alone costs $4.50; ⊤847-3511;
ⓦwww.bishop.hawaii.org.

The best museum of **Hawaiian history**, **anthropology** and **natural history** – and the world's finest collection of the arts of the Pacific – is in an otherwise obscure district two miles northwest of downtown.

The **Bishop Museum** was founded in 1889 by Charles Reed Bishop to preserve the heirlooms left by his wife, Princess Bernice Pauahi, the last direct descendant of Kamehameha the Great. Spread across three principal buildings on a twelve-acre hillside estate, it sets out to demonstrate the reality of Polynesian culture, as opposed to the fakery of Waikīkī.

After you buy your tickets, the first section you come to – Hawaii's only **planetarium** – relates to the current "Hawaiian Renaissance." Master navigator Nainoa

LIKELIKE HIGHWAY

Thompson of the *Hōkūle'a* studied the virtual sky here to reinvent traditional Polynesian navigational techniques, as used in the voyages mentioned on p.69. A 45-minute film, shown regularly, explains how it was done, and is complemented by displays in the adjoining **observatory**. An attendant helps visitors to make their own observations, and you can also take a look at the real night sky after the evening planetarium shows on Fridays and Saturdays.

TheBus #2 from Waikīkī stops on Kapalama Street, two blocks east of the Bishop Museum. If you're driving, take the first exit on the right as you head up Likelike Highway

----

The huge main building of the museum houses the bulk of its historic exhibits. To the right of the entrance, the **Hawaiian Hall** consists of a large ground-level room overlooked by two tiers of wood-paneled balconies. Suspended in the central well is the skeleton of a sperm whale, half clad in papier-mâché skin. Among the priceless ancient artifacts down below are carved stone and wooden images of gods, including what may be at least one of the legendary "poisonwood gods" from Molokai, which were said to possess such powerful magic that only Kamehameha the Great could handle them, and Kamehameha's own personal image of the war god Kūkā'ilimoku, found in a cave in Kona on the Big Island. You'll also see *koa* platters and calabashes, and multicolored feather *leis* and capes.

A scale model of the Big Island's Waha'ula *heiau*, built in 1903 using stones from the site, now serves as a valuable record of an important piece of Hawaiian history. The original – thought to have been founded thirty generations ago by the warrior-priest Pā'ao from Tahiti – was recently overrun by lava from the Kīlauea volcano. Nearby stands a sharkskin drum once used to announce human sacrifices in a similar *luakini* temple on the seaward slopes of Diamond

Head – the only such drum known to have survived the overthrow of the *kapu* system. A full-sized *hale,* or traditional hut, brought here from Hā'ena on Kauai, stands as usual on a platform of smooth stones; it's windowless, and thatched with *pili* grass.

On the lower of the Hawaiian Hall's balconies you'll find weapons, including swords embedded with sharks' teeth, plus exhibitions on whaling, the nineteenth-century distribution of land known as the Great Mahele (see p.244) and the creation and dyeing of *tapa* (the bark-cloth also known as *kapa*). The higher balcony is devoted to the contributions of Hawaii's immigrants, with costumes and artifacts from such countries as Germany, Spain, Portugal, Puerto Rico, the Philippines, Japan, Korea and China.

The **Polynesian Hall**, above the entrance in the same building, emphasizes the full diversity of Polynesia. After the breaking of the *kapu* (see p.243), the Hawaiians themselves set about destroying the relics of their ancient religion; most other Polynesian cultures have preserved far more of their heritage. Stunning exhibits here include woven-grass masks and dance costumes from Vanikoro, modeled skulls and figures from Vanuato, stark white and red sorcery charms from Papua New Guinea, and stick charts used by Pacific navigators. The Maoris of New Zealand are represented by the facade of a storehouse, carved in high relief with human figures and inlaid with abalone-shell eyes.

On the top floor, the **Hall of Hawaiian Natural History** explains the origin of the Hawaiian islands with a large-scale relief model of the entire chain, then covers the development of life here, from the first chance arrivals to recently introduced pests.

The new **Castle Building** next door houses top-quality temporary exhibitions. At the back of the adjacent **Pākī Hall**, the Hawaii Sports Hall of Fame – more of a hallway

BISHOP MUSEUM

than a hall, if truth be told – honors figures who will probably mean more to locals than to tourists. Among the names you're most likely to recognize are Duke Kahanamoku, whose gold medals are on display; Buster Crabbe, a fellow Olympic medalist who's best remembered as Flash Gordon and Tarzan; and All-American footballer Squirming Herman Wedemeyer, who played Duke Lukela in *Hawaii Five-O*.

The Bishop Museum holds an excellent bookstore as well as *Woody's Snack Bar* (daily 9am–4pm). On the first Sunday of every month, known as **Family Sunday**, Hawaii residents are allowed in free and the lawns play host to food stalls, *hula* performances and all sorts of other activities.

Pearl Harbor

Ancient Hawaiians knew the vast inlet of Pearl Harbor, reaching deep into the heart of Oahu, as Wai Momi, "water of pearl," on account of its pearl-bearing oysters. Their canoes had no need of deep-water anchorages, but Westerners came to realize that dredging its entrance would turn it into the finest harbor in the Pacific. With its strategic potential, the desire to control Pearl Harbor played a large role in the eventual annexation of Hawaii by the United States. The US first received permission to develop installations here in 1887, in return for granting Hawaiian sugar duty-free access to US markets, and construction of the naval base commenced in 1908.

To this day, the 12,600-acre Pearl Harbor Naval Complex is the headquarters from which the US Pacific Fleet patrols 102 million square miles of ocean. The entire fleet consists of 265 ships, 1900 aircraft and 268,000 personnel, while Pearl Harbor itself is the home port for twenty surface vessels and twenty nuclear submarines.

Except for the offshore **USS Arizona Memorial**, commemorating the surprise **Japanese attack** with which Pearl Harbor remains synonymous, almost the whole area is off-limits to civilians.

THE ATTACK ON PEARL HARBOR

As the winter of **1941** approached, with German soldiers occupying most of Europe and moving into Soviet Russia, and Japanese forces advancing through Southeast Asia, the United States remained outside the global conflict. However, negotiations to halt Japanese progress had stalled, and on November 27 the US government sent secret "war warnings" to its military units throughout the world. The version received by the commanding general in Hawaii read: "Japanese future action unpredictable but hostile action possible at any moment. If hostilities cannot, repeat cannot, be avoided the United States desires that Japan commit the first overt act."

A few days earlier, a Japanese attack fleet, with six aircraft carriers among its 33 vessels, had sailed from northern Japan. By maintaining strict radio silence, it dodged American surveillance. The conventional wisdom was that it must be heading toward the Philippines, site of the most distant US base in the Pacific, and a detachment of B-17 "Flying Fortress" aircraft was sent from Hawaii to bolster the islands' defenses. In fact, however, Hawaii itself, where **Pearl Harbor** had since the previous spring been the headquarters of the US Pacific Fleet, was the target. The Japanese fleet sailed there along an icy, rarely used northerly course, keeping well clear of usual shipping lanes. The Japanese did not expect to achieve complete surprise, and were prepared to engage the US fleet in battle if they met them on the open sea, but reconnaissance flights from Pearl Harbor only covered the likeliest angle of attack, from the southwest, and the Japanese approach was not detected. By the early morning of December 7, the fleet was in position north of Kauai, and 230 miles northwest of Oahu.

The first wave of the attack, consisting of 183 aircraft, was launched at 6am. As the planes passed over the western

Wai'anae mountains, they were picked up by radar screens at a nearby mobile tracking station. When the operators called Honolulu with news that a large group of aircraft had been spotted, they were told "Well, don't worry about it," in the belief that these were replacement B-17s from the mainland. Meanwhile, the cloud cover had lifted to give the attackers a perfect view of Pearl Harbor, where seven of the US fleet's nine battleships lay at anchor along "Battleship Row." At 7.53am, Commander Mitsuo Fuchida sent the code word "*Tora! Tora! Tora!*" (Tiger! Tiger! Tiger!) to his flagship, the *Akagai*, signalling that a surprise attack was under way.

Within two hours the US Navy lost eighteen warships – eight battleships, three light cruisers, three destroyers and four auxiliary craft – and 87 planes. Simultaneous attacks on other bases on Oahu destroyed 77 Air Force planes and damaged 128 more. Following recent warnings, the planes were parked wingtip-to-wingtip on the airfields. This was supposed to make them easier to protect against sabotage by Japanese agents among the *nisei* (Hawaiian residents of Japanese ancestry); instead it left them utterly exposed to aerial attack. During the onslaught, the expected squadron of B-17s arrived from California; several were shot down.

In total, 2403 US military personnel were killed, and 1178 wounded. The Japanese lost 29 aircraft, plus five midget submarines that had sneaked into Pearl Harbor during the previous night in the hope of torpedoing damaged ships. Ten hours later, Japanese aircraft did indeed attack Clark Airfield in the Philippines, and there too they destroyed large numbers of aircraft on the ground. The next day, declaring the United States to be at war with Japan, President Franklin D. Roosevelt condemned the "dastardly" Pearl Harbor attack as "a date which will live in infamy."

The official postwar **inquiry** into "the greatest military and naval disaster in our nation's history" set out to explain why the attack was possible, let alone successful. Answering the issue of the fleet being based in Hawaii, instead of the relative safety of the US West Coast, the inquiry explained that not fortifying Pearl Harbor would have signaled a lack of will to resist Japanese expansion in the Pacific. As to whether the fleet's vulnerability had invited the attack, Japanese plans were drawn up expecting a much larger fleet at Pearl Harbor, and they were disappointed to find that both US aircraft carriers were out of port. The fact that the Japanese withdrew from Hawaii almost immediately, instead of destroying port installations such as the vast oil tanks, and thereby crippling US Navy operations for years – let alone invading the islands – suggests that they overestimated US defenses.

No hard evidence has been produced to support **revisionist assertions** that Roosevelt knew the attack was coming, but allowed it to happen because he wanted an excuse to join the war, or that the British knew, and they deliberately failed to warn the Americans for the same reason. It makes no sense, if Roosevelt did know, that he didn't at least alert US defenses a few hours in advance, when an unprovoked Japanese attack was imminent.

Mistakes were certainly made. Among the most glaring was the fact that Navy authorities were never told of intercepted messages from Tokyo in which the Japanese consulate in

USS ARIZONA MEMORIAL

Map 1, G7. Daily 7.30am–5pm; tours 8am–3pm; free; ⊤ 422-0561.
Almost half the victims of the December 1941 Japanese attack on Pearl Harbor were aboard the battleship **USS Arizona**. Hit by an armor-piercing shell that detonated its magazine

Honolulu was asked to divide the moorings in Pearl Harbor into five separate areas and specify which ships were anchored in each section. Perhaps the clearest explanations can be gleaned from each side's post-attack reports: the Japanese commander, reporting to his superiors a fortnight later, wrote that "good luck, together with negligence on the part of the arrogant enemy, enabled us to launch a successful surprise attack." Admiral Husband E. Kimmel, in charge of the US Pacific Fleet, asked why he had left the ships exposed in Pearl Harbor, replied that he never thought the Japanese "could pull off such an attack, so far from Japan." Although Kimmel was stripped of his rank in the immediate aftermath, he was posthumously promoted back to admiral by both Senate and Congress in 1999, but that still-controversial move has yet to be ratified by the president.

In the long run, the Japanese decision to provoke the US into all-out **war in the Pacific** proved suicidal. What's more, most of the vessels damaged and even sunk at Pearl Harbor eventually returned to active service. Only the *Arizona* and the *Utah* could not be salvaged, while the *Oklahoma* sank once again, 500 miles off the Big Island. By contrast, just two Japanese ships that were involved in the attack survived the war; four of the anti-aircraft carriers were sunk during the Battle of Midway. In 1945, the *West Virginia*, risen from the waters of Pearl Harbor, was in Tokyo Bay to witness the Japanese surrender.

and lifted its bow twenty feet out of the water, it sank within nine minutes. Of its crew of 1514 – who had earned the right to sleep in late that Sunday morning by finishing second in a military band competition – 1177 were killed.

The *Arizona* still lies submerged where it came to rest, out in the waters of the harbor along "Battleship Row,"

USS ARIZONA MEMORIAL

next to Ford Island. Its wreck is spanned (though not touched) by the curving white **USS Arizona Memorial**, maintained by the National Park Service in honor of all the victims of the attack; small boats ferry a stream of visitors out from the mainland.

The **visitor center** for the memorial is six miles west of Honolulu, just over a mile after Kamehameha Highway cuts off to the left of H-1. It takes anything from fifteen minutes up to an hour to drive across town from Waikīkī; as you approach, follow signs for the *Arizona* rather than "Pearl Harbor," which as an active installation remains off-limits. In addition to TheBus #20, overpriced commercial tours run direct from Waikīkī for around $20. On arrival, pick up a numbered ticket for the free memorial tour; in peak season, it can be two or three hours before you're called to board the ferry. Many people try to beat the crowds by arriving early, but if anything your chances of a short wait may be better in the afternoon.

**TheBus #20 takes just over one hour
to reach Pearl Harbor from Waikīkī.**

Perhaps because so many of the 1.5 million annual visitors are Japanese, the displays in the visitor center are surprisingly even-handed, calling the attack "a daring gamble" by Admiral Yamamoto to knock out the US fleet and give the Japanese time to conquer Southeast Asia. The center has long been scheduled to hold a new **museum**, designed to trace the events leading up to the attack, the bombing, and the course of the war in the Pacific. Only a few exhibits were in place as this book went to press, however, including models of both the *Arizona* and the Japanese flagship, the IMS *Akagi*; an aerial torpedo; and some personal items salvaged from the wreck.

Until the museum is completed, the best place to get a

sense of what happened is in the waterfront **garden** outside. From here, you see the low and undramatic mountain ridges that ring Pearl Harbor, together with the gap down the center of the island through which the first planes arrived. Captioned photographs clearly illustrate the disposition of the ships moored along "Battleship Row" on the fateful morning, as well as their eventual fate. Survivors of the attack are often on hand to tell their stories.

When your number finally comes up, you're first shown a twenty-minute film that pays tribute to "one of the most brilliantly planned and executed attacks in naval history." A pained female voice narrates the course of the attack, over footage of Japanese planes taking off from their aircraft carriers.

The USS *Arizona* memorial was partly financed by Elvis Presley's 1961 Honolulu concert, his first show after leaving the Army.

Crisp-uniformed Navy personnel then usher you onto open-sided boats, which they steer for ten minutes across a tiny fraction of the naval base. At the memorial, whose white-marble walls are inscribed with the names of the dead, you disembark for the twenty minutes until the next boat arrives. The outline of the *Arizona* is still discernible in the clear blue waters, and here and there rusty metal spurs poke from the water. All those who died when the *Arizona* went down remain entombed in the wreckage, occasionally joined by veteran survivors who choose to be buried here.

USS Bowfin Submarine Museum and Park

Map 1, G7. Daily 8am–5pm; sub and museum adults $8, under-13s $3, or combined with *Missouri*, adults $18, ages 4–12 $9; museum only, adults $4, under-13s $2.

USS BOWFIN SUBMARINE MUSEUM AND PARK

Near the *Arizona* visitor center, the **USS Bowfin Submarine Museum and Park** serves as an additional stop if you have a couple of hours to wait before your ferry. Its main focus, the claustrophobic *Bowfin* itself, is a still-floating, 83-man submarine that survived World War II unscathed, having sunk 44 enemy vessels. Once you've explored it on a self-guided audio tour – complete with a first-person account of one of the *Bowfin*'s most hair-raising missions, narrated by the captain in charge – you can learn more about the whole story of twentieth-century submarines in the adjoining museum.

The park outside, to which access is free, holds various missiles and torpedoes, including the Japanese naval equivalent of a *kamikaze* airplane, a *kaiten*. Such manned, single-seater torpedoes were designed for suicide attacks on larger ships; only one, piloted by its inventor, ever succeeded in sinking a US Navy ship.

USS Missouri

Map 1, G7. Daily 9am–5pm. Adults $14, ages 4–12 $7, or combined with *Bowfin*, adults $18, ages 4–12 $9; guided tours $6 extra per person. ℡ 973-2494; ⊛ www.ussmissouri.com.

Since 1998, the decommissioned battleship **USS Missouri**, also known as the "Mighty Mo," has been permanently moored close to the USS Arizona Memorial. The last battleship to be constructed by the United States, her keel was laid in January 1941, and she was christened in January 1944. After service in the Pacific and Korean wars, she was decommissioned in 1955 and then remained mothballed until being refitted in 1986. Operation Desert Storm saw the *Missouri* firing Tomahawk missiles against Iraq, but she was finally retired once more in 1992, by which time she was the last operational battleship in the world. Should the need arise, she's still capable of being recommissioned in 45–90 days.

USS MISSOURI

Several different US locations competed for the honor of providing a final berth for the *Missouri*. Pearl Harbor won, on the basis that the place where World War II began for the United States should also hold the spot where it ended; the Japanese surrender of September 2, 1945, was signed on the deck of the *Missouri*, then moored in Tokyo Bay. In addition to being a monument in her own right, part of the battleship's new role is as a recruiting tool for the US Navy; it's even possible to arrange kids' sleep-over parties on board.

Because the battleship is alongside Ford Island, which is officially part of the naval base, visitors can only reach it by shuttle bus. These depart from the USS *Bowfin* visitor center, which is also where you purchase tickets. Having crossed the harbor via one of only six retracting bridges in the world, you're deposited at the entrance gate. If you've paid extra to join one of the regular hour-long guided tours, you're then shepherded toward your guide.

The overwhelming first impression for all visitors is the *Missouri*'s sheer size; at 887 feet long, she's the length of three football fields. Next you're likely to focus on her colossal twin gun turrets, each of which is equipped with three guns. By contrast, once you go below decks, the crew's quarters are cramped in the extreme, bringing home the full claustrophobic reality of her long and dangerous missions. The principal highlights are the dimly-lit Combat Engagement Center, set up as it was during the Gulf War but now looking very antiquated; the surrender site, on the deck nearby; and the spot where a kamikaze fighter careered into the side of the ship, as captured in a dramatic photo. Thus far, however, the *Missouri*'s four engine rooms are not open to the public.

USS MISSOURI

The rest of Oahu

U nless you see more of Oahu than Waikīkī and Honolulu, you may never get a real sense of the island's beauty, or of how it must have looked before the arrival of foreigners. By using the myriad routes offered by TheBus, as detailed on p.16, it's a small enough island that you can visit anywhere as a day-trip from the capital. With a car, one day is just about sufficient for an exploration of Oahu. What you can't do, however, is make a complete circuit along the coast; the northwestern tip of the island, Ka'ena Point, is accessible only on foot.

The most popular short excursion from Honolulu is down to the **southeast** corner of Oahu, where the superb snorkeling waters of **Hanauma Bay** are sheltered in an extinct volcanic caldera. If you want to spend a full day touring, however, a more manageable route sets off directly inland from Honolulu, climbing across the dramatic Ko'olau Mountains. The green cliffs of the **windward coast** on the far side are awe-inspiring, lined with safe, secluded beaches and indented with remote time-forgotten valleys. Towns such as **Kailua**, **Kāne'ohe** and **Lā'ie** may be far from exciting, but you're unlikely to tire of the sheer beauty of the shoreline drive – so long as you time your forays to miss the peak-hour traffic jams.

Driving the full length of the windward coast brings you to the eastern end of the **North Shore**, the world's premier

surfing destination. Mere mortals can only marvel at the winter waves here; for anyone other than experts, entering the water at that time is almost suicidal. However, **Waimea**, **Sunset** and **'Ehukai** beaches are compelling spectacles, little **Hale'iwa** makes a refreshing contrast to Waikīkī, and in summer you may manage to find a safe spot for a swim. From Hale'iwa, a much shorter drive across the agricultural plains of **central Oahu** can get you back to your hotel within an hour.

Although the **west** (or **leeward**) **coast** of Oahu also holds some fine beaches – including the prime surf spot of **Mākaha** – it remains very much off the beaten track. There's just one route in and out of this side of the island, and the locals are happy to keep it that way.

Hotels and restaurants all over Oahu are reviewed in chapters 9 and 10, respectively.

Southeast Oahu

The high crest of the Ko'olau Mountains curves away to the east beyond Honolulu, providing Oahu with its elongated **southeastern promontory**. The built-up coastal strip is squeezed ever more tightly between the hills and the ocean, but not until you reach **Koko Head**, eight miles out from Waikīkī and eleven from downtown, do you really feel you've left the city behind. Thereafter, however, the shoreline is so magnificent – punctuated by towering volcanoes, sheltered lagoons and great beaches – that there have been serious proposals to designate the entire area as a state park devoted to ecotourism, under the Hawaiian name of **Ka Iwi**.

KĀHALA AND HAWAII KAI

H-1 ends at the Kāhala Mall, just beyond Diamond Head, to become Hwy-72, or **Kalaniana'ole Highway**. Both **Kāhala** itself, and **Hawaii Kai** further along, are upmarket residential communities that have little to attract visitors, and no desire to encourage them. Hawaii Kai spreads back inland to either side of the large Kuapā Pond, an ancient fishpond remodeled to create the Koko Marina. The one reason to stop is to eat at *Roy's* gourmet restaurant (see p.195). None of the beaches along this stretch merits a pause.

HANAUMA BAY

Map 8, C8. Daily except Tues 7am–6pm; admission is $3 for adults, free for under-13s; parking costs an additional $1.

Beautiful **Hanauma Bay** is barely half a mile beyond Hawaii Kai, just across the volcanic ridge of Koko Head. So curved as to be almost round, the bay was created when part of yet another volcano – southeast Oahu is one long chain of volcanic cones – collapsed to let in the sea.

> TheBus #22 ("The Beach Bus") from Waikīkī
> runs by Hanauma Bay every forty minutes.

This spellbinding spot, where a thin strip of palms and sand nestles beneath a green cliff, has long been famous as Oahu's best place to **snorkel**. Unfortunately, however, the sheer quantity of Waikīkī-based beach-lovers who come here poses a constant threat to the fragile underwater environment. Since the 1960s, Hanauma Bay has been a Marine Life Conservation District, and organized tour parties are now banned, but most of the inshore coral reef has died.

Though the sea still holds enough brightly colored fish to satisfy visitors, they're sustained these days by handouts of fish food; the minute coral creatures that should underpin the food chain have gone.

Visiting Hanauma Bay

A series of ambitious and controversial proposals have been advanced in recent years to restrict the number of visitors to Hanauma Bay, and to enhance their experience. By the time you read this, a large new **visitor center** may well have opened on the hilltop above Hanauma, adjoining the **parking lot** just off the highway, but hidden from the view of anyone in the bay itself. The plan is that first-time visitors will be required to watch a video about Hanauma and marine conservation in general. As this book went to press, a run-down pavilion on the beach served as the place both to buy snacks and rent **snorkel equipment**, at around $6 per day (you'll be asked to leave some form of deposit; rental car keys, but not hotel keys, are acceptable). In the long run, however, all facilities will probably relocate up to the new visitor center.

The beach is five-minutes' walk from the visitor center, down a gently winding road used only by an open-sided "trolley" (50¢ down, $1 up). As you walk down, the ridge rises like a rich green curtain ahead of you, but the vegetation on the more exposed northeast side of the bay, off to your left, is generally dry and faded. From here you can see patches of reef in the turquoise water, standing out against the sandy seabed, and swarms of fish are clearly visible. The largest gap in the reef, at the parking lot end of the bay, is known as the **Keyhole**.

Even if the crowds spoil the romance a little, it's worth spending a few hours at Hanauma Bay whether or not you go in the water. The crisp green lawns along the foot of the *pali*,

HANAUMA BAY

103

dotted with banyan trees, are ideal for picnics. At either end of the beach you can walk along the rocky ledge that rings the old crater walls, just above sea level, though there is a real risk of being swept off by the waves. Just before the open ocean, at the far northeastern limit of the bay, the indelicately named **Toilet Bowl** is a natural hole in the lava that repeatedly fills with gushing sea water and then gurgles dry. On the western limit of the bay, the similar **Witch's Brew** fills and empties like a whirlpool. You may see people jumping into these pools, but that doesn't mean it's safe to do so.

Snorkeling at Hanauma is a bit like snorkeling in an aquarium; although you'll see a lot of fish, it can all feel rather tame. The water is so shallow near the shore that it's hard to stay off the reef, but it's essential to try – walking on the coral kills the reef, and can cause cuts that take weeks to heal. Reasonably skilled swimmers who want to see living coral, and bigger fish, can swim out to the deeper waters beyond the inner reef. However, the currents through the reef are notoriously strong, and the one that sweeps across the mouth of the bay is known as the "Molokai Express" because it's capable of sucking you all the way to Oahu's easterly neighbor.

KOKO HEAD AND KOKO CRATER

Right after the highway turnoff for Hanauma Bay, a dirt road climbs straight along the bare ridge above the beach. It's not always open to hikers but, if it is, it affords great views of the 642-foot summit of **Koko Head**, roughly a fifteen-minute walk away. From the summit you can see back to Diamond Head and walk down a footpath to peek into the southern end of Hanauma Bay.

Koko Head Regional Park, which covers Koko Head and Hanauma Bay, extends another couple of miles northeast to take in **Koko Crater**. The youngest of southeastern

Oahu's volcanic cones, this is considerably higher than Koko Head and makes a very impressive spectacle. Like its neighbor, it is topped by a double crater. The road up its far side – reached from Hawaii Kai, or by doubling back farther along the coastal highway – comes to a dead end at Koko Crater Stables. Alongside you'll find the barely developed **Botanic Garden** (daily 9am–4pm; free), where a twenty-minute stroll is rewarded by a grove of sweet-smelling, heavy-blossomed plumeria trees. The crater's rim, however, is inaccessible to hikers.

HĀLONA BLOWHOLE

A couple of miles beyond Hanauma Bay, where Kalaniana'ole Highway squeezes between Koko Crater and the ocean, a roadside parking lot enables drivers – and a *lot* of tour buses – to stop off for a look at the **Hālona Blowhole**. The coastline consists of layers of flat lava, each sheet set back from the one underneath to form a stairway up from the sea. Here, the waves have carved out a cave below the visible top layer, and as each new wave rushes in it's forced out through a small hole to create a waterspout up to fifty feet high. The hole itself does not go straight down, but is stepped; if you fall in, it's almost impossible to get out.

Little **Hālona Cove**, to the right of the Blowhole overlook and sheltered by tall cliffs, holds enough sand to make a welcome private beach, if you're lucky enough to have it to yourself. Only swimming within the cove itself is safe, and even then only in summer.

SANDY BEACH

Avoiding the crowds is not at all the point at **Sandy Beach**, half a mile farther on as the shoreline flattens out between Koko Crater and Makapuʻu Head. Kids from both sides of Oahu meet up here for the best **body-surfing** and **boogie-boarding** in Hawaii. This is also one of the few places where the waves remain high enough in summer to tempt pro surfers. Tourists who try to join in soon find that riding surf of this size takes skill and experience; Sandy Beach is notorious for serious injuries. If you just want to watch, settle down in the broad sands southwest of the central lava spit; swimming is never safe at Sandy Beach, and beyond the spit it's all but suicidal.

MAKAPUʻU POINT

The rising bulk of Oahu's easternmost point, **Makapuʻu Head**, pushes Hwy-72 away from the coastline as it swings round to run back up the island's windward flank. Shortly before the last low incline of the Koʻolau Ridge, there's just about room to park beside the road at **Makapuʻu State Wayside**.

A dirt road here snakes off to the right, soon curving south toward the hillock of Puʻu O Kīpahulu. An hour-long hike (there and back) wends around the hill, and back north along the coastal cliffs to **Makapuʻu Point**. From the viewing platform at the end, you can look straight down the cliffs to the Makapuʻu lighthouse below, out to Molokai on the horizon, back to Koko Head and up along the spine of eastern Oahu.

Rounding Makapuʻu Point on the highway – especially if you manage to stop at the small official **lookout** at the top – is equally memorable. The coastal *pali* suddenly soars away to your left, while straight out to sea a couple of tiny islands stand out in misty silhouette. The larger of the two, Mānana, is also known as **Rabbit Island**, thanks to its population of wild rabbits. They share their home only with seabirds – both Mānana and its neighbor,

Kāohikaipu or Turtle Island, are bird sanctuaries, and off-limits to humans.

Makapuʻu Beach County Park

Few drivers who miss the lookout can resist stopping to drink in the views as they descend from Makapuʻu Point. The first proper parking lot, however, is down below, at **Makapuʻu Beach County Park**. In summer, this is a broad and attractive strip of sand; in winter, pounded by heavy surf, it's a rocky straggle. Swimming is rarely safe even at the best of times – ask the lifeguards if you're in doubt. Like Sandy Beach, however, it's a greatly loved **body-surfing** and **boogie-boarding** site, and with the same propensity to lure unwary tourists into the water, it boasts a similarly dismal record of fatalities.

Sea Life Park

Map 8, F5. Mon–Thurs & Sat 9.30am–5pm, Fri 9.30am–10pm; adults $24, ages 4–12 $12. Call ⓣ259-7933 for details of free shuttle buses from Waikīkī. TheBus #22 ends its route here.

Immediately opposite the Makapuʻu Beach parking lot stands the entrance to the expensive **Sea Life Park**, which tends to hold greater appeal for children than for their parents. It has recently been reported to be in economic difficulty, and it's conceivable it may have closed down by the time you read this. For the moment, along with the predictable dolphin and porpoise shows, which feature human co-stars dressed up as pirates and princesses, there's a giant Reef Tank, a penguin enclosure, and a hospital for injured monk seals. The park also raises rare green sea turtles for release into the ocean and has even bred a **wholphin** – half-whale, half-dolphin. With a couple of snack bars, where live entertainment is provided by some unidentifiable

MAKAPUʻU POINT

costumed characters who have yet to secure their own TV series, plus a bar run by the *Gordon Biersch Brewery*, it's all too possible to find yourself spending an entire day here.

WAIMĀNALO

WAIMĀNALO, four miles on from Makapu'u, holds one of the highest proportions of native Hawaiians of any town on Oahu and has become a stronghold for advocates of Hawaiian sovereignty. The main drag, lined with fast-food joints, is far from picturesque, but as long as you take care not to intrude, you can get a real glimpse of old-time Hawaii by exploring the back roads. The small family-run farms and nurseries along Waikupanaha Street, which runs inland along the base of the *pali*, are particularly rural and verdant.

The most compelling reason to come to Waimānalo, however, is its **beach**. At over three miles long, it's the longest stretch of sand on Oahu, and the setting, with high promontories to either end and a green cradle of cliffs behind, is superb. The most accessible place to park, and also the safest swimming spot, is **Waimānalo Beach County Park** at its southern end, but wherever you start you're likely to feel tempted to stroll a long way along the seemingly endless sands.

About a mile farther north, where the fir trees backing the beach grow thicker again beyond a residential district, you come to **Waimānalo Bay State Recreation Area**. The waves here are a little rougher than those at the county park, but it feels even more secluded, and you can **camp** for up to five days with a permit from the state parks office in Honolulu ($5; closed Wed & Thurs; see p.166).

Farther on still, access to pristine **Bellows Field Beach Park** – ideal for lazy swimmers and novice body-surfers – is controlled by the adjoining Air Force base. The public is

allowed in only between noon on Friday and 8am on
Monday. This time it's the county parks office (see p.166)
that runs the **campground**, also open weekends only.

Windward Oahu

Less than ten miles separate downtown Honolulu from
Oahu's spectacular **windward coast**. Climb inland along
the **Pali Highway**, the **Likelike Highway**, or **Hwy-3**,
and at the knife-edge crest of the Ko'olau Mountains you're
confronted by amazing views of the serrated *pali* that
sweeps from northwest to southeast. As often as not, the
abrupt transition from west to east is marked by the arrival
of **rain** – it has, after all, been raining on this side of the
island for several million years, cutting away at the cliffs to
create a long, sheer wall.

The mountain highways drop down to the twin residential communities of **Kailua** and **Kāne'ohe**, both of which,
apart from their fine beaches, possess minimal appeal for
visitors. On a day's tour of Oahu you'd probably do better
to avoid them altogether, and head straight north on **Hwy-
83**. This clings to the coastline all the way up to Oahu's
northernmost tip, sandwiched between a tempting fringe of
golden sand and a ravishing belt of well-watered farmland
and tree-covered slopes. On most Hawaiian islands, the
windward shore is too exposed to be safe for swimming,
but here a protective coral reef makes bathing possible at a
long succession of narrow, little-used **beaches**. Oahu is also
exceptional in having a chain of picturesque little **islets** just
offshore; you're unlikely to set foot on any of them, but
they provide a lovely backdrop.

Though driving through such luscious scenery is a real
joy, there are few specific reasons to stop. The **Byōdō-In**

WINDWARD OAHU

Temple provides a great photo opportunity, while further north the **Polynesian Cultural Center** attracts a million visitors each year; otherwise you might want to spend an hour or two hiking in the backcountry, somewhere like **Kahana Valley** or **Hau'ula**.

KAILUA

The shorefront town of **KAILUA** stretches along Kailua Bay roughly four miles down from the Nu'uanu Pali lookout, and four miles north of Waimānolo. Now little more than an exclusive suburb of Honolulu, it was once a favorite dwelling place for the chiefs of Oahu, surrounded by wetlands and rich soil ideal for growing *taro*. Exploring the little side streets that lead off Kalāheo Avenue as it parallels the bay may fuel your fantasies of relocating to Hawaii, but inquiring about real-estate prices will bring you back to reality, and any time you have here is best spent on the **beach**.

Kailua Beach County Park, which fills the colossal main curve of the bay, is utterly gorgeous and makes an ideal family swimming spot year-round. The soft wide sands slope down into turquoise waters much used by **windsurfers**; windsurfing equipment, as well as **kayaks**, can be rented from vans and stalls along the park approach road or on the beach itself. Just be sure to keep away from the polluted area around the Ka'elepulu Canal.

Head north from here, and you'll soon reach **Kailua Beach**, where the waves hit a little harder, so there's less sand, but swimming conditions are generally safe. On the other hand, walking south beyond Alāla Point swiftly brings you to the similar but less crowded **Lanikai Beach**.

Lanikai consists of just a few short streets of priceless homes, all but cut off from the rest of Kailua by Ka'iwa Ridge. The coastal road beyond the beach park becomes a one-way loop immediately south of the ridge, forcing you to turn slightly inland on A'alapapa Road. Take the second right here (Ka'elepulu St) and park near the gate of the Mid-Pacific Country Club. Here you'll see the **Ka'iwa Ridge Trail** leading away to the left. Just a few minutes' steep climbing is rewarded with superb views up and down the coast and out to the tiny islands in the bay.

Almost the only vestige of Kailua's past is **Ulupo Heiau**, an ancient temple once used for human sacrifice. This long, low platform of rounded lava boulders looks out across the Kawainui Marsh from a hillock to the left of Kailua Road. To get there, take Uluo'a Road, the first left after Kailua Road breaks away from Kalaniana'ole Highway, and then turn right.

As for Kailua itself, the only area that feels much like a genuine community lies around the intersection of Kailua and Ku'ulei roads, a few hundred yards inland from the beach park. Here you'll find assorted neighborhood stores as well as the **Kailua Shopping Center** mall.

THE MŌKAPU PENINSULA

Kailua's northern limit is defined by Oneawa Ridge, stretching toward the ocean and culminating in the **Mōkapu Peninsula**. More of an island than a peninsula, joined to the rest of Oahu by two slender causeways, Mōkapu is entirely taken up by a Marine base, and no public access is permitted. It was to connect the base with Pearl Harbor that Hwy-3, the new trans-Ko'olau highway, was originally commissioned. Archeologists have found the extensive sand dunes along Mōkapu's northern shore to be the richest ancient burial site in all Hawaii.

KĀNE'OHE

Slightly smaller than Kailua, and boasting a far less robust economy, as well as considerably fewer amenities for visitors,

KĀNE'OHE is seldom seen as an exciting destination in its own right. That's largely because none of its silty beaches are suited for swimming. However, seven-mile **Kāne'ohe Bay**, reaching northwards from the Mōkapu peninsula, is the largest bay in Hawaii and, once you're outside the main built-up strip, one of the most beautiful. If you want to join the local pleasure-boaters out on the calm waters of the bay, take a one-hour **cruise** from He'eia Kea Pier on the glass-bottomed *Coral Queen* (Mon–Sat 10am, 11am, noon & 1.30pm; adults $8, under-13s $4; ⊤235-2888).

He'eia State Park, on the headland immediately before the pier, is a landscaped area set aside largely for its views of the adjoining **He'eia Fishpond**. Ancient Hawaiians built the low curving stone walls that enclose this saltwater lagoon; it's now once more being used to raise mullet. What little you see from the park probably won't hold your attention long, however. Tiny **Coconut Island**, out to sea, is used for marine research by the University of Hawaii, but is better known from the credits sequence of *Gilligan's Island*.

Inland, Kāne'ohe holds several attractive public **gardens**. Among the quietest and most relaxing is the nature reserve of **Ho'omaluhia Botanical Garden** (daily 9am–4pm; free; ⊤233-7323), at the top of Luluku Road, which loops back into the hills off Kamehameha Highway between Pali and Likelike highways. Several short trails lead swiftly into the wilderness; **camping** is free by arrangement on Friday, Saturday and Sunday nights only.

For a more commercial display of flowers, fruits and orchids, head instead for **Senator Fong's Plantation**, near Kahalu'u in northern Kāne'ohe (daily 9am–4pm; adults $10, children $6), where trams whisk visitors along the paved walkways. The smaller, free **Ha'ikū Gardens**, just off Hwy-83 at the entrance to glorious **Ha'ikū Valley**, is a nice little lily pond designed to lure diners into

Body surfing, Sandy Beach

Waikīkī Beach and Diamond Head

Waikīkī seen from the sea

Kodak Hula Show, Waikīkī

USS Missouri and USS Arizona, Pearl Harbour

Hanauma Bay

GREG EVANS

Sunset Beach, North Shore

GREG WARD

The windward coast

the on-site *Hale'iwa Joe's* restaurant (☏247-6671; for a review of the branch in Hale'iwa, see p.197).

Byōdō-In Temple

A clearly marked side road *mauka* of Hwy-83 (Kahekili Highway) just beyond central Kāne'ohe leads to the inter-denominational cemetery known as the **Valley of the Temples** (daily 8.30am–4.30pm; adults $2, under-12s $1). Several religions have chapels and monuments here, but casual visitors are always drawn to the Buddhist **Byōdō-In Temple**, built in the 1960s to celebrate a hundred years of Japanese immigration to Hawaii. This replica of a 900-year-old temple at Uji in Japan looks absolutely stunning, its red pagodas standing out from the trees at the base of the awesome *pali*.

Having parked outside the temple gates, you cross an arching footbridge to stroll through the peaceful gardens. A fishpond here is so full of orange, gold and mottled carp that they squeeze each other out of the water in their frenzy for fish food. Before you reach the main pavilion, you're encouraged to use a suspended battering ram to ring a three-ton brass bell; you'll probably have heard it echoing through the valley as you arrive. Once inside, you're confronted by a nine-foot meditating Buddha made of gilded, lacquered wood.

KUALOA PARK AND MOKOLI'I

At **Ka'alaea**, a mile north of the Byōdō-In Temple, Kahekili Highway joins Kamehameha Highway on its way up from He'eia State Park, and the two then run on together as Kamehameha Highway. The tumbling waterfalls at the heads of Waihe'e and Waiāhole valleys, visible as you look inland, are superb, but the next point worthy of a halt is at the northern tip of Kāne'ohe Bay.

From the crisp green lawns of **Kualoa Point**, out on the headland, you can look through a gap-toothed straggle of windswept coconut palms to conical **Mokoli'i Island**. To ancient Hawaiians, this picturesque little outcrop was the tail of a dragon; its more banal modern nickname is "Chinaman's Hat." At low tide, you can wade out to it along the reef – the water should never rise more than waist high, and reef shoes are an absolute must – to find a tiny hidden beach on its northern side. Otherwise, content yourself with a swim from the thin shelf of sand at Kualoa Park.

Kualoa Ranch

Map 1, J4. For full details, including rates and schedules for specific activities, contact ☎237-7321 or ⓦwww.kualoa.com. By way of example, a "Three Activity Adventure Tour," including round-trip transportation from Waikīkī, costs $99.

Roughly 200 yards north of Kualoa Park, a driveway *mauka* of the highway (left as you head north) leads into the expansive grounds of **Kualoa Ranch**. Until recently a conventional cattle ranch, it now plays host to flocks of Japanese tourists. Individual travelers are welcome to sign up for any of a wide range of activities – such as horse riding, bicycling, helicopter rides, para sailing and snorkeling, as well as a "Haunted House" in a natural cave at the foot of the *pali* – but the place is dominated by large groups of honeymooners.

Ka'a'awa

Several more good beaches lie immediately north of Kāne'ohe Bay. There's no danger of failing to spot them; in places the highway runs within a dozen feet of the ocean. So long as the surf isn't obviously high, it's generally safe to park by the road at any of the consecutive **Kanenelu**, **Kalae'ō'io**, and **Ka'a'awa** beaches, and head straight into the water. Only **Swanzy Beach County Park**, a little further along, really demands caution because of its unpredictable currents. It became a beach park thanks to a rich Kailua resident of the 1920s who donated this land on the condition that no other public parks would be created nearer her home.

Just beyond Swanzy, by which time the beach has often narrowed away to nothing, you'll probably have trouble recognizing the rock formation known as the **Crouching Lion**, one of windward Oahu's best-known landmarks.

KAHANA VALLEY

The whole of the deeply indented **Kahana Valley**, tucked in behind a high serrated *pali* around the corner from the Crouching Lion, is a state park. The basic economic unit of ancient Hawaii was the *ahupua'a*, a wedge of land reaching from the mountain peaks down to the ocean; Kahana is now the only *ahupua'a* to be entirely owned by the state. Still farmed by thirty native Hawaiian families, it aims to be a "living park," though what that means has never quite been settled. In theory, the residents educate visitors in Hawaiian traditions, but while traditional crops are still grown they don't dress up or pretend to *be* ancient Hawaiians. There's a friendly, helpful **visitor center** (Mon–Fri 7.30am–4pm; ☎237-7766) a little way back from the highway as it curves around Kahana Bay, but most people who call in have come simply to **hike**. Be sure to bring waterproof clothing if you plan to join them; upper Kahana Valley receives 300 inches of rain per year.

KAHANA VALLEY

Kahana trails

The easiest of Kahana Valley's attractive **trails** starts by following the dirt road that heads to the right in front of the visitor center. After passing a few houses, it enters a lush meadow scattered with fruit trees, and then veers left at a far-from-obvious junction to climb into the woods. It soon reaches a clearing where you can gaze across the valley to the high walls on the far side, and watch as it recedes away inland. Not far beyond, a few weather-worn stones mark the site of the **Kapa'ele'ele Ko'a** fishing shrine. A steep climb then leads up to **Keaniani Kilo**, a vantage point from which keen-eyed Hawaiians would watch for schools of fish, and signal canoes waiting below to set off in pursuit. There's nothing here now, but it's a lovely spot. The trail drops down to the highway, and you can make your way back along the beach.

To take the **Nakoa Trail**, which heads for the back of the valley, leave your car at the visitor center. Assuming that it hasn't been raining (in which case the valley streams will be too high to cross – check at the visitor center), walk along the main valley road for a mile or so before a gate bars the way. The trail then rambles up and around the valley walls for roughly four miles, with some great views and plenty of mosquitoes for company. In 1999, two Danish women who ventured farther back into Kahana Valley were lost for eight days before being rescued; be sure to carry a map and supplies. For a shorter adventure, simply head left at the start and you'll soon come to an idyllic little swimming hole in **Kahana Stream**.

Kahana Bay

The beach at **Kahana Bay**, straight across from the park entrance, hangs onto an ample spread of fine sand year-round, and is very safe for swimming. It's possible to **camp** in the woods that line its central section; $5 permits are issued by the park visitor center, or the state parks office in Honolulu (see p.166).

HAU'ULA AND PUNALU'U

Beyond Kahana, the highway continues to cling to every curve of the coastline, and traffic moves slowly. Maps show **HAU'ULA** and **PUNALU'U** as distinct towns, but on the ground it's hard to tell where one ends and the next begins. Both are quiet little local communities that barely reach a hundred yards back from the shore.

Of the half-dozen named beaches in this stretch, **Punalu'u Beach Park**, the farthest south, is the best for swimming, so long as you keep away from the mouth of Wai'ono Stream. The strip of sand is so thin here that the coconut palms rooted in the lawns behind it manage to curve out over the waves. **Hau'ula Beach Park**, a few miles along, is equally sheltered, but only snorkelers derive much pleasure from swimming out over the rocks.

Sacred Falls State Park

A very inconspicuous parking lot, *mauka* of the highway a mile past Punalu'u, is the trailhead for **Sacred Falls**. Two miles up from here – half through flat and featureless fields, and half hacking through the undergrowth beside Kalanui Stream – the **Kaliuwa'a Falls** plummet eighty feet from a green crevice in the hillside.

Although this area remains a state park, it has been closed to the public since the disaster of May 1999, when a sudden land-slide killed eight hikers immediately below the falls. That was merely the most recent of several such landslides. In another notorious incident, a tourist group was held up at gunpoint. The park is not expected to reopen in the near future.

Hau'ula trails

Three exhilarating but muddy trails enable hikers to explore **Ma'akua Gulch**, behind central Hau'ula. To reach them, park at the *mauka* end of Hau'ula Homestead Road, which starts opposite the northern limit of Hau'ula Beach Park. Having walked a hundred yards up the track (officially Ma'akua Rd) from here, you'll see a small driveway on the left, with a mailbox-style check-in station to write down your details before you set off.

The best short hike, the **Hau'ula Loop Trail**, branches off to the right just beyond the entrance gate. In something under two hours, with a few stretches of steep climbing, it carries you up and over the high ridge to the north, through sweet-smelling forests of ironwood and pine. As well as ocean views, you get amazing panoramas of neighboring Kaipapa'u Valley, reaching far inland and looking as though no human has ever entered it.

The similar but more overgrown **Ma'akua Ridge Trail** twists its own circuit around the southern wall of the Gulch, while the **Ma'akua Gulch Trail** follows the central stream back toward the mountains. As the gulch narrows, you have to hike more and more in the streambed, which can be dangerous after rain. Otherwise, it's a good opportunity to see the luscious blossoms for which Hau'ula – meaning "red *hau* trees" – is named.

LĀ'IE

The town of **LĀ'IE**, three miles on from Hau'ula, owes its neat, prim appearance to the fact that it was founded by Mormons in 1864, and remains dominated by the Latter-Day Saints to this day. This was the second major Mormon settlement in Hawaii; the first, on Lanai, was abandoned when church elders discovered that its President, William

Gibson, had registered all its lands in his own name. Gibson went on to be Prime Minister of Hawaii, while his congregation moved to Oahu. Lāʻie now has an imposing **Mormon Temple**, built in 1919 as the first such temple outside the continental United States – the temple itself is not open to the public, though a separate visitor center is (daily 9am–9pm) – and a branch of the Mormon-run **Brigham Young University**. Lāʻie, however, is best-known to visitors for a less obviously Mormon enterprise, the **Polynesian Cultural Center**.

Mormon colleges tend not to spawn lively alternative scenes, and Lāʻie is no exception. Local students do at least get to body-surf the heavy waves at **Pounders Beach** at the south end of town, but don't join in if you lack their know-how. **Kokololio Beach** just south of that is an attractive curve of sand where swimming is only safe in summer, while **Lāʻie Beach** in the center of town is prone to strong currents. The two-part **Mālaekahana Bay State Recreation Area** farther north provides the best local recreational swimming, and also makes an excellent place to camp; pick up a free state permit in Honolulu (see p.166). At low tide, you can wade out to **Goat Island**, a bird sanctuary that has a beautiful protected beach on its north shore.

The Polynesian Cultural Center

Map 9, G4. Mon–Sat 12.30–9pm; adults $27, ages 5–11 $16. Extra charges for *lūʻau* and IMAX movie show; the full "Ambassador Package" works out at $95 for adults, $63 for children. For reservations, call ⊤293-3333; ⊚www.polynesia.com. Two hours from Ala Moana on TheBus #52.

An incredible one million customers per year pay to visit Lāʻie's **Polynesian Cultural Center**. Part entertainment (with joke-telling guides and displays of fire-walking) and

LĀʻIE

119

part educational (with step-by-step demonstrations of traditional crafts), it's a haphazard mixture of real and bogus Polynesia. Kids tend to love it, while adults think of it either as uproarious kitsch or insulting.

Daytime visits consist of touring seven themed "villages" – by tram, on foot or in a canoe – to learn about seven Polynesian groups. Unless you time your visit to each village to coincide with the daily schedule of presentations, there's very little to see, so if you come at all be prepared to spend at least half a day altogether. In addition to those of Hawaii, Tahiti and the Marquesas, the farther-flung cultures of Fiji, Tonga, Samoa and the Maori are represented. University students comprise most of the staff, and they don't necessarily come from the relevant parts of the Pacific. Some milder-mannered Mormons scarcely look suitably ferocious when pretending to be Maori warriors, for example. Also bear in mind that their information is laced with Mormon theology; thus the Polynesians are said to be descended from one of the lost tribes of Israel, who migrated from Central America under the leadership of a certain Hagoth. Come in the evening, pay extra, and you can eat bad lūʻau food and watch a banal program of amateurish song-and-dance routines.

KAHUKU

KAHUKU, a couple of miles on from Lāʻie, may look run-down by comparison, but it is considerably more atmospheric. Though the plantation it served went out of business in 1971, the rusting hulk of the **Kahuku Sugar Mill** still overshadows this small town. Assorted outbuildings now house a half-hearted shopping mall. Unidentified lumps of machinery are dotted around the courtyard, painted in peeling pastel blues and yellows. Most of the old mill workings remain in place; some parts are color-coded according to their former function, as you'll see while exploring inside on the metal walkways (Mon–Sat 9am–5pm; free).

Behind the sugar mill, a few dirt lanes lead to tin-roofed plantation homes. The long **beach** beyond is not suitable for swimming, but stretches a full five miles up to Turtle Bay if you fancy a solitary, bracing hike.

Beyond Kahuku, the highway veers away from the shore to run alongside the **Amorient Aquafarms**. Fresh shrimp from this series of ponds can be bought from trucks and vans stationed along the highway nearby. The Walsh Farms complex of small, brightly painted shacks at the far end sells fresh fruit, shrimp, and an entertaining mixture of antiques and junk.

TURTLE BAY

Just before Kamehameha Highway rejoins the ocean on the North Shore, an obvious spur road leads *makai* past some expensive condos and private homes to end at **Turtle Bay**. Here photogenic beaches lie to either side of **Kuilima Point** – long, wave-raked Turtle Bay to the west, and the sheltered artificial lagoon of Kuilima Cove to the east – but you'd only choose to come here if you were staying at the luxury **hotel** on the point, reviewed on p.164.

Central Oahu

Thanks to the island's butterfly-like shape, the quickest route from Honolulu to the North Shore lies across the flat agricultural heartland of **central Oahu**. Cradled between the mountains, the **Leilehua Plateau** was created when lava from the Ko'olau eruptions lapped against the older

Wai'anae Range. Sugar cane and pineapples raised in its rich soil were the foundation of the Hawaiian economy until less than fifty years ago. As commercial farming has dwindled, however, the area has become neglected and dejected. More people than ever live in towns such as **Waipahu** and **Wahiawā** – many of them personnel from the military bases tucked into the hillsides – but there's little here to interest tourists. If you plan to drive around Oahu in a single day, you'd do better to press straight on to Hale'iwa (see p.126).

'AIEA AND PEARL CITY

Whichever road you follow, you have to drive a long way **west of Honolulu** before reaching open countryside. H-1, the main "interstate," curves past the airport and Pearl Harbor, while Hwy-78 sticks closer to the Ko'olau foothills, but they eventually crisscross each other to run through the nondescript communities of **'AIEA** and **PEARL CITY**. Restaurants where commuters can grab a quick meal loom on all sides, but neither town has a center worth stopping for.

Keaīwa Heiau State Park

Only hilltop **Keaīwa Heiau State Park**, in suburban **'Aiea Heights** above 'Aiea proper, merits a detour from the highway, and even that appeals more to local residents than to outsiders. The road up heads right from the second stoplight after the 'Aiea Stadium turnoff on Hwy-78, and then twists for almost three miles through a sleepy residential area.

Keaīwa Heiau, whose ruined walls are on the left as soon as you enter the park, was a center where healers, such as Keaīwa – "the mysterious" – himself, practiced herbal medicine, using plants cultivated in the surrounding gardens. Lots of *ti* plants, together with a few larger *kukui* trees, still grow within the otherwise well-maintained precinct, which also holds a little shrine and a central ring of stones that encloses a small lawn. This layout is largely conjectural, however, as the *heiau* was severely damaged during the sugar-plantation era.

There are no views from the *heiau*, but a mile-long **loop road** circles the ridge beyond, where the ironwood forest is punctuated with meadows and picnic areas looking out over Pearl Harbor. Halfway around, the **'Aiea Loop Trail** traces a five-mile circuit through the woods, offering views of the interior valleys as well as Honolulu. The highlight is the wreckage of a World War II cargo plane that crashed into a remote gully.

Camping at the park's cool, secluded campground (closed Wed and Thurs) costs $5, with a state permit.

WAIPAHU

Just beyond Pearl City, both Hwy-2 and Kamehameha Highway branch away to head north across the central plateau. Only a mile or so west, however, the small town of **WAIPAHU** holds one of Hawaii's best historical **museums**, an evocative memorial to the early days of immigration. It's also home to the unexpectedly upmarket **Waikele Center** shopping mall, with a giant Borders bookstore, and lots of discount "factory outlets."

Hawaii's Plantation Village

Map 1, F7. Mon–Fri 8am–3pm, Sat 10am–3pm; guided tours only, hourly until 3pm; adults $7, seniors $4, under-13s $3; ⓣ 667-0110. A mile south of H-1 in Waipahu, just below the sugar mill to which it owes its existence, stands **Hawaii's Plantation**

WAIPAHU

Village. It's a loving not-for-profit re-creation of the living conditions of the almost 400,000 agricultural laborers who migrated to Hawaii between 1852 and 1946, and were largely responsible for spawning the ethnic blend of the modern state.

Enthusiastic guides lead visitors around a small museum, and then through a "time tunnel" on to the former plantation estate. Simple houses – some always stood on this site, others have been brought in – contain personal possessions, illustrating both how much the migrants brought with them, and how different groups mingled to create a common Hawaiian identity. Cumulatively, the domestic details – pots, pans, buckets, family photographs, even the tiny boxing gloves used to train Filipino fighting cocks – make you feel the occupants have merely stepped out for a minute. The most moving artifacts are the *bangos*, the numbered metal badges that helped the *lunas* (whip-cracking Caucasian plantation supervisors) to distinguish each worker from the next. Goods could be obtained in the company store by showing your *bango*, with the cost deducted from your next pay packet.

WAHIAWĀ

All routes across central Oahu – whether you take Hwy-2 or Kamehameha Highway from Pearl City, or the more scenic **Kunia Road** through the fields from Waipahu – pass through the large town of **WAHIAWĀ** in the heart of the island. The main drag holds the dismal array of bars, fast-food outlets and gun stores that you'd expect to find this close to the **Schofield Barracks**, Oahu's largest military base (which by all accounts is actually very pretty, if you can get through the gates).

A couple of mildly diverting sites lie just outside the town. The **Wahiawā Botanical Gardens** (daily

9am–4pm; free), a mile east, is a reasonably attractive enclave of tropical trees and flowers, but nothing special by Hawaiian standards. To the north, on Whitmore Avenue off Kamehameha Highway, what look like faintly marked reddish-brown lava boulders in a pineapple field actually constitute an archeological site known as **Kukaniloko**, or the **Birthing Stones**. Tradition had it that any chief hoping to rule Oahu should be born here.

Dole Plantation

Map 1, F4. Daily 9am–6pm; free. Maze daily 9am–5.30pm; $4.50.

The single-story building of the **Dole Plantation** stands east of Kamehameha Highway a mile north of Wahiawā. Though all the cars and tour buses parked outside might lead you to expect something more interesting, the plantation is basically a large covered mall-cum-marketplace, which sells the usual assortment of tacky souvenirs and craft items, as well as fresh pineapples and pineapple products such as juices and frozen "whips."

The gardens alongside the mall hold what the *Guinness Book of Records* considers to be the world's largest **maze**, composed of Hawaiian plants. The aim here is not to reach the center, let alone escape; instead you're expected to traipse around in the hot sun to find six separate color-coded "stations." If you'd rather do that than head for the beach, go right ahead. Visitors can also wander around the back into a small display garden of pineapple species, and read a perfunctory history of the Dole family business.

WAHIAWĀ

The North Shore

Although the **surfing beaches** of Oahu's **North Shore** are famous the world over, the area as a whole is barely equipped for tourists. **Waimea**, **Sunset** and **'Ehukai** beach parks are all laid-back roadside stretches of sand, where you can usually find a quiet spot to yourself. In summer, the tame waves may leave you wondering what all the fuss is about; see them at full tilt in the winter, between October and April, and you'll have no doubts.

If you plan to do some surfing – and this is no place for casual amateurs – then you'd do best to base yourself in **Pūpūkea** (see p.132). Otherwise, you can see all there is to see in an easy day-trip from Waikīkī, with a pause to shop and snack in **Hale'iwa**.

HALE'IWA

The main town on the North Shore stands at the point where Kamehameha Highway reaches the ocean, 24 miles north of Honolulu. For most visitors, **HALE'IWA** (pronounced "*ha-lay-eve-a*") comes as a pleasant surprise. Despite the fact that tourists have been coming here ever since the opening of a train line from Honolulu in 1899, it's one of the very few communities on Oahu whose roots have not been obscured by a century of rebuilding and development.

Since the 1960s, Hale'iwa has become a mecca for **surfers** from all over the world. Many of the originals, lured here from California by the movie *Endless Summer*, seem to have remained not only in Hawaii, but also in the 1960s. The town is bursting with half-hippie businesses such as surf shops, tie-dye stores, organic restaurants and galleries of ethnic knick-knacks. Add those to a scattering of upfront tourist traps, and local stores and diners, and you've got an intriguing, energetic blend that entices many travelers to stay for months.

Cafés and restaurants in Hale'iwa are reviewed on p.197.

That said, there's precious little to see in Hale'iwa. Its main street, **Kamehameha Avenue**, runs for a mile from the Paukauila Stream to the Anahulu River, far from the ocean, passing a cluster of gas stations and then a succession of low-rise malls. In the largest of these, the **North Shore Marketplace**, Strong Current is the most interesting of the **surf shops**, for devotees and idle browsers alike. As well as selling nine-foot boards for anything from $700 up to $2500 (no rentals), it has a small section set aside as the **Hale'iwa Surf Museum**, crammed with historic boards, books, memorabilia and videos. Another nearby building, still within the North Shore Marketplace, also calls itself a **Surf Museum** (open "most of the time"; free), this time with slightly more justification. It traces the history of Hawaiian surfboards from the hollow wooden boards of the 1930s through early fiberglass models from the 1950s, and holds shrines to Duke Kahanamoku in particular and the 1960s in general.

Only as you approach the river do you finally come to the heart of Hale'iwa, a short stretch of old-fashioned boardwalk lined with false-front wooden buildings. One of these houses Matsumoto's, a Japanese grocery store renowned for its heavenly **shave ice** – the Hawaiian equivalent of a sno-cone, a mush of ice saturated with flavored syrup.

Beyond that, narrow Rainbow Bridge crosses Anahulu River, with great views upstream toward the green slopes of the Anahulu Valley. Traffic congestion led to the opening in 1995 of the Hale'iwa Bypass. Now that tourists circling

HALE'IWA

●

HALE'IWA EQUIPMENT RENTAL

The best known surf outfitter in Hale'iwa is Surf'n'Sea, to the left of the highway immediately across Rainbow Bridge (62-595 Kamehameha Hwy; ☎ 637-9887 or 1-800/899-SURF; ⓦ www .surfnsea.com). As well as renting surfboards ($5 per hour, $24 per day), body-boards ($4/$20), windsurfing boards ($12/$45) and snorkel equipment ($6.50 half-day, $9.50 all day), they organize good-quality dive trips (one tank $65, two tanks $90), provide lessons in surfing and windsurfing ($65 for two hours, $150 all day), and sell new and used boards and souvenirs.

Raging Isle, in the North Shore Marketplace (☎ 637-7700), also sells surfboards and rents mountain bikes ($40 for 24hr).

Oahu can avoid Hale'iwa altogether, the town is having to work a little harder to lure them in – hence the highway signs that plead "Don't Bypass Hale'iwa." Even so, the decrease in business should ensure that the delightfully rural back roads that lead away from Kamehameha Avenue, such as **Pa'ala'a Road**, will remain unspoiled for many years to come.

The small bay at the river mouth is **Waialua Bay**, with Hale'iwa Harbor sheltered by a breakwater on its southwestern side. Southwest of the harbor, **Hale'iwa Ali'i Beach Park** is a favorite place for local kids to learn to surf – there are even **free surfing lessons** on weekend mornings in winter – but inexperienced outsiders who have a go are taking their lives in their hands. The peril of the surf was the excuse for making this the fictional location of TV's *Baywatch Hawaii*, a short-lived state-subsidized experiment in relocating the Californian show to Hawaii that cost Hawaiian taxpayers dearly.

Just to reach the waves at Hale'iwa Ali'i, you have to pick

your way across a tricky shallow coral reef; once you're out there, you're at the mercy of strong cross-currents. Swimming at **Hale'iwa Beach Park**, on the northeast shore of the bay, is much safer.

WAIMEA BAY

Long **Kawailoa Beach** stretches for almost five miles northeast of Hale'iwa, interrupted repeatedly by rocky reefs and swept by fierce currents. Driving along the highway, however, the first glimpse you get of the ocean comes as you crest a small promontory to look down on **Waimea Bay**.

Waimea Bay is the most famous **surfing** spot in the world, thanks to what many say are the biggest rideable waves on the planet. During the summer, it's often calm as a lake, but in winter the break off its craggy headlands can remain more than twenty feet high for days at a time. Anywhere else, even the waves right on the beach would count as monsters, and lethal rip currents tear along the shoreline. While entering the ocean at Waimea in winter is extremely dangerous for anyone other than expert surfers, the beautiful sands of **Waimea Bay Beach County Park** are usually crowded with swimmers, snorkelers and boogie-boarders in summer, and with awe-struck spectators in winter.

Until a huge flood in 1894, the Waimea River flowed freely into the sea, and the valley behind was densely populated. Most of its farms and homes were destroyed, however, and the mouth of the river is now blocked by a sandbar that forms part of the beach park.

Waimea Valley and Adventure Park

Map 9, D4. Daily 10am–5.30pm; adults $24, ages 4–12 $12;
ⓣ 638-8511.

All of Waimea Valley inland of the highway bridge is now
occupied by the commercially run **Waimea Valley and
Adventure Park**. In theory, the intention of this tame
exploitation of the island's most beautiful valley is to intro-

DEATH IN WAIMEA VALLEY

In 1779, shortly after Captain Cook's death at Kealakekua Bay
on the Big Island (see p.242), one of his ships, the *Resolution*,
put in at Waimea to collect water for the long voyage north.
Waimea Bay, the first spot on Oahu to be visited by foreigners, was described by the new Captain Clerke as "by far the
most beautifull Country we have yet seen among the Isles . . .
bounteously cloath'd with Verdure, on which were situate
many large Villages and extensive plantations."

Thirteen years later, on May 12, 1792, one of Clerke's crew
returned to Waimea. **Lieutenant Richard Hergest**, in command of the *Daedalus*, had become separated from the rest of
an expedition led by Captain George Vancouver. By this time,
Kamehameha the Great's access to European weapons was
enabling him to defeat all his rivals. However, when locals
eager to barter for arms came aboard the *Daedalus*, Hergest
refused to trade and threw their leader overboard, leaving him
to swim ashore ignominiously.

Hergest then took a party ashore, landing in Waimea Bay
just west of the river mouth. As his men filled their casks, he
set off to explore inland. Accompanying him were a young
astronomer, **William Gooch** – who just a week earlier had
stayed as an overnight guest in Kamehameha's hut in
Kealakekua – and a Portuguese sailor named Manuel. A mile

duce Hawaii and its natural history to first-time visitors; it's considerably higher-minded than the Polynesian Cultural Center (see p.119), for example. However, the park has been in financial crisis for several years, amid allegations that its previously sensitive attempts to preserve and cultivate rare Hawaiian plant species have been all but abandoned. It may well have closed down altogether by the time you read this, though the city of Honolulu has been

or so up the valley – a site between the aviaries of Waimea Falls Park – the unarmed men were alarmed to see a group of Hawaiians rushing down the slopes toward them from the Pu'u O Mahuka *heiau* (see p.133). Each was a fearsome **pahupu** or "cut-in-two" warrior, having tattooed half his body – either top to bottom, or his entire head – completely black. Hergest, Gooch and Manuel were swiftly cut down, and their corpses taken as sacrificial offerings to another *heiau* at Mokulō'ia, to be baked and stripped of their flesh.

Waimea was then under the control of warrior priests who lived at the Pu'u O Mahuka *heiau*. Their leader, Koi, had been stationed here by Chief Kahekili of Maui to guard the traditionally rebellious north coast of Oahu; he was probably the man whom Hergest pushed into the ocean, and it was probably he who took his revenge. Nonetheless, when Vancouver called into Waikīkī the next year and demanded that the culprits be handed over for trial, he was presented with three men picked virtually at random. Although no one seriously believed they were guilty, they were summarily executed as an example of British justice. In 1799, the tattooed Koi was pointed out to another visiting captain at Waikīkī, who shot and wounded him in his canoe, and then hanged him.

For a fuller account of this story, read *The Death of William Gooch*; see Books, p.258.

WAIMEA VALLEY AND ADVENTURE PARK

trying to put together a rescue package to keep it open in some form.

Assuming it's still possible to enter the valley, its most prominent historical relic is the restored *Hale O Lono* or "House of Lono," an ancient *heiau* whose three stone terraces rise next to the main gate; in fact you could take a look without entering the park. If you pay to go in, once past the entrance complex of gift stores and snack bars you can wander along streamside walkways that lead past botanical gardens, aviaries and the fenced-off ruins of further *heiaus* and ancient burial sites. Almost a mile up from the gates, beyond a *hula* demonstration area and a mock-Hawaiian village of thatched huts, the path reaches the double **Waimea Falls** at the head of the valley. Cliff divers regularly leap sixty feet into the pool below.

PŪPŪKEA

Immediately beyond Waimea Bay, Kamehameha Highway starts to cruise beside a succession of magnificent surfing beaches. Driving demands patience; at the best of times, vehicles pull off without warning, while during major competitions traffic slows to a standstill.

Pūpūkea Beach County Park, which, like Hanauma Bay (see p.102), is a Marine Life Conservation District, stretches for well over a mile from the mouth of Waimea Bay. At its western end, the Three Tables surf break is named after three flat-topped chunks of reef, where plenty of unwary swimmers have come to grief, while **Shark's Cove** to the east, riddled with submarine caves, is a popular site for snorkelers and scuba divers in summer.

Bumper stickers all over Oahu carry the slogan "Save the North Shore," a reference to the planned Lihi Lani real-estate development on the cliffs above **PŪPŪKEA**. For the moment, Pūpūkea is a low-key community composed largely of international surf-bums, with a few stores and no restaurants. It offers by far the best **accommodation** along the North Shore, however, in the shape of the *Backpacker's Vacation Inn* (see p.164).

Pu'u O Mahuka Heiau State Monument

For a superb view of Waimea Valley and the bay, head up to the **Pu'u O Mahuka Heiau**, perched on the eastern bluff above the mouth of the river. As Oahu's largest temple of human sacrifice, this was once home to a terrifying brotherhood of *pahupu* ("cut-in-two") warrior-priests, who tattooed half their bodies completely black. To reach it, turn off the highway at the Foodland supermarket, a few hundred yards beyond the bay. Climb the hill on twisting Pūpūkea Road, then turn right onto a narrow track that skirts the cliff-edge for just under a mile.

The parking lot at the end stands alongside the higher of the temple's two tiers. The meadow that from here appears to lie just beyond the *heiau* is in fact on the far side of the deep cleft of Waimea Valley. **Trails** lead around and partly through the old stone walls, within which the outlines of several subsidiary structures can be discerned; most were originally paved with water-worn stones carried up from Waimea Bay. The main "altar" at the *mauka* end is usually covered with wrapped offerings and probably bears little resemblance to its original configuration. From the little loop path around the java plum trees nearby, you can see right along the North Shore to Ka'ena Point in the western distance.

Kaunala Trail

Beyond the *heiau* turnoff, Pūpūkea Road heads inland for another two miles, to end at the gates of a Boy Scout Camp. From here, the five-mile **Kaunala Trail**, open on

PŪPŪKEA

weekends only, runs along the thickly wooded crest of a high mountain ridge. As well as views of the deep and inaccessible gorges to either side, if the clouds clear you'll eventually get to see Oahu's highest peak, 4020-foot **Mount Ka'ala**, far across the central plains.

SUNSET BEACH

With its wide shelf of yellow sand, lined by palm trees, **Sunset Beach**, northeast of Pūpūkea, is perhaps the most picture-perfect beach on Oahu. Only occasional gaps between the oceanfront homes allow access, but once there you're free to wander for two blissful miles of paradise-island coastline. Unless you come on a calm and current-free summer's day (ask the lifeguards), stay well away from the water; the "Sunset Rip" can drag even beachcombers out to sea.

In winter, when the waves are stupendous, Sunset Beach fills with photographers in search of the definitive surfing shot, while reckless pro surfers perform magazine-cover stunts out on the water. Each of the breaks here has its own name, the most famous being the **Banzai Pipeline**, where the goal is to let yourself be fired like a bullet through the tubular break and yet manage to avoid being slammed down onto the shallow, razor-sharp reef at the end. To watch the action, walk a few hundred yards west (left) from **'Ehukai Beach County Park**, where a small patch of lawn separates the beach from the road.

Sunset Beach, a mile past 'Ehukai, was where North Shore surfing first took off in the early 1950s, and remains the venue for many contests. The break known as **Backyards** is renowned as especially lethal, though it's a popular playground for windsurfers. **Kaunala Beach** beyond that, home to the **Velzyland** break, is the last surf spot before the highway curves away toward Turtle Bay (see p.121) and the windward coast. Velzyland offers reliable rather than colossal waves, but riding them with any degree of safety requires immense precision.

WEST FROM HALE'IWA: WAIALUA AND MOKULE'IA

The coast of northern Oahu to the **west of Hale'iwa** lacks suitable surfing beaches, and is so rarely visited that most people don't really count it as part of the North Shore at all.

The area's principal landmark is the **Waialua Sugar Mill**, gently rusting away at the foot of the Wai'anae mountains since the local sugar company closed in 1996. A moderately interesting driving tour leads down the backroads of the village of **Waialua** and along oceanfront Crozier Drive to even smaller **Mokulē'ia**. From here, you have attractive views of Hale'iwa in the distance, but with not much to do, you might as well go straight to Hale'iwa itself.

KA'ENA POINT

The westernmost promontory of Oahu, **Ka'ena Point** is accessible only on foot or mountain bike; it's not possible to drive all the way around from the North Shore to the Leeward Shore. As Farrington Highway runs west of Waialua and Mokulē'ia, the landscape grows progressively drier, and the road eventually ends a couple of miles beyond Dillingham Airfield.

On the far side of the gate, you can follow either a bumpy, dusty dirt road beside the steadily dwindling Wai'anae Ridge or a sandy track that straggles up and down across the coastal rocks. The only sign of life is likely to be the odd local fisherman, perched on the spits of black lava reaching into the foaming ocean.

After roughly an hour of hot hiking, the ridge vanishes altogether, and you squeeze between boulders to enter the **Ka'ena Point Natural Area Reserve**. This flat and extremely windswept expanse of gentle sand dunes, knitted together with creeping ivy-like *naupaka*, is used as a nesting site in winter by Laysan **albatrosses**. At the very tip, below a rudimentary lighthouse – a slender white pole topped by flashing beacons – tiny beaches cut into the headland. Winter waves here reach over fifty feet high, the highest recorded anywhere in the world. That's way beyond the abilities of any surfer, though humpback whales often come in close to the shore.

From Ka'ena Point, you can see the mountains curving away down the leeward coast, as well as the white "golfball" of a military early-warning system up on the hills. Just out to sea is a rock known as **Pōhaku O Kaua'i** ("the rock of Kauai"); in Hawaiian legend, this is a piece of Kauai, which became stuck to Oahu when the demi-god Maui attempted to haul all the islands together.

The Leeward Coast

The **west** or **leeward coast** of Oahu, cut off from the rest of the island behind the Wai'anae mountains, is accessible only via the **Farrington Highway** that skirts the southern end of the ridge. Customarily dismissed as "arid," it may not be covered by tropical vegetation, but the **scenery** is still spectacular. As elsewhere on Oahu, the mountains are pierced by high green valleys – almost all of them inaccessible to casual visitors – while fine beaches such as Mākaha Beach Park line the shore.

However, the traditionally minded inhabitants of towns

such as **Nānākuli** are not disposed to welcome the encroachment of hotels and golf courses, and visitors tend to be treated with a degree of suspicion. The further north you go, the stronger the military presence becomes, with soldiers in camouflage lurking in the hillsides. It's not possible to drive all the way up to Ka'ena Point.

TheBus #51 from the Ala Moana Center runs up the Wai'anae coast as far as Mākaha.

THE SOUTHWEST CORNER

The strip development that characterizes both sides of H-1 from Honolulu to Waipahu finally comes to an end as you enter the **southwest** corner of Oahu. Long-cherished plans by the state authorities to turn this region into a major tourism and residential center seem finally to be approaching fruition, however, as the former plantation settlement of **'Ewa** becomes ever more overshadowed by the burgeoning modern community of **Kapolei**.

'Ewa

A couple of miles south of Farrington Highway along Fort Weaver Road, **'EWA** is a picturesque little hamlet of wooden sugar-plantation homes arranged around a well-kept village green. Other than snapping a few photos along the back lanes, the only reason to come here is to take a **train excursion** with the Hawaii Railway Society, based just west of town along Renton Road. Their souvenir store and museum is open all week (Mon–Sat 9am–3pm, Sun 10am–3pm; free), but only on Sunday afternoons (at 12.30pm and 2.30pm) does the restored *Waialua #6* locomotive set out on its ninety-minute round-trip journey (adults \$8, seniors and under-13s \$5; ☎681-5461; Ⓦhttp://0/members.aol.com/hawaiianrr/index.html) to the Ko Olina Resort (see opposite). On the second Sunday of each month, by reservation only, you can have a private narrated tour in a luxury parlor car (\$15).

'Ewa Beach Park, three miles south of the village, is an attractive oceanfront park popular with sailors from the nearby base. It has plenty of sand, and views across to Diamond Head, but the water tends to be too murky for swimming, and there's an awful lot of seaweed around.

Kapolei

Until very recently, the name **KAPOLEI** did not appear on even the most detailed maps of Oahu. Now, however, it's the island's fastest-growing town, stretching alongside H-1 as it approaches its end in the southwest corner of the island. Homes, movie theaters and shopping malls have sprung up at an astonishing rate, but the new town has so far made only one bid to attract tourists, in the shape of the **Hawaiian Waters Adventure Park**, at 400 Farrington Hwy (hours vary; adults \$30, ages 4–11 \$20; ☎674-9283; Ⓦwww.hawaiianwaters.com). Hawaii's first water park follows the model of its predecessors in California, Florida and elsewhere, with lots of swirling plastic tubes for visitors to raft or simply slide down, children's play areas, and an exhilarating wave pool. It's all great fun, though with so many wonderful beaches on the island to compete with, it hasn't yet attracted great numbers of visitors. In principle, it's open daily from 10.30am until dusk, but it often seems to close its gates as early as 4pm; call ahead before you make the drive.

Ko Olina Resort

During the 1980s, a great deal of money was poured into landscaping the **Ko Olina Resort**, just north of **Barbers Point** at the southwest tip of the island. Four successive artificial lagoons were blasted into the coastline, each a perfect semicircle and equipped with its own crescent of white sand. Work also began on creating a marina for luxury yachts at the Barbers Point Harbor. While the construction work continues to proceed, of the projected residential estates, condo buildings, shopping centers and hotels, only the *Ihilani Resort*, reviewed on p.165, has so far materialized. Its one neighbor, the relentlessly tacky *Paradise Cove lū'au* site (see p.170), is something of a poor relation.

NĀNĀKULI

Farrington Highway reaches the Wai'anae coast at **Kahe Point Beach Park**, near the section known as "Tracks" because of the adjacent railroad tracks. As well as being a small but pretty strip of sand, this is Oahu's most popular year-round **surfing** site. The waves offshore remain high (but not overpoweringly so) even in summer, and break much closer to the shore than usual. Since the bay itself is relatively sheltered, swimming usually becomes dangerous only in the depths of winter.

A couple of miles further on, **NĀNĀKULI** is the southernmost of a string of small coastal towns. According to local legends, its name means either "look at knee" or "pretend to be deaf" – neither of which seems to make much sense. The population is largely Hawaiian, and there's little attempt to cater to outsiders. **Nānākuli Beach Park**, which runs alongside the highway all through town, is another good summer swimming beach, while **Zablan Beach** at its southern end is much used by scuba divers.

NĀNĀKULI

The beach immediately north of Nānākuli is called **Ulehawa**, or "filthy penis," after a particularly unsavory ancient chief.

WAI'ANAE

WAI'ANAE, five miles up the coast, centers on curving **Pōka'ī Bay**. Thanks to the breakwaters constructed to protect the boat harbor at its northern end, the main sandy beach here is the only one on the Leeward Coast where swimming can be guaranteed safe all year-round. The high-walled valley behind provides an irresistible backdrop.

Beyond a flourishing coconut grove at the tip of the flat spit of land that marks the southern end of Pōka'ī Bay stand the ruined walls of **Kū'īlioloa Heiau**. Unusual in being virtually surrounded by water, this three-tiered structure is said to mark the place where the first coconut tree was planted in Hawaiian soil.

MĀKAHA

MĀKAHA, or "savage," the last of the leeward towns, was once the hideout of a dreaded band of outlaws. Now famous for the savagery of its **waves**, it began to attract surfers in the early 1950s. Before World War II, virtually all Oahu surfing was concentrated in Waikīkī. When changes in the ocean conditions there, and the development of new techniques and equipment led surfers to start looking elsewhere, Mākaha was the first place they hit on. The waves at its northern end are said to be the largest consistently reliable surf in Hawaii, and several major surfing contests are still held at **Mākaha Beach Park** each year. In summer, when sand piles up in mighty drifts, it's often possible to swim here in safety, and Mākaha retains enough sand to remain a beautiful crescent beach even in winter. You'll probably notice what look like hotels along the oceanfront nearby, but they're all long-term rental condos intended for local families.

Kāne'āki Heiau

Map 1, C5. Tues–Sun 10am–2pm; free.

A couple of miles back from the ocean in Mākaha Valley, beyond the defunct *Sheraton Mākaha Resort*, a private driveway leads to **Kāne'āki Heiau**. The most thoroughly restored ancient temple in Hawaii, it was excavated by Bishop Museum archeologists in 1970 and can now be visited with permission from the security guards at the gate; you must leave a driver's license or passport as security. Its principal platform of weathered, lichen-covered stones is topped by authentic thatched structures such as the *anu'u* ("oracle tower"), as well as carved images of the gods. The *heiau* originated as an agricultural temple to the god Lono in the fifteenth century. Two hundred years later, it was converted into a *luakini,* where human sacrifices were dedicated to the god Kū.

THE ROAD TO KA'ENA POINT

Beyond Mākaha, the highway traces a long, slow curve up the coast to Yokohama Bay. Barely populated, and splendidly bleak, this region attracts few visitors other than a handful of daredevil surfers prepared to risk its sharks, currents and mighty waves.

Looking inland, the rolling green slopes of **Mākua Valley** also conceal dangerous secrets. Used by the Air Force for bombing practice during and after World War II, the valley is still barred to the public due to the possible presence of unexploded war toys. Gaping **Kāneana Cave** to the south is too vandalized to be worth investigating.

Not even the sturdiest four-wheel-drive vehicle could negotiate the dirt road that continues from the end of the highway. In any case, the dunes beyond were designated as the **Ka'ena Point Natural Area Reserve** to help repair damage done by military jeeps and motorbikes. However, an exposed one-hour hike along the route of the old railroad tracks will bring you to the very tip of the island. The walk is substantially similar to the corresponding trail along the North Shore, described on p.135.

LISTINGS

LISTINGS

Accommodation

Virtually all the **accommodation** available in the city of Honolulu, and on the entire island of Oahu for that matter, is confined to **Waikīkī**, which holds an extraordinary concentration of hotels in all price ranges. Unless you're happy to spend hundreds of dollars per night for world-class luxury, however, Waikīkī rooms are far from exciting. Most are in anonymous tower buildings, charging at least $100 for a standard en-suite double room, with another $50 for an ocean view, and $50 more again if they're right on the seafront. Few have any sort of personal touch, and there are no local B&Bs.

The very cheapest accommodation option is a $14–20 dorm bed in one of Waikīkī's half-dozen **hostels**, all of which are geared heavily towards young international backpackers. However, so long as you don't mind missing out on a sea view, or having to walk a few minutes to the beach, it's normally possible to find an adequate hotel room for around $50 per night. Note that the Hawaiian word *lānai* is universally used to mean "balcony."

The telephone area code for all Hawaii is ⊤ 808.

Except for the very top-of-the-line properties, there's little point choosing a hotel with a **swimming pool** – most

ACCOMMODATION PRICE CODES

All the accommodation prices listed here have been graded with the symbols below, which refer to the quoted rates for a double room in high season (Dec to March), not including state taxes of 11.25 percent. In low season, Waikīkī hotels in categories ❹, ❺ and ❻ tend to drop their rates by $10 to $30 per night, and some offer intermediate summer rates in July and August.

❶ up to $40   ❷ $40–70   ❸ $70–100
❹ $100–150   ❺ $150–200   ❻ $200–250
❼ $250–300   ❽ $300–400   ❾ over $400

are squeezed onto rooftop terraces, overlooked by thousands of rooms in the surrounding high-rises and attracting all the dirt and fumes of the city.

To get your first-choice hotel in peak season, be sure to **reserve** well in advance. That said, even if you arrive in Hawaii with nowhere to stay, it's seldom hard to find a room on short notice. In the baggage claim area at Honolulu Airport, a board lists discounted rates in assorted Waikīkī hotels, together with courtesy phones to make your reservation.

As for possibilities away from Waikīkī, **Honolulu** proper offers a small selection of hotels and B&Bs aimed primarily at business travelers, and a couple more hostels, while the rest of the island holds very few alternatives. The only hotels **elsewhere on Oahu** are the *Hilton* and *Ihilani* resorts, at the far northeast and southwest corners, respectively, while the bargain *Backpackers Vacation Inn* caters for the surf crowd on the North Shore. Other than a few tiny B&Bs in Kailua and Kāneʻohe on the windward coast, that's about it.

There are no **campgrounds** in Waikīkī, and camping at Honolulu's only site, in Sand Island State Park (see p.70), is

ACCOMMODATION

not recommended. Other Oahu campgrounds are reviewed on p.166.

WAIKĪKĪ HOSTELS

Banana Bungalow Waikīkī Beach Hostel

Map 3, G4. 2463 Kūhiō Ave, Waikīkī, HI 96815 ⓣ924-5074 or 1-888/2-HOSTEL, ⓕ924-4119;

ⓦ www.bananabungalow.com. Part hostel, part bargain-rate hotel, this central tower block is an invaluable resource for budget travelers. All its sixty or so rooms have en-suite bathrooms, balconies, phones and TVs; roughly half are six-to-eight-bed dorms priced at $18 per person, the rest are $55 private doubles. There's cheap internet access downstairs, free airport pick-up, and island tours run several days per week; parking costs $7 per night. ❶–❷

Hale Aloha Hostel (Hostelling International Waikīkī)

Map 3, G4. 2417 Prince Edward St, Waikīkī, HI 96815 ⓣ926-8313, ⓕ922-3798.

Official but informal youth hostel in the heart of Waikīkī, in a turquoise four-story building a couple minutes from the beach. Dorm beds in four-person rooms are $17 ($19 for nonmembers), while double rooms cost $42–48; guests share a kitchen and patio. Office open 7am–3am; no curfew. Reservations recommended, especially the four double rooms. ❶–❷

Hawaiian Hostel

Map 3, D2. 419 E Seaside Ave, Waikīkī, HI 96815 ⓣ924-3303 or toll-free 1-866/924-3303, ⓕ923-2111;

ⓦ www.hawaiianhostel.com. Basic, unofficial hostel, for travelers with passports and onward flight tickets only (US citizens included.) Tucked back from the street around a courtyard, it's a few blocks from the beach in a quiet area of central Waikīkī.

WAIKĪKĪ HOSTELS

A bed in a six-person dorm costs $17, in two-person dorm it's $20, and a private double is $52; discounts for stays of three or more days, seventh night free. No curfew, free breakfasts, $5 dinners, free airport shuttle, and internet access. **❶–❷**

Island Hostel

Map 4, E3. Hawaiian Colony Building, 1946 Ala Moana Blvd, Waikīkī, HI 96815 ⓣ & ⓕ 924-8748.

Unofficial, good-value hostel, a little way back from the *Hilton Hawaiian Village,* in western Waikīkī. Not quite in the thick of things, but a good base. Beds in four-person dorms $17 per night or $105 per week, doubles with kitchenette and TV $50 per night. No curfew. **❶–❷**

Polynesian Hostel Beach Club

Map 4, I4. 2584 Lemon Rd, Waikīkī, HI 96815 ⓣ 922-1340 or 1-877/504-2924, ⓕ 923-4146; ⓦ www.hostelhawaii.com. Former motel converted into clean, private, air-conditioned hostel, a block from the sea at

the Diamond Head end of Waikīkī. All rooms have en-suite bathrooms; some hold four bunk beds priced at $15 for one or $26 for two, while others serve as private doubles ($39) and studios ($51). Cash only. Van tours of the island are offered, and meals are served in the communal area some nights. Free snorkels, boogie boards and internet access. **❶–❷**

Waikīkī Beachside Hotel & Hostel

Map 4, I4. 2556 Lemon Rd, Waikīkī, HI 96815 ⓣ 923-9566, ⓕ 923-7525; ⓦ www.hokondo.com. Motel near the park in eastern Waikīkī that has been rather perfunctorily rejiggered as a private hostel; it looks a lot smarter from the outside than it does once you go in. It offers dorm beds ($17.50) and double rooms ($70), some of which are two-room suites capable of sleeping four guests, which isn't a bad deal if you're traveling as a group. An additional night's rent is taken as a deposit. **❶–❸**

HONOLULU YMCAS AND HOSTELS

Central Branch YMCA

Map 4, D3. 401 Atkinson Drive, Honolulu, HI 96814 ⓣ941-3344, ⓕ941-8821. Set in attractive grounds opposite the Ala Moana shopping mall, just outside Waikīkī, with an on-site swimming pool and a beach nearby. Accommodations include plain rooms with shared bath for men only, at $30 single or $41 double, plus some nicer en-suite doubles available to women too, at $38 single, $53 double. All guests must reserve at least two weeks in advance, and have a definite check-out date; no walk-ins are accepted. ❷

Fernhurst YWCA

Map 2, G4. 1566 Wilder Ave, Honolulu, HI 96822 ⓣ941-2231, ⓕ949-0266; ⓔfernywca@get.net. Women-only lodging, not far west of the university and quite a way from the ocean, that's intended primarily for locals in need. Double rooms share a bathroom with one other room, and cost $25 per person; some can be rented by single travelers for $30. Rates include simple buffet breakfasts and dinners served Mon–Sat; a $30 membership is compulsory. ❶–❷

Honolulu International AYH Hostel (Hostelling International Honolulu)

Map 2, G4. 2323-A Seaview Ave, Honolulu, HI 96822 ⓣ946-0591, ⓕ946-5904. Youth hostel in college residence, a couple of miles from Waikīkī, across from the University of Hawaii in Mānoa. There's no direct bus from the airport: change at Ala Moana on to TheBus #6 or #18; get off at Metcalfe St/University Ave, one block south of the hostel. Office hours 8am–noon and 4pm–midnight; no curfew. Dorm beds are $13.50 for AYH/IYHA members, $16.50 for nonmembers, and there's a three-night maximum stay for nonmembers. ❶

Nu'uanu YMCA

Map 5, E2. 1441 Pali Hwy, Honolulu, HI 96813 ⓣ 536-3556, ⓕ 533-1286.
Basic single rooms, sharing bath, for men only at $30 per night. The well-equipped new building is just up from downtown and easily accessible by bus. ❷

WAIKĪKĪ HOTELS: BUDGET

Aloha Punawai

Map 3, A5. 305 Saratoga Rd, Waikīkī, HI 96815 ⓣ & ⓕ 923-5211; ⓦ www.alternative-hawaii.com/alohapunawai/.
Miniature hotel, opposite the post office, whose well-priced studios and apartments – with and without air conditioning – are furnished in a crisp, vaguely Japanese style. All units have kitchens, bathrooms, balconies and TV. Small discounts for weekly stays. ❸

The Breakers

Map 3, A5. 250 Beach Walk, Waikīkī, HI 96815 ⓣ 923-3181 or 1-800/426-0494, ⓕ 923-7174; ⓦ www.breakers-hawaii.com.
Small, intimate hotel on the western edge of central Waikīkī, offering two-person studio apartments and four-person garden suites; all have kitchenettes and TV, and there's a bar and grill beside the flower-surrounded pool. ❸–❹

Hale Pua Nui

Map 3, A6. 228 Beach Walk, Waikīkī, HI 96815 ⓣ 923-9693, ⓕ 923-9678.
Small, unprepossessing but clean motel-like hotel, among the cheapest deals in central Waikīkī. The studio apartments are far from fancy, but all have two twin beds, kitchenettes, cable TV and free local calls. Reserve well ahead. ❷

Hawaiian Waikīkī Beach Hotel

Map 4, I4. 2570 Kalākaua Ave, Waikīkī, HI 96815 ⓣ 922-2511 or 1-800/877-7666, ⓕ 923-3656; ⓦ www.hawaiianWaikīkī beach.com.
A 25-story behemoth at the

Diamond Head end of Waikīkī, notable for its above-average nightly entertainment. Rooms further back from the ocean – especially in the separate Mauka Tower – are much better value than those overlooking the beach. ❸–❺

Hawaiiana Hotel

Map 3, A4. 260 Beach Walk, Waikīkī, HI 96815 ⓣ923-3811, 1-800/628-3098 (HI) or 1-800/367-5122 (US & Can), ⓕ926-5728; ⓦwww.hawaiianahotelatWaikīkī .com.

Pleasant low-rise family motel close to the heart of Waikīkī. Rooms – all with kitchenettes, but equipped to varying degrees of luxury – are arranged around two pools. ❸–❺

Kai Aloha

Map 3, A5. 235 Saratoga Rd, Waikīkī, HI 96815 ⓣ923-6723, ⓕ922-7592; ⓔkaialoha@gte.net.

Tiny, very central hotel. *Lānai* studios plus apartments sleeping up to four, all with kitchenettes, bathrooms, TV and air-con. ❸

Royal Grove

Map 3, H4. 151 Uluniu Ave, Waikīkī, HI 96815 ⓣ923-7691, ⓕ922-7508; ⓦwww.royalgrovehotel.com.

Small-scale, family-run hotel with a personal touch in central Waikīkī. The facilities improve the more you're prepared to pay, but even the most basic rooms, which lack air-conditioning, are of a reliable standard. There's also a courtyard pool, making the *Royal Grove* one of Waikīkī's best bets for budget travelers. Special weekly rates apply April–Nov only. ❷

Waikīkī Gateway Hotel

Map 4, F3. 2070 Kalākaua Ave, Waikīkī, HI 96815 ⓣ955-3741 or 1-800/247-1903, ⓕ923-2541; ⓦplanet-hawaii .com/sand/gateway.

High-rise hotel on the western side of central Waikīkī, budget-oriented by local standards. Free continental breakfast on sixteenth-floor *lānai*. The highly rated lobby restaurant, *Nick's Fishmarket*, is reviewed on p.183. ❸

Waikīkī Prince

Map 3, H5. 2431 Prince Edward St, Waikīkī, HI 96815 ⓣ922-1544, ⓕ924-3712. Slightly drab but perfectly adequate and very central budget hotel. All rooms offer air conditioning, en–suite baths and basic cooking facilities, but no phones; the "very small" and "small" categories are even cheaper than "economy" units. Office open 9am–6pm only; seventh night free April–Nov. ❷

Most mid-priced Waikīkī hotels work out much cheaper if booked as part of a package; see p.3.

WAIKĪKĪ HOTELS: MID-RANGE

Aston Coral Reef Hotel

Map 3, E4. 2299 Kūhiō Ave, Waikīkī, HI 96815 ⓣ922-1262, 1-800/321-2588 (HI) or 1-800/922-7866 (US & Can), ⓕ922-8785; ⓦwww.aston -hotels.com.
Relatively inexpensive but still classy hotel, a couple of blocks back from the beach near the International Marketplace. The extra-large rooms sleep three or four people, while room rates drop by $25 April–June and Sept–Christmas. ❻

Aston Pacific Monarch

Map 3, H4. 2427 Kūhiō Ave, Waikīkī, HI 96815 ⓣ923-9805, 1-800/321-2588 (HI) or 1-800/922-7866 (US & Can), ⓕ924-3220; ⓦwww.aston-hotels.com.
Tall condo building in the heart of Waikīkī, having small studios with kitchenettes, plus larger four-person suites with full kitchens and balconies. ❹–❺

Aston Waikīkī Beachside Hotel

Map 3, H6. 2452 Kalākaua Ave, Waikīkī, HI 96815 ⓣ931-2100, 1-800/321-2588 (HI) or 1-800/922-7866 (US & Can), ⓕ931-2129; ⓦwww.aston-hotels.com.

An elegant oceanfront option, with a marble lobby, and paneled chinoiserie in the bathrooms. Though it styles itself as "the only luxury boutique hotel in Waikīkī," the cheapest rooms are worth avoiding: glibly promoted as "inside cabins," they have no windows. There's no restaurant, but a continental breakfast is included, and guests can charge meals at the *Hyatt Regency* to their accounts. Standard ❻, partial ocean view ❼, deluxe ❽.

Aston Waikīkī Circle Hotel

Map 3, H6. 2464 Kalākaua Ave, Waikīkī, HI 96815 ⓣ 923-1571, 1-800/321-2500 (HI) or 1-800/922-7866 (US & Can), ⓕ 926-8024; ⓦ www.aston-hotels.com.

Bright and cheery tower, dwarfed by its surroundings but one of the cheapest options along the oceanfront. Each of its thirteen circular floors is divided into eight identical rooms, with prices varying according to how much sea you can see. The hotel is the base for Aloha

Express Tours; see p.219. City view ❹, ocean view ❺.

Ilima Hotel

Map 3, E2. 445 Nohonani St, Waikīkī, HI 96815 ⓣ 923-1877 or 1-800/367-5172 (US & Can), ⓕ 924-8371; ⓦ www.ilima.com.

Good-value small hotel near the canal on the *mauka* side of central Waikīkī and catering to a mainly local clientele. Spacious condo units, each with two double beds, its own kitchen, and free local calls. ❹

Imperial of Waikīkī

Map 3, B7. 205 Lewers St, Waikīkī, HI 96815 ⓣ 923-1827 or 1-800/347-2582 (US & Can), ⓕ 923-7848; ⓦ www.imperialofWaikīkī.com.

Studio rooms and one- or two-bedroom balcony suites in a tower building set slightly back from the beach, just south of Kalākaua Ave. A bit hemmed in by the oceanfront giants, but not bad for groups traveling together. The best views are from the terrace around the 27th-floor pool. ❹

WAIKĪKĪ HOTELS: MID RANGE

OUTRIGGER AND OHANA HOTELS

Until 1999, the family-oriented **Outrigger** chain ran twenty hotels in Waikīkī, with a total of more than 7500 rooms. To convey the differences among its various properties, the Outrigger company has now divided them into two separate categories. The five most luxurious kept the Outrigger brand name, while the rest have become **Ohana** (which means "family") hotels. By Waikīkī standards, all remain competitively priced. Even the fanciest of the Outriggers, the oceanfront *Reef on the Beach*, is less opulent than places like the *Hyatt Regency* or the *Hilton Hawaiian Village*, and costs significantly less per night. The Ohana properties all charge between $110 and $140 per night for a clean, well-maintained room with standard upmarket hotel furnishings, and offer discounted "Simple Saver" rates in low season (April–June and Sept to mid-Dec).

A high proportion of Outrigger and Ohana guests are on all-inclusive vacation packages. If you contact either chain directly – reservations are handled centrally, at the numbers opposite – be aware that both offer one free night to guests who stay six nights or more, and a plethora of room-and-car deals. Standard room rates, however, remain constant year-round; where the price codes below indicate ranges, these refer to the rate for a standard double room with and without ocean views.

Outrigger Hotels:

East, 150 Ka'iulani Ave (Map 3, F4)   ⑤

Islander Waikīkī, 270 Lewers St (Map 3, B5)   ⑤

Reef on the Beach, 2169 Kālia Rd (Map 3, A7)   ⑥–⑧

Waikīkī on the Beach, 2335 Kalākaua Ave (Map 3, E6)   ⑥–⑧

Waikīkī Shore, 2161 Kālia Rd (Map 3, A7)   ⑥

Outrigger Reservations Ⓦ www.outrigger.com
US & Canada Ⓣ 1-800/688-7444
Australia Ⓣ 0011-800/688-74443
New Zealand Ⓣ 00-800/688-74443
UK & Ireland Ⓣ 001-800/688-74443

Ohana Hotels:

Ala Moana Towers, 1700 Ala Moana Blvd (Map 4, D3) ❹
Maile Sky Court, 2058 Kūhiō Ave (Map 4, F3) ❹
Ohana Surf, 2280 Kūhiō Ave (Map 3, D3) ❹
Waikīkī Coral Seas, 250 Lewers St (Map 3, B5) ❹
Waikīkī Edgewater, 2168 Kālia Rd (Map 3, A7) ❹
Waikīkī Hobron, 343 Hobron Lane (Map 4, D3) ❹
Waikīkī Malia, 2211 Kūhiō Ave (Map 3, C3) ❹
Waikīkī Reef Lānai, 225 Saratoga Rd (Map 3, A6) ❹
Waikīkī Reef Towers, 227 Lewers St (Map 3, B5) ❹
Waikīkī Royal Islander, 2164 Kālia Rd (Map 3, A7) ❹
Waikīkī Surf, 2200 Kūhiō Ave (Map 3, B3) ❹
Waikīkī Surf East, 422 Royal Hawaiian Ave (Map 3, C2) ❹
Waikīkī Tower, 200 Lewers St (Map 3, B7) ❹
Waikīkī Village, 240 Lewers St (Map 3, B6) ❹
Waikīkī West, 2330 Kūhiō Ave (Map 3, F3) ❹

Ohana Reservations Ⓦ www.ohanahotels.com
US & Canada Ⓣ 1-800/462-6262
Worldwide (US) Ⓣ 303/369-7777

OUTRIGGER AND OHANA HOTELS

●

Island Colony – A Marc Suite

Map 3, D2. 445 Seaside Ave, Waikīkī, HI 96815 ☎ 923-2345; reserve through Marc Resorts ☎ 922-9700 or 1-800/535-0085 (US & Can), ⓕ 922-2421 or 1-800/633-5085 (US & Can); ⓦ www.marcresorts.com. Anonymous-looking high-rise at the quieter inland side of Waikīkī, still within five-minutes' walk of the beach. Despite the name, it has conventional hotel rooms as well as more luxurious suites; all are furnished to a high standard and have their own balconies. Hotel rooms ❹, studios ❺, suites ❻.

New Otani Kaimana Beach Hotel

Map 2, G7. 2863 Kalākaua Ave, Waikīkī, HI 96815 ☎ 923-1555 or 1-800/421-8795, ⓕ 922-9404; ⓦ www.kaimana.com. Intimate, Japanese-owned, Japanese-toned hotel on quiet and secluded Sans Souci

Beach (see p.38), a half-mile east of the bustle of central Waikīkī and boasting lovely backdrops of Diamond Head. The *Hau Tree Lānai* restaurant is reviewed on p.182. ❹

Pacific Beach Hotel

Map 3, I6. 2490 Kalākaua Ave, Waikīkī, HI 96815 ☎ 922-1233, 923-4511 or 1-800/367-6060, ⓕ 922-8061; ⓦ www.pacificbeachhotel.com. The *Pacific Beach* boasts 830 rooms in two separate towers, at the Diamond Head end of Kalākaua Ave. The high central tower contains the Oceanarium – a three-story fishtank that's the focus for diners in the *Neptune* and *Oceanarium* (see p.176) restaurants. ❻–❼

Queen Kapiʻolani

Map 4, I4. 150 Kapahulu Ave, Waikīkī, HI 96815 ☎ 922-1941, 1-800/533-6970 or 1-800/367-5004 (US & Can), ⓕ 922-2694; ⓦ www.castle-group.com. One of Waikīkī's older high-

---

Note that almost all Waikiki hotels charge guests around $8–12 per night to park in their garages.

---

rises, overlooking Kapi'olani Park and Diamond Head at the east end of town. Recently spruced up, it's a relatively good value, so long as you don't get one of the handful of undersized rooms. **❹–❺**.

Sheraton Princess Ka'iulani

Map 3, F5. 120 Ka'iulani Ave, Waikīkī, HI 96815 ☏ 922-5811 or 1-800/782-9488, ⓕ 931-4577; ⓦ www.sheraton-hawaii.com.
Tower-block hotel, not quite on the seafront but big enough to command wide views of ocean and mountains. A spacious and attractive garden surrounds the tiny street-level pool. Standard **❻**, ocean view **❼**.

Waikīkī Beachcomber

Map 3, D5. 2300 Kalākaua Ave, Waikīkī, HI 96815 ☏ 922-4646 or 1-800/622-4646 (US & Can), ⓕ 923-4889; ⓦ www.Waikīkī beachcomber.com.
A gleaming and centrally located white tower, just "297 steps" from the beach. The 500 rooms are all but identical, with private balconies and above-average comforts – though all have showers, not baths. Ask about special room/car deals. **❻**.

Waikīkī Joy

Map 3, B4. 320 Lewers St, Waikīkī, HI 96815 ☏ 923-2300, 1-800/321-2588 (HI) or 1-800/922-7866 (US & Can), ⓕ 924-4010; ⓦ www.aston-hotels.com.
Friendly, small-scale hotel. Marble decor throughout, from the airy garden lobby through the well-appointed rooms – all of which contain Jacuzzis. **❹–❺**.

Waikīkī Parc

Map 3, C7. 2233 Helumoa Rd, Waikīkī, HI 96815 ☏ 921-7272 or 1-800/422-0450, ⓕ 923-1336; ⓦ www.Waikīkīparc.com.
Modern high-rise set slightly back from the beach, operated by the same management as the *Halekūlani* opposite, and offering a taste of the same luxury at more affordable prices. Conventional top-of-the-line rooms, plus two good restaurants: *Kacho* (see p.182) and the *Parc Café* (see p.183). Standard **❺**, ocean view **❻**.

WAIKĪKĪ HOTELS: MID-RANGE

Waikīkī Royal Suites

Map 3, B5. 255 Beach Walk, Waikīkī, HI 96815 ☎ 926-5641; reserve through Marc Resorts, ☎ 922-9700 or 1-800/535-0085 (US & Can); ℱ 922-2421 or 1-800/633-5085 (US & Can); ⓦ www.marcresorts.com.

Plush all-suite property in the heart of Waikīkī. The building itself is not all that large, which gives it a friendly atmosphere, but each individual suite, complete with living room and *lānai*, offers extensive living space for families. ❻

Waikīkī hotels and restaurants are shown on maps 3 and 4

WAIKĪKĪ HOTELS: EXPENSIVE

Halekūlani

Map 3, C7. 2199 Kālia Rd, Waikīkī, HI 96815 ☎ 923-2311 or 1-800/367-2343, ℱ 926-8004; ⓦ www.halekulani.com. Stunning oceanfront hotel, arranged around an exquisite courtyard and pool in a prime location for views along the beach to Diamond Head, but aloof from the Waikīkī bustle. Probably the most luxurious option in the area, and home to the highly rated *La Mer* restaurant. The open-air *House Without a Key* bar (see p.202) is perfect for sunset cocktails. Garden view ❽, ocean view ❾.

Hilton Hawaiian Village

Map 4, E4. 2005 Kālia Rd, Waikīkī, HI 96815 ☎ 949-4321 or 1-800/221-2424, ℱ 947-7898; ⓦ www.hiltonhawaiianvillage.com. The biggest hotel in Hawaii, with more than 2500 rooms and counting, the *Hilton* is a scaled-down version of all of Waikīkī, having almost a hundred of the exact same stores and restaurants you'd find out on the streets. The center of Waikīkī is a 15min walk away, and with a good pool, a great stretch of beach (see p.36), and even its own flamingo-filled lagoon, there's little incentive to leave the hotel precincts – which is, of course, the point. If you like this kind of self-contained resort, however, there are better ones on the other islands. Garden view ⑥, ocean view ⑧.

Hyatt Regency Waikīkī

Map 3, G6. 2424 Kalākaua Ave, Waikīkī, HI 96815 ⓣ 923-1234 or 1-800/233-1234, ⓕ 923-7839; ⓦ www.hyatt.com. Very lavish, very central property, across the road from the heart of Waikīkī Beach, and consisting of two enormous towers engulfing a central atrium equipped with cascading waterfalls and tropical vegetation. Also holds a sixty-store shopping mall, a third-story open-air pool, a nightclub, 1230 "oversized" rooms, a spa, and six restaurants, of which three, *Ciao Mein*, *The Colony* and *The Texas Rock'n'Roll Sushi Bar*, are reviewed on pp.179–181. ⑦–⑨

The Royal Hawaiian

Map 3, D7. 2490 Kalākaua Ave, Waikīkī, HI 96815 ⓣ 922-7311 or 1-800/782-9488, ⓕ 931-7840; ⓦ www.sheraton-hawaii.com.
The 1920s "Pink Palace" (see p.42), now owned by Sheraton, remains one of Waikīkī's best-loved landmarks. The original building still commands a great expanse of beach, and looks over the terrace gardens to the sea, but is now flanked by a less atmospheric tower block holding the most expensive suites. ⑧ ⑨

Sheraton Moana Surfrider

Map 3, F6. 2365 Kalākaua Ave, Waikīkī, HI 96815 ⓣ 922-3111 or 1-800/782-9488, ⓕ 923-0308; ⓦ www.sheraton-hawaii.com.
Waikīkī's oldest hotel, built at the end of the nineteenth century (see p.42). Despite

---

Our humble price category barely does justice to Waikīkī's top hotels, which can charge as much as $4000 per night for their most sumptuous suites.

---

extensive restoration, the "Colonial" architectural style of the original building – now the focus of the Banyan wing – remains intact, though these days it's flanked by two huge towers. The main lobby, with its wooden walls, plush settees and old-time atmosphere, is a delight. City view ❼, ocean view ❾.

Sheraton Waikīkī Hotel
Map 3, C7. 2255 Kalākaua Ave, Waikīkī, HI 96815 ☎ 922-4422 or 1-800/782-9488, Ⓕ 923-8785; Ⓦ www.sheraton -hawaii.com.
Ultramodern, 1715-room skyscraper on Waikīkī Beach, with beachside gardens and pool. The rooms are deluxe, but can't compete with the thrill of the high-speed, glass-

sided, ocean view elevators. The separate *Sheraton Manor* wing offers much cheaper and smaller rooms with poor views. *Sheraton Manor* ❺, *Sheraton Waikīkī* city view ❼, ocean view ❾.

W Honolulu
Map 2, G7. 2885 Kalākaua Ave, Waikīkī, HI 96815 ☎ 922-1700 or 1-877/W-HOTELS, ⒻG 923-2249; Ⓦ www.whotels.com.
Intimate, very chic little fifty-unit oceanfront hotel, just over half a mile east of Waikīkī, and part of an exclusive international chain. All rooms have balconies, CD players and cordless phones, and the *Diamond Head Grill* restaurant (see p.181) is downstairs. Rooms ❽, suites ❾.

HONOLULU HOTELS AND B&BS

Ala Moana Hotel
Map 4, D2. 410 Atkinson Drive, Honolulu, HI 96814 ☎ 955-4811, 1-800/446-8990 (HI) or 1-800/367-6025 (US & Can), ⒻG 944-2974; Ⓦ www.alamoanahotel.com.

Thousand-room tower block right alongside the Ala Moana Center, just down the road from the Convention Center, and five-minutes' walk from Waikīkī. Though it's targeted primarily at

AIRPORT ACCOMMODATION

If you find yourself stuck at **Honolulu Airport** and desperate for sleep, the ideal solution is right there in the main lobby. The *Honolulu Airport Mini Hotel* (℡ 836-3044, ⓕ 834-8985; ❷) – also known as *Sleep & Shower* – offers tiny but clean private rooms, for single occupancy only, at $30 for eight hours or $17.50 for two hours, including shower.

Nearby on North Nimitz Highway, and served by complimentary shuttle buses, there's a *Best Western Plaza* (3253 N Nimitz Hwy ℡ 836-3636 or 1-800/528-1234, ⓕ 834-7406; ❸) and a *Holiday Inn* (3401 N Nimitz Hwy; ℡ 836-0661 or 1-800/800-4683, ⓕ 833-2349; ❹).

business visitors and shopaholics, it offers the lively *Rumours* nightclub and some good restaurants, and there's an excellent beach close at hand (see p.71). ❺

Aston at the Executive Center Hotel

Map 5, F5. 1088 Bishop St, Honolulu, HI 96813 ℡ 539-3000, 1-800/321-2588 (HI) or 1-800/922-7866 (US & Can), ⓕ 523-1088; ⓦ www.aston-hotels.com.
All-suite downtown hotel, enjoying great harbor views from the top of a 40-story skyscraper. Geared to business travelers, but with prices that compare well with similar standard Waikīkī hotels. ❺

Mānoa Valley Inn

Map 2, F2. 2001 Vancouver Drive, Honolulu, HI 96822 ℡ 947-6010, ⓕ 946-6168; ⓦ www.aloha.net/~wery/.
One of Honolulu's most relaxing options: a plush, antique-filled B&B inn, near the University in lush Mānoa Valley. Waikīkī feels a lot farther away than the mile it really is. Eight rooms, some sharing bathrooms and some en-suite. Sit in one of the wicker chairs on the back porch and linger over breakfast. ❹–❺

HONOLULU HOTELS AND B&BS

161

Pagoda Hotel

Map 6, G1. 1525 Rycroft St,
Honolulu, HI 96814 ⓣ 923-4511
or 1-800/367-6060, ⓕ 922-
8061; ⓦ www.pagodahotel.com.
Roughly halfway between
downtown Honolulu and
Waikīkī, within easy walking
distance of Ala Moana mall,
and offering two pools and
three restaurants. The *Pagoda*
has conventional, comfortable
hotel rooms plus one- and
two-bedroom suites. ❹

For a selection of top-quality B&Bs on all the Hawaiian
islands, contact Hawaii's Best Bed & Breakfasts, PO Box
563, Kamuela, HI 96743 ⓣ 885-4550 or 1-800/262-9912,
ⓕ 885-0559; ⓦ www.bestbnb.com.

THE REST OF OAHU

KAILUA

Akamai B&B

Map 1, L7. 172 Kuʻumele
Place, Kailua, HI 96734 ⓣ 261-
2227 or 1-800/642-5366;
ⓦ www.planet-
hawaii.com/akamaibnb.
B&B half a mile back from
Kailua Beach, where two
small, well-equipped en-suite
units, each with basic
cooking facilities, share use of
a pool and laundry room. ❸

Hale Makai

Map 1, L7. 68 Laiki Place,
Kailua, HI 96734; reserve
through Hawaii's Best Bed &
Breakfasts, PO Box 563,
Kamuela, HI 96743 ⓣ 885-4550
or 1-800/262-9912, ⓕ 885-
0559; ⓦ www.bestbnb.com.
Friendly and very hospitable
B&B accommodation in
private home on a quiet street
barely a minute's walk from
lovely Kailua Beach. The
attractive guest bedroom has
its own attached bathroom. ❸

Lanikai B&B

Map 1, L7. 1277 Mokulua
Drive, Kailua, HI 96734 ⓣ 261-
1059 or 1-800/258-7895,
ⓕ 262-2181;

Ⓦ www.lanikaibb.com.
Long-established B&B
across from Lanikai Beach,
which has a studio room
facing the mountains and a
larger seaview apartment.
Three-night minimum stay.
❸–❹

Sharon's Serenity
Map 1, L7. 127 Kakahiaka St,
Kailua, HI 96734 Ⓣ 262-5621 or
1-800/914-2271.
Very comfortable B&B,
alongside a golf course just
back from Kailua Beach,
where the two good-value
guest bedrooms share use of a
bathroom. Three-night
minimum stay. ❸

KĀNE'OHE

Ali'i Bluffs Windward B&B
Map 1, K6. 46-251 Iki'iki St,
Kāne'ohe, HI 96744 Ⓣ 235-
1124 or 1-800/235-1151;
Ⓦ www.hawaiiscene.com
/aliibluffs.
Two-room antique-furnished
B&B on a suburban
Kāne'ohe street, complete
with pool, ocean view and

en-suite facilities. Three-
night minimum stay. ❸

Hula Kai Hale
Map 1, K6. 44-002 Hulakai
Place, Kāne'ohe, HI 96744
Ⓣ 235-6754;
Ⓦ www.lava.net/hulakai.
Delightful B&B overlooking
Kāne'ohe Bay, in which the
two guestrooms have en-suite
bathrooms, kitchen facilities
and access to a swimming
pool. Three night minimum
stay. ❸

Kāne'ohe Bay B&B
Map 1, K6. 45-302 Pu'uloko
Place, Kāne'ohe, HI 96744;
reserve through Hawaii's Best
Bed & Breakfasts, PO Box 563,
Kamuela, HI 96743 Ⓣ 885-4550
or 1-800/262-9912, Ⓕ 885-
0559; Ⓦ www.bestbnb.com.
One guest B&B room, with
en-suite facilities, is available
in this gorgeous open-plan
home, perched immediately
above Kāne'ohe Bay with its
own private mooring. The
friendly owners are absolute
island experts. Two-night
minimum stay. ❹

KĀNE'OHE

LĀ'IE

Best Inn – Hukilau Resort

Map 9, G4. 55-109 Laniloa St, Lā'ie, HI 96762 ⊤ 293-9282, 1-800/237-8466 or 1-800/526-4562, ⓕ 293-8115; ⓦ www.hawaiibestinn.com.
Clean, modern **motel** – anonymous and well away from the ocean, but quite good value – less than a hundred yards north of the Polynesian Cultural Center (see p.119). Each room has its own *lānai* overlooking the swimming pool; rates include free calls and breakfast. It shares its driveway with the oddest *McDonalds* you ever saw, converted from a leftover section of the Polynesian Cultural Center and still featuring an entrance carved to resemble a South Seas longhouse. ❸

TURTLE BAY

Turtle Bay Hilton Golf and Tennis Resort

Map 9, E2. 57-091 Kamehameha Hwy, PO Box 187, Kahuku, HI 96731 ⊤ 293-8811 or 1-800/221-2424, ⓕ 293-9147; ⓦ www.turtlebayresort .hilton.com.
Thousand-acre resort at the northeastern tip of Oahu, having almost five hundred oceanview rooms, as well as two golf courses, ten tennis courts and four restaurants. Handily positioned for the North Shore, but priced far beyond the pockets of the surfing crowd, it feels oddly out of place in this remote corner and, apart from children enthralled by the nearby beaches, most guests seem to end up wondering what they're doing here. It does, however, have three good restaurants; the *Sea Tide Room*, *The Cove*, and *Palm Terrace*. Ocean view ❻, oceanfront ❼.

THE NORTH SHORE

Backpacker's Vacation Inn

Map 9, C3. 59-788 Kamehameha Hwy, Hale'iwa, HI

96712 ⓣ 638-7838 or 1-888/628-8882 (HI only), ⓕ 638-7515; ⓦ www.backpackers-hawaii.com.

The North Shore's best accommodation option, in tiny Pūpūkea (see p.132), was founded by Mark Foo, a daredevil Hawaiian surfer who died surfing in California in 1994. Its rambling main building, *mauka* of the highway, has dorm beds for $18 per night in high season, and simple private double rooms sharing kitchen and bath for $60. Across the street in low oceanfront blocks, dorm beds cost $21 a night, and good-value studio apartments with great views start at $95. *The Plantation Village*, a hundred yards down the road, across from the sea and run by the same management, consists of nine restored plantation cabins, with dorm beds, private rooms and larger cabins at similar rates. All rates are discounted for stays of a week or longer, and drop by fifteen percent April–Nov. Communal buffet dinners on Tues, Wed, Fri & Sun cost

$6, and there's a free daily bus to Honolulu Airport. They also provide free snorkeling equipment and boogie boards, offer Net access at $7 per hour, and arrange island tours, plus scuba diving in summer. ❶–❸.

LEEWARD OAHU

Marriott Ihilani Resort and Spa

Map 1, D8. 92-1001 Olani St, Ko Olina Resort, Kapolei, HI 96707 ⓣ 679-0079 or 1-800/626-4446, ⓕ 679-0080; ⓦ www.ihilani.com.

The *Ihilani*, in the far southwest corner of Oahu, opened in 1993 as the island's closest approximation to the resorts elsewhere in the state. If you can afford it, it's an absolute idyll; fifteen stories of state-of-the-art rooms are equipped with every high-tech device imaginable, from computerized lighting and air-conditioning systems to CD players and giant-screen TVs. The adjoining spa boasts thalasso therapy and sauna facilities, plus rooftop tennis

LEEWARD OAHU

courts and a top-quality golf course. The in-house restaurants are excellent – a meal at the least expensive, the poolside *Naupaka*, will set you back at least $50, though its delicate Pacific Rim fish dishes are well worth trying; alternatives include the formal *Azul* grill. **8**–**9**

CAMPING

You can **camp** in county parks on Oahu for free, and in state parks for $5 per night, with a permit from the relevant office. However, few sites are worth recommending, and none of those is especially convenient for Honolulu. Furthermore, all county and state campgrounds are closed on both Wednesday and Thursday nights, and you can't stay at any one site for more than five days in one month. The best options among the state parks are those at Keaīwa Heiau (see p.122), Mālaekahana Bay (p.119), Waimānolo Bay (p.108), and Kahana Valley (p.115); appealing county parks include Bellows Field Beach (p.108), and Kaiaka Beach Park, a mile out of Hale'iwa near the mouth of Kaiaka Bay.

The **state parks office**, which accepts postal applications seven to thirty days in advance, is in Room 310, 1151 Punchbowl St, Honolulu, HI 96813 (Mon–Fri 8.30am–3.30pm; ☏587-0300). **County** permits can be obtained, in person only, from 650 S King St (Mon–Fri 7.45am–4pm; ☏523-4525), or from the subsidiary "City Hall" in the Ala Moana Center (Mon–Fri 9am–4pm, Sat 8am–4pm; ☏973-2600).

Eating

T
hanks to two major factors, Honolulu and Waikīkī boast a restaurant scene to rival any in the world. First of all, there's Hawaii's ethnic diversity; national dishes and recipes brought from all over the world by nineteenth-century immigrants have subsequently mingled to create intriguing new flavors and specialties. Second, the presence of millions of tourists, eager to pay top rates for good food, means that the city holds more superb restaurants than its own population could ever sustain.

Almost all the hotels in **Waikīkī** have at least one on-site restaurant. As you'd expect, the standards in the major hotels are high, but out on the streets the emphasis is on keeping the price down, rather than the quality up. Many better restaurants don't bother to open for lunch, but take-outs, fast-food chains and snack bars are everywhere you turn; the largest concentrations are along Kūhiō Avenue and, with more of a Japanese emphasis, on Kalākaua Avenue west of Lewers Street.

No single district of **Honolulu** can quite match Waikīkī for its sheer concentration and range of eating options. Although **downtown** is all but deserted at night, nearby **Chinatown** abounds in inexpensive Chinese and Vietnamese places, and the malls along the **waterfront** – especially Aloha Tower Marketplace, Restaurant Row, and

HONOLULU AND WAIKĪKĪ FAVORITES

Breakfast	*Shore Bird Beach Broiler*	Waikīkī	p.172
Buffet	*Todai Seafood Buffet*	Waikīkī	p.180
Chinese	*Indigo*	Honolulu	p.186
Fast food	*International Marketplace*	Waikīkī	p.173
	Maunakea Marketplace	Honolulu	p.187
Gourmet	*Alan Wong's*	Honolulu	p.192
Greek	*Olive Tree Café*	Honolulu	p.194
Italian	*Arancino*	Waikīkī	p.173
Japanese	*L'Uraku*	Honolulu	p.191
Korean	*Yakiniku Canellia*	Honolulu	p.193
Local	*Kaka'ako Kitchen*	Honolulu	p.190
Pacific Rim	*Bali By The Sea*	Waikīkī	p.180
	Sansei	Honolulu	p.192
Pizza	*California Pizza Kitchen*	Honolulu	p.188
Seafood	*Sam Choy's Breakfast, Lunch & Crab*	Honolulu	p.194
Steak	*The Colony*	Waikīkī	p.181
Thai	*Singha Thai Cuisine*	Waikīkī	p.179
Vietnamese	*Maxime*	Honolulu	p.188

the Ward Centre – hold an abundance of delectable alternatives. Many of Honolulu's finest restaurants are also tucked away in tourist-free zones, for example around the university or in more upscale residential areas.

Within the last dozen years, chefs trained in both Eastern and Western traditions have returned to Hawaii to open restaurants that serve an exciting hybrid cuisine known variously as **Pacific Rim**, **Hawaii Regional**, or **New Hawaiian**. Drawing on fresh local ingredients and strong spices, they have placed Hawaii among the world's hottest culinary destinations. Roy Yamaguchi, of *Roy's* in Hawaii Kai, is generally credited as being the instigator of this movement;

EATING

other practitioners include Alan Wong and Sam Choy.

For inexpensive eating, Honolulu has its fair share of the national fast-food chains, but typical budget restaurants, diners and takeout stands, serve **"local food"** – a blending of the US mainland along with Japan, China, Korea and the Philippines, all given a slight but definite Hawaiian twist. **Breakfast** in these places tends to be the standard combination of eggs, meat, pancakes, muffins or toast. At midday, the usual dish is the **plate lunch**, served on a molded tray holding meat and rice as well as potato or macaroni salad and costing from $5 to $8. **Bento** is the Japanese equivalent, with mixed meats and rice; in Filipino diners, you'll be offered **adobo**, which is pork or chicken stewed with garlic and vinegar. Korean barbecue, **kal bi** – prepared with sesame – is especially tasty, while **saimin** (pronounced *sigh-min* not *say-min*), a bowl of clear soup filled with noodles and other ingredients, has become something of a national dish. Finally, the carbohydrate-packed **loco moco** is a fried egg served on a hamburger with gravy and rice.

Food in general is often referred to as **kaukau**, and it's also worth knowing that **pūpūs** (pronounced *poo-poos*) is a general term for little snacks, the kind of finger food that is given away in early-evening Happy Hours.

WAIKĪKĪ – INEXPENSIVE

Waikīkī restaurants are keyed on maps 3 and 4.

China Garden
Map 3, E3. *Aston Coral Reef Hotel*, 2299 Kūhiō Ave ☎923-8383.
Daily 11am–10pm.
Inexpensive Chinese restaurant serving $6 lunch specials and $9 one-plate dinners with rice and soup. Entrees cost $9–14; set meals for two or more are $14–18 per person.

LŪʻAUS

All too many visitors to Hawaii – largely those reared on a steady diet of Elvis movies – arrive in the islands determined to attend a "traditional Hawaiian feast" or *lūʻau*. Local families do indeed celebrate holidays with beachside picnics they call *lūʻaus*, but the only *lūʻaus* a tourist can hope to attend are strictly commercial affairs. Besides pseudo-Polynesian entertainment, these always involve mass catering and canteen-style self-service. Though the food tends to be indifferent at best, they do provide the opportunity to sample such dishes as *kālua pork*, an entire pig wrapped in *ti* leaves and baked all day in an underground oven known as an *imu*; *poi*, a purple-gray paste produced by pounding the root of the *taro* plant; *poke*, which is raw fish, shellfish, or octopus, marinated with soy and Oriental seasonings; and *lomi-lomi*, made with raw salmon.

If you insist on going to a *lūʻau* while you're in Waikīkī, go to the *Royal Hawaiian Hotel* on Monday at 6pm (☎923-7194). Their *lūʻau* costs around $80, but the food's not bad, the Waikīkī Beach setting is romantic, and you can get there and back easily.

The two biggest *lūʻaus* on Oahu, which you'll see advertised everywhere, are *Germaine's* (nightly; ☎1-800/367-5655 or 949-6626; ⓦwww.germainesluau.com) and *Paradise Cove* (nightly; ☎973-5828). What the ads don't tell you is that they are both thirty miles from Waikīkī, in the far southwestern corner of the island. The price – reckon on $40 from an activity center – includes an hour-long bus trip each way (singalongs compulsory), and your reward at the end is the chance to spend hours looking at tacky overpriced souvenirs, eating indifferent food, drinking weak cocktails and watching third-rate entertainment.

LŪʻAUS

Eggs'n'Things

Map 4, E3. 1911B Kalākaua Ave ☎ 949-0820.
Daily 11pm–2pm.
All-night diner drawing a big breakfast crowd for its bargain omelettes, waffles and crepes. The Early Riser (before 9am) and Late Riser (1–2pm) specials give you three pancakes or two eggs for just $3.

Ezogiku

Map 4, I4. 2546 Lemon Rd ☎ 923-2013.
Daily 7–10am & 11am–11pm.
Plain and very inexpensive Japanese diner, with three branches in Waikīkī – the others are at 2420 Koa Ave and 2146 Kalākaua Ave. Ramen soups plus rice and curry dishes, all at $6–7, to eat in or takeout

Hawaii Seafood Paradise

Map 4, D3. 1830 Ala Moana Blvd ☎ 946-4514.
Daily 6.30am–3am.
Almost three restaurants in one, not far from the *Hilton* at the Ala Moana end of Waikīkī. At breakfast, the food is American and very inexpensive. Chinese-style lunch specials cost around $7, and only in the evening is it really a "seafood paradise," with high-quality Chinese and Thai entrees such as crispy oysters and steamed catfish generally priced at $10–15.

La Cucaracha

Map 3, E3. 2310 Kūhiō Ave ☎ 922-2288.
Daily 2pm–mdnight.
Budget Mexican food, served from early afternoon until late in a party atmosphere. Standard Mexican favorites like enchiladas and chimichangas are about $10; fancier seafood combos cost $20 or so.

Leonard's Bakery

Map 4, I1. 933 Kapahulu Ave ☎ 737-5591.
Sun–Thurs 6am–9pm, Fri & Sat 6am–10pm.
Longstanding Portuguese bakery on the northeastern fringes of Waikīkī, renowned for its delicious desserts and *malasadas*. Most of the pastries cost under $1.

WAIKĪKĪ – INEXPENSIVE

Moose McGillycuddy's
Map 3, B4. 310 Lewers St
T 923-0751.
Mon, Tues & Sun 7.30am–2am,
Wed–Sat 7.30am–4am.
Nightclub and drinking
venue, with booths in the bar
downstairs, and a dining
room on the second floor.
Among the breakfast options
is a $2 special that includes
two eggs and bacon. Later on
you can get burgers and
sandwiches for $6–9, snacks
like quesadillas, wings, or
nachos for $5–8, or full
dinners of fajitas, pasta, steak,
or chicken for $10–15. Youth
Hostel Association members
receive a fifteen percent
discount on all entrees.

Perry's Smorgy
Map 3, G3. 2380 Kūhiō Ave
T 926-0184.
Daily 7–11am, 11.30am–2.30pm
& 5–9pm.
Bland all-you-can-eat buffets,
served indoors or in a nice
little garden. The food is
filling but the place is always
crowded, and hardly anything
actually tastes that great. The
$5.25 breakfast includes ham,
beef, sausages, pancakes,

pastries and juices; the $6.25
lunch consists of *mahi mahi*,
Southern-fried chicken, garlic
bread, rice, baked macaroni
and desserts; and the $9.25
dinner features beef, shrimp,
ribs, turkey and teriyaki
chicken. (Note that there's
another *Perry's* at the *Ohana
Coral Seas*, 250 Lewers St,
Map 3, B6, but it's indoor-
only and less appealing.)

Ruffage Natural Foods
Map 3, H4. 2443 Kūhiō Ave
T 922-2042. Mon–Sat
9am–7pm.
Tiny wholefood grocery with
a takeout counter and patio
seating. Avocado and bean-
sprout sandwiches, plus salads
and vegetables with pasta or
tofu all cost under $7, and they
do great real-fruit smoothies.
The front part of the shop
becomes an inexpensive sushi
bar from 6pm onwards.

Shore Bird Beach Broiler
Map 3, A7. *Outrigger Reef on
the Beach*, 2169 Kālia Rd
T 922-2887.
Daily 7–11am & 4.30–10pm.
Open-air hotel restaurant on
the oceanfront serving an

WAIKĪKĪ MALL DINING

Waikīkī's most convenient fast-food option must be the International Food Court, in the International Marketplace on Kalākaua. Takeout counters with self-explanatory names – *Joe's Hamburger Grill*, *Yummy Korean B-B-Q*, *Bautista's Filipino Kitchen*, etc. – surround a sheltered area of tables, and there's often free musical entertainment of some kind. There's a similar, smaller food court beneath the Waikīkī Shopping Plaza at 2250 Kalākaua Ave, while *Starbucks* coffee outlets are in the **Waikīkī Trade Center** at Kūhiō and Seaside and the **Discovery Bay Center** at 1778 Ala Moana Blvd.

If you want to cook for yourself, try the Food Pantry, a good-value 24-hour supermarket at the northwest corner of Kūhiō Avenue and Walina Street. Wholefood enthusiasts will probably prefer Down to Earth Natural Foods, a mile or so out of Waikīkī near the University, at 2525 S King St (℡947-7678).

$8 breakfast buffet, and dinner with an open salad bar for $13–19, depending on your choice of entree. There's a communal grill on which guests cook their own meat or fish. Excellent value, especially if you use the $1-off coupons in the free magazines.

WAIKĪKĪ – MODERATE

Arancino
Map 3, B6. 255 Beach Walk ℡923-5557.
Daily 11.30am–2.30pm &
5–10pm.
Surprisingly authentic Italian trattoria – albeit decorated an unlikely lurid orange – in

Tokyo Noodle House
Map 3, A4. 2113 Kalākaua Ave ℡922-3479. Daily 11am–2am.
Clean, glass-fronted Japanese eatery offering large, tasty servings of ramen noodle soups, fried noodles and rice dishes, all priced at $6–7.
Cash only.

central Waikīkī. The basic dinner menu of pasta dishes and pizza ($8–12) is supplemented by tasty specials such as a steamed clams appetizer for ($7.50) and *spaghetti alla pescator* ($14.50), with all kinds of fish swimming in olive oil and garlic. There's always plenty of Chianti to go around.

Banyan Veranda

Map 3, F6. *Sheraton Moana Surfrider*, 2365 Kalākaua Ave ⓣ 922-3111.
Mon–Sat 7–11am, 1–4.30pm & 5.30–10pm; Sun 9am–1pm, 3–5pm & 5.30–10pm.
Poolside hotel café on Waikīkī Beach. A full $19 breakfast buffet is available daily except Sunday, when the lavish brunch costs $35. Instead of lunch, they perform the time-honored ritual of serving tea every afternoon: $18 buys a plate of scones and pastries and a pot of tea to be enjoyed as you listen to a Hawaiian guitarist. The nightly sunset buffet costs $27 and includes dim sum and sushi as well as the usual meat and fish entrees;

your meal is accompanied by Hawaiian music from 5.30 to 7.30pm, followed by a pianist from 7.30 to 10.30pm.

Cheeseburger in Paradise

Map 3, I6. 2500 Kalākaua Ave ⓣ 923-3731.
Daily 8am–midnight.
The Waikīkī outlet of this successful Maui burger joint occupies a prime position facing the ocean and shares its twin's retro 1950s South Seas/beachcomber style. The food, however, is uninspired – the $7 cheeseburgers are adequate, the $7–11 salads less so – and the service perfunctory.

Duke's Canoe Club

Map 3, E6. *Outrigger Waikīkī on the Beach*, 2335 Kalākaua Ave ⓣ 922-2268.
Daily 7am–1am.
Open-air beachfront restaurant/bar named after legendary surfer Duke Kahanamoku, and boasting a great view of the waves. The good-value buffet breakfasts (until 11am) are available with hot items ($10) or just

cold ($8); the fairly basic lunch buffets are $10. At night, there's a full (if unimaginative) dinner menu with a $10 salad bar and chicken, beef and fish entrees at around $20. The bar stays open until after midnight and features live music.

Genki Sushi

Map 4, I1. 900 Kapahulu Ave ⓣ735-8889.
Mon–Thurs 11am–3pm & 5–9pm, Fri 11am–3pm & 5–10pm. Closed Sat & Sun.
Weekdays-only conveyor-belt sushi bar, a mile or so northeast of Waikīkī. Each plate is color-coded according to price, with two pieces of sushi starting at just $1.20, so grab whatever you fancy from the very broad range as it drifts by. Other Honolulu locations of this popular chain offer drive-through sushi.

Golden Dragon

Map 4, E4. *Hilton Hawaiian Village*, 2005 Kalia Rd ⓣ946-5336.
Tues–Sun 6–9.30pm.
The classiest Chinese restaurant in Waikīkī, with garden seating overlooking a lagoon, and a tasteful indoor dining room. The food is good too, and the prices surprisingly low. Entrees such as crispy lemon chicken, roast duck, and noodles with fish or chicken cost under $15, while set menus start at $29.50 per person.

Hard Rock Café

Map 4, D2. 1837 Kapi'olani Blvd ⓣ955-7383.
Mon–Thurs & Sun 11.30am–11pm, Fri & Sat 11.30am–11.30pm.
Just across the Ala Wai Canal from Waikīkī, this is one of the earliest *Hard Rock Cafés*, here since 1971, and is usually jammed with memorabilia-hungry tourists. The food – ribs, burgers, and so on – is predictable but not at all bad, and most menu items cost under $10. The drinking and the music get progressively heavier as the night wears on.

House Without a Key

Map 3, B7. *Halekūlani*, 2199 Kālia Rd ⓣ923-2311.
Daily 7.30am–10pm.

Waikīkī's classiest venue for an open-air sunset cocktail (see p.202) is open all day, every day, and serves good, relatively simple food at prices well below what you might imagine. True, the ample breakfast buffet costs $20, but a Greek salad with shrimp at lunchtime is just $7, and dinner entrees like roasted half chicken and lump-crab-crusted *mahimahi* are less than $20.

Keo's in Waikīkī
Map 3, F3. 2028 Kūhiō Ave
℡951-9355.
Daily 7.30am–2pm & 5–10.30pm.
Although *Keo's* has only recently moved to central Waikīkī, it has long proclaimed itself to be Hawaii's best Thai restaurant. Its walls are festooned with photos of celebrities enticed by trademark dishes such as the "Evil Jungle Prince" curries, made with basil, coconut milk and red chili. The increasing worldwide familiarity of Thai cooking means that *Keo's* is no longer a novelty, and its menu may seem unexceptional, but the food tastes as good as ever,

and with all entrees under $15, the prices are reasonable. Breakfast is both American and Asian; lunch and dinner are entirely Thai. The several other Keo's branches in Honolulu include *Keoni* by *Keo's* at 150 Ka'iulani Ave in Waikīkī, and one at the Ward Centre (see p.216).

Lewers Street Fish Company
Map 3, B6. 247 Lewers St
℡971-1000.
Daily 5–10pm.
Basement fish restaurant below the *Ohana Reef Towers*, where they make their own pasta (the linguini is good) and serve it with grilled or sautéed island fish. Steaks are available as well. Most of the menu has a strong Italian twist, with dishes typically priced at $17–20, but there's also *mahimahi* fish'n'chips for $8. Selected specials cost $6 between 5pm and 6pm.

Oceanarium
Map 3, I6. *Pacific Beach Hotel*, 2490 Kalākaua Ave ℡922-6111.
Daily 6am–2pm & 5–10pm.
Minimally furnished

HAWAIIAN FISH

Although the ancient Hawaiians were expert offshore fisher-
men as well as sophisticated fish farmers, the great majority of
the fish eaten in Hawaii nowadays is imported. Local fishing is
on too small a scale to meet the demand, and in any case
many of the species that tourists expect to find on menus
thrive in much cooler waters. Thus salmon and crab come
from Alaska, and mussels from New Zealand, although Maine
lobsters are now being farmed in the cold waters of the deep
ocean off the Big Island.

However, if you feel like being adventurous, you should get
plenty of opportunity to try some of the Pacific species caught
nearby. If the list below still leaves you in the dark, personal
recommendations include *opah*, which is chewy and salty like
swordfish; the chunky *'ōpakapaka*, which because of its red
color (associated with happiness) is often served on special
occasions; the succulent white *ono* (which means "delicious"
in Hawaiian); and the dark *'ahi*, the most popular choice for
sashimi.

'ahi	yellow-fin tuna	*mano*	shark
a'u	swordfish or marlin	*moi*	thread fish
		onaga	red snapper
'ehu	red snapper	*ono*	mackerel or tuna-like fish
hāpu'upu'u	sea bass		
hebi	spear fish	*'ōpae*	shrimp
kākē	barracuda	*opah*	moonfish
kalekale	pink snapper	*'ōpakapaka*	pink snapper
kāmano	salmon	*pāpio*	pompano
kēmē	red goat fish	*uhu*	parrot fish
lehi	yellow snapper	*uku*	gray snapper
mahi mahi	dorado or dolphin fish	*ulua*	jack fish
		weke	goat fish

restaurant with a big gimmick, which is more fun for kids than for adults – one wall of the dining room is a gigantic aquarium, so as you eat your meal you can watch (and be watched by) 400 live fish, plus the occasional scuba diver. The day starts with a continental breakfast (6–11am) for $7.50 or a $9.50 buffet. Lunchtime noodles, burgers, salads or sandwiches all cost under $10, while the dinner menu features seafood pancakes for $24 or prime rib for $18.50, as well as surf'n'turf combos.

Peacock Room & Garden Lanai

Map 4, I4. Third Floor, *Queen Kapiʻolani Hotel*, 150 Kapahulu Ave ⊺931-4451.
Daily 6.30–10am, 11am–2pm & 5.30–9pm.
Buffet-style restaurant in an old-fashioned Waikīkī hotel. The $11 breakfast buffet features fruit, eggs, meat and so on. Lunch and dinner both feature the same types of

food: Mon–Wed it's Hawaiian *à la carte*; Thursday features a Japanese buffet; and Fri–Sun there's a Hawaiian buffet. The Japanese lunch buffet is $13, the Hawaiian one, $11. Dinner buffets cost $17, or $8 if you just choose from the salad bar.

Planet Hollywood

Map 3, B4. 2155 Kalākaua Ave ⊺924-7877.
Daily 11am–2am.
Frenetic theme restaurant enlivened by faux zebra-skin and neon trimmings and cases of movie memorabilia (Hawaii-related where possible, so there's an abundance of discarded *Waterworld* costumes), but with very little substance – the food, be it $10 burgers and pizzas or $15 chicken or pork chops, is glossy but mediocre. You may have to wait as much as an hour for a table – kill time by looking at Michael J. Fox's high school yearbook, and reading house instructions on how to go about tipping.

Waikīkī restaurants are keyed on maps 3 and 4.

Restaurant Suntory

Map 3, C5. Third Floor, Royal
Hawaiian Shopping Center,
Orchid Court, 2233 Kalākaua
Ave ⓣ 922-5511.
Mon–Fri 11.30am–1.30pm &
5.30–9.30pm, Sat & Sun
5.30–9.30pm.

The teppanyaki menu,
cooked at your table in this
viewless Japanese restaurant,
features squid or steak for
around $16, and shrimp or
scallop for more like $20, as
well as mixed sashimi for
$27; there's also a full sushi
bar. Weekday lunches with
sushi and steak cost $10, but
set dinners range from $55
to $100.

Singha Thai Cuisine

Map 4, E3. 1910 Ala Moana
Blvd ⓣ 941-2898.
Mon–Fri 4–11pm.
Bright, modern, dinner-only
place that serves delicious
Thai food with a definite
Hawaiian tinge. All sorts of
fresh fish and scallop dishes,
plus curries, pad thai, and
hot and sour tom yum
soups; vegetables are
organic, and salads available
fat-free. Typical entrees cost

$15–20, while set menus
start at $35 per person. Thai
dancers perform nightly
7–9pm.

Tanaka of Tokyo

Map 3, G5. Third Floor, King's
Village, 131 Ka'iulani Ave
ⓣ 922-4233. Mon–Fri
11.30am–2pm & 5.30–10pm,
Sat & Sun 5.30–10pm.
Large, open Japanese place,
serving teppanyaki cuisine
sizzled at your table by chefs-
cum-jugglers. You'll be
squashed up with a bunch of
strangers, but the food is
good – and the experience is
fun. A full steak meal comes
to around $25, scallops and
shrimps about the same, and
there's a salmon special for
$19.

Texas Rock 'n' Roll
Sushi Bar

Map 3, G5. *Hyatt Regency
Hotel*, 2424 Kalākaua Ave
ⓣ 923-7655.
Full restaurant menu daily
6–10pm, sushi daily
6–11.30pm.
A high-concept, postmodern
restaurant/bar on the first
floor of the giant *Hyatt*

WAIKĪKĪ – MODERATE

Regency, the *Rock 'n' Roll Sushi Bar* is part Hawaiian *paniolo* cowboy, part Japanese, and part *Hard Rock Café*. They've largely given up their previous mix'n'match approach, so they no longer serve seaweed-wrapped beef sushi, for example; instead you can get conventional sushi specialties for around $8, and straightforward barbecue beef, ribs and chicken for $17–20. It all tastes surprisingly good, with full meals featuring both cuisines at $21–31.

Todai Seafood Buffet

Map 4, E3. 1910 Ala Moana Blvd ⓣ947-1000.
Sun–Thurs 11am–2.30pm & 5–9pm, Fri & Sat 11am–2.30pm & 5–10pm.
Stylish-looking outlet of an upmarket Japanese chain, in western Waikīkī, with huge curved windows outside and a 160ft buffet bar inside. Lunch costs $15 and dinner $26, but the range and quality of the food makes it a real bargain; there's plenty of sushi, shrimp, crab and lobster, as well as chicken and pork.

Before dining at any of the *Hyatt Regency* restaurants, pick up a free coupon book in the hotel lobby, for a 10–15 percent discount on your check.

WAIKĪKĪ – EXPENSIVE

Bali By The Sea

Map 4, E4. *Hilton Hawaiian Village*, 2005 Kālia Rd ⓣ941-2254.
Mon–Sat 6–9pm.
Highly refined gourmet restaurant, with the tables arrayed along a curving window that offers irresistible views of the full length of Waikīkī. Very tasteful modern Hawaiian cuisine, with appetizers such as seared *ahi* or the succulent Island Bouillabaisse at $9–12, and entrees like rack of lamb, roasted duck breast or *'ōpakapaka* with kaffir lime

more like $30. The wine list is enormous, with bottles from $22 up to $4000, and the desserts do as claimed make a "Grand Finale"; one is a chocolate Diamond Head overflowing with dry ice. Though the atmosphere is formal, formal dress is not required.

Ciao Mein
Map 3, G5. *Hyatt Regency Waikīkī*, 2424 Kalākaua Ave ⊤923-2426.
Daily 6–10pm.
Huge restaurant, serving an odd but successful mixture of Chinese and Italian cuisine. Not all dishes actually combine the two, though "Collision Cuisine" specials at around $16 include "Hot Bean Salmon *alla Siciliana*" and Chinese Roast Duck cannelonni. In general, the Italian dishes are more sophisticated and less expensive. There's an excellent focaccia appetizer for under $7, and most pasta entrees cost $15. Chinese entrees include sizzling Mongolian beef ($17), honey walnut shrimp ($23) and

steamed fish ($27), and there are vegetarian options, too. Set meals cost from $29 per person.

The Colony
Map 3, G5. *Hyatt Regency Waikīkī*, 2424 Kalākaua Ave ⊤923-1234 ext 6510.
Daily 6–10pm.
Appetizers at this, the most traditional of the *Hyatt's* restaurants, include a three-onion soup for $5. Steaks, which cost from $19, are available in all sorts of combinations (steak with lobster is $55), and you can also get a delicious fresh catch for $22, or a "Hukilau" of steamed seafood for two or more diners at $28 per person.

Diamond Head Grill
Map 2, G7. *W Honolulu*, 2885 Kalākaua Ave ⊤922-3734.
Mon–Fri 7–10.30am & 6–11.30pm, Sat & Sun 7–11.30am & 6–11.30pm.
Ultramodern, over-chic hotel restaurant, kitted out with lots of gleaming metal and specializing in Pacific Rim cuisine. The food is fussy,

WAIKĪKĪ – EXPENSIVE

perhaps, but very good, with appetizers like ginger-glazed macadamia nut oysters baked with spinach ($10) and entrees such as juicy lemongrass and Asian pesto-scented rotisserie chicken ($22). However, little about the ambience is at all Hawaiian – when there's not smooth Latin or jazz playing live, it's Elton John on the stereo – and despite the name, the only views you get at dinner time are of the long curving bar. Breakfast is rather more ordinary hotel food, while a limited bistro menu is served 10–11.30pm.

Hanohano Room

Map 3, C7. *Sheraton Waikīkī Hotel*, 2255 Kalākaua Ave ☏ 922-4422.
Mon–Fri 6.30–10.30am & 6–10pm, Sat 6–10pm, Sun 8am–1pm & 6–10pm.
Glamorous restaurant, stacked thirty stories above Waikīkī, with nightly dancing to "contemporary jazz." Fixed-price menus with a contemporary Pacific Rim tinge range from $53 to $75; *à la carte* dishes average $32,

whether you go for one of the rich array of meats with sauces, or for the broiled fresh fish.

Hau Tree Lanai

Map 2, G7. *New Otani Kaimana Beach Hotel*, 2863 Kalākaua Ave ☏ 921-7066.
Mon–Sat 7–11am, 11.30am–4pm & 5.30–9pm, Sun 7–11am, noon–4pm & 5.30–9pm.
Intimate oceanfront restaurant, set beneath the shade of a magnificent spreading *hau* tree beside Sans Souci Beach, and perfect for romantic sunsets. Cuisine is mostly continental/American, but with added Pacific Rim touches: choose from top-quality breakfasts (go for the $13 eggs Benedict), lunches ranging from sandwiches to crabcake burgers or chicken curry for under $15, or dinner entrees like beef Madagascar or pan-roasted seafood risotto at $25–35.

Kacho

Map 3, E6. *Waikīkī Parc*, 2233 Helumoa Rd ☏ 921-7272 ext 6045.
Daily 6–10am, 11.30am–2pm, &

5.30–10pm.

Superb Japanese restaurant, with typically understated decor. The menu emphasizes Kyoto cuisine, with lots of raw and pickled fish; look for crab *sunomono* (in vinegar), and the delicious, cod-like butterfish. A basic salmon dinner costs $21, a bento box or sushi assortment more like $30–40, and the full chef's dinner is $65 per person.

Matteo's

Map 3, D3. *Marine Surf Hotel* 364 Seaside Ave ☎922-5551. Daily 5.30–11pm

Dinner-only Italian restaurant, with added flavor drawn from modern Southwest (chili, sundried tomato) and Hawaiian cuisine. Quite pricey and formal, but the food is well above average. Appetizers (around $10) are predominantly seafood; the highlight is the spicy clams. A $10 Early Bird Special is served nightly 5.30–6.30pm, but otherwise entrees start at $18 for ravioli, and range through grilled fish and meats up to a $33 rack of Molokai lamb.

Nick's Fishmarket

Map 4, F3. *Waikīkī Gateway Hotel*, 2070 Kalākaua Ave ☎955-6333.
Mon–Thurs & Sun 5.30–10pm, Fri & Sat 5.30–11pm.

Waikīkī's top fish restaurant, with dark leatherette seating, glittering glass and mirrors, and a formal atmosphere. The cooking is not especially innovative and the sauces are rich, but the preparation is meticulous and the range of choices amazing. Appetizers, generally priced $10–13, include sautéed crab and steamed mussels. A typical main dish like Hawaiian swordfish costs around $30, a mixed seafood grill $35, and lobsters up to $50. The same menu is served until midnight nightly in the less formal adjoining café, which also has live music.

Parc Café

Map 3, C7. *Waikīkī Parc*, 2233 Helumoa Rd ☎931-6643.
Mon–Sat 5.30–10.30am, 11.30am–2pm & 5.30–9.30pm Sun 11am–2pm & 5.30–9.30pm.

Upmarket hotel restaurant boasting the best buffets in

WAIKĪKĪ – EXPENSIVE

Waikīkī. Breakfast costs $13, while the lunchtime choice is either Hawaiian *lū'au* food (Wed & Fri; $17), a pan-Asian spread (Mon, Tues, Thurs & Sat; $16), or Sunday's sushi brunch ($26). Depending on the day, the dinner buffet features prime rib alone (Mon, Tues & Thurs; $19), Hawaiian food once again (Wed; $19), or prime rib plus high-quality Japanese, Hawaiian and American seafood (Fri, Sat & Sun; $27). *À la carte* entrees are also available.

Sam Choy's Diamond Head

Map 4, I1. 449 Kapahulu Ave ℡ 732-8645.

Mon–Thurs 5.30–9.30pm, Fri & Sat 5–10pm, Sun 9.30am–2pm & 5–10pm.

Very popular, dinner-only "New Hawaiian" restaurant, a mile or so northeast of Waikīkī. TV chef Sam Choy has a reputation for feeding his customers to the bursting point, and the portions of the $20–30 entrees such as seafood *laulau* (steamed in *ti* leaves) and veal *ossobucco* are truly enormous in addition to being deliciously flavored with local herbs and spices. The $25 Sunday brunch buffet features Choy's trademark fried *poke* (diced fish).

DOWNTOWN HONOLULU

Cafe Laniakea

Map 5, G5. YWCA, 1040 Richards St ℡ 524-8789. Mon–Sat 10.30am–2.30pm, Sun 8.30am–2pm.

Lunch-only downtown cafeteria, very close to 'Iolani Palace, and run by a not-for-profit adult training organization. Lots of inexpensive vegetarian dishes, such as a $1.25 mini *manapua* and a $7 plate lunch with *taro* and sweet potato salad and pesto pasta, plus meat sandwiches and burgers. On Sundays, the mood changes for a jazz brunch, with *à la carte* New Orleans specialties like gumbo and softshell crab at $9–13.

Café Peninsula
Map 5, E5. 1147 Bethel St
Ⓣ 533-2233.
Mon–Fri 6.30am–5.30pm.
Oddly groovy Chinatown coffee shop, near the Hawaii Theater, with sprawling rattan armchairs and a hip soundtrack. It serves simple plate lunches, such as spam and egg ($5) and *saimin* ($3.50), as well as

sandwiches, croissants and espressos.

Honolulu Coffee Co
Map 5, F7. 741 Bishop St
Ⓣ 533-1500.
Mon–Fri 6am–5pm.
Busy, large downtown coffee bar, at the south end of Bishop St near the Aloha Tower, with seating indoors and out. Open weekdays only, it serves espressos and smoothies plus gourmet salads and sandwiches for $6–7, and daily specials such as $9.50 crab cakes.

To combine fine food with sightseeing, try the cafés at the Contemporary Museum (p.75) and the Academy of Arts (p.58).

CHINATOWN

Duc's Bistro
Map 5, C5. 1188 Maunakea St
Ⓣ 531-6325.
Mon–Fri 11.30am–2pm & 5.30–10pm, Sat 5.30–10pm, closed Sun.
Sophisticated Asian-influenced French restaurant in Chinatown, which hosts live jazz in the evenings.

Dinner appetizers ($7–8) include gravadlax, escargots and crabcakes; a basic lemongrass chicken entree costs $14, fancier options like duck breast in Grand Marnier or flambéed steak are $20–25. Portions and prices are significantly smaller at lunchtime.

CHINATOWN

HONOLULU MALL DINING

The *Makai Market Food Court*, downstairs on the ocean side of the **Ala Moana Center**, offers twenty fast-food counters, covering the spectrum through French, Italian, Filipino, Korean, Chinese, Japanese, American, and Hawaiian. All share a central seating area, and the standard is generally high. Actual restaurants include the Italian *Assaggio* at street level (see p.195), and the *California Pizza Kitchen* (see p.188) and *Bubba Gump's* on the top-level deck. Look also for the food hall upstairs in the Shirokiya department store, where there's a huge deli plus a buffet of delicious hot and cold Japanese specialties (Mon–Sat 3.30–8.15pm).

Both the **Ward Centre** and the adjacent **Ward Warehouse**, farther west along Ala Moana Boulevard toward downtown, hold several dining options. The former boasts the good-value *Kaka'ako Kitchen* (see p.190), a *Keo's*, and a nice espresso-cum-deli bar – and there's a *Starbucks* across the street from Borders – while the larger Ward Warehouse is geared more toward fast food.

Indigo
Map 5, D5. 1120 Nu'uanu Ave
ⓣ 521-2900.
Tues–Fri 11.30am–2pm &
6–9.30pm, Sat 6–9.30pm,
closed Sun & Mon.
Chinatown's classiest option
serves delicious nouvelle
Chinese–Californian
crossover food. In addition
to the bargain $13 lunch
buffet, dim sum ranges from
taro dumplings and goat's

cheese wontons for around
$6, to mussels in black bean
and cilantro oil for $10.
Dinner entrees, under $20,
include duck confit, *miso*-
grilled salmon, cacao bean
curried shrimp and grilled
lamb.

Legend Seafood
Restaurant
Map 5, B4. 100 N Beretania St
ⓣ 532-1868.

The **Aloha Tower Marketplace** offers eleven food outlets, including *Big Island Steak House*, the tacky *Hooters*, and *Baja Betty's Southwestern Bar & Grill*, as well as *Chai's* (see p.189) and *Gordon Biersch* (see p.189). Its small Kau Kau Food Court features fast food like *Yokozuna's* and *Villa Pizza*. Nearby, Restaurant Row is a mall that consists entirely of fully fledged restaurants; *Ocean Club* and *Sansei* are reviewed on p.191, the *Sunset Grille* is a dependable all-round alternative.

For quick lunches, downtown office workers head for the various takeouts along pedestrian-only Fort Street or in Bishop Square, which can provide anything from *saimin* or Korean sushi to *piroscki* and a cappuccino. Chinatown's **Maunakea Marketplace**, off Hotel and Maunakea streets, holds a ravishing assortment of inexpensive fast-food counters, with bargain Thai, Chinese, Vietnamese, Indian, Malaysian, Filipino, Japanese and Italian places. A big lunch, say of *saimin* with shrimp, can cost as little as $3.

Mon–Fri 10.30am–2pm & 5.30–10pm, Sat & Sun 8am–2pm & 5.30–10pm. Chinatown seafood specialist in a modern building whose big plate-glass windows look out over the Nu'uanu Stream. The lunchtime dim sum trolleys are piled with individual portions at $2–3; full Chinese meals, with entrees including whole lobster or crab at $8–16, are served at both lunch and dinner.

Legend Vegetarian Restaurant

Map 5, B4. 100 N Beretania St ☎ 532-8218.
Daily except Wed 10.30am–2pm & 5.30–9pm. Bright, clean Chinese vegetarian restaurant in the heart of Chinatown, looking out across the Nu'uanu

CHINATOWN

●

Stream. The menu features faux beef balls, cuttlefish, pork ribs and tenderloin – all the dishes are actually tofu or other organic, vegetarian ingredients shaped and flavored to resemble specific meats and fishes. There's also a wide selection of vegetarian dim sum, plus conventional vegetable dishes. Entrees are priced well under $10; set meals for four or more work out at under $10 per person. No alcohol is served.

Maxime
Map 5, C5. 1134 Maunakea St ☎545-4188.
Daily 10am–9pm.
This bright, clean, Chinatown restaurant is the best place to sample Vietnamese pho (noodle soup). Some is served with tripe, but *pho tai*, with thin slices of beef, is a reliable option ($6.25). There are also lots of other noodle dishes for around $7, plus Vietnamese crepes, seafood specials and even a catfish soursoup at $9. Wash it all down with *chanh muoi* (sweet and sour lemon juice), for $1.75.

Mei Sum
Map 5, D4. 65 N Pauahi St at Smith ☎531-3268.
Daily 7am–9pm; dim sum until 3pm only.
Plain but appealing traditional dim sum restaurant, serving a wide assortment of lunchtime snacks at $2–3 each. Tasty options include seafood or mushroom chicken dumplings, turnip cake, and *char siu* buns. Noodle, rice and wonton entrees, featuring chicken, prawn, scallops or calamari, are served later in the day for $7–10 per plate. A full dinner for four is just $32.

WATERFRONT HONOLULU

California Pizza Kitchen
Map 1, F5. Ala Moana Mall ☎941-7715.
Sun–Thurs 11am–10pm, Fri & Sat 11am–1am.
Postmodern pizzeria, on a bright deck on the top floor of the Ala Moana mall. One-

person pizzas ($10) – such as goat's cheese and bacon or Peking duck and wonton – are served in a high-tech, new-Asia sort of atmosphere, and they also have pasta with ginger and black-bean sauce ($12), and focaccia sandwiches ($7–8).

Chai's Island Bistro

Map 5, J9. Aloha Tower Marketplace, 101 Ala Moana Blvd ⓣ 585-0011.
Mon–Fri 11am–10pm, Sat 4–10pm, Sun 10am–10pm.
Very busy, very smart place, half indoors and half out at the inland side of the Aloha Tower Marketplace, so there are no ocean views. Though it's owned by the same chef as Waikīkī's *Singha Thai* (see p.179), the food is not so much Thai as pan-Asian, and it's every bit as exquisite as the decor. For dinner, the prices are extremely high, but that's largely because *Chai's* books the absolute crème de la crème of Hawaiian musicians to perform live, currently including Hapa on Thursdays and Fridays, and the Makaha Sons on Mondays. Miss the show, scheduled for 7–8.30pm, and you'll be paying well over the norm for delicious entrees like Chinese-style steamed onaga ($37) or grilled Mongolian lamb chops ($38). Lunchtime prices are half that, except for Sunday's $35 buffet brunch. Note that at the time this book went to press, on-going problems concerning the immigration status of the Thai owner, Chai himself, were threatening his restaurant's continued existence.

Gordon Biersch Brewery Restaurant

Map 5, J9. Aloha Tower Marketplace, 101 Ala Moana Blvd ⓣ 599-4877.
Mon–Thurs 10.30am–10pm, Fri–Sun 10.30am–11pm; bar open until midnight Mon–Wed & Sun, 1am Thurs–Sat.
This restaurant with a built-in brewery is one of Aloha

WATERFRONT HONOLULU

There's another *California Pizza Kitchen* in the Kahala Mall, 4614 Kilauea Ave (ⓣ 737-9446).

Tower's more stylish options. Seating is either outdoors on a large dockside terrace, or indoors, near a long bar that's brimming with beers from around the globe. For lunch ($10–11) try a pizza, hummus salad, a burger or grill item, or the cashew chicken stir-fry. The dinner menu offers the same pizzas and salads, plus Hawaiian regional dishes such as peppered *ahi* ($19) and kaffir lime-grilled chicken ($15), and Japanese, Thai and even Tahitian specialties. Live music Wed–Sat evenings.

Kaka'ako Kitchen

Map 6, E4. Ward Centre, 1200 Ala Moana Blvd ⊤ 596-7488. Mon–Fri 7–10am & 10.30am–9pm, Sat 7–11am & 11.30am–9pm, Sun 7–11am & 11.30am–5pm.

Mall diner, with easy off-street parking on the Auahi St side, that dishes up Hawaiian-style fast food. Having ordered at the counter, you eat it from styrofoam boxes with plastic cutlery, at plain indoor and outdoor tables but the food is of a uniformly high quality. Pretty much everything, from the hamburger stew to the signature dish chicken linguini, costs $6–9, and there's a rota of daily $7.25 specials like meat loaf or pot roast. Credit cards accepted for checks of $50 and over only.

La Mariana Sailing Club

Map 2, C3. 50 Sand Island Access Rd ⊤ 848-2800. Daily 11.30am–11.30pm.

An atmospheric oceanside restaurant – technically a yacht club – on a *very* obscure stretch of Honolulu's industrial waterfront, *La Mariana* is bursting with *tiki* images and South Seas decor rescued from the ever-dwindling 1950s-style bars and clubs of Waikīkī. The decor is great, and the food's pretty good too. There are hearty appetizers like *taco poke* (marinated octopus) for $9, full dinners such as seafood brochette or *ahi* Cajun for well under $20, and a good-value $14 buffet brunch on Sundays. However, the real reason to come is for the impromptu semi-professional performances of Hawaiian music on Friday and Saturday evenings, from 9pm until late; for more details, see p.202.

L'Uraku

Map 6, F2. 1341 Kapi'olani Blvd ⊤ 955-0552.
Daily 11am–2pm & 5.30–10pm. Quirky, hip Japanese restaurant – the name means "happiness" – on a busy street a block inland from the Ala Moana mall. The interior is festooned with crudely hand-painted umbrellas that trace the saga of artist Kiyoshi's lost Somalian cat. Most of the menu is solidly Japanese, with lots of soy marinades and stir-fried bok choy, but there's a strong Italian flavor as well, including a daily pasta special. Appetizers range from a single baked oyster ($2.50) up to a bento box filled with goodies ($13), and for once, the entrees ($18–25), including steamed fish and garlic steak at $18–25, are just as good as the starters. A dinner "tasting" menu is $34 ($47

with wine), while at lunchtime on weekends they offer a bargain $15 set meal.

Ocean Club

Map 5, J9. Restaurant Row, 500 Ala Moana Blvd ⊤ 526-9888.
Tues–Fri 4.30pm–3am, Sat 6pm–3am. Closed Sun & Mon. Big, loud, and very glitzy bar that's a major hangout for downtown's after-work crowd, and won't admit anyone under 23 years old or wearing a T-shirt. The extensive menu of excellent finger-food (all seafood) is served at roughly half-price before 8pm, with teriyaki steak at $8, coconut shrimp, crab dip or sashimi for under $4, *poke* for $3, and a *kalua* pig wrap just $2.50.

OnJin

Map 6, E3. 401 Kamake'e St ⊤ 589-1666.
Mon 11am–2pm, Tues–Thurs 11am–2pm & 5–9pm, Fri 11am–2pm & 5–10pm, Sat 5–10pm. Closed Sun. Bright, smart little café, one block inland from the Ward Centre, offering quality cooking at very reasonable

rates. At lunchtime, when orders are taken at the counter, pretty much everything costs $6–7 – and that includes the crispy snapper in lemon *beurre blanc*, and the daily specials like Thursday's roast leg of lamb, as well as wraps, burgers, sandwiches. The service is more formal in the evening, and the prices are significantly higher, with entrees such as half a duck in Grand Marnier for $17.50 and bouillabaisse for $22.

Sansei
Map 5, J9. Restaurant Row, 500 Ala Moana Blvd ☏ 536-6286.

Restaurant daily 5–10pm; karaoke, with food service daily 10pm–1am.
The Restaurant Row setting may not be particularly attractive, but whether you go for the full Pacific Rim menu or stick to the sushi bar, the food is excellent and very well priced. Sushi starts at $4 (a fruity mango crab salad roll is $8), while entrees like grilled *opah* on succulent chanterelle mushrooms, Japanese jerk chicken, or Peking duck breast are mostly around $20. The adjoining karaoke bar gets going when the restaurant closes, and serves a limited half-price menu.

MĀNOA AND THE UNIVERSITY DISTRICT

Alan Wong's
Map 2, G4. 1857 S King St ☏ 949-2526.
Daily 5–10pm.
Though expensive and hard to find – it's tucked away on the fifth floor in a nondescript area southwest of the university – *Alan Wong's* has nonetheless rapidly become Honolulu's most

fashionable gourmet rendezvous, thanks to its superb food. Besides changing daily specials, appetizers always include the signature "*Da Bag*," a giant foil bag holding clams steamed with *kalua* pig, shiitake mushrooms and spinach ($11.50), and salads such as marinated eggplant with Maui onions and seared *ahi* ($6). Typical entrees ($25–35) include ginger-crusted *onaga* (snapper) and a spicy Hawaiian reinterpretation of paella. There's a five-course tasting menu each night ($65). Valet parking only.

Coffee Cove Online

Map 2, G5. 2600 S King St ☎ 955-2683.
Mon–Fri 7.30am–11pm, Sat & Sun 10am–11pm.
Grungy espresso bar at King and University that offers pastries and cereal for breakfast, simple snacks and sandwiches ($4–6) later on, and internet access at $7 per hour.

Coffeeline Campus Coffeehouse

Map 2, G4. 1820 University Ave ☎ 947-1615.
Mon–Fri 7am–4pm, Sat 7am–noon.
Inconspicuous student café, upstairs in the Atherton YMCA volunteer center at Seaview Ave, across from the University of Hawaii campus, and handy to the *Honolulu International Hostel* (see

p.149). It's basically a takeout counter, with terrace seating, and serves a small selection of snacks along with espresso coffees. There's a ten percent discount on food for Youth Hostel Association members.

Down to Earth

Map 2, G5. 2525 S King St ☎ 947-7678.
Daily 7.30am–10pm.
Longstanding wholefood store near the university. It offers a full vegetarian menu of deli dishes, baked pies and pastas – some with tofu, some with cheese – plus a varied salad bar at $5 per pound and a hot bar at $6 per pound.

Yakiniku Canellia

Map 2, G4. 2494 S Beretania St ☎ 1-800/331-9698.
Daily 11am–10pm.
Korean buffet restaurant about a mile north of Waikīkī, just south of the university, with very simple decor; the few English speakers who venture in have to fend for themselves. Whether at lunch ($10) or dinner ($16), the food is a treat; you select slices of marinated beef, chicken or

pork from refrigerated cabinets and grill them yourself at the gas-fired burners set into each table. There are also lots of vegetables, which you can cook or not as you choose, as well as a wide assortment of interesting salads, including octopus, pickles and delicious tiny dried fish.

ELSEWHERE IN HONOLULU

Olive Tree Café

Map 2, I6. 4614 Kilauea Ave
☎ 737-0303.
Mon–Fri 5–10pm, Sat & Sun 11am–10pm.
Simple but tasteful Greek deli, adjoining but not technically within Kāhala Mall, with some outdoor seating. The value is unbeatable, and the food is great, ranging from refreshing tomato and feta cheese salads to a lovely ceviche of New Zealand mussels ($5), to souvlaki skewers of chicken ($7) or fish ($9).

Sam Choy's Breakfast, Lunch and Crab

Map 2, D3. 580 N Nimitz Hwy
☎ 545-7979.
Restaurant Mon–Sat 6.30am–10pm, Sun 9am–10pm, brewery daily 10.30am until late.
A mile or two west of downtown, sandwiched so tightly between the west- and east-bound sides of Nimitz Highway that it only offers valet parking, this updated version of a local Hawaiian diner looks unenticing from the outside. It's a different story inside, however, where you'll find a full-sized sampan fishing boat, the gleaming *Big Aloha* microbrewery and mosaic floors, plus crowds of diners seated at the many tables or along the stainless-steel counter facing the vast open-plan kitchen. Plate lunches, at around $10, come very big indeed – the fried *poke* is a must – and there's a $13 brunch on Sundays (9am–noon). Evening entrees, at $17–27, include fresh fish, paella, crabs' legs and roasted or steamed whole crabs. The desserts are enormous, and beer is half-price daily 3–6pm.

HAWAII KAI

Roy's

Map 8, B7. #110, Hawaii Kai
Corporate Plaza, 6600
Kalanianaʻole Hwy, Hawaii Kai
T 396-7697.
Mon–Thurs 5.30–10pm, Fri–Sun
5–10pm

Dinner-only gourmet
restaurant, just yards from the
sea alongside Hwy-72 ten
miles east of Waikīkī, which
opened in 1988 as chef Roy
Yamaguchi's first Hawaiian
venture. His innovative
Pacific Rim cuisine swiftly
became the benchmark for all
the top restaurants in Hawaii,
and Roy himself has opened
branches throughout the
state. While renowned as one
of Oahu's finest restaurants, it
attracts far more locals than
tourists; getting here is simply
too much of an effort for
most Waikīkī-based visitors.
It's a noisy, hectic place,
where diners can choose
between watching the
goings-on in the open
kitchen or enjoying the views
out over Maunalua Bay. The
food is consistently excellent,
with $6–13 appetizers
including individual pizzas,
crab cakes, and blackened *ahi*,
and $17–26 entrees ranging
from garlic-mustard short ribs
to the *hibachi*-style salmon
selected by President Clinton
when he dropped by.

KAILUA

Assaggio

Map 1, L7. 354 Uluniu Rd,
Kailua T 261-2772.
Mon–Thurs 11.30am–2.30pm &
5–9.30pm, Fri & Sat
11.30am–2.30pm & 5–10pm,
Sun 5–9.30pm.

This wildly popular upmarket
Italian restaurant is always busy,
despite being hidden on a
quiet side street a block north
of central Kailua. As well as
dozens of pasta dishes for
under $15, like fettuccini
Alfredo and eggplant
parmigiani, they offer nine
styles of chicken, including
stuffed with ricotta cheese for

HAWAII KAI • KAILUA

$15, and fish of the day cooked as you choose for around $20.

Morning Brew
Map 1, L7. 572 Kailua Rd, Kailua ⊤ 262-7770.
Mon–Thurs 6am–9pm, Fri 6am–10pm, Sat 6.45am–10pm, Sun 6.45am–8pm.
Friendly local coffee bar in central Kailua, with a full range of coffee drinks, pastries and snacks, that's bravely clinging on despite the arrival of *Starbuck's* opposite.

Otaru
Map 1, L7. 572 Kailua Rd, Kailua ⊤ 263-4482.
Mon–Fri 11am–2pm & 5–9.30pm, Sat & Sun 5–9.30pm.

This welcoming mall restaurant calls itself Pacific Rim, but most of the menu is straightforward, good-value Japanese, with sushi rolls starting at $4 or combos at $14; full steak and fish dinners are well under $20.

Saeng's Thai Cuisine
Map 1, L7. 315 Hahani St, Kailua ⊤ 263-9727.
Mon–Fri 11am–2pm & 5–9.30pm, Sat & Sun 5–9.30pm.
High-quality Thai restaurant, where the menu of good-value soups and noodle dishes features plenty of vegetarian options. Pad thai goes for $7.50, green and red curries are $9, and typical daily specials include lobster at around $10.

PUNALU'U

Ahi's
Map 9, H6. Punalu'u ⊤ 293-5650.
Mon–Sat 11am–9pm.
Appealing single-story local restaurant, nestling beneath the palm trees at a curve in Hwy-83 half a mile south of

Punalu'u Beach Park, and marked by a vintage delivery truck parked permanently outside. The specialty is delicious fresh shrimp served in a variety of different ways; a $9.50 sampler plate allows you to try four options.

HALE'IWA

Café Hale'iwa

Map 9, B6. 66-460
Kamehameha Hwy, Hale'iwa
☎ 637-5516.
Daily 7am–2pm.

This venerable local diner dates back to the old days of the Hale'iwa surf scene, and still serves as a rendezvous for surfers to plot the day's events as they look out toward the mountains Mexican and American breakfasts cost $4 to $8, while lunch consists of sandwiches, quesadillas or salads, at similar prices.

Cholo's Homestyle Mexican

Map 9, B6. North Shore Marketplace, Hale'iwa ☎ 637-3059.
Daily 8am–9pm.

Busy, plain but very lively Mexican joint, with some outdoor seating, with a big menu of the expected favorites at $8–10, and plenty of combos at up to $15. They also serve juices and espressos.

Hale'iwa Joe's

Map 9, B5. 62-540
Kamehameha Hwy, Hale'iwa
☎ 637-4336.
Mon–Thurs & Sun 11.30am–9.30pm, Fri & Sat 11.30am–10.30pm.

Breezy, attractive steak and seafood place, with an outdoor terrace overlooking the mouth of the Anahulu River. For lunch, good sandwiches and salads are around $10, but otherwise much the same menu is offered all day, with only a slight upwards shift in prices in the evening, when sushi or *poke* appetizers cost around $7, and entrees range from herb-roasted chicken at $13 to grilled salmon for $17.50 up to a $20 New York steak.

There's another dinner-only *Hale'iwa Joe's* at Ha'ikū Gardens, 46-336 Ha'ikū Rd, Kāne'ohe (☎ 247-6671).

HALE'IWA

Jamesons by the Sea

Map 9, B5. 62-540
Kamehameha Hwy, Hale'iwa
℡ 637-4336.
Daily 11am–9pm.

Conventional steakhouse near Hale'iwa harbor, facing west from the far side of the river for unbeatable sunset views. Reserve early if you want an oceanfront table for the sunset specials (Wed–Sun 5–9pm), when a full shrimp or seafood meal costs around $20, and teriyaki chicken, steak or fresh fish is more like $15; or just turn up and try to squeeze on to the shaded *lānai* of the bar downstairs, where you can grab a simple snack.

Paradise Found Café

Map 9, B6. 66-443
Kamehameha Hwy, Hale'iwa
℡ 637-4540.
Snack bar Mon–Fri 9am–5pm, Sun 10am–5pm; store Mon–Fri 9am–6.30pm, Sun 10am–6pm; both closed Sat.

Small wholefood snack bar, consisting of a few tables at the back of the Celestial Natural Foods store, where you can pick up breakfast or lunch for $5–6, or a big smoothie for $3. Fresh avocado sandwiches and pitta pockets are very much the thing here.

SUNSET BEACH

Taste of Paradise

Map 9, B6. Rocky Point, Sunset Beach ℡ 348-5886.
Mon–Fri 11am–6pm, Sat & Sun 11am–8pm.

This quintessential North Shore hangout is not so much a restaurant as a greenhouse-like awning with a van parked at the far end, six miles north of Hale'iwa between Sunset and 'Ehukai beaches. You can't miss it – a giant totem pole dedicated to Maui Pōhaku Loa stands guard. In addition to cheap fruit smoothies, they sell sandwiches, burgers and kebabs for $4–7, shrimp plates for around $10, and a tiger shrimp and *ahi* combo for $12.50.

Entertainment and nightlife

Most of Honolulu's nightlife concentrates on Waikīkī, where fun-seeking tourists set the tone. On the whole, however, entertainment tends to be bland. Hawaii is usually bypassed by touring mainstream musicians, so if you enjoy live music you'll probably have to settle for little-known local performers (even rising stars of contemporary Hawaiian music try to keep their credibility by not playing in Waikīkī too often). As for bars, Chinatown has the most raucous in town, but they're way too hair-raising for most tastes.

Various magazines and papers will keep you abreast of what's going on; the best are the free *Honolulu Weekly* newspaper (ⓦ www.honoluluweekly.com), and the "TGIF" section of Friday's *Honolulu Advertiser* (ⓦ www.honolulu advertiser.com).

Annual events and festivals in Honolulu are listed on p.229.

HAWAIIAN ENTERTAINMENT

The popular image of Hawaiian tourism may still revolve around lilting ukuleles and swaying grass skirts, but it's surprisingly difficult to find good **Hawaiian entertainment** in Waikīkī or Honolulu, and genuine *hula* performances are rare. By far the best idea is to look for events that are arranged for Hawaiian (rather than tourist) audiences, such as the frequent one-time performances and benefit concerts at downtown's beautiful Hawaii Theatre (see p.61). Otherwise, settle for evoking bygone days with a sunset cocktail at one of Waikīkī's grander hotels, most of which regularly feature accomplished Hawaiian musicians.

A number of regular **free shows** also take place each week, most of greater appeal to older travelers. In addition to the **Pleasant Hawaiian Hula Show** at the Waikīkī Shell (see p.45), there are Polynesian-themed performances in Waikīkī at the Royal Hawaiian Shopping Center (Tues & Thurs 6.30pm) and the DFS Galleria at Royal Hawaiian and Kalākaua avenues (daily 7pm), and in Honolulu at the Aloha Tower Marketplace (Mon & Wed–Fri 11.30am). In addition, the **Royal Hawaiian Band** gives free hour-long performances on Fridays at noon on the lawns of 'Iolani Palace downtown.

Typical prices in Waikīkī cocktail bars are $4–6 for bottled beer, $6–9 for a Mai Tai.

Banyan Court

Map 3, F6. *Sheraton Moana Surfrider*, 2365 Kalākaua Ave, Waikīkī ☏ 922-3111.
Open-air beach bar that was home to the nationally syndicated *Hawaii Calls* radio show from the 1930s to the 1970s. Steel guitar and *hula* dancers nightly 5.30–7.30pm, followed by a pianist 7.30–10.30pm. No cover but a one-drink minimum.

IZ: MAY 20, 1959 – JUNE 26, 1997

In the summer of 1997, the contemporary Hawaiian music scene lost the man who was in every sense its biggest star. **Israel Kamakawiwoʻole**, who started out singing in the Makaha Sons of Niihau, and then went solo in 1990, died of respiratory difficulties in a Honolulu hospital. During his twenty-year career, "Iz" came to epitomize the pride and the power of Hawaiian music. His extraordinary voice adapted equally well to rousing political anthems, delicate love songs, pop standards and Jawaiian reggae rhythms, while his personality, and his love for Hawaii, always shone through both in concert and on record. Like his brother Skippy before him – also a founding member of the Makaha Sons – Iz eventually succumbed to the health problems caused by his immense size. At one point, his weight reached a colossal 757 pounds; he needed a fork-lift truck to get on stage, and could only breathe through tubes. His strength in adversity did much to ensure that he was repeatedly voted Hawaii's most popular entertainer, and after his death he was granted a state funeral, with his body lying in state in the Capitol. His enduring legacy will be the music on his four solo albums – *Ka Anoʻi* (1990), *Facing Future* (1993), *E Ala Ē* (1995), and *'n Dis Life* (1996) – while his haunting rendition of "Hawaiʻi 78" (featured on *Facing Future*) has become the signature song of the Hawaiian sovereignty movement.

Chai's Island Bistro

Map 5, J9. Aloha Tower Marketplace, 101 Ala Moana Blvd ☎ 585-0011. Mon–Fri 11am–10pm, Sat 4–10pm, Sun 10am–1pm.

Sumptuous and very expensive Thai restaurant, currently under a cloud due to its owner's legal battle to remain in Hawaii, with a policy of booking the very finest Hawaiian musicians to perform for diners nightly 7–8.30pm. With a roster including Maui's Hapa on

HAWAIIAN ENTERTAINMENT

Thursdays and Fridays, and the Makaha Sons on Mondays, it's the best venue to hear top-class Hawaiian music – so long as you don't mind paying premium prices for the food (reviewed on p.189).

Duke's Canoe Club

Map 3, E6. *Outrigger Waikīkī on the Beach*, 2335 Kalākaua Ave, Waikīkī ☏ 923-0711. Smooth Hawaiian sounds wash over this oceanfront cocktail bar nightly from 4–6pm and 10pm–midnight. On weekends, the afternoon show is usually a big-name "Concert on the Beach." No cover charge.

House Without a Key

Map 3, C7. *Halekūlani*, 2199 Kālia Rd, Waikīkī ☏ 923-2311. This romantic beach bar was named after a Charlie Chan mystery that was written by Earl Derr Biggers after a stay at the hotel. The name of both book and bar alludes to the fact that no one in Honolulu used to lock their doors; in fact the *House Without A Key* barely has walls, let alone a door. Old-time Hawaiian classics

performed nightly 5–8.30pm, with *hula* dancing by a former Miss Hawaii. No cover.

La Mariana Sailing Club

Map 2, C3. 50 Sand Island Access Rd ☏ 848-2800. Waterfront restaurant – the food is reviewed on p.190 – with a wonderful 1950s feel, hidden away amid the docks of Honolulu. Pianist Ron Miyashiro and a group of semiprofessional singers gather each Fri & Sat, from 9pm onward, to work their way through a nostalgic set of classic Hawaiian songs. Daily 11am–11pm.

Lobby Bar

Map 4, H4. *Hawaiian Regent Hotel*, 2552 Kalākaua Ave, Waikīkī ☏ 922-2611. A consistently good roster of Hawaiian musicians performs at this cocktail bar Mon–Wed, Fri & Sat from 7pm onward, and Sun from 8pm onward. The highlight of the week comes on Thursdays, however, when the magnificent falsetto singer Auntie Genoa Keawe appears 5.30–7pm. No cover.

HAWAIIAN ENTERTAINMENT

Mai Tai Bar

Map 3, D7. *Royal Hawaiian*, 2259 Kalākaua Ave, Waikīkī ☎923-7311.
Another atmospheric open-air bar on Waikīkī Beach, which puts on live Hawaiian and/or *hula* performances nightly at 5.30pm.

Pier Bar

Map 5, E8. Aloha Tower Marketplace ☎536-2166.
Open-air bar whose waterfront stage features live nightly performances by top Hawaiian musicians until late, plus regular lunchtime and sunset entertainment. No cover.

BARS, LIVE MUSIC AND DANCING

There's rarely a clear distinction between **bars**, **live music venues** and **nightclubs** in Honolulu, and many restaurants get in on the act as well. While there's plenty of live music around – especially in Waikīkī – the overall standard tends to be disappointing. In addition, few Waikīkī clubs get to build a regular clientele, so the atmosphere is unpredictable. The biggest touring acts tend to appear at Pearl Harbor's Aloha Stadium (☎545-4000); watch for announcements in the local press.

If you're especially keen to find live **jazz**, your best bet is in restaurants such as the *Diamond Head Grill* in the *W* in Waikīkī's *W Hotel* (see p.181), *Duc's Bistro* in Chinatown (see p.185), and *Cafe Laniakea* in Honolulu's downtown *YWCA* (see p.184), which hosts a Sunday jazz brunch.

You can drink alcohol in Hawaii only if you're over 21, and have the ID to prove it.

There's a cover charge at the venues listed below unless otherwise noted.

Anna Banannas

Map 2, G4. 2440 S Beretania St, Honolulu ☎946-5190.
A university district bar with

reasonable prices, live R&B and reggae most nights, and a hectic weekend atmosphere. Daily 9pm–2am.

The Blue Room

Map 6, C4. 327 Keawe St ⓣ 585-5995.
Major student hang-out near the Ward Centre. Between the two diminutive dance floors, the music runs the gamut: hip-hop, drum and bass, trance, reggae and just plain "alternative." Tues–Sat 10pm until late.

The Cellar

Map 4, B6. 205 Lewers St, Waikīkī ⓣ 923-9952.
Basement joint in central Waikīkī that calls itself "Waikīkī's coolest Top 40 Dance Club" and attracts a predominantly tourist crowd. Daily except Mon 9pm–4am.

Lewers Lounge

Map 3, C7. *Halekūlani*, 2199 Kālia Rd, Waikīkī ⓣ 923-2311.

Sophisticated nightspot that looks more like an English drawing room than a Waikīkī bar. Live jazz nightly 9pm–12.30am, at its best Tues–Sat, when Bruce Hamada performs.

Nashville Waikīkī

Map 3, F3. 2330 Kūhiō Ave, Waikīkī ⓣ 926-7911.
If you're hankering to hoe down in Hawaii, this country music club below the *Outrigger West* has plenty of room to show off your rhinestones. Check ahead, though; it also hosts hip-hop and DJ nights. There are pool tables and darts, too. Daily 4pm–4am.

Ocean Club

Map 5, J9. Restaurant Row, 500 Ala Moana Blvd, Honolulu ⓣ 526-9888.
Flamboyant, frenetic downtown bar-cum-restaurant, which serves inexpensive food in the early evening (see p.191) and turns into a wild dance club as the

Gay bars and clubs in Honolulu are listed in Chapter 12.

BARS, LIVE MUSIC AND DANCING

night wears on. Over-22s only; no T-shirts. Open until at least 2am Tues–Sat.

Rolando's Salsa Club

Map 2, H5. Kāhala Mall ℡677-3642.

Long a fixture of Honolulu's nightlife scene, Rolando Sanchez and his Salsa Hawaii Band now have their own place to do their Latin thing. They perform Thurs–Sat nights and also tend to join the Sunday-night Latin jazz jam. On other nights the dance music is provided by DJs instead. Mon–Tues 9pm–midnight, Wed 9.30pm–midnight, Thurs–Sat 10pm–1am, Sun 9–11pm.

Rose and Crown

Map 3, G4. King's Village, 2400 Koa Ave, Waikīkī.

Not a bad approximation of an English pub; the beer pumps are fake, but it's appropriately dark and gloomy even at noon. From 11am until 7.30pm a draft Bud or Miller costs $1.50, and there's a Happy Hour 4.30–7.30pm. No cover. Daily 11.30am–2am.

Rumours

Map 4, D2. *Ala Moana Hotel*, 410 Atkinson Drive, Honolulu ℡955-4811.

Mainstream disco in a business hotel behind the Ala Moana mall, extremely popular with the after-work local crowd. Friday's '70s night is a fixture on many calendars. Daily 5pm onward.

Sand Island Restaurant and Bar

Map 2, C3. 197 Sand Island Access Rd, Honolulu ℡847-5001.

Honolulu's one real blues venue, en route to Sand Island (p.70), in an area where you're unlikely to see any tourists. Gigs are usually scheduled for Wed–Sat, starting at 9pm.

Warriors Lounge

Map 4, E4. *Hale Koa Hotel*, 2055 Kālia Rd, Waikīkī ℡955-0555.

Only military personnel can stay at this seafront hotel, but the no-cover dance floor is open to all, and features a changing program of country, Latin, big band,

BARS, LIVE MUSIC AND DANCING

205

and contemporary Hawaiian music, plus karaoke most nights. Daily 5pm–midnight.

Wave Waikīkī

Map 4, E2. 1877 Kalākaua Ave, Waikīkī ☎ 941-0424. Insofar as Waikīkī has an alternative rock scene, this is it. Large venue, with a bar upstairs and dance floor down below, and DJs rather than live bands most nights. No cover before 10pm. Open nightly 9pm–4am.

World Café

Map 2, D3. Nimitz Business Center, 1130 N Nimitz Hwy, Honolulu ☎ 599-4450. Three-level club not far west of Chinatown that boasts Hawaii's largest dance floor and offers differing themed dance nights as well as live big-name acts. Hip-hop, house and trance music predominates. As one of the few local clubs to admit under-21s, it tends to be crammed with hyped-up youngsters. Daily 9pm until late.

SHOWS AND SPECTACULARS

The days when every major Waikīkī hotel put on its own Las Vegas-style, big-budget extravaganza seem to be over. Nonetheless, there are still a few nightly shows. For most of the shows below, specific prices are not listed because you can get much better deals by buying **reduced-price tickets** through "activity centers" (see p.219). Expect to pay $20–25 if it's possible to book for the show alone (and bear in mind you'll be expected to drink once you're there), or more like $50 if you eat as well.

Creation – A Polynesian Odyssey

Map 3, F5. Ainahau Showroom, *Sheraton Princess Ka'iulani*, 120 Ka'iulani Ave, Waikīkī, HI 96815 ☎ 931-4660.

Lavish new Polynesian revue, complete with fire-dancing, *hula*, and a buffet dinner and aimed at tempting the middle-of-the-road customers who might otherwise head for the

Polynesian Cultural Center or the big commercial *lū'aus*. Hotel guests get a discount for the early-evening performance. Daily 5.15pm & 8pm.

Legends in Concert
Map 3, D5. Aloha Showroom, Royal Hawaiian Shopping Center, Waikīkī ☎971-1400. An enjoyable tribute show of quick-fire impersonations, though your tastes have to stretch pretty wide to want to see Elvis, Prince, Jackie Wilson, Michael Jackson, Judy Garland and Dolly Parton (to name but a few)

on the same bill. You can get the general idea from free "taster" shows on the mall's open-air stage, at odd times throughout the day. Two shows nightly at 6.30pm & 9pm; dinner served at 5pm.

Society of Seven
Map 3, E6. *Outrigger* Main Show Room, 2335 Kalākaua Ave, Waikīkī ☎922-6408. *Very* long standing song-and-dance ensemble that performs Broadway musical routines and pop hits with amazing energy. Mon 8.30pm, Tues–Sat 6.30pm & 8.30pm.

HONOLULU MOVIE THEATERS

The best spot to catch a new **movie** in Honolulu is on one of the nine screens at Restaurant Row, near downtown (☎526-4171). Alternative offerings are shown at the Academy of Arts (900 S Beretania St ☎532-8768) and the Movie Museum (3566 Harding Ave ☎735-8771). The only choice in Waikīkī lies between the two screens of the Waikīkī Theaters (Seaside at Kalākaua Ave ☎971-5133).

The giant-screen **Imax Theater** in Waikīkī, 325 Seaside Ave (☎923-4629), has hourly showings of films such as *Cyberworld*, *Extreme* and *Hidden Hawaii* (daily 11am–9pm, adults $7.50 one show, $12 two, $15 three; under-12s $5/$8/$10). They also put on laser shows and rock-concert films.

Gay and lesbian Honolulu

Hawaii ranks among the world's most appealing destinations for **gay and lesbian** travelers, and nowhere is the gay presence more conspicuous than in Honolulu. While the social climate of the state is undeniably liberal, recent media attention has tended to exaggerate how much progress has been made in Hawaii on issues such as **same-sex marriage**. A series of court rulings that seemed to clear the way for same-sex unions – which would be of special significance because every US state is obliged by the Constitution to recognize marriages deemed legitimate in any other state – have been consistently thwarted by cautious, conservative state politicians. No such officially sanctioned marriages have yet taken place.

In addition, although Honolulu's gay scene still has plenty to offer visitors, its longstanding epicenter suffered a major blow in 1998. Until then, a single block of **Kūhiō Avenue** in central Waikīkī housed virtually all Oahu's best-known gay businesses, including the legendary *Hula's Bar and Lei Stand*. That entire block has now been bulldozed, and developers have set about constructing a major shopping complex on the site. Only *Hula's* has found a permanent new home; see overleaf.

For gay travelers intending to throw themselves into the Waikīkī scene, an evening at *Hula's* is the obvious first step. Step two would be to join one of the two weekly **catamaran cruises**; *Hula's* organizes one on Saturdays at 3pm ($10), *Angles* (see overleaf) another on Sunday mornings at 11am (also $10).

The two most popular **beaches** among gay travelers are **Queen's Surf**, across from Kapi'olani Park at the edge of Waikīkī (see p.37), and **Diamond Head Beach Park**, a mile or so further on (see p.39).

SERVICES FOR GAY TRAVELERS

Pacific Ocean Holidays (PO Box 88245, Honolulu, HI 96830-8245 ☎923-2400 or 1-800/735-6600, ℱ923-2499; ⓦwww.gayhawaii.com/vacation/index.html) organizes all-inclusive **package vacations** in Hawaii for gay and lesbian travelers. It also publishes the thrice-yearly *Pocket Guide to Hawaii*, a useful booklet of gay listings throughout the state (available free in Hawaii, or by mail for $5 per issue, one year's subscription $12). Other useful sources of **information** include Matthew Link's *Rainbow Handbook* (ⓦwww.rainbowhandbook.com), a self-published guide book to all the Hawaiian islands available from local book-stores for $15.

Beechman Agencies, 234 Beach Walk, Waikīkī (☎924-2855), is a **travel agency** specializing in gay travelers, while Lambda Travel Hawaii (☎922-5176; ⓦwww.global-aloha.com/lambda.html) can arrange gay **marriage ceremonies**, as well as accommodation and hiking and biking **tours** of Oahu for gay and lesbians. Taking The Plunge (☎922-2600; ⓦwww.takemediving.com) is a highly recommended gay-friendly **scuba diving** company. A gay **hiking** club, Likehike (℗455-8193; ⓦhttp://gayhawaii.com/likehike/index.html), organizes different group hikes on alternate Sundays at 9am.

GAY COMMUNITY RESOURCES

For general information on gay life in Honolulu, contact the **Gay & Lesbian Community Center**, at 2424 S Beretania St, Honolulu (℗951-7000), which operates a library and resource center. In addition, the **Life Foundation**, #226, 233 Keawe St, Honolulu, HI 96813 (℗521-2437), offers counseling and support to all persons with HIV/AIDS, and the **Honolulu Gay Support Group** (℗532-9000) provides similar services.

GAY BARS AND CLUBS

Angles Waikīkī

Map 3, D3. 2256 Kūhiō Ave, Waikīkī ℗926-9766 or 923-1130; ⓦwww.gayhawaii.com/angles.
Dance club with lively bar and street-view patio, plus bar games, including pool and darts. Daily 10am–2am.

Fusion

Map 3, D5. 2260 Kūhiō Ave, Waikīkī ℗924-2422 ⓦwww.gayhawaii.com/fusion.
Wild, split-level nightclub, with male strippers, female impersonators and special drink discounts.
Mon–Thurs 9pm–4am, Fri & Sat 8pm–4am, Sun 10pm–4am.

Hula's Bar and Lei Stand

Map 4, 14. *Waikīkī Grand Hotel*, 134 Kapahulu Ave, Waikīkī ℗923-0669.
Waikīkī's most popular and longstanding gay club now occupies a suite of ocean-view rooms on the second floor of the *Waikīkī Grand*, across from the Honolulu

Zoo. In addition to a state-of-the-art dance bar equipped with giant video screens, there's a more casual lounge area. Daily 10am–2am.

In-Between
Map 3, B3. 2155 Lau'ula St, Waikīkī ⓣ 926-7060.
Local gay bar in the heart of Waikīkī, open Mon–Sat 4pm–2am, Sun 2pm–2am.

GAY BARS AND CLUBS

●

Shopping

Despite the millions of dollars invested by big business in the attempt to persuade visitors otherwise, shopping is one of the least exciting ways to spend time in Honolulu. The retail scene in both Honolulu and Waikīkī is dominated by large, characterless malls, whose primary function is to give Asian customers easy access to the wonders of the American marketplace. Almost nowhere will you find neighborhoods or even streets of traditional independent stores.

According to official figures, the average Japanese tourist in Hawaii spends $120 per day on clothes and accessories; US visitors are reckoned to spend a mere $20 per day. That makes the downturn in the Asian economy very bad news indeed for Hawaiian shopkeepers; quite possibly, the frantic race to build ever-swankier malls is finally about to collapse.

If you're simply looking for **souvenirs**, the prints, posters and T-shirts piled high along the sidewalks of Waikīkī are all well and good for anyone who thinks that whales are interplanetary voyagers from another dimension, but stores and galleries selling high-quality indigenous arts and crafts are few and far between.

Colorful Hawaiian **clothing**, such as *aloha* shirts and the cover-all "Mother-Hubbard"-style *muʻumuʻu* dress, is on sale everywhere, though classic designs are surprisingly rare

HONOLULU BOOKSTORES AND MUSIC STORES

Bookstores

Barnes & Noble, Kahala Mall (☎737-3323).

Best Sellers, 1001 Bishop St (☎528-2378) and Hilton Hawaiian Village (☎953-2378).

Bishop Museum, 1525 Bernice St (☎848-4158).

Borders Books & Music, Ward Centre (☎591-8995).

Rainbow Books & Records, 1010 University Ave at King St (☎955-7994).

Rand McNally, Ala Moana Center (☎944-6699).

Waldenbooks, Waikiki Shopping Plaza (☎922-4154), Waikiki Trade Center (☎924-8330), Kahala Mall (☎737-9550), and several other Honolulu locations.

Music Stores

Barnes & Noble, as above.

Borders Books & Music, as above.

Hungry Ear Records & Tapes, 1518E Makaloa St (☎944-5044).

Rainbow Books & Records, as above.

Tower Records, 611 Ke'aumoku Ave (☎941-7774), Kahala Mall (☎737-5088), and two other outlying Honolulu locations.

and you tend to see the same stylized prints over and over again. The prevailing trend these days is for muted "reverse-print" designs, in which the cloth is effectively worn inside-out; for more stimulating ideas, seek out clothing designed by **Sig Zane** from the Big Island, who depicts spiritually significant Hawaiian plants and animals using traditional colors and dyes, or **Tori Richard**, whose fabrics have a playful, contemporary garishness.

Otherwise, the main **local crafts** to look for are **lau hala weaving**, in which mats, hats, baskets and the like are

LEIS

Some of the most attractive products of Hawaii are just too ephemeral to take home. That goes for virtually all the orchids and tropical flowers on sale everywhere, and unfortunately it's also true of *leis*.

Leis (pronounced *lays*) are flamboyant decorative garlands, usually composed of flowers such as the fragrant *melia* (the plumeria or frangipani) or the bright-red *lehua* blossom (from the *'ōhia* tree), but sometimes also made from feathers, shells, seeds or nuts. They're worn by both men and women, above all on celebrations or gala occasions – election-winning politicians are absolutely deluged in them, as are the statues of Kamehameha the Great and Queen Lili'uokalani on state holidays.

The days are gone when every arriving tourist was festooned with a *lei*, but you'll probably be way-*leied* at a *lū'au* or some such occasion, while if you're around for Lei Day (May 1), everyone's at it. If you want to buy one, Chinatown is the acknowledged center of the art, with one or two stores on every street displaying a supply of fresh flower *leis* in refrigerated cabinets. Recommended outlets include Cindy's Flower & Lei Shoppe, 1034 Maunakea St (☎536-6538); Lita's Leis, 59 N Beretania St (☎521-9065); and Lin's Lei Shop, 1017A Maunakea St (☎537-4112).

created by plaiting the large leaves (*lau*) of the spindly legged pandanus (*hala*) tree, and **wood turning**, with fine bowls made from native dark woods such as *koa*.

WAIKĪKĪ SHOPPING

If you want to buy a T-shirt, a beach mat or a monkey carved out of a coconut, Waikīkī is the place for you. Kalākaua and Kūhiō avenues especially are lined with cut-price souvenir stores; there are 38 shops in the ABC chain alone, all open daily from 7am to midnight and selling basic groceries along with postcards, sun block and other tourist essentials.

Waikīkī's largest malls, the monolithic **Royal Hawaiian Shopping Center** and the five-floor **Waikīkī Shopping Plaza**, across the street at 2250 Kalākaua Ave, are aseptic upmarket enclaves, packed with designer clothing shops, jewelry stores and sunglasses emporiums. The trend these days is for the major hotels to build their own upscale shopping malls; the two largest, the *Hyatt Regency* and, especially, the *Hilton Hawaiian Village*, now hold conglomerations of stores to rival any in Honolulu.

For the moment, the venerable 1950s style open-air **International Marketplace**, 2330 Kalākaua Ave, still survives. With its simple wooden stalls scattered among the trees, it has a lot more atmosphere, though it has to be admitted that the "crafts" on sale tend to be made-in-Taiwan, while the "psychic readers" are as a rule devoid of paranormal powers.

It's harder than you'd expect to find that quintessential emblem of old Hawaii, the authentic **aloha shirt**; try Bailey's, 517 Kapahulu Ave (☏734-7628).

For eating options in the malls of Waikīkī, see p.173.

HONOLULU SHOPPING

For many years, the **Ala Moana Center**, between downtown Honolulu and Waikīkī, held sway as the premier mall for serious shoppers. However, its success has meant that new rivals now seem to be springing up all the time, with its close neighbor, the **Ward Centre**, as its most serious competitor.

Away from the malls, probably the best places to shop for unusual gifts and souvenirs are the stores in Honolulu's major museums and galleries. Those at the **Bishop Museum** (see p.87), are especially good, stocking a wide range of books, cards, clothing and crafts objects. The Academy Shop at the **Honolulu Academy of Arts** (see p.58) specializes in high-quality traditional arts and crafts, including jewelry and fabrics, while the more eclectic Gift Shop at the **Contemporary Museum** (see p.75) carries flamboyant and original gift items, most of them irresistible despite being of little if any practical use.

MALLS AND MARKETPLACES

Ala Moana Center

Map 6, G3. 1450 Ala Moana Blvd; Mon–Sat 9.30am–9pm, Sun 10am–7pm; ⓦ www.alamoana.com.

The **Ala Moana Center**, a mile west of Waikīkī, has since 1959 been Hawaii's main shopping destination; neighbor-island residents fly to Honolulu to shop here. One of the largest open-air malls in the world, it holds several major department stores, including Sears, JC Penney, Neiman Marcus, and Hawaii's own Liberty House. (The direct descendant of a ships' chandlery store that opened downtown in 1849, Liberty House has hit financial trouble of late, amid accusations of neglecting its traditional customers in pursuit of the elusive yen.) Be sure to explore the Japanese Shirokiya, which has a fabulous upstairs food hall, piled high with sushi and poi, and also stocks a great array of bargain electronic goodies. In addition, the Ala Moana Center is home to a couple of hundred smaller specialty stores, with all the big international names – Emporio Armani, Gucci, Dior, Tiffany, Louis Vuitton, etc – rubbing shoulders with the likes of The Gap, The Body Shop, and Banana

Republic. There's also a branch of the resolutely downmarket Hilo Hattie's, which specializes in inexpensive aloha-wear and souvenirs for tourists – so there's less point than ever in joining the bus parties that trek out to the main Hilo Hattie's, en route to the airport. The whole complex is rounded off by a central performance area, a food court (see p.186), a satellite city hall, and a post office.

Ward Centre and Ward Warehouse

Map 6, E4. 1050 Ala Moana Blvd. Mon–Sat 10am–9pm, Sun 10am–5pm.

Stretching along and back from Ala Moana Blv from a couple of blocks west of the Ala Moana Center, the various **Ward** malls – the Centre, Warehouse, Farmers Market and Village Shops – have been greatly spruced up in the last few years. Anchored by a giant Borders, the **Ward Centre** in

particular has become a serious rival to the Ala Moana Center, with a more intimate atmosphere and a much better selection of bars and restaurants. Its finest stores include the Kamehameha Garment Company, for aloha-wear, and Handblock, selling household linens. Among highlights in the longer-established **Ward Warehouse** alongside are the Nohea Gallery, which sells contemporary artwork from paintings and ceramics to woodcarvings, and distinctive clothing boutiques such as Aloha Tower Traders and Mamo Howell

Aloha Tower Marketplace

Map 5, E8. Mon–Thurs & Sun 9am–9pm, Fri & Sat 9am–10pm.

Downtown's **Aloha Tower Marketplace** (see also p.67) has yet to lure significant numbers of tourists away from Ala Moana, but the

For eating options in the malls of Honolulu, see p.186

MALLS AND MARKETPLACES

dockside setting makes it a fun place to wander around. Most of the stores are one-of-a-kind rather than chain outlets, and souvenir possibilities range from the fake vomit at Monty's World of Magic and the grunting "Mr Bacon" pigs at Magnet Five-O to the beautiful and very expensive *koa*-wood furniture and aloha-wear at Martin & MacArthur.

Kāhala Mall

Map 2, I6. 4211 Waialae Ave; Mon–Sat 10am–9pm, Sun 10am–5pm; ⓦwww.Kahalamallcenter.com. Only a couple of miles from Waikīkī, *mauka* of Diamond Head, the **Kāhala Mall** is almost as chic as – and far less frenzied than – Ala Moana. As well as Liberty House,

Longs Drugs, Banana Republic, The Gap, an eight-screen movie theater and a fine assortment of restaurants, it holds a large Tower Records and an excellent Barnes & Noble bookstore.

Aloha Flea Market

Map 1, H7. Aloha Stadium, Pearl Harbor; Wed, Sat & Sun 6am–3pm. Admission 50¢. More than a thousand diverse traders ensure that the **Aloha Flea Market**, held thrice weekly at the Aloha Stadium in Pearl Harbor, provides an entertaining opportunity to look for (mostly second-hand) bargains. The Aloha Flea Market Shuttle Bus (ⓣ955-4050) runs there from Waikīkī, charging $7 round-trip, including admission.

Ocean activities

Hawaii's vast tourism industry is rooted in the picture-book appeal of its endless palm-fringed sandy beaches and crystal-clear, fish-filled turquoise ocean. The opportunities for sea sports on Oahu are almost infinite, ranging from swimming through snorkeling, scuba diving, fishing and whale-watching, to Hawaii's greatest gift to the world, the art of surfing.

For landlubbers, a list of Oahu's best
golf courses appears on p 234.

ACTIVITY CENTERS

Aloha Express, *Waikīkī Circle Hotel*, 2464 Kalākaua Ave ☎924-4030.

Magnum Tickets & Tours, 2134 Kalākaua Ave ☎923-7825.

Pacific Monarch Travel, 2426 Kūhiō Ave ☎924-7717.

Polynesian Express, Kūhiō Mall, 2301 Kūhiō Ave #22 ☎922-5577 or 1-800/903-9970.

Tours 4 Less, 159 Ka'iulani Ave ☎923-2211.

If you're prepared to shop around a little, you can find much lower rates for most activities than those quoted by the island's many activity companies; look for discount coupons in the free magazines, and in the handbills distributed on every street corner. In particular, independent "**activity centers**" throughout Waikīkī sell tickets for every conceivable island activity, including the various waterborne pursuits described in this chapter, as well as land-based tours (see p.20), and excursions to *lū'aus* (p.170) and the Polynesian Cultural Center (p.119). They can also

OCEAN SAFETY

It's all too easy to forget that Hawaiian beaches can be deadly as well as beautiful; Hawaii is the remotest archipelago on earth, so waves have two thousand miles of the misnamed Pacific Ocean to build up their strength before they come crashing into the islands. People born in Hawaii are brought up with a healthy **respect for the sea** and learn to watch out for all sorts of signs before they swim. You'll be advised to throw sticks into the waves to see how they move, or to look for disturbances in the surf that indicate powerful currents; unless you have local expertise, however, you're better off sticking to the official beach parks and most popular spots, especially those that are shielded by offshore reefs. Not all beaches have lifeguards and warning flags, and unattended beaches are not necessarily safe. Look for other bathers, but whatever your experience elsewhere, don't assume you'll be able to cope with the same conditions as the local kids. Always ask for advice, and above all follow the cardinal rule – **Never turn your back on the water**.

The beaches that experience the most accidents and **drownings** are those where waves of four feet or more break offer air tickets and packages to the other Hawaiian islands, and discounts on airport shuttle vans.

Aim to pay perhaps $20–25 per person for a basic cruise (including a buffet dinner), increasing to around $50 for a submarine ride and anything up to $90 for a better standard of food, and perhaps $40–50 for anything like jet-skiing or scuba diving. For activities not based in central Waikīkī, the price should include round-trip transport to the departure point.

directly onto the shore. This varies according to the season, so beaches that are idyllic in summer can be storm-tossed death traps between October and April. If you get caught in a rip current or undertow and find yourself being dragged out to sea, stay calm and remember that the vast majority of such currents disappear within a hundred yards of the shore. Never exhaust yourself by trying to swim against them, but simply allow yourself to be carried out until the force weakens, and swim first to one side and then back to the shore.

Sea creatures to avoid include *wana* (black spiky **sea urchins**), Portuguese man-o'-war **jellyfish**, and **coral** in general, which can give painful, infected cuts. **Shark attacks** are much rarer than popular imagination suggests; in 2000, 79 occurred worldwide, of which ten were fatal. Two of the non-lethal attacks were in Hawaii, both off Maui. Those that do happen are usually due to "misunderstandings" caused by surfers idling on their boards who look a bit too much like turtles from below.

Emergency Numbers

Police, Fire and Ambulance ☏ 911

Ocean Search and Rescue ☏ 1-800/552-645

OCEAN SAFETY

DINNER AND SIGHTSEEING CRUISES

Ali'i Kai Catamaran

℡ 539-9400 or 1-800/831-5541.

Giant catamaran that offers nightly sunset cruises along Waikīkī Beach – though you're bused to and from Honolulu before and after your voyage – with differing rates according to whether you eat a buffet supper or a full steak and seafood dinner. To get the most from the experience, you need to enjoy – or at least be oblivious to – kitsch.

Dream Cruises

℡ 592-2000 or 1-800/400-7300; ⓦ www.dream-cruises.com.

Lunch and sunset cruises from either Kewalo Basin in Honolulu or Waianae Small Boat Harbor on the North Shore, with snorkel equipment available. Dolphins can be seen year-round. Whale-watching cruises are available in winter.

Navatek I

℡ 973-1311; ⓦ www.go-atlantis.com.

Giant catamaran, operated by Atlantis and based at Pier 6 in Honolulu, which prides itself on offering the smoothest sailing experience on Oahu. The lunchtime buffet cruise costs $45, while the sunset version, complete with *Blue Hawaii*-era Elvis impersonator strumming a *ukulele*, is $49.

Paradise Cruise

℡ 983-7827.

The *Star of Honolulu* cruises between Diamond Head and Pearl Harbor, starting alongside Aloha Tower. $38 morning sightseeing excursions, with whale-watching in winter, and sunset dinner cruises from $58 up to $200 per person. Also snorkeling trips in the *Starlet*.

SUBMARINES

Atlantis Submarines

T 973-9811 or 1-800/548-6262; W www.go-atlantis.com. Passengers leave Waikīkī's *Hilton Hawaiian Village* by motorboat, then transfer onto a genuine submarine out in the ocean for a 45min dive down to the seabed, where you cruise past two sunken airplanes and an artificial reef before circling a full-sized shipwreck. You may see sharks and turtles, but be prepared for the muted underwater colors. The whole experience lasts around 2hr; departures daily from 7am, but many are narrated in Japanese.

Voyager Submarines

T 539-9400 or 1-800/831-5541; W www.robertshawaii.com. After a five-minute catamaran trip from Kewalo Basin, passengers rendezvous with the "yellow submarine" above a natural reef, and take a 35min tour along the ocean floor, culminating in the atmospheric shipwreck of the *Sea Tiger.* The same company also runs catamaran excursions.

SURFING

The nation that invented **surfing** – long before the foreigners came – remains its greatest arena. A recurring theme in ancient legends has young men frittering away endless days in the waves rather than facing up to their duties; now young people from all over the world flock to Hawaii to do just that. The sport was popularized early in the twentieth century by champion Olympic swimmer **Duke Kahanamoku**, the original Waikīkī Beach Boy; see p.40. He toured the world with his sixteen-foot board, demonstrating his skills to admiring crowds and was responsible for introducing surfing to Australia.

Waikīkī lost its best surf breaks when it was relandscaped at the start of the tourist boom. Today, with advances in techniques and technology, surfing has never been more popular. Oahu's fabled **North Shore** – see p.126 onward – is a Mecca for surf-bums, who ride the waves around Waimea Bay and hang out in the coffee bars of Hale'iwa. However, surfing at such legendary sites is for experts only. Whatever your surfing experience at home, you need to be very sure you're up to it before you have a go in Hawaii, so start by sampling conditions at lesser surf-spots to be found on all the islands.

Concession stands near the Duke Kahanamoku statue in central Waikīkī rent out surfboards for around $10 per hour, and offer **surfing lessons** for beginners costing more like $40 per hour, including board rental. Lessons are great fun, and they really work; with the aid of a friendly push at the right moment, almost everyone manages to ride a wave within the hour. An equally exhilarating way to get a taste for the surf is to start out by using a smaller **boogie board**, which you lie on.

WINDSURFING

Since Oahu's Robbie Naish won the first world championship in the 1970s, at the age of 13, Hawaii has also been recognized as the spiritual home of **windsurfing**. Maui tends to be regarded as the prime goal for enthusiasts from around the world, but Oahu also has some excellent spots, not least Kailua Beach on the windward shore (see p.110). Once again, be warned that Hawaiian waters present challenges on a vastly different scale from what you may be familiar with at home.

Naish himself now operates Naish Windsurfing Hawaii at 155-C Hamakua Drive, Kailua Beach (☎ 261-3539; ⓦ www.naish.com), offering equipment rental from $25 per half-day and private lessons from $60. A similar service on the North Shore is provided by Surf'n'Sea, 62-595 Kamehameha Hwy, Hale'iwa (☎637-9887 or 1-800/899-SURF; ⦿www.surfnsea.com); see p.128.

SNORKELING

Probably the easiest ocean activity for beginners is **snorkeling**. Equipped with mask, snorkel and fins, you can while away hours and days having face-to-face encounters with the rainbow-colored populations of Hawaii's reefs and lava pools. A description of Oahu's best-known site, **Hanauma Bay**, appears on p.102. As a rule, conditions in the waters close to Waikīkī tend to be less enticing; the best spot in the vicinity is Sans Souci Beach (see p.38).

Operators of snorkel cruises and similar activities provide equipment to their customers, and there's a concession stand at Hanauma Bay, but you may prefer to **rent** better stuff from a specialist such as Snorkel Bob's, 700 Kapahulu Ave, Waikīkī (☎735-7944; ⦿www.snorkelbob.com), or Surf'n'Sea in Hale'iwa (see above). Typical rates start at $5 per day, or $20 per week.

SCUBA AND SNUBA

Scuba diving is both expensive and demanding, but with endless networks of submarine lava tubes to explore, and the chance to get that bit closer to some amazing marine life forms, Hawaii is a great diving destination. Aficionados do not usually rank Oahu as highly as the Big Island or Maui, in part because there are few stellar dives accessible directly from the shoreline.

Nonetheless, there are still some superb sites a short distance offshore, particularly in the southeast. Even a few yards out to sea from central Honolulu, the clarity of the Pacific waters is remarkable. From Kewalo Basin, for example, a five-minute boat trip takes you to the wreck of the *Sea Tiger*, 100ft underwater, where it's possible to stand on the bridge and watch the submarines go by. By contrast, boat diving along the North Shore is rarely feasible, and even shore diving is recommended only on calm summer days. For medical reasons. don't dive within 24 hours of flying.

A typical rate for a two-tank dive trip should be around $90. Operators include the Aloha Dive Shop at Koko Marina, not far from Hanauma Bay (☏395-5922); Surf'n'Sea in Hale'iwa, as overleaf; Ed Masucci's Taking The Plunge (☏922-2600; ⒲www.takemediving.com); and Ocean Concepts (☏677-7975 or 1-800/808-3483; ⒲www.oceanconcepts.com).

An unusual variation on conventional scuba diving is offered by Bob's Hawaii Adventure at Koko Marina (☏943-8628). "Bob" here stands for "Breathing Observation Bubble," a sort of **underwater moped**, on which the rider's head is enclosed within a giant plexiglass helmet, fed by an oxygen supply held in the body of the vehicle. No diving experience is required, and the $110 fee includes half an hour's instruction and a half-hour ride along the ocean floor.

For an easier taste of what it's all about, you might like to try **snuba**, which is basically snorkeling from a boat equipped with a longer breathing tube. Many snorkel cruises offer snuba for an extra charge, or you could contact Snuba Tours of Oahu (☏396-6163), which organizes specialist snuba cruises to Hanauma Bay and other destinations for around $85.

KAYAKING

Kayaks for inshore expeditions can readily be rented in both Waikīkī (Prime Time Sports; ☏949-8952) and Kailua (Kailua Sailboards & Kayaks; ☏262-7341). The best organized **kayak tours**, at less than $50 for two hours, are run by Kayak Oahu Adventure, which has bases in Waikīkī at the *New Otani Kaimana Beach Hotel*, adjoining Sans Souci Beach (☏923-0539), and on the North Shore at Waimea Park (☏638-8189).

WATER-SKIING AND PARASAILING

Traditional **water-skiing** is available in southeast Oahu's Koko Marina with Suyderhoud's Waterski Center (☏395-3773), which charges around $50 per half-hour. For a similar price, also try **parasailing** – you soar several hundred feet up into the air beneath a parachute. Companies operating brief flights off Waikīkī include Aloha Parasail (☏521-2446) and Hawaiian Parasail (☏591-1280).

FISHING

Big-game **fishing**, for marlin especially, is a year-round attraction for many visitors to Hawaii. Most of Oahu's wide range of charter vessels are based at Koko Marina in the southeast, though they're usually prepared to pick up clients at Kewalo Basin in Honolulu. Rates for a day's expedition with outfits such as Kono Fishing Charters (☏593-8472) and Ku'u Huapala (☏596-0918) vary from $50 per person up to as much as $1000 for a whole boat.

Details on fishing regulations, and thirty-day licenses for freshwater fishing ($3.75), can be obtained from the Department of Land and Natural Resources, 1151 Punchbowl St, Room 311, Honolulu, HI 96813 (☏587-0077).

WHALE-WATCHING

A large proportion of the North Pacific's three thousand **humpback whales** winter in Hawaiian waters between

WATER-SKIING AND PARASAILING • FISHING • WHALE-WATCHING

late November and early April. They're especially fond of the shallow channels between Maui, Molokai and Lanai, and prefer not to linger in the rougher seas off Oahu. Nonetheless, a couple of Oahu-based boats run regular **whale-watching** expeditions in season; *Navatek I* (see p.222; ☎973-1311), and Dream Cruises (see p.222; ☎592-2000). Note that looking for whales tends to involve cruising a few miles out to sea, which can mean pretty rough waters. Expect to pay a little under $50 for a 2hr 30min cruise.

WHALE-WATCHING

Festivals and holidays

The following calendar includes all federal and state holidays celebrated in Hawaii, together with Oahu's major annual festivals and sporting events. Note that the exact dates of surfing contests, and in some cases the venues as well, depend on the state of the waves.

Jan 1	New Year's Day; public holiday
Early Jan	Morey Bodyboards World Championships, Banzai Pipeline
3rd Mon in Jan	Dr Martin Luther King Jr's Birthday; public holiday
Jan /Feb	Narcissus Festival, Chinese New Year, Chinatown
Feb	Buffalo's Big Board Surfing Classic, Mākaha Beach
3rd Mon in Feb	Presidents Day; public holiday. Great Aloha Run, from Aloha Tower to Aloha Stadium.
March 17	St Patrick's Day Parade, Waikīkī

March 26	Prince Kūhiō Day; public holiday, state wide celebrations
Easter Sunday	Easter Sunrise Service at dawn, Punchbowl, Honolulu
Easter Monday	public holiday
April	Hawaiian Professional Championship Rodeo, Waimānolo
May 1	May Day, Lei Day; public holiday, state-wide celebrations
May 2	*Lei* ceremony at Royal Mausoleum, Honolulu
late May	Molokai–Oahu kayak race ends at Hawaii Kai
late May	Maui–Oahu Bankoh Hoʻomanaʻo canoe race ends at Waikīkī Beach
late May	Outrigger Hotels Hawaiian Oceanfest; island-wide watersports
Last Mon in May	Memorial Day; public holiday
late May/early June	State Fair, Aloha Stadium, Honolulu
June 11	Kamehameha Day; public holiday, statewide celebrations, Honolulu to Waikīkī parade
late June	King Kamehameha *Hula* Festival, Blaisdell Center, Honolulu
July 4	Independence Day; public holiday
early July	Nā Wāhine O Hawaii; Hawaiian women performers, Ala Moana Park
mid- July	Hawaii International Jazz Festival, Honolulu
3rd Sat in July	Prince Lot Hula Festival, Moanalua Gardens, Honolulu
mid-Aug	Floating Lantern Ceremony, Waikīkī

3rd Fri in Aug	Admission Day; public holiday
1st Mon in Sept	Labor Day; public holiday
mid-Sept	Aloha Festival, islandwide
late Sept	Molokai–Oahu women's outrigger canoe race ends at Waikīkī
late Sept	Makahiki Festival, Waimea Falls Park
early Oct	Molokai–Oahu men's outrigger canoe race ends at Waikīkī
2nd Mon in Oct	Columbus Day; public holiday
Oct 31	Halloween parade, Waikīkī
early Nov	World Invitation Hula Festival, Honolulu
Nov 11	Veterans' Day; public holiday
Nov	Hawaii International Film Festival, Honolulu
mid-Nov	Triple Crown of Surfing; Hawaiian Pro, Ali'i Beach Park, Hale'iwa
Last Thurs in Nov	Thanksgiving; public holiday
late Nov/early Dec	Triple Crown of Surfing; World Cup, Sunset Beach
early Dec	Triple Crown of Surfing; Pipe Masters, Banzai Pipeline
2nd Sun in Dec	Honolulu Marathon
Dec 25	Christmas Day; public holiday. Aloha Bowl Football Classic, Aloha Stadium, Honolulu
Dec 31	First Night Festival, downtown Honolulu

FESTIVALS AND HOLIDAYS

Directory

AREA CODE The telephone area code for the whole state of Hawaii is ☎ 808.

BANKS For details of banks in Honolulu and Waikīkī, see p.26.

CLIMATE For details of the climate on Oahu, see the "Introduction" on p.xiii.

CONSULATES Neither Britain, New Zealand nor Canada has a consulate in Honolulu. There is, however, an Australian consulate, at 1000 Bishop St, Honolulu, HI 96813 (☎ 524-5050).

CONVENTION CENTER The showpiece new Hawaii Convention Center (☎ 923-1811; Ⓦ www.hvcb.org/hconv) stands on the western edge of Waikīkī at Kalākaua Ave at Kapiolani Blvd, close to the Ala Moana Center.

DENTISTS The Hawaii Dental Association (☎ 536-2135) can provide lists of recommended dental practitioners, and operates a 24hr emergency service (☎ 593-7956).

DOCTORS All Waikīkī hotels keep a list of doctors to recommend to guests requiring minor medical help; Doctors on Call (☎ 971-6000) maintains 24hr clinics at the *Hilton*, *Hyatt Regency*, *Sheraton Princess Ka'iulani*, *Royal Hawaiian*, and *Hawaiian Regent* hotels.

ELECTRICITY Hawaii's electricity supply, like that on the US mainland, uses 110 volts AC. Plugs are standard American two-pins.

FISHING For full details on Hawaii's fishing regulations write to Division of Aquatic Resources, Dept of Land and Natural Resources, Kalanimoku Building, 1151 Punchbowl St, Room 330, Honolulu, HI 96813.

GOLF The annual *Hawaii Golf Guide*, published by the Aloha Section PGA (#715, 770 Kapi'olani Blvd, Honolulu, HI 96813; ☏593-2230) carries complete listings and details of all Hawaii's golf courses. Stand-By Golf (☏1-888/645-2265) is a company that specializes in finding discounted and short-notice golfing opportunities on all the Hawaiian islands.

HOSPITALS Honolulu hospitals providing 24-hour assistance include Kuakini Medical Center, 347 Kuakini St (☏536-2236); Moanalua Medical Center, 3288 Moanalua Rd (☏834-5333);

the Queens Medical Center, 1301 Punchbowl St (☏538-9011); and the Straub Clinic and Hospital, 888 S King St (☏522-4000). In emergencies call ☏911.

INOCULATIONS No inoculations or vaccinations are required by law in order to enter Hawaii, though some authorities suggest a polio vaccination.

LAUNDROMATS Among public laundromats in Waikīkī are those at the *Ohana Waikīkī Coral Seas*, 250 Lewers St; the *Outrigger Waikīkī on the Beach*, 2335 Kalākaua Ave; and the *Ohana Waikīkī West*, 2330 Kūhiō Ave.

LIBRARY Honolulu's best public library is the Hawaii State Library, 478 S King St at Punchbowl downtown (Mon, Fri & Sat 9am–5pm; Tues & Thurs 9am–8pm; Wed 10am–5pm ☏586-3500).

POST OFFICES The major post offices in Honolulu and Waikīkī are listed on p.28.

OAHU'S GOLF COURSES

Ala Wai Golf Course, Honolulu; $42	☎ 733-7387
Bayview Golf Links, Kāne'ohe; $45	☎ 247-0451
Coral Creek Golf Course, 'Ewa Beach; $125	☎ 441-4653
'Ewa Beach Golf Club, 'Ewa Beach; $80	☎ 689-8317
Hawaii Country Club, Wahiawā; $45	☎ 621-5654
Hawaii Kai Golf Course	
Championship Course; $90	☎ 395-2358
Executive Course; $28.50	☎ 395-2358
Hawaii Prince Golf Club, 'Ewa Beach; $135	☎ 944-4567
Honolulu Country Club, Honolulu; $55	☎ 833-4541
Kahuku Golf Course, North Shore; $20	☎ 293-5842
Kapolei Golf Course, Ko 'Olina; $70	☎ 674-2227
Ko'olau Golf Course, Kāne'ohe; $125	☎ 236-4653
Ko 'Olina Golf Club, Ko 'Olina; $145	☎ 676-5300
Luana Hills Country Club, Kailua; $95	☎ 262-2139
Mākaha Resort Golf Club, Mākaha; $100	☎ 695-9544
Mākaha Valley Country Club, Mākaha; $55	☎ 695-9578
Mililani Golf Club, Mililani; $89	☎ 623-2222
Moanalua Golf Club, Honolulu; $20	☎ 839-2411
New 'Ewa Beach Golf Club, 'Ewa Beach; $115	☎ 689-8351
Olomana Golf Links, Waim*analo; $65	☎ 259-7926
Pali Golf Course, Kāne'ohe; $42	☎ 266-7612
Pearl Country Club, 'Aiea; $65	☎ 487-3802
Ted Makalena Golf Course, Waipahu; $42	☎ 675-6052
Turtle Bay Hilton Country Club	
The Links at Kuilima, Kahuku; $135	☎ 293-8574
Turtle Bay Country Club, Kahuku; $90	☎ 293-8574
Waikele Golf Club, Waipahu; $107	☎ 676-9000
West Loch Golf Course, 'Ewa Beach; $42	☎ 296-2000

OAHU'S GOLF COURSES

PUBLIC TOILETS Some public toilets are labeled in Hawaiian: *Kanes* means Men, *Wahines* means Women.

QUARANTINE Very stringent restrictions apply to the importation of all plants and animals into Hawaii. Cats and dogs must stay in quarantine for 120 days; if you were hoping to bring an alligator or a hamster into the state, forget it. For full regulations call ☎ 861-8490.

SENIOR TRAVELERS US residents aged 50 or over can join the American Association of Retired Persons, 601 E St NW, Washington, DC 20049 (☎ 1-800/424-3410; membership hotline ☎ 1-800/515-2299 or 202/434-2277; ⓦ www.aarp.org), for discounts on accommodation and vehicle rental.

TIME Unlike most of the US, Hawaii does not observe Daylight Saving Time. Therefore, from 2am on the last Sunday in April until 2am on the last Sunday in October, the time difference between Hawaii and the US West Coast is three hours, not the usual two; the difference between Hawaii and the mountain region is four hours, not three; and the islands are six hours later than the East Coast, not five. Hawaiian time is from ten to eleven hours behind the UK. In fact it's behind just about everywhere else; although New Zealand and Australia might seem to be two and four hours, respectively, behind Honolulu time, they're on the other side of the International Date Line, so are actually almost a full day ahead.

TIPPING Waiting staff in restaurants expect tips of fifteen percent, in bars a little less. Hotel porters and bellhops should receive around $1 per piece of luggage and housekeeping staff $2 per night.

TRAVELERS WITH DISABILITIES Copies of the *Aloha Guide to Accessibility in the State of Hawaii*, and additional information on facilities for travelers with disabilities on Oahu, can be obtained from the State Commission on Persons with Disabilities, 919 Ala Moana Blvd, #101, Honolulu, HI 96814 (☏586-8121). Accessible Vans of Hawaii (☏879-5521; ⓦwww.accessiblevans.com) rent out wheelchair-accessible vans and also run island tours and shuttle services, while C R Newton, 1575 S Beretania St (☏949-8389; ⓦwww.crnewton.com) rent wheelchairs, scooters and crutches. Most TheBus vehicles are adapted to suit passengers with physical disabilities.

WEDDINGS To get married in Hawaii, you need a valid state license, which costs $50 from the Department of Health, Marriage License Office, 1250 Punchbowl St, Honolulu, HI 96813 (Mon–Fri 8am–4pm ☏586-4545;

ⓦwww.hawaii.gov), and is valid for thirty days. You also need proof of rubella immunizations or screening, which can be arranged through the Department of Health. Most resorts offer their own marriage planners, while companies that specialize in arranging weddings include Aloha Wedding Planners (☏943-2711 or 1-800/288-8309; ⓦwww.alohaweddingplanners.com), Affordable Weddings of Hawaii (☏923-4876 or 1-800/942-4554), or Traditional Hawaiian Weddings (☏671-8420 or 1-800/884-9505).

WORK For details on finding paid employment in Hawaii – an option only open to US citizens – contact the State Department of Labor & Industrial Relations, 830 Punchbowl St, Honolulu, HI 96813.

WEDDINGS–WORK

CONTEXTS

A brief history

J ust two thousand years ago, Oahu was an unknown speck in the vast Pacific, populated by the few organisms that had been carried here by wind or wave. Exactly when and where its first human settlers arrived remains unknown, in part because rising water levels have almost certainly submerged the very earliest settlements. However, carbon dating of sites at Kahana Valley and Bellows Field on the windward coast suggests that there were people on Oahu by around 200 AD.

For a full account of the daily life, traditions and culture of the ancient Hawaiians, see p.253.

These first inhabitants were **Polynesians**, probably from the Marquesas Islands. Except perhaps for their first chance landfall, they came equipped to colonize, carrying goats, dogs, pigs, coconut palms, bananas and sugar cane among other essentials. Their ancestors spread from Asia to inhabit Indonesia and the Solomon Islands 30,000 years ago. Such migrations, across coastal waters shallower than they are today, involved hopping from island to island without crossing open ocean. There then followed a 25,000-year hiatus, while the techniques were acquired to venture farther. Just over three thousand years ago, the voyagers reached Fiji;

A BRIEF HISTORY

239

they then spread via Tahiti to populate the "Polynesian Triangle," extending from Easter Island in the east to Hawaii in the north and New Zealand in the south.

Recent archeological and scientific investigations have shed more light on the ancient history of Hawaii, while throwing a number of long-cherished beliefs into doubt. Thanks to DNA testing, for example, it is now certain that the Polynesians did indeed enter the Pacific from southeast Asia. Thor Heyerdahl's argument for a North American origin, as promulgated by the Mormon church in Oahu's Polynesian Cultural Center, has been finally disproved. On the other hand, historians are no longer sure whether traditional accounts of Hawaii being settled by successive waves of migrants at widely spaced intervals are in fact true. According to that model, Marquesas Islanders continued to arrive until the eighth century and were followed by Tahitians between the eleventh and fourteenth centuries, with each group violently supplanting its predecessors. One piece of evidence that does point to a Tahitian influx is the name "**Hawaii**" itself, which is known previously to have been an alternative, "poetic" name for the largest of the leeward Tahitian islands, Raiatea, the home of the voyaging temple of Taputapuatea. Whether or not Tahitians did reach Hawaii in significant numbers, it remains unquestioned that by the time the Europeans appeared, no two-way voyaging between Hawaii and the South Pacific had taken place for around five hundred years.

Before the coming of the foreigners, Oahu was probably the least significant of the four major Hawaiian islands. Nonetheless, the windward valleys of the east coast are thought to have held sizeable agricultural populations, while the sheltered coastline of Pearl Harbor supported an intricate network of fishponds. Not until the eighteenth century, however, did any individual chief become powerful enough to subdue the whole island, and by that time the rulers of Maui and Hawaii (the Big Island) were capable of launching successful invasions.

The coming of the foreigners

No Western ship is known for certain to have chanced upon Hawaii before that of **Captain Cook**, in January 1778; the first European to sail across the Pacific, the Portuguese Ferdinand Magellan, did so without seeing a single island.

There is, however, considerable circumstantial evidence of pre-Cook contact between Hawaiians and Europeans. **Spanish** vessels disappeared in the northern Pacific from the 1520s onward, while during the two centuries, starting in 1565, that the "Manila Galleons" made annual voyages across the Pacific between Mexico and the Philippines, at least nine such ships were lost. Cook observed that the first Hawaiians he encountered were familiar with iron, and even suggested that some bore European features. Hawaiian legends speak of what may have been Spanish mariners being shipwrecked on the north coast of Lanai during the sixteenth century, and again off Maui some time later, while the log of the Dutch ship *Lefda* in 1599 spoke of eight seamen deserting to an unknown island at this latitude. A map captured by the British in 1742 appears to show a group of islands, labelled La Mesa, Los Monges, and La Desgraciada in the correct location, and Cook's crew debated whether these were the same islands that they had found.

Spanish influence might explain the similarity of the red-and-yellow feather headdresses of Hawaiian warriors – unknown elsewhere in Polynesia – to the helmets of Spanish soldiers, and account for what seemed the phenomenal speed with which syphilis spread through the islands after it was supposedly introduced by the Cook expedition. The skeleton of a young woman was recently unearthed on Oahu who appears to have died of syphilis in the mid-seventeenth century; other contemporary burials have been shown to contain small scraps of sailcloth.

When Cook first encountered Hawaii, on his way to the north Pacific in search of the Northwest Passage, he missed Maui and the Big Island altogether, and only glimpsed Oahu before making his first footfall upon Kauai. When he returned to the "**Sandwich Islands**" at the end of the year, he again bypassed Oahu en route to the Big Island, where he met his death in a skirmish in Kealakekua Bay on February 14, 1779.

Shortly after Cook's death, one of his ships, the *Resolution*, put in at Waimea Bay on Oahu's North Shore to collect water for the long voyage north. The new Captain Clerke described the first spot on Oahu to be visited by foreigners as "by far the most beautiful country we have yet seen among the Isles... bounteously cloath'd with verdure, on which were situate many large villages and extensive plantations."

By the time the next foreign expedition reached Oahu in 1792, led by Cook's former midshipman George Vancouver, the island had been conquered by Chief **Kahekili** of Maui. Kahekili's ferocious *pahupu* or "cut-in-two" warriors, who tattooed half of their bodies completely black, killed two of Vancouver's crew in Waimea Valley.

After news of Cook's discoveries reached the outside world, the Sandwich Islands became a port of call for traders of all kinds, especially those carrying furs from the Pacific Northwest to China. In 1793, Captain William Brown, a British fur trader in command of HMS *Butterworth*, found a safe anchorage near the spot where the Nu'uanu Stream had created a gap in the coral reef fringing southeastern Oahu. The Hawaiians knew this as *He Awa Kou*, "the harbor of Kou," but Brown renamed it "fair haven," which was soon translated into Hawaiian as **Honolulu**. That name in turn attached itself to the small fishing village that stood nearby, which until then had been too insignificant even to deserve its own name.

The rise and fall of the Hawaiian monarchy

The acquisition of European military technology made it possible for a single chief to conquer the entire archipelago. The first to do so was the astute young Big Island warrior **Kamehameha**, who was by some accounts Kahekili's own bastard son. Kahekili himself died at Waikīkī in 1794, and Kamehameha won control of Oahu the following year, defeating the armies of Kahekili's heir Kalanikūpule in an epic battle at Nuʻuanu Valley (see p.85).

Kamehameha originally based himself in a grass hut beside the beach at Waikīkī. Within ten years, however, Honolulu had turned into a cluster of shacks surrounding the semi-permanent adobe homes of sixty foreigners, and Kamehameha had built himself a palace, known as *Halehui*, at what is now the foot of Bethel Street. Another ten years on – by which time Kamehameha had moved his capital back to the Big Island, and then died – Honolulu was a thriving port, complete with bars and taverns.

Kamehameha was succeeded as king by two of his sons – Liholiho or **Kamehameha II**, who died of measles during a visit to England, and Kauikeaouli or **Kamehameha III**. Under both rulers, Kamehameha's widow Queen Kaʻahumanu was the real power behind the throne. She was largely responsible for the overthrow of the ancient *kapu* system of Hawaiian religion (see p.257) – motivated to some extent by the fact that the *kapu* denied women any political authority – and her subsequent conversion to Christianity was a principal factor in the success of Hawaii's first Christian **missionaries**.

In the years that followed, **whaling** ships en route between the Arctic and Japan began to call in twice-yearly to pick up provisions, drop off their haul, and catch up on a little entertainment. In Honolulu, the whalers were originally hauled in by Hawaiians standing on the reef; later on, teams of oxen did the job, and for many years an immense rope reached up Alakea Street to loop around a capstan at the foot of Punchbowl Street. By 1830, the city had a population of ten thousand, with a dominant American presence, and the basic grid of downtown streets was in place. Tensions between the missionaries and the lawless whaling crews were high, and both the seat of Hawaiian government and the epicenter of the whaling industry moved back and forth between Honolulu and Lahaina on Maui. Only in the 1840s did Honolulu become definitively established as the capital of Hawaii.

The Great Mahele

Kamehameha III's government was dominated by foreign-born fortune-seekers. Fourteen of the king's closest advisers were white, including his three most important ministers. The various foreign powers jostled for position; it is easy to forget now that it was not inevitable that the islands would become American. In 1843, a British commander captured Honolulu, claiming all Hawaii for Queen Victoria; and it was six months before word arrived from London that it had all been a mistake. A French admiral did much the same thing in 1849, but this time everyone simply waited until he got bored and sailed away.

The most important obstacle to the advance of the foreigners was that they could not legally own land. In the old Hawaii there was no private land; all was held in trust by the chief, who apportioned it to individuals at his continued pleasure only. After a misunderstanding with the British consul almost resulted in the islands' permanent cession to Britain, the king was requested to "clarify" the situation. A land commission was set up, under the direction of a missionary, and its deliberations resulted in the **Great Mahele**, or "Division of Lands," in 1848. In theory all the land was parceled out to native Hawaiians only, with sixty percent going to the crown and the government, 39 percent to just over two hundred chiefs, and less than one percent to eleven thousand commoners. Claiming and keeping the land involved complex legal procedures and required expenditures that few Hawaiians, paid in kind not cash, were able to meet. In any case, within two years the *haoles* (non-Hawaiians) were also permitted to buy and sell land. The much repeated jibe that the missionaries "came to Hawaii to do good – and they done good" stems from the speed with which they amassed vast acreages; their children became Hawaii's wealthiest and most powerful class.

Many Hawaiians were denied access to the lands they had traditionally worked, arrested for vagrancy, and used as forced labor on the construction of roads and ports for the new landowners. Meanwhile, a simultaneous **water grab** took place, with new white-owned plantations diverting water for their thirsty foreign crops from the Hawaiian farmers downstream.

The sugar industry

At the height of the whaling boom, many newly rich entrepreneurs began to put their money into **sugar**. Hawaii's first sugar plantation started in 1835 in Kōloa on Kauai, and it swiftly became clear that this was an industry where large-scale operators were much the most efficient and profitable. By 1847 the field had narrowed to five main players, four of whom had started out by provisioning whale ships. These **Big Five** were Hackfield & Co (later to become Amfac), C Brewer & Co, Theo Davies Co, Castle & Cooke (later Dole) and Alexander & Baldwin. Thereafter, they worked in close co-operation with each other, united by common interests and, often, family ties.

Hawaii was poised to take advantage of the coming of Civil War, when the markets of the northern US began to cast about for an alternative source of sugar to the Confederate South. The consequent boom in the Hawaiian sugar industry, and the ever-increasing integration of Hawaii into the American economic mainstream, was the major single factor in the eventual loss of Hawaiian sovereignty.

The Civil War also coincided with the decline of the whaling industry. Several ships were bought and deliberately sunk to blockade Confederate ports, while the discovery of petroleum had diminished the demand for whale oil. The final disaster came in 1871, when 31 vessels lingered in the Arctic too long at the end of the season, became frozen in, and had to be abandoned.

By the 1870s, canefields were spreading across all the islands. The ethnic mixture of modern Hawaii is largely due to the search for laborers prepared to submit to the draconian conditions on the plantations. Once the Hawaiians had demonstrated their unwillingness to knuckle under, agents of the Hawaiian Sugar Planters Association scoured the world in search of peasants eager to find new lives.

As members of each ethnic group in turn got their start on the plantations, and then left to find more congenial employment or establish their own businesses, a new source of labor had to be found. It soon became clear that few single men chose to stay on the plantations when their contracts expired – many left for California to join the Gold Rush – so the planters began to try to lure families to Hawaii, which meant providing better housing than the original basic dormitories.

First came the **Chinese** (see p.62), recruited with a $10 inducement in Hong Kong, shipped over for free, and then signed to five-year contracts at $6 or less per month. The **Portuguese** followed, brought from Madeira and the Azores from 1878 onward by planters who thought they might adjust more readily than their Asian counterparts to the dominant *haole*-Hawaiian culture. **Koreans** arrived during the brief period between 1902, when they were first allowed to leave their country, and 1905, when it was invaded by the **Japanese**, who themselves came in great numbers until 1907, when the so-called Gentleman's Agreement banned further immigration. **Filipinos**, whose country had been annexed by the US in 1898, began to arrive in their stead, to find the climate, soil and crops were all similar to their homelands.

The end of the Kingdom of Hawaii

> *Hawaii is ours. As I look back upon the first steps in this miserable business, and as I contemplate the means used to complete the outrage, I am ashamed of the whole affair.*

US President Grover Cleveland, 1893

After sugar prices dropped at the end of the Civil War, the machinations of the sugar industry to get favorable prices on the mainland moved Hawaii inexorably toward **annexation** by the US. In 1876 the Treaty of Reciprocity abolished all trade barriers and tariffs between the US and the Kingdom of Hawaii; within fifteen years sugar exports to the US had increased tenfold.

By now, the Kamehameha dynasty had come to an end, and the heir to the Hawaiian throne was chosen by the national legislature. The first such king, William Lunalilo, died in 1874, after barely a year in office. In the ensuing elections, **Queen Emma**, the Anglophile widow of Kamehameha IV (see p.83), lost to **King David Kalākaua**. .

THE RISE AND FALL OF THE HAWAIIAN MONARCHY

THE HAWAIIAN MONARCHY

Kamehameha I	1791–1819
Kamehameha II (Liholiho)	1819–1824
Kamehameha III (Kauikeaouli)	1825–1854
Kamehameha IV (Alexander Liholiho)	1854–1863
Kamehameha V (Lot Kamehameha)	1863–1872
William C. Lunalilo	1873–1874
David Kalākaua	1874–1891
Lili'uokalani	1891–1893

The "Merrie Monarch" is affectionately remembered today for his role in reviving traditional Hawaiian pursuits such as *hula* and surfing, but he was widely seen as being pro-American, and a riot protesting his election in 1874 virtually destroyed Honolulu's Old Court House. King Kalākaua was to a significant extent the tool of the plantation owners. In 1887 an all-white (and armed) group of "concerned businessmen" forced through the "Bayonet Constitution," in which he surrendered power to an assembly elected by property owners (of any nationality) as opposed to citizens. The US government was swiftly granted exclusive rights to what became Pearl Harbor.

Kalākaua died in San Francisco in 1891, shortly after recording a farewell address to his people on a newly invented Edison recording machine. In his absence, he had appointed his sister **Lili'uokalani** to serve as his regent, and she now became queen. When she proclaimed her desire for a new constitution, the same group of businessmen, who had now convened themselves into an "**Annexation Club**," called in the US warship *Boston*, then in Honolulu, and declared a provisional government. President Grover

Cleveland (a Democrat) responded that "Hawaii was taken possession of by the United States forces without the consent or wish of the government of the islands . . . [It] was wholly without justification . . . not merely a wrong but a disgrace." With phenomenal cheek, the provisional government rejected his demand for the restoration of the monarchy, saying the US should not "interfere in the internal affairs of their sovereign nation." They found defenders in the Republican US Congress, and declared themselves a **republic** on July 4, 1894, with **Sanford Dole** as their first President.

Following an abortive coup attempt in 1895, Lili'uokalani was charged with **treason**. She was placed under house arrest, first in 'Iolani Palace, and later at her Honolulu home of Washington Place (see p.53). Though she lived until 1917, hopes of a restoration of Hawaiian independence were dashed in 1897, when a Republican president, McKinley, came to office claiming "annexation is not a change. It is a consummation." The strategic value of Pearl Harbor was emphasized by the Spanish–American War in the Philippines, and on August 12, 1898, Hawaii was formally **annexed** as a territory of the United States.

A Territory and a State

At the moment of annexation there was no question of Hawaii becoming a state; the whites were outnumbered ten to one and had no desire to afford the rest of the islanders the protection of US labor laws, let alone to give them the vote. Furthermore, as the proportion of Hawaiians of Japanese descent (*nisei*) increased (to 25 percent by 1936), Congress feared the prospect of a state whose inhabitants might consider their primary allegiance to be to Japan. Consequently, Hawaii remained for the first half of the twentieth century the virtual fiefdom of the Big Five, who, through their control of agriculture (they owned 96 percent of the sugar crop), dominated transport, banks, utilities, insurance and government.

Things began to change during World War II. The Japanese bombing of Pearl Harbor, on December 7, 1941, detailed on p.92, meant that Hawaii was the only part of the United States to be attacked in the war, and it demonstrated just how crucial the islands were to the rest of America. Military bases and training camps were established throughout Hawaii, many of which remain operational to this day. In addition, Hawaiian troops played an active role in the war. Veterans of the much-decorated 442nd Regimental Combat Team – composed of Japanese Hawaiians and, for obvious reasons, sent to fight in Europe – became a leading force in Hawaiian politics for more than fifty years.

The main trend in Hawaiian history since the war has been the slow decline of agriculture and the rise of **tourism**. Strikes organized along ethnic lines in the sugar plantations had consistently failed in the past, but from 1937 on, labor leaders such as Jack Hill and Harry Bridges of the International Longshoremen's and Warehousemen's Union began to organize workers of all races and all crafts, in solidarity with mainland unions. In September 1946, the plantation workers won their first victory. Thanks to the campaigns that followed, the long-term Republican domination of state politics ended, and Hawaii's agricultural workers became the highest paid in the world. Arguably, this led to the eventual disappearance of all their jobs in the face of Third World competition; fifty years later almost all the sugar mills had closed.

Hawaii finally became the fiftieth of the United States in 1959, after a plebiscite showed a 17-to-1 majority in favor, with the only significant opposition coming from the few remaining native Hawaiians. **Statehood** coincided with the first jet flight to Hawaii, which halved the previous nine-hour flight time from California. These two factors triggered a boom in tourism – many visitors had had their first sight of Hawaii as GIs in the war – and also in migration from the mainland to Hawaii. As detailed on p.32, Waikīkī, has been repeatedly relandscaped and rebuilt to cope with its emergence as the main focus of the tourist industry.

Official figures showing the growth of the Hawaiian economy since statehood conceal a decline in living standards for many Hawaiians, with rises in consumer prices far outstripping rises in wages. Real estate prices in particular have rocketed, so that many islanders are obliged to work at two jobs, others end up sleeping on the beaches, and young Hawaiians emigrate in droves with no prospect of being able to afford to return.

The sovereignty movement

Since the late 1980s, broad-based support has mushroomed for the concept of **Hawaiian sovereignty**, meaning some form of restoration of the rights of native Hawaiians. Pride in the Polynesian past has been rekindled by such means as the voyages of the *Hōkule'a* canoe (see p.69), and the successful campaign to claim back the island of Kahoolawe, which had been used since the war as a Navy bombing range.

The movement has reached the point where everyone seems to expect that sovereignty is coming, but no one knows what form it will take. Of the three most commonly advanced models, one sees Hawaii as an independent nation once again, recognized by the international community, with full citizenship perhaps restricted either to those born in Hawaii or prepared to pledge sole allegiance to Hawaii. Another possibility would be the granting to native Hawaiians of nation-within-a-nation status, as with Native American groups on the mainland. Others argue that it would be more realistic to preserve the existing political framework within the context of full economic reparations to native Hawaiians.

Even the US government has formally acknowledged the illegality of the US overthrow of the Hawaiian monarchy with an official **Apology to Native Hawaiians** signed by President Clinton in November 1993. A separate but related problem, indicative of the difficulties faced in resolving this issue, is the failure by both federal and state governments to manage 200,000 acres set aside for the benefit of native Hawaiians in 1921. The state has now agreed to pay Hawaiians more than $100 million in compensation, though disputes remain over where the money will come from and to whom it will go.

The sovereignty issue attained such a high profile in 1998, thanks to the centenary of annexation, that it provoked something of a backlash among elements of the state's non-native (and particularly Caucasian) population. The Office of Hawaiian Affairs, the body responsible for looking after the interests of native Hawaiians and, potentially, distributing compensation, had long been run by a Board whose members were elected by voting among native Hawaiians only. In a landmark ruling in February 2000, the US Supreme Court declared such race-based elections to be unconstitutional; new elections later that year were open to all state residents and produced one new non-native Board member. Hawaiian activists fear that their movement is in jeopardy, with state programs liable to be dismantled by the courts. Nonetheless political support appears to remain strong for, at the very least, federal recognition of the status of native Hawaiians as being equivalent to that of native peoples elsewhere in the country, and US Senator Daniel Akaka of Hawaii has repeatedly introduced drafts of a bill to that end in Washington.

Ancient culture and society

No written record exists of the centuries between the arrival of the Polynesians and the first contact with Europeans. However, sacred chants, passed down through the generations, show a history packed with feuds and forays between the islands, and oral traditions provide a detailed picture of the day-to-day life of ordinary Hawaiians.

Developing a civilization on the most isolated islands in the world, without metals and workable clays, presented many challenges. Nevertheless, by the late eighteenth century, Hawaii was home to around a million people. Two hundred years later, the population has climbed back to a similar level, though its distribution is utterly different. The Big Island probably held several hundred thousand, and Maui perhaps 200,000, compared to around 100,000 each today, while Oahu, which formerly sheltered well under 100,000 inhabitants, now boasts around 900,000. Furthermore, virtually no pure-blooded Hawaiians remain, and the islands are not even close to being self-sufficient in terms of food.

Daily life

In a sense, ancient Hawaii had no economy, not even barter. Although then as now most people lived close to the coast, each island was organized into wedge-shaped land divisions called ahupua'a, stretching from the ocean to the mountains. The abundant fruits of the earth and sea were simply shared among the inhabitants within each *ahupua'a*.

There's some truth in the idea of pre-contact Hawaii as a leisured paradise, but it had taken a lot of work to make it that way. Coconut palms had to be planted along the seashore to provide food, clothing and shade for coastal villages, and bananas and other food plants distributed inland. Crops such as sugar cane were cultivated with the aid of complex systems of terraces and irrigation channels. *Taro*, whose leaves were eaten as "greens" and whose roots were mashed to produce *poi*, was grown in the windward valleys.

Most **fishing** took place in shallow inshore waters. Fish-hooks made from human bone were believed to be especially effective; the most prized hooks of all were made from the bones of chiefs who had no body hair, so those unfortunate individuals were renowned for their low life expectancy. Nets were never cast from boats, but shallow bays might be dragged by communal groups of wading men drawing in *hukilau* nets (Elvis did it in *Blue Hawaii*, and you occasionally see people doing it today). In addition, the art of **aquaculture** – fish-farming – was more highly developed in Hawaii than anywhere in Polynesia.

Ordinary commoners – the **maka'āinana** – lived in simple windowless huts known as *hales*. Most of these were thatched with *pili* grass, though in the driest areas they didn't bother with roofs. Buildings of all kinds were usually raised on platforms of stone, using rounded boulders taken from river beds. Matting covered the floor, while the pounded tree bark called *kapa* (known as *tapa* elsewhere in the Pacific, and decorated with patterns) served as clothing and bedding. Lacking pottery, households made abundant use of gourds, wooden dishes and woven baskets.

The ruling class, the **ali'i**, stood at the apex of Hawaiian society. In theory, heredity counted for everything, and great chiefs demonstrated their fitness to rule by the length of their genealogies. In fact the *ali'i* were educated as equals, and chiefs won the very highest rank largely through physical prowess and force of personality. To hang on to power, the king had to be seen to be devoutly religious and to treat his people fairly.

The most popular pastime was **surfing**. Ordinary people surfed on five- to seven-foot boards known as *alaia*, and also had *paipus*, the equivalent of the modern boogie board; only the *ali'i* used the thick sixteen-foot *olo* boards, made of dark oiled *wiliwili* wood. On land the *ali'i* raced narrow sleds on purpose-built, grass-covered *hōlua* slides and staged boxing tournaments.

Religion

It's all but impossible now to grasp the subtleties of ancient Hawaiian **religion**. So much depends on how the chants and texts are translated; if the word *akua* is interpreted as meaning "god," for example, historians can draw analogies with Greek or Hindu legends by speaking of a pantheon of battling, squabbling "gods" and "goddesses" with magic powers. Some scholars however prefer to translate *akua* as "spirit consciousness" – which might correspond to the soul of an ancestor – and argue that the antics of such figures are peripheral to a more fundamental set of attitudes regarding the relationship of humans to the natural world.

The **Kumulipo**, Hawaii's principal creation chant, has been preserved in full. It tells how after the emergence of the earth "from the source in the slime . . . [in] the depths

RELIGION

of the darkness," more complicated life forms developed, from coral to pigs, until finally men, women and "gods" appeared. Not only was there no Creator god, but the gods were much of a kind with humans. It took a hundred generations for Wākea, the god of the sky, and Papa, an earth goddess, to be born; they were the divine ancestors of the Hawaiian people.

Not all Hawaiians necessarily shared the same beliefs; different groups sought differing ways of augmenting their *mana*, or spiritual power. Only the elite *ali'i* may have paid much attention to the bloodthirsty warrior god Kū, while ordinary families, and by extension villages and regions, owed their primary allegiance to their personal *'aumākua* – a sort of clan symbol, possibly a totem animal such as a shark or owl, or a more abstract force, such as that embodied by Pele, the volcano goddess.

Spiritual and temporal power did not lie in the same hands, let alone in the same places. Hawaiian "priests" were known as **kahunas** ("men who know the secrets"), and were the masters of ceremonies at temples called **heiaus**. A *heiau* consisted of a number of separate structures set on a rock platform (*paepae*). These might include the *hale mana* ("house of spiritual power"), the *hale pahu* ("house of the drum") and the *anu'u* ("oracle tower"), from the top of which the *kahunas* conversed with the gods. Assorted *ki'i akua*, wooden images of different gods, stood on all sides, and the whole enclosure was fenced or walled off. In addition to the two main types of *heiau* – **luakinis**, dedicated to the war god Kū, which held *leles* or altars used for human sacrifice, and **māpeles**, peaceful temples to Lono, an errant former ruler of the Big Island who had become deified as patron of the annual *makahiki* (renewal) festival – there were also *heiaus* to such entities as Laka, goddess of the *hula*. Devotees of Pele, on the other hand, did not give their protectress formal worship at a *heiau*. Most *heiaus* were built for some specific occasion, and did not remain in constant use; the largest on Oahu was the **Puʻu O Mahuka Heiau**, overlooking Waimea Valley on the North Shore (see p.133).

Hawaiian religion in the form encountered by Cook was brought to the islands by the Tahitian warrior-priest Paʻao, who led the last great migration to Hawaii. Paʻao is also credited with introducing the complex system of **kapu** – the Hawaiian version of the Polynesian *tahu*, or *taboo* which circumscribed the daily lives of all Hawaiians. Some of its restrictions served to augment the power of the kings and priests, while others regulated domestic routine or attempted to conserve natural resources. Many had to do with food. Women were forbidden to prepare food or to eat with men; each husband was obliged to cook for himself and his wife in two separate ovens and to pound the *poi* in two distinct calabashes. The couple had to maintain separate houses, as well as a *Hale Noa*, where a husband and wife slept together. Women could not eat pork, bananas or coconuts, or several kinds of fish. Certain fish could only be caught in specified seasons, and a *koa* tree could only be cut down once two more were planted in its place.

No one could tread on the shadow of a chief; the highest chiefs were so surrounded by *kapus* that some would go out only at night. The ruling chiefs did not necessarily possess the highest spiritual status. One of Kamehameha's wives was so much his superior that he could only approach her naked and on all fours.

The only crime in ancient Hawaii was to break a *kapu*, and the only punishment was death. It was possible for an entire *ahupuaʻa* to break a *kapu* and incur death, but that penalty was not always exacted. One way guilty parties could avoid execution was by hotfooting it to a *puʻuhonua*, or "place of refuge."

Books

An extraordinary number of books have been written about Hawaii and all matters Hawaiian, though you're likely to come across most of them only on the islands themselves. Honolulu bookstores are listed on p.212.

Unless otherwise specified, all the publishers below are based in the US.

History

Gavan Daws, *Shoal of Time* (University of Hawaii Press). Definitive if dry single-volume history of the Hawaiian Islands, tracing their fate from European contact to statehood.

Greg Dening, *The Death of William Gooch* (University of Hawaii Press). Elaborate anthropological and metaphysical speculations spun around the 1792 murder of three European sailors in Oahu's Waimea Valley.

Michael Dougherty, *To Steal a Kingdom: Probing Hawaiian History* (Island Style Press). An eccentric and entertaining look at Hawaiian history, which focuses on the famous names of the nineteenth century and pulls no punches.

Bob Dye (ed), *Hawaii Chronicles* (University of Hawaii Press). A collection of entertaining short essays on little-known aspects of Hawaiian history, culled from *Honolulu* magazine.

Glen Grant, *Waikīkī Yesteryear* (Mutual Publishing). Short but well-illustrated history of Hawaii's premier playground.

Liliʻuokalani, *Hawaii's Story by Hawaii's Queen* (Mutual Publishing). Autobiographical account by the last monarch of Hawaii of how her kingdom was taken away. Written in 1897 when she still cherished hopes of a restoration.

Jeannette Peek, *Stepping Into Time* (Mutual Publishing). Attractively presented volume of historical accounts of Honolulu's major landmarks, ably illustrated by the author.

Gordon W. Prange, *At Dawn We Slept* and *The Verdict of History* (Penguin). Definitive best-selling analysis of the attack on Pearl Harbor. Over two volumes, Prange exhaustively rebuts revisionist conspiracy theories.

A. Grenfell Price (ed), *The Explorations of Captain James Cook in the Pacific* (Dover). Selections from Cook's own journals, including entries about his first landfall on Kauai and his ill-fated return to the Big Island.

Luis I. Reyes, *Made in Paradise* (Mutual Publishing). Lovingly prepared coffee-table history of how Hollywood has depicted Hawaii, with some great illustrations.

Ronald Takaki, *Pau Hana* (University of Hawaii Press). Moving history of life on the sugar plantations, and the trials experienced by generations of immigrant laborers.

Ancient Hawaii

Nathaniel B. Emerson, *Unwritten Literature of Hawaii – The Sacred Songs of the Hula* (Charles E. Tuttle Co). Slightly dated account of ancient Hawaii's most important art form. Published in 1909, its wealth of detail ensures that it remains required reading for all students of the *hula*.

Samuel M. Kamakau, *The People of Old* (Bishop Museum Press, three vols). Anecdotal essays, published in Hawaiian as newspaper articles in the 1860s. Packed with fascinating information, they provide a compendium of Hawaiian oral traditions. Kamakau's longer *Ruling Chiefs of Hawaii* (Bishop Museum Press) details all that is known of the deeds of the kings.

Patrick Kirch, *Feathered God and Fishhooks* and *Legacy of the Past* (both University of Hawaii Press). The former is the best one-volume account of ancient Hawaii, though non-specialists may find the minutiae of specific archeological digs hard going. The latter is an excellent guide to specific Hawaiian sites.

David Malo, *Hawaiian Antiquities* (Bishop Museum Press). Nineteenth-century survey of culture and society, written by a Maui native who was brought up at the court of Kamehameha the Great.

Contemporary Hawaii

Michael Kioni Dudley and Keoni Kealoha Agard, *A Call for Hawaiian Sovereignty* (Nā Kāne O Ka Malo, two vols). The first of these short books attempts to reconstruct the world view of the ancient Hawaiians; the second is the clearest imaginable account of their dispossession.

Randall W. Roth (ed), *The Price of Paradise* (Mutual Publishing, two vols). Assorted experts answer questions about life and society in Hawaii in short essays that focus on economic and governmental issues. Of most interest to local residents or prospective migrants, but a useful introduction to ongoing island debates, which sadly has now become somewhat dated.

Haunani Kay Trask, *From A Native Daughter: Colonialism and Sovereignty in Hawaii* (University of Hawaii Press). A stimulating and impressive contribution to the sovereignty debate, from one of Hawaii's best-known activists.

Travelers' tales

Isabella Bird, *Six Months in the Sandwich Islands* (University of Hawaii Press). The enthralling adventures of an Englishwoman in the 1870s, whose escapades on the Neighbor Islands are interspersed with acute observations of the Honolulu social scene.

James Macrae, *With Lord Byron at the Sandwich Islands in 1825* (Petroglyph Press). Short pamphlet of extracts from the diary of a Scottish botanist, including descriptions of Honolulu as a small village and the first-known ascent of Mauna Kea.

Andy Martin, *Walking on Water* (Minerva, UK). An English journalist attempts to immerse himself in the surfing culture of Oahu's North Shore.

Robert Louis Stevenson, *Travels in Hawaii* (University of Hawaii Press). The Scottish novelist spent several months in Hawaii in the late nineteenth century, and struck up a close friendship with King David Kalākaua.

Mark Twain, *Letters from Hawaii* (University of Hawaii Press). Colorful and entertaining accounts of nineteenth-century Hawaii; much of the best material was reworked for inclusion in *Roughing It* (Penguin, UK and US).

Hawaii in fiction

Herman Melville, *Typee* (Penguin). Largely set in the Marquesas Islands, but with echoes of his time in Hawaii, Melville's wildly romanticized version of the South Seas – originally published as nonfiction – makes a perfect escapist read.

W. S. Merwin, *The Folding Cliffs* (Alfred Knopf). A compelling, visually evocative blank-verse retelling – in more than three hundred pages – of the story of Koolau the Leper, by one of America's leading contemporary poets.

James Michener, *Hawaii* (Random House). Another romanticized romp, whose success was a major factor in the growth of Hawaiian tourism.

Paul Theroux, *Hotel Honolulu* (Houghton Mifflin US, Hamish Hamilton UK). This funny and very entertaining slice of reportage brilliantly captures the flavor of life in Oahu, packed with tourists passing through as well as local characters; there's even a cameo appearance from Iz himself (see p.201).

Richard Tregaskis, *The Warrior King* (Falmouth Press). This fictionalized biography of Kamehameha the Great serves as a readable introduction to a crucial period in Hawaiian history.

Kathleen Tyau, *A Little Too Much is Enough* (Farrar, Straus & Giroux US, The Women's Press UK). Atmospheric and amusing account of growing up as a Chinese-Hawaiian, with an appetizing emphasis on food.

Natural sciences

Gordon A. Macdonald and Agatin A. Abbott, *Volcanoes in the Sea* (University of Hawaii Press). Thorough technical examination – sadly not illustrated in color – of how fire and water have shaped the unique landscapes of Hawaii.

Frank Stewart (ed), *A World Between Waves* (Island Press). Stimulating collection of essays by authors such as Peter Matthiessen and Maxine Hong Kingston, covering all aspects of Hawaiian natural history.

Language

The Hawaiian language is an offshoot of languages spoken elsewhere in Polynesia, with slight variations that arose during the centuries when the islands had no contact with the rest of Polynesia. Among its most unusual features is the fact that there are no verbs "to be" or "to have," and that, although it has no word for "weather," it distinguishes between 130 types of rain and 160 types of wind.

Although barely two thousand people speak Hawaiian as their mother tongue, it remains a living language and has experienced a revival in recent years. While visitors to Hawaii are almost certain to hear Hawaiian-language songs, it's rarely spoken in public, and there should be no need to communicate in any language other than English. However, everyday conversations tend to be sprinkled with Hawaiian words, and you'll also spot them in many local place names.

The Hawaiian alphabet

Hawaiian became a written language only when a committee of missionaries gave it an alphabet. The shortest in the world, it consists of just twelve letters – *a*, *e*, *h*, *i*, *k*, *l*, *m*, *n*, *o*, *p*, *u*, and *w* – plus two punctuation marks. When the missionaries were unable to agree on the precise sounds of the language, they simply voted on which letter to include – thus *k* beat *t*, and *l* beat *r*.

Hawaiian may look hard to **pronounce**, but in fact with just 162 possible syllables – as compared to 23,638 in Thai – it's the least complicated on earth. The letters *h, l, m* and *n* are pronounced exactly as in English; *k* and *p* are pronounced approximately as in English but with less aspiration; *w* is like the English *v* after an *i* or an *e*, and the English *w* after a *u* or an *o*. At the start of a word, or after an *a, w* may be pronounced like a *v* or a *w*.

The **glottal stop** (') creates the audible pause heard in the English "oh-oh." Words without macrons (¯) to indicate stress are pronounced by stressing alternate syllables working back from the penultimate syllable. Thanks to the frequent repetition of syllables, this is usually easier than it may sound. "Kamehameha," for example, breaks down into the repeated pattern *Ka–meha–meha*, pronounced *Ka–mayha–mayha*.

a	*a as in above*	*ē*	*ay as in day*
e	*e as in bet*	*ī*	*ee as in bee*
i	*γ as in pity*	*ō*	*o as in hole (but slightly*
o	*o as in hole*		*longer)*
u	*u as in full*	*ū*	*oo as in moon*
ā	*a as in car*		

Note that, strictly speaking, the word Hawaii should be written Hawai'i, with the glottal stop to show that the two "i"s are pronounced separately. However, this book follows the convention that words in common English usage are written without their Hawaiian punctuation. Maui itself is unique among the islands in that its correct name features neither a macron nor a glottal stop, while all the other island names – Hawaii, Oahu, Kauai, and so on – appear in their familiar English form.

Glossary

'A'ā rough lava

Ahupua'a basic land division, a "slice of cake" from ocean to mountain

'Āina land, earth

Akua god, goddess, spirit, idol

Ali'i chief, chiefess, noble

Aloha love; hello; goodbye.

'Aumākua personal god or spirit; totem animal

Hala tree (pandanus, screw pine)

Halāu long house used for *hula* instruction; also a *hula* group

Hale house, building

Hana work

Haole (white) non-native Hawaiian, whether foreign or American resident

Hapa half, as in *hapa haole*, or half-foreign

Hāpu'u tree fern

Heiau ancient place of worship

Honua land, earth

Hui group, club

Hula dance/music form (*hula 'auana* is a modern form, *hula kahiko* is traditional)

Imu pit oven

Kahuna priest(ess) or someone particularly skilled in any field; *kahuna nui* chief priest

Kai sea

Kālua to bake in an *imu* (underground oven)

Kama'āina Hawaiian from another island; state resident

Kāne man

Kapa the "cloth" made from pounded bark, known elsewhere as *tapa*

Kapu forbidden, taboo, sacred

Kaukau food

Keiki child

Kiawe thorny tree, mesquite

Ki'i temple image or petroglyph

Koa dark hardwood tree

Kōkua help

Kona leeward (especially wind)

Lānai balcony, terrace, patio

Lau leaf

Lehua *or* **'Ōhi'a Lehua** native red-blossomed shrub/tree

Lei garland of flowers, feathers, shells or other material

Liliko'i passion fruit

Limu seaweed

Lomi Lomi massage or raw salmon dish

Luakini temple of human sacrifice

Lū'au traditional Hawaiian feast

Mahalo thank you

Makai direction: away from the mountain, towards the sea

Malihini newcomer, visitor

Mana spiritual power

Mauka direction: away from the sea, towards the mountain

Mele ancient chant

Menehune in legend, the most ancient Hawaiian people, supposedly dwarfs

Mu'umu'u long loose dress

Nēnē Hawaiian goose – the state bird

Nui big, important

'Ohana family

'Ōhelo sacred red berry

'Ōhi'a Lehua see *lehua*

'Ono delicious

'Ō'ō yellow-feathered bird

'Ōpae shrimp

Pāhoehoe smooth lava

Pali sheer-sided cliff

Paniolo Hawaiian cowboy

Pau finished

Pili grass, used for thatch

Poi staple food made of *taro* root

Poke raw fish dish

Pua flower, garden

Pūpū snack

Pu'u hill, lump

Taro Hawaiian food plant

Tsunami tidal wave

Tūtū grandparent, general term of respect

Wahine woman

Wai water

Wikiwiki hurry, fast

INDEX

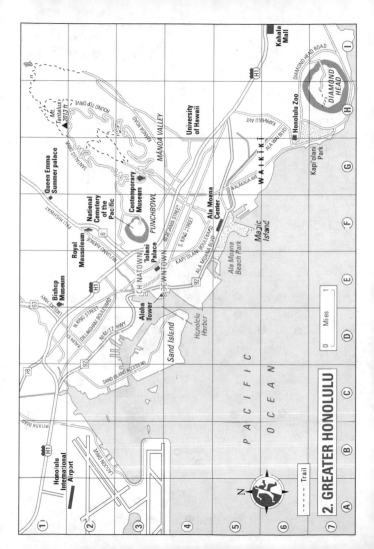

2. GREATER HONOLULU

- - - - - Trail

0 — 1 Miles

PACIFIC OCEAN

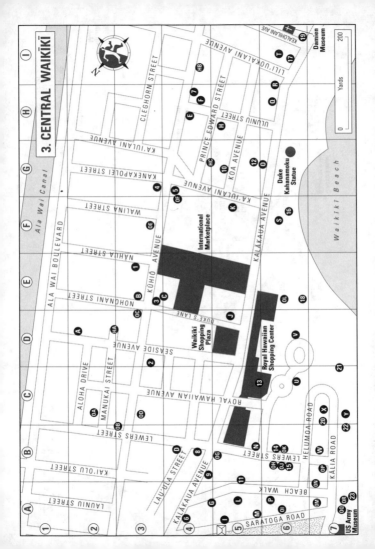

Ala Wai Canal

LAUNIU STREET
KAI'OLU STREET
LEWERS STREET
LAU'ULA STREET
NOHONANI STREET
NAHUA STREET
WALINA STREET
KANEKAPOLEI STREET
CLEGHORN STREET

ALA WAI BOULEVARD

SEASIDE AVENUE
MANUKAI STREET
ALOHA DRIVE

KA'IULANI AVENUE
PRINCE EDWARD STREET
ULUNIU STREET
LILI'UOKALANI AVENUE

KŪHIŌ AVENUE

KOA AVENUE

KA'IULANI AVENUE

ROYAL HAWAIIAN AVENUE

KALAKAUA AVENUE

DUKE'S LANE

International Marketplace

Waikīkī Shopping Plaza

Royal Hawaiian Shopping Center

HELUMOA ROAD

KĀLIA ROAD

SARATOGA ROAD

BEACH WALK

KALAKAUA AVENUE

Duke Kahanamoku Statue

Waikīkī Beach

US Army Museum

Damien Museum

KEALOHILANI AVE

0   Yards   200

N

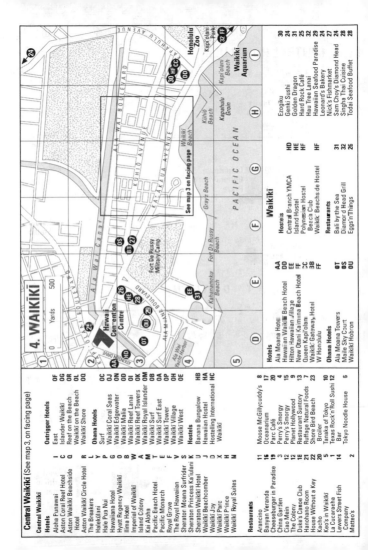

4. WAIKĪKĪ

Central Waikīkī (See map 3, on facing page)

Central Waikīkī

Hotels

Aloha Punawai	I
Aston Coral Reef Hotel	C
Aston Waikīkī Beachside Hotel	Q
Aston Waikīkī Circle Hotel	R
The Breakers	L
Halekūlani	Y
Hale Pua Nui	P
Hawaiiana Hotel	G
Hyatt Regency Waikīkī	O
Ilima Hotel	B
Imperial of Waikīkī	N
Island Colony	A
Kai Aloha	M
Pacific Beach Hotel	T
Pacific Monarch	E
The Royal Hawaiian	F
Royal Grove	S
Sheraton Moana Surfrider	U
Sheraton Princess Ka'iulani	J
Sheraton Waikīkī Hotel	D
Waikīkī Joy	X
Waikīkī Parc	H
Waikīkī Prince	M

Outrigger Hotels

East	OF
Islander Waikīkī	OG
Reef on the Beach	OR
Waikīkī on the Beach Hotel	OL
Waikīkī Shore	OQ

Ohana Hotels

Surf	OC
Waikīkī Coral Seas	OJ
Waikīkī Edgewater	OD
Waikīkī Malia	OO
Waikīkī Reef Lanai	OI
Waikīkī Reef Towers	OK
Waikīkī Royal Islander	OM
Waikīkī Surf	OB
Waikīkī Surf East	OA
Waikīkī Tower	OP
Waikīkī Village	OH
Waikīkī West	OE

Hostels

Banana Bungalow	HB
Hawaiian Hostel	HA
Hostelling International Waikīkī	HC

Restaurants

Arancino	11
Banyan Veranda	16
Cheeseburger in Paradise	19
China Garden	3
Ciao Mein	15
The Colony	12
Duke's Canoe Club	18
Hanohano Room	13
House Without a Key	23
Kacho	20
Keo's Waikīkī	5
La Cucaracha	14
Lewers Street Fish Company	
Matteo's	2
Moose McGillycuddy's	8
Oceanarium	17
Parc Café	20
Perry's Smorgy	4
Perry's Smorgy	9
Planet Hollywood	
Restaurant Suntory	12
Ruffage Natural Foods	21
Shore Bird Beach Broiler	22
Tanaka of Tokyo	10
Texas Rock'n'Roll Sushi Bar	12
Tokyo Noodle House	6

Waikīkī

Hotels

Ala Moana Hotel	AA
Hawaiian Waikīkī Beach Hotel	DD
Hilton Hawaiian Village	EE
New Otani Kaimana Beach Hotel	FF
Queen Kapi'olani	CC
Waikīkī Gateway Hotel	BB
W Honolulu	FF

Ohana Hotels

Ala Moana Towers	OT
Maile Sky Court	OS
Waikīkī Hobron	OU

Hostels

Central Branch YMCA	HD
Island Hostel	HE
Polynesian Hostel Beccia Club	HF
Waikīkī Beachs de Hostel	HF

Restaurants

Bali by the Sea	31
Diamond Head Grill	32
Eggs'n'Things	26
Ezogiku	30
Genki Sushi	24
Golden Dragon	31
Hard Rock Café	25
Hau Tree Lanai	32
Hawaiian Seafood Paradise	29
Leonard's Bakery	29
Nick's Fishmarket	27
Sam Choy's Diamond Head	24
Singha Thai Cuisine	24
Todai Seafood Buffet	28

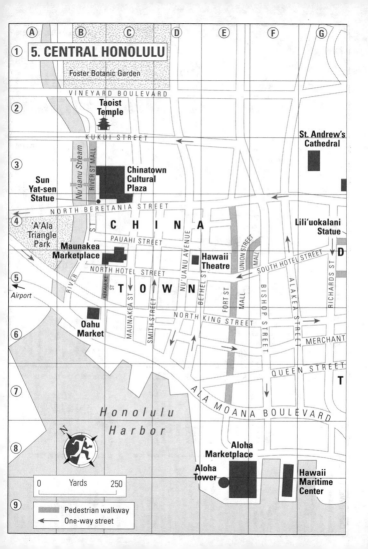

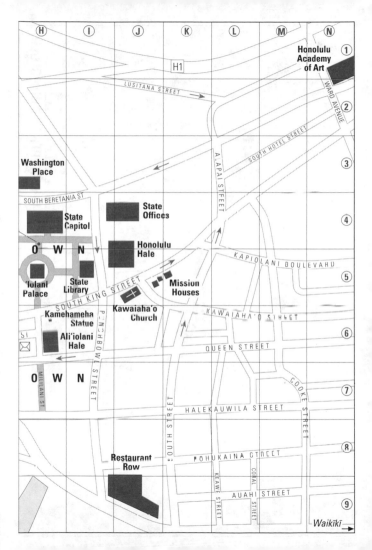

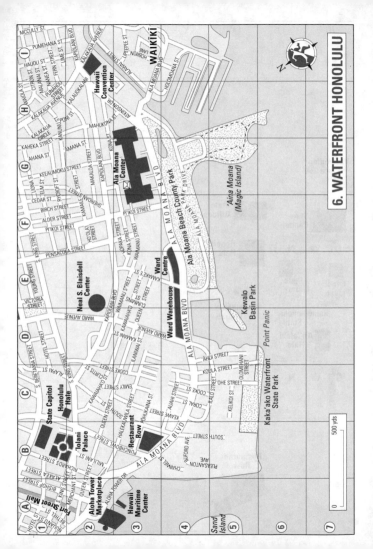

6. WATERFRONT HONOLULU

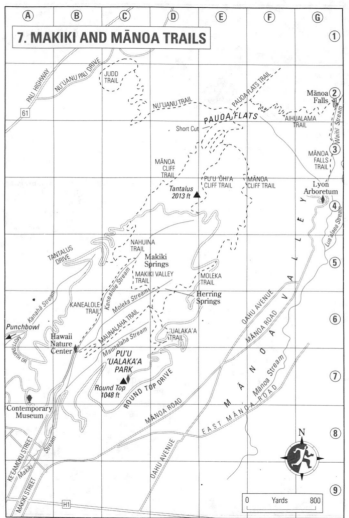

7. MAKIKI AND MĀNOA TRAILS

A B C D E F G

PALI HIGHWAY

NU'UANU PALI DRIVE

JUDD TRAIL

61

NU'UANU TRAIL

PAUOA FLATS TRAIL

Mānoa Falls

Short Cut

PAUOA FLATS

AIHUALAMA TRAIL

MĀNOA CLIFF TRAIL

PU'U 'ŌHI'A CLIFF TRAIL

MĀNOA CLIFF TRAIL

MĀNOA FALLS TRAIL

Tantalus 2013 ft

Lyon Arboretum

Waihī Stream

Lua'alaea Stream

TANTALUS DRIVE

NAHUINA TRAIL

Makiki Springs

Kanahā Stream

Kanealole Stream

MAKIKI VALLEY TRAIL

MOLEKA TRAIL

MĀNOA VALLEY

KANEALOLE TRAIL

Moleka Stream

Herring Springs

OAHU AVENUE

MĀNOA ROAD

Punchbowl

MAUNALAHA TRAIL

'UALAKA'A TRAIL

Mānoa Stream

Hawaii Nature Center

Maunalaha Stream

PU'U 'UALAKA'A PARK

ROUND TOP DRIVE

Round Top 1048 ft

MĀNOA ROAD

EAST MĀNOA ROAD

Contemporary Museum

OAHU AVENUE

KE'EAUMOKU STREET

Makiki Stream

MAKIKI STREET

H1

N

0 Yards 800

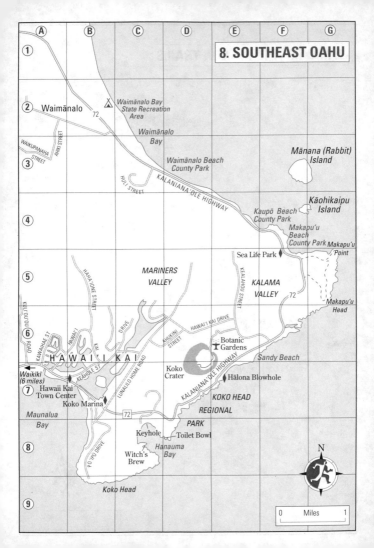

8. SOUTHEAST OAHU

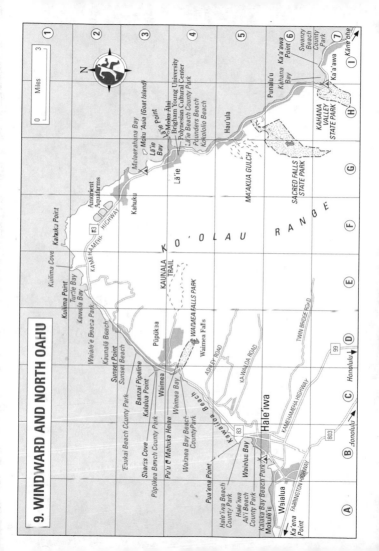

9. WINDWARD AND NORTH OAHU

0 Miles 3

N

Kāne ohe →

① ② ③ ④ ⑤ ⑥ ⑦

Ⓐ Ⓑ Ⓒ Ⓓ Ⓔ Ⓕ Ⓖ Ⓗ

KO'OLAU RANGE

Kahuku Point
Kuilima Cove
Kuilima Point
Turtle Bay
Kawela Bay
'Ehukai Beach County Park
Waiale'e Beach Park
Kaunala Beach
Sunset Point
Sunset Beach
Banzai Pipeline
Kalalua Point
Sharks Cove
Pūpūkea Beach County Park
Pūpūkea
Waimea
Pu'u e Mahuka Heiau
Waimea Bay
Waimea Bay County Park
Waimea Falls
Kawailoa Beach
Pua'ena Point
Hale'iwa Beach County Park
Hale'iwa
Hale'iwa Ali'i Beach County Park
Kaiaka Bay Beach Park
Mokulē'ia
Waialua
Ka'ena Point
FARRINGTON HIGHWAY

KAMEHAMEHA HIGHWAY
KAMEHAMEHA HIGHWAY

Amorient Aquafarms
Kahuku

KAUNALA TRAIL
WAIMEA FALLS PARK

ASHLEY ROAD
KA WALOA ROAD
TWIN BRIDGE ROAD

Honolulu →
Honolulu ↓
Honolulu →

99
803
83
83
83

Melaerahana Bay
Maku 'Auia (Goat Island)
Lā'ie Point
Lā'ie Bay
Moku 'Aki
Brigham Young University
Polynesian Cultural Center
Lā'ie Beach County Park
Pounders Beach
Kokololio Beach
Lā'ie
Hau'ula

MA'AKUA GULCH

SACRED FALLS STATE PARK

Punalu'u
Kahana Bay
Ka'a'awa Point
Swanzy Beach County Park
KAHANA VALLEY STATE PARK
Ka'a'awa

"The ———— ————————— said, —————— —————————

"Let them. It will keep them from all manner of foolishness on the trail." Lily glanced at her hand, still captured by his, and then at her skillet. "The turnovers will burn."

Jack didn't care. He wanted to pull her into his lap, bend her over his arm and kiss those red lips.

"Jack. Let go."

He did, and she went about as if nothing had happened. But her cheeks flushed and her nostrils flared as they had when they had climbed that final slope. So, the brief encounter rattled her, as well. It was both disquieting and satisfying to know that he was not alone in his desire.

***

Gold Rush Groom
Harlequin® Historical #1055—September 2011

JENNA
GOLD RUSH GROOM
KERNAN

TORONTO NEW YORK LONDON
AMSTERDAM PARIS SYDNEY HAMBURG
STOCKHOLM ATHENS TOKYO MILAN MADRID
PRAGUE WARSAW BUDAPEST AUCKLAND

ISBN-13: 978-0-373-29655-2

GOLD RUSH GROOM

Dedication

With love and gratitude to my prospecting partner
and husband who understands that
what matters is not the treasure, but the hunt.

Author Note

I'm so excited to bring you a story set during the Yukon gold rush. Some of you know that gold prospecting is a hobby of mine and I've hunted from North Carolina to Alaska. I've learned how alluring and elusive gold can be and that surprising things often happen when out on an adventure. In my case that has included keeping a watchful eye out for copperheads while dredging in a North Carolina river and being startled by a bull moose while prospecting in the Brooks Mountain Range.

In this story, Jack Snow, a greenhorn prospector, discovers too late that his steamer ticket does not include transport of his goods from the waterline to the shore. This one unforeseen circumstance nearly costs him everything. He is rescued from disaster by Lily Shanahan, a singer determined to find a partner to get her to Dawson City.

I hope you fall in love with Lily and Jack as you share their dangerous journey.

For more about Jack and Lily please visit me on the web and check out my Story Behind the Story section at www.jennakernan.com.

And, as always, enjoy the adventure!

Chapter One

Dyea, Alaska, Fall 1897

Who among them might be willing to accept an unconventional arrangement? From her vantage point on the muddy beach, Lily Shanahan eyed the newly arrived greenhorns, fresh from the steamer just arrived from Seattle. She knew the wrong choice would mean the end for her, for God only knew the journey to Dawson was perilous, especially now that the freeze-up had begun.

The ship had set anchor far out in the Taiya Inlet to avoid the bore tide that now rushed down the narrow passage. Trapped between the mountains, the water surged forward in long curling waves, hurling the overloaded scows toward the mudflats. The men clung to the gunwales, their faces grim and their eyes wide.

She had seen many arrive this way and depart for the goldfields soon afterward, while she had remained anchored like a rock in a stream. Lily had stopped asking the best candidates. They were not stupid or desperate enough to take her. That left only the ones with obvious flaws. So far they had turned her down as well.

Lily heard her mother's voice as clearly as she had on that final day her mother died. *Sell it all, right down to the sheets I'm lying on and have yourself a life worth remembering.*

And what could be more memorable than joining the mad pulsing rush of stampeders pouring north on the way to the goldfields? But somehow she didn't think her mother had intended her to be marooned by circumstance in these stinking mudflats.

How could she have known, when she spent her last dollar for her ticket, that Dawson City was five hundred miles inland, over mountains and down rivers, a place so wild there were no roads or trains, not even a telegraph? How could she have guessed that it was a journey she could not make alone?

So her search for a partner began. But after nearly a month in this swamp, hauling freight from the muddy beach to the tent town with her dog cart, she'd made a tidy bankroll and had been turned down more times than she could count. Lily longed to be in Dawson by the spring break-up. It was October now, and already the winds blew colder than January in

San Francisco. Would she even see Dawson by next summer?

The first boat scraped up on the mud, beaching as the wave dissipated. The next one rolled in ten feet behind. She knew what would happen next. The poor men would lose everything to the greedy water, while the rich ones would buy protection, paying whatever the haulers demanded to move their precious goods to high ground.

Lily chose potential customers with care, seeking a possible match. Her huge Newfoundland mix, Nala, and her small cart could not handle the larger loads.

Most of the men climbed over the sides into knee-high surf, sucking in their breaths or swearing as the icy water bit through their clothing. The first had just reached the wet mud when the crew began tossing their belongings out like so much rubbish.

One man clutched a single valise, his eyes wide with terror. A wave caught the boat as he tried to jump and fell into the sea. Lily held her breath as he disappeared beneath the crashing water. The oarsman used the paddle to nudge the submerged man toward shore. He came up sputtering and lost his grip on the bag. The tide cast it far past him and then dragged it back before he could wipe the stinging seawater from his eyes. The next wave knocked him down again, but brought his case close to her. Lily lifted her skirts and plucked the soggy suitcase from the surf, hauling it out of harm's way. Nala whined, unhappy when her mistress ventured too close to the sea.

"It's all right, girl." She righted the case and stooped to pat her dog. "Maybe this one will take me."

The man crawled up on the mudflats, spitting up seawater. She had to admit he was a scrawny fellow, but beggars could not be choosers. She felt winter's fast approach like a killing frost. She must get through the pass before the real cold came.

She waited for the man to straighten. He looked even more poorly prepared for Dyea than she had been. He reached for his bag.

"Thanks, missus. You sure saved me."

"You need a cart?" she asked.

"No, missus. I only got this here." He clutched the handle, showing her the suitcase she'd rescued.

"How about a partner?"

"You know a man looking?"

"*I'm* looking."

The little pipsqueak actually had the audacity to laugh.

"Oh, now, I might just as well tie an anvil round my neck as try and haul a woman to Dawson."

She scowled, until she noticed him shivering.

"Camp's that way." She thumbed over her shoulder toward the dunes, beyond which a tent city grew in the mud like mushrooms on a rotting log.

Lily gathered her flagging confidence.

"Come on, Nala."

She picked up several fares and collected her fees. Her purse had never been so large. But her adventure lay over the passes. *A life worth living,* her mother had said, but what had she meant? Lily wasn't sure; death had taken her before she could ask.

Lily lifted her collar against the cold wind that blew off the water. If she made it to Dawson City, would she have enough stories to fill her up like a pitcher of milk, with warm memories and satisfaction?

Stories to tell her children and grandchildren. Lily smiled.

Did you know your old granny once climbed the Chilkoot Pass?

"Did you know she failed and had to go home with her tail between her legs?" Lily pressed her lips together and shook her head. No, she wouldn't.

She lifted her chin and scanned the passengers in the next dinghy hoping, praying for a chance to do as she had promised.

The boat grounded and newcomers scrambled overboard trying vainly to avoid a soaking in icy water. Most had little in the way of property and scampered up the beach like crabs—all except one man. He remained in the punishing surf accepting box after box from the oarsman and tossing them, one after another, the eight-foot distance to the shore.

The undertow should have taken him off his feet, but somehow he held his position.

Lily measured him with her gaze. His clothing looked new and expensive. She judged him to be one of the idle rich who came north out of boredom, unlike those who were driven here by desperate circumstances. He had more gear than any other passenger on the beach. A rich fool, then, with no notion of what to pack and what to leave. Probably had his bloody silver tea service in one of those crates. She hated him on sight, for hadn't she worked sixteen-hour days for men just like this one? But no more. Now she answered only to herself. Her mother would like that.

She expected Pete to cut in front of her, offering his mule team to haul the dandy's gear, but he was far down the beach attending the three launches that had arrived just before this one.

The dandy was all hers. Anticipation coiled in her belly, as she fixed her eyes on the dark-haired man like a hungry rat eyeing an apple core.

She stepped closer. He certainly was big, with none of the flab she associated with men who could afford to eat regularly. She glanced at his hands, noting their size and substance. His shoulders were more than just wide; they seemed to be hung with some quantity of useful muscle. Did he get them boxing in some men's club?

He had secured the load on shore, but now the

next waves shot over his boots to lap at the mountain of cargo, lifting two large crates and dragging them back into the water. He caught both and easily hauled them back to safety. She noted the bulging muscles beneath his fancy new coat as well as the power and agility with which he moved. She estimated the distance of the high-tide line and the speed of the current.

He'd never save it all—not alone anyway. What was in those boxes? Would he do anything to save them?

He looked strong enough, but stamina was needed as well and a drive born from the fear that rich men lacked. A man foolish enough to come here with this many boxes might be foolish enough to accept her offer.

She took a definitive step toward him and then pulled herself up short. What if he turned her down, too? Her cheeks burned with humiliation at the thought. It was one thing to be cast off by one of her own, quite another to be sent packing by this greenhorn dandy. She liked the term greenhorn, once someone had explained that it meant an inexperienced newcomer and compared the men to young animals with new, or green, horns.

He had not noticed her yet, intent as he was at singlehandedly bringing his belongings to high ground. He continued his frantic dance for many minutes, finally coming to complete stillness as he stared out at the inlet. He'd seen it now, the second wave of water reaching ten feet as it rushed toward him. His chin nearly touched his chest. Ah, now that was an expression she recognized—for hadn't she seen that look in the faces of so many hopeless men and women when the jobs dried up back there?

It was a rare thing to witness one of his class brought so low. She savored the moment.

He glanced up. Their eyes met and held. He recognized the truth now; that even he couldn't save it all. She would offer her services and see just what sort of a man fate had cast in her path. It wasn't the offer she wanted to make, but best to test the waters first. She stooped to pat Nala, who sat with her long pink tongue lolling.

Part of her hoped he would turn her down. But surely he couldn't tell by looking at her what she was or where she had come from. She wore fine clothing now and had paid good money for lessons to help eliminate the traces of her Irish heritage that had clung to her every word like cold porridge to a bowl.

Could he?

She set her jaw, gathering her courage. Her desperation eased the next step.

"Would you like help moving your belongings?" She had concentrated hard not to drop the *h* in help.

"*You're* a hauler?"

His clipped New England accent held no hint of the gentle brogue of the Irish. He managed his *h* effortlessly, while simultaneously adding a definite inflection of skepticism. She inclined her head, dignified as a queen.

She took in his black hair and a straight nose that spoke of a childhood which did not include being clouted in the face.

Lily fingered the bump at the bridge of her own nose then dropped her hand, suddenly very self-conscious. All the Shanahans were fighters. No shame in that.

She met his gaze, inhaling sharply at his soulful whiskey colored eyes. He wore no hat and his unruly hair brushed his wide brow. His skin glowed from the exertion with perfect good health. Why he was young, she realized, perhaps only twenty, the same age as Lily. Had his size made her think he was older? He held her gaze and for some reason she couldn't seem to breathe as he looked at her. Her gaze fixed on the curve of his upper lip, the twin lines upon his cheeks that flanked his mouth, the dark stubble that he'd likely scraped away before leaving the steamship this morning. His jaw was wide and the muscles looked strong as if he spent a good deal of his time clenching his teeth.

When she met his eyes again, she felt off-balance and slightly dizzy, as if she were the one who had been dashing in and out of the shifting waves.

The man was handsome as sin, but Lily forced herself to breathe, if a bit more quickly than customarily, for she'd not be caught gawking at him like a child at a candy store window.

"How much?" he asked.

This time she noticed that the rich timbre of his deep voice seemed to vibrate through her insides. She pressed a hand to her middle to gather her flagging resolve.

"I'm not interested in your money."

He frowned. Was he so used to buying everything he needed? She pushed back her indignation. No time for that now.

He quirked a brow, finally fixing her with those arresting eyes before taking the bait. "What would you have from me then?"

"I find myself in need of a partner to Dawson."

His jaw dropped and then he recovered himself and grinned.

"You're joking." He cocked his head. "Are you serious?"

"Deadly."

"Well, I rather think you would be a liability."

She didn't argue, but only glared at him as another three-foot wave beat against his legs, rocking his foundation.

"Well, you're a dark horse yourself, but I'm in a gambling mood."

His eyes widened at the insult. "You think *I'm* a liability? How so?"

How so? She wanted to smack the smug arrogance off his handsome face.

"A greenhorn dandy, with not enough sense to secure his own supplies. Did you think that servants lined the rivers here with the nuggets?"

He lifted his hands to stop her as another wave hit. Two crates smashed together, spilling wood shavings onto the mud.

"Not to worry," she called, "with luck that bore tide will drag you right back to Seattle."

That seemed to strike a nerve, for his face reddened.

A vicious wave crashed into his goods, washing away his indignation. He scrambled to keep hold of his possessions. The ten-foot tidal wave had made half the distance to the shore, rolling a hundred yards beyond the steamer. Lily hoped they had placed the vessel on a long line. She'd seen similar tides take down ships even larger than this one.

"Come, Nala." She placed a hand on her dog's harness and her hound rose.

"A trade," he offered, his voice tinged with desperation. "I have goods."

She turned away.

Damn him and his ten-dollar words. *Liability, my ass.* Doubtful he'd keep his word anyway. Few ever did. Lily gripped Nala's harness and started off. She had wasted enough time.

"Wait!"

She didn't, making him run after her.

He blocked her path, wet to the waist and panting with the exertion of keeping what was more than any one man had a right to hold.

"Be reasonable," he begged.

She laughed, making no attempt to hold down her brogue. "To hell with dat!"

Another wave hit, cresting her boots. It swept away one of his boxes, taking it too far for him to recover, but he tried, rushing into the surf to his knees, preparing to dive and then thought better of it. That showed some sense. Water this cold could cramp the muscles of even the strongest swimmer. She bet he could swim. Probably had private lessons in a pool in Newport. She had learned when her brother had thrown her off a pier one hot July afternoon.

She watched his shoulders droop.

"You need dat?" she called.

He glanced back. His entire face had changed. He looked like a man standing beside an open grave.

"I can't succeed without it."

"If you take me to Dawson, I'll get it fer ye."

He glanced at the box, already twenty yards out and drifting fast. He shook his head in bewilderment. "Yes. I will."

"*All* the way to Dawson?" she clarified.

"Yes!"

With speed born of practice, Lily released Nala's harness and pointed at the box. "Fetch, girl."

Nala barked excitedly and charged into the surf. The dog's webbed feet helped her swim and her thick oily coat seemed impervious to the icy water. Lily stood beside the man, watching her hound cut through the breakers like a black swan, reaching the crate and gripping the edge in her powerful jaws. Nala had it now and Lily knew she'd not let go. In only a few moments the dog had the box ashore and was dragging it over rock and mud with the determination of a St. Bernard making a rescue.

He turned to her, his smile bright with excitement and relief, pinning her with his whiskey eyes. She felt her stomach flutter for the second time. Sand clung to the wet fabric of his new clothing making it look dirty and worn. She took in his disheveled hair and wide flaring nostrils, and realized what was happening between them. Lily tamped down her rising desire. She'd sooner drink seawater than fall for a charmer.

So why did the hair on her neck rise up?

Nala barked excitedly, breaking their trance. The Newfoundland cross frolicked beside the rescued crate, justifiably proud of her accomplishment.

Lily's eyes narrowed on the man. "We have a deal?"

He nodded.

"And in return, I'll look out for you all I can, even after we hit Dawson."

He smiled indulgently, as if he thought a woman could be of little assistance, but offered his hand. She eyed it with suspicion. It was big and broad, the kind that could break a woman's jaw with a moment's carelessness. She pressed her lips together and extended her hand. Long fingers wrapped about hers, cold as seaweed, yet still her stomach fluttered as if just awakening from a long sleep. Lily stepped back from the threat she recognized too late. He felt it, too; she knew it from the new speculation now glittering in his startling eyes.

Suddenly her decision to cast her lot with this stranger seemed more dangerous than the trip to Dawson, because the menace he posed was far more immediate. She knew a man like this could cost her everything. Well, she'd not allow it. She drew herself up, resisting the pull between them as she moved to stand beside her dog even as she eyed him. This was the one she feared would come, the one her mother had warned her about, and she'd just convinced him to spend six months with her as his partner.

Chapter Two

Jack Snow rested one hand on the final crate and stared out at the water that had almost claimed his only chance. They had saved the lot. Together, and with her horse of a hound, they'd reached safety with all his equipment and tools intact. He had read about the tidal bores, of course, but that couldn't compare to riding the mountainous waves that heaved through the narrow inlet. He'd never imagined having to fight one. Now that he and all his goods were past the high-water mark, he stared a moment, finding the phenomenon fascinating. His father would love to see this!

That thought dashed Jack's exaltation as memories rolled in, relentless as any rising tide. There was no sense in looking back. If he was to be his own man, his future lay ahead.

The big dog whined, anxious to get under way. Jack glanced at the beast, happy for the distraction.

The black bitch was strong as any mule, she could swim better than a Labrador and in water as cold as an ice bath. He eyed the huge shaggy creature. How much weight could one dog pull?

The dog's mistress stepped beside her, grounding Jack's thoughts firmly in the here and now. Their eyes met.

Damn it to hell.

The permanence of their arrangement crept over him slowly like a thin layer of ice on a mill pond. He felt sick to his stomach as he thought of all the things that might happen to her while she was in his keeping. Another female in his care, the idea pressed down upon his shoulders, making it hard to breathe. But if he hadn't agreed, then what would become of the two he'd left behind? His carefully laid plans had already begun to crumble like old masonry. He thought he might be sick.

To provide for the two at home, he had to save his gear, and that meant there really was no choice at all. The little hellion had entrapped him as neatly as any spider. With luck, she'd find someone better and drop him like yesterday's news, just like his fiancée had done when she'd heard of his family's ruin.

Why hadn't the available information about the Yukon included something about this mayhem arrival? Jack had planned and studied, taking into account the cold, snow and ice, anticipated river travel and mountain-climbing. He had calculated his supplies and equipment with the excruciating exactitude of the mechanical engineer he had nearly become, taking in every eventuality but one. He had not, in his wildest dreams, imagined that the Pacific Coast Steamship Company would not have constructed a proper dock in Dyea on which to moor their vessel.

Sunk by unforeseen circumstances. Was he no wiser than his father, risking all on one wild venture?

Perhaps not, but he was stronger than his sire, for he'd not cut and run at the first sign of adversity. He might look the part of a dandy, as his new partner had assumed, but he was that man no longer. Circumstances had changed him. Now he needed to succeed just as badly as anyone here. More, in fact. Jack needed to seize the glimmering opportunity to restore what his father had lost—their good name, the respect of his peers, the ability to care for what was left of his family and the future that he still craved. He would reach that gold-bearing gravel in Eldorado Creek so he could try his invention, even if he had to carry this female all the way to Forty Mile.

He glanced at the woman—his partner—giving her a critical once-over. The lift of her pointed chin, the slight curve fixed upon her lips and the narrowing of her eyes made her look both beautiful and wary. No doubt she was trying to size him up as well. He knew she was surprisingly strong for one stricken with such a diminutive body, but she was still only a woman and so his physical and mental inferior. She stood motionless in her crimson coat. Her cuffs and hood were adorned with lush dark fur, possibly wolf. The tight fit showed her to be petite, curvaceous and trim, exactly the type of woman he'd like to bed, but not at all the kind he would choose as a traveling companion. The only thing about her that did not speak of feminine grace was the large Colt repeater strapped to her hip. It seemed impossibly large against her small frame as evidenced by the extra bore holes that kept the wide belt from sliding off her flaring hips. She wore it cinched at the narrowest part of her waist, entirely too high for a quick draw. He wondered if the ancient weapon even fired.

Jack raked both hands through his hair, stopping to cradle his head for a moment as he searched the beach for help. When his gaze finally returned it was to find her studying him.

The woman arrested him with her stunning blue eyes, framed by spiky dark lashes and raven brows that arched as she stared at him in silence. His arms dropped to his sides.

What was she doing here in the first place? Didn't she have family or friends to shelter her? A strong wind might blow her off the mountain.

Surely he could make her see reason. He knew

females had a knack for self-preservation and a proclivity to latch on to the best provider, at least that's what Nancy had done, returning his ring and taking up with Jonathan Martin as quickly after his father's death as propriety permitted. He was a good choice, all in all, with his family's mills lining the Connecticut River from Hartford to Springfield. Was this one like her? If so, he need only find her a better partner to be rid of her.

She leaned forward and he was unable to prevent himself from doing the same. She drew him to her as surely as a magnet draws iron and he could not resist her allure. Her voice was sultry and low, as her breath brushed his cheek like a summer breeze off the Narragansett Bay.

"Don't even think about reneging on our agreement."

He straightened, affronted by her accusation, until he realized he had been thinking that exactly. He'd made an agreement, given his word and yet here he was trying to wiggle out of the deal. He knew what his father would have done in similar circumstances and that made the choice easy.

He met the accusation in her gaze.

"I won't. I'm yours until Dawson."

She laughed. "That's fine then."

What could the little minx possibly think to do inland? She couldn't hope to be a miner—could she?

The work alone would kill her before the ice even froze to the river bottoms.

"What is there in Dawson for you?" he asked, considering that she might be more than she appeared, for here she was alone on a beach making her way without help. If the circumstances were reversed, could he have done as well? He gave her a grudging respect for her pluck.

"Adventure and gold, of course."

Why was he not surprised that she was after riches?

He narrowed his eyes on her, wondering what kind of a woman he had partnered with.

"Adventure?"

She nodded.

"But what will you do there?"

"I can sew or cook or sing. I've done all those and more to make my way here."

"A singer?"

Could he possibly have found a woman who would be more useless on the trail?

"Aren't you the sharp tack? Bet you graduated first in your class."

He hadn't graduated, though he'd been in line to be valedictorian. Likely be Francis Cobbler now. *No, don't think about those days, back when you had everything ahead of you, before the world crumbled beneath your feet.*

If she noticed his sour mood turning icy cold, she

gave no sign, merely laughed, a musical tinkling sound that made the muscles of his abdomen tighten.

"Gold is quite difficult to extract."

Her smile turned his insides to oatmeal. "Oh, there's more to life than gold. And anyway, I'll not starve." She placed a hand on her hip and smiled coquettishly. "And I've a life to live, if I can get over those fool mountains." She gave him a direct stare, reminding him without a word of the promise he had made. He'd never met a woman like her. And what was she talking about, life being more than gold? Obviously, but most of those here were not arriving for the fun of freezing in the passes. He could not figure her.

She gave him a questioning look, her sculpted brows lifting. "We will make it, won't we?"

He couldn't think when he looked at her. Why was he thinking about kissing her? Perhaps it was the nearly irresistible temptation of her raspberry-colored lips.

As the woman waited for some response, she rested her hand easily on the grip of her pistol as if it were a walking stick. Did she not expect him to uphold his end of the bargain? Well, he would.

He couldn't keep the growl from rumbling in his throat. "We'll make it."

That made her smile.

"Yes, we will." She stroked the black dog's head. The beast closed its eyes to savor her mistress's touch and Jack found himself suddenly and unreasonably jealous.

"I'm Jack Snow," he said.

"Lily Delacy Shanahan. And this," she indicated her hound, "is Nala." She nodded and then pressed both fists to her hips, regarding him as if he had just tracked mud onto her clean kitchen floor. "You're shivering."

Her expression was so dark he found himself resisting the urge to tremble, succeeding momentarily, before the jerking spasms sent his teeth knocking together again.

"Follow me." She tugged at the dog's harness and set the cart in motion.

"What about my things?"

She turned away from Jack and let loose an ear-splitting whistle, which brought a scrappy young man to her. "Watch these." She told him as she pressed something into his palm.

"You betcha," said the lad.

Lily looked back at him and then set off again, bringing less than half of his gear along. He stood for a minute torn between following and remaining with the rest of his belongings. Could this be an elaborate scheme to rob him?

In the end, his shivering got the better of him and he hurried to catch up. They followed a hard-packed trail up over the rocky beach. Everywhere, men stacked bags and boxes of their belongings. Some had even staked their tents right there where the rock met the scrappy willow. As they continued, the hum of eager conversation and shouted orders drowned out the crashing waves that had almost destroyed him.

The road widened as they crossed through the willows. Her dog strained to pull his things up the incline. Lily glanced back at him.

"Well? Push!"

He scowled, far more used to giving orders than taking them. But he did as she bade, and together, he and the hound managed to crest the rise. The dog received all of the praise, while he did not even gain a backward glance. He frowned, more at the realization that he wanted her attention than from the lack of it. That would not do. He refused to become bewitched by a little firebrand like this. He was stuck with her, but he didn't have to like it.

Ahead lay Dyea, a large tent city with stripped logs for street posts and only a few timber structures. Cold, dark mud turned the streets to quagmire and crept up the canvas that passed for buildings here. Some of the tents were large enough to hold a circus, but instead of sawdust and prancing white ponies, they held rows of rough-hewn tables with hungry men eating in makeshift restaurants. They passed Brackett's Trading Post, singular for its two stories and five glass windows, though no one had yet painted the exterior, which had already weathered to a dark gray. A steady stream of stampeders picked their way along with horses and mules. He wished he could trade places with any one of them.

Each of the tents had a stovepipe poking from the roof like the stem of an apple. He was glad he had one himself, a very light efficient stove that burned nearly five hours on just two split logs. Lily turned down this road and up the next until he was thoroughly lost in the maze of identical canvases.

She stopped before an unremarkable tent that looked hardly big enough for one, let alone two.

"This is it," she said.

He frowned.

"You're not much of a poker player, I imagine," she said.

He glanced at her, trying to understand the cryptic comment but she only laughed and patted him amiably on the shoulder, then began unloading his gear. She was so petit. How would she endure the journey? In a few moments they had his belongings stacked beside the tent flap.

"You have clothes in here?" She indicated the pile.

He stared in mute astonishment as he realized his duffel with all his personal belongings lay back with the unknown lad. He could not fathom the oversight. Jack needed to do better if he was to succeed. The Yukon would be no more forgiving than the banks back home had been. He gritted his clattering teeth.

There was no way to recapture what was lost. His only choice was to start again.

His mother disagreed. This expedition terrified her. She had told him that having lost her husband she could not bear the thought of losing her only son, as well. It pained him to worry her and he did fear what would become of them should he not return. Were it up to his mother, he'd be safe at home looking for a wife with a fortune. The thought turned his stomach. He would be his own man, despite the risks. Her latest telegram had reached him in Seattle, begging him to reconsider. He'd written that he was pressing on. He'd earn his fortune and return to have his pick of the New York debutants. He'd have his old life back or return like a whipped dog.

He looked up to find her staring at him.

She shook her head in dismay. "Go on in and strip out of those things. Take a blanket off my bed and heat the coffee. It's in the pot. You do know how to rake coals and start a fire?"

"Of course."

She made a harrumphing sound as if she did not believe it. It occurred to him suddenly that he might not be her ideal partner, either, though he could not see her objection. She turned the dog cart and stopped. "Leave the flap open or your crates will likely walk away on you. You have a pistol?"

"Not on me."

"I find they do more good when they are carried

in plain sight." She patted the handle of her Colt. "You're not at Yale now, college boy. There are thieves everywhere here."

With that she set the cart in motion, as he wondered if she were among the thieves. Was this even her tent?

"Princeton, actually."

She shrugged and continued on.

He shouted after her. "And how do you know I went to college?"

She called back without stopping. "Only an educated man would be fool enough to carry a crate of books to the Yukon. Might make good tinder, I suppose."

He looked at the broken crate, lid askew. On top lay his copy of *The Notebooks of Leonardo da Vinci*, edited by Jean Paul Richter. The woman acted as if it were a box of dumbbells or some other useless fodder.

Eventually his shivering forced him into retreat, but he kept the tent flap up. The woman was shrewd with the kind of knowledge that did not come from a classroom, he'd give her that.

The inside of her tent was much more spartan than he had anticipated. In his experience, women shared a pack rat's propensity for dragging home bits of glitter and fluff. Lily Delacy Shanahan's tent looked as if it belonged to a new cadet. Her bed was made with sharp corners. Her wood supply was ample and well away from the stove. She had a small, neat kitchen area all set up, including the coffeepot. He sloshed the contents and found it still half-full. Jack stoked the coals and added kindling, sighing in relief as the flames lapped around the slender branches. She had one crate beside the bed and a sack, sewn from a piece of canvas, hanging from a tent post. He shrugged at the oddness of her private quarters. His shivering made it difficult to unbutton his sodden coat. Jack's trembling fingers looked ghostly white from lack of blood as he wrestled with his sweater and flannel shirt. Then he peeled out of his union suit, bringing it down to his waist. Only when he was holding his soaked garments did he notice the clothesline stretched tight over the stove. He added *organized* to her list of attributes as he threw his things over the line and then held his hands out to the stove. It was no good. The shaking was worse and his skin was as puckered-up as a plucked chicken's. A glance at his nail beds startled him. The blue tinge had him doing as she had instructed, removing the red Hudson's Bay blanket from her bed and wrapping it over his shoulders. The coarse wool grazed his damp skin as her scent reached him and he paused to inhale—cinnamon. The shivering brought him close to the stove. He set the coffeepot on the top and then jumped up and down until his numb feet began to tingle.

A few minutes later the coffeepot steamed and

he poured himself a hot mug. He inhaled the aroma and hummed in pleasure.

"Take off your boots!" Lily harped from the street.

Jack nearly dropped his coffee. He glanced down at the ground and saw it was hard-packed earth, making her request totally illogical.

"You can't track dirt onto dirt," he said, thinking that reasoning with a woman was as productive as explaining physics to a cocker spaniel.

"Your feet are wet. You have to warm them or you'll get frostbite."

She was correct again, though he wouldn't say so aloud. She knelt before him, muttering as her agile fingers worked the laces from the eyelets. Then she slapped his calf as if he were a horse needing his hooves picked clean. He shifted his weight, giving her his foot and trying very hard not to drop the hot coffee on her head. She pulled and the boot came away.

"I was about to get to those," he muttered. *Just as soon as I can feel my fingers again.*

She cast him a displeased glance. "And leave a toe or two here in Dyea? Now that I've got you, I'll be damned if I'll let your toes turn black."

"It's barely below freezing."

She ignored that and returned her attention to his feet. He'd only wanted to warm his hands a moment first and then she'd blown in like a March wind. His jaws now tapped like the signal key of a telegraph.

"The other," she ordered and repeated the process. But this time the blanket slipped to the floor. He placed the cup on the top of the stove and then stooped to recover it, just as she did the same.

They nearly banged heads and came up standing face-to-face with the blanket stretched between them. It was only then that he realized she was staring wide-eyed at his naked torso. His impulse was to grab the blanket and cover himself, but something about her startled expression stayed him. Her cheeks flushed and her lips separated as she inhaled. He recognized the look of carnal desire and couldn't move now if he tried, for she had arrested him. His entire body tensed. Her azure eyes lifted from his chest to stare up at him. She inched closer.

The cold that had gripped him like an icy fist melted in the heat of her gaze, warming him inside and out.

She lifted her free hand and reached for him. His heart galloped into a wild pulsing rhythm, sending fountains of blood to his groin. Dear Lord in heaven, she managed to arouse him without so much as a touch. The touch came an instant later when she used her index finger to stroke his chest, as if skimming cream from a bowl.

"You're cold," she whispered, her voice a second caress.

His mind filled with all the ways she could warm him and he took an aggressive step in her direction, lifting his hands to capture her shoulders, needing to bring her against him. But she resisted and he let go. She stumbled back, now gripping the blanket with both hands. Her expression had changed in that instant, going from an open invitation to one of ill-concealed horror. Her fists clenched, holding the coarse wool before her as if it were some kind of magic shield that would protect her from him.

It wouldn't.

"We're not that kind of partners," she said.

His brain knew it, but his body was still beating the order to advance. He listened to his body, stepping forward, reaching again in an effort to recapture what was already lost, that heat she had given him with her flashing eyes and that one single touch.

She stepped back. "No."

Even with his blood pounding through his ears like hoofbeats, he was gentleman enough to understand that. He halted. His current befuddlement had nothing whatsoever to do with the cold. No, this was all to do with this woman. He wanted her.

She shook out the blanket and then held it up.

He turned and she wrapped the red wool about his shoulders, her arms encircling his neck for just an instant before she retreated again.

Jack turned, now cloaked in his cape. She blew out a breath as one does after a narrow escape. But she had not escaped yet. Why had she done it? Had his nakedness precipitated her rash action? It gave him a sense of power he'd never felt before and filled his mind with possibilities.

"Lily?" He had no idea what to say beyond that. How did a man express such a physical desire to a woman he had met scarcely two hours earlier? He couldn't. His heartbeat returned to a more normal pace and the erection, which had sprung to action like a soldier to the signal to charge, now returned to at-ease. He began to shiver again.

"Drink your coffee," she instructed.

He didn't. Instead he held her gaze.

"Why did you touch me like that?"

Chapter Three

Why *had* she touched him like that? Lily was at a loss to explain herself. Clearly she'd lost her damned mind. The bold action brought to mind her mother's warning. *If you need a man, then take one, but don't give him your heart, Lily, for he'll only break it with his leaving.* Lily had decided that she'd not be needing a man in that way. Men propositioned her, of course, one or two had even tried to take what they wanted. But she had been unaffected, until now. In all her years she had never reached out and stroked a man as if he were her pet cat.

Seeing all that muscle did something to her thinking. She'd known on the beach that she was attracted to him, but she had told herself she could control her desire. Now the demons of doubt plagued her. What if the only difference between her and her ma was that, until today, she had not yet met the right sort of temptation?

She shivered. If Jack Snow was her weakness, she should break the deal that he so clearly wanted broken and send him off this very minute. She weighed the risk of being hurt against the possibility of ever again finding a partner as strong as this one.

What terrible luck to find a man who made her belly flutter like a flag in a windstorm. It would lead her to a bad end. But wasn't this exactly how her mother described it—the irresistible pull of one to the other. Carrie Delacy had been unable to resist big, handsome charmers who had not a penny in their pockets or the least inclination to work. Lily stared at her partner and stilled at her realization. Was Jack just like them? Would he leave her, too?

"Lily?" he asked, waiting for her to say something.

Her stomach no longer trembled. Now it tightened with that sick feeling that she would not be able to control this desire that stood between them like a living thing. Why was he so handsome? Even with his whiskers coming in and his hair falling over his eyes, she had the devil's own time not to take what he offered. She didn't want to be hurt, used like her mother and then abandoned by careless men.

Her mother wanted more for her daughter than this. One child, then another and before Lily knew it, she'd be leaning over the same washboard wondering where her life had gone wrong. Right here was where. It was exactly what her mother had *not* wanted for her.

That realization struck her hard. Yield to him and she'd be just like her mother, stuck in these mudflats forever, hauling freight and darning socks, while Jack waltzed away to have the adventure she coveted.

"No, thank you," she said aloud. "I'm heading out, so get your things off my cart."

He had to abandon the blanket and pull up his wet union suit, but he did as she asked, unloading his gear and stacking it with the rest. She did not look back as she hurried Nala away.

On the beach she paid another hauler to take the rest of his gear to her tent. She earned several more fares, staying longer than customary to stay clear of him. Soon that would be an impossibility.

Late in the day, she came upon a man struggling with his crates and suitcases. He was thin, dark-haired and wore a small white fringed apron beneath his gray vest. She offered her cart, but he had nothing with which to pay her.

"I'll pay you twice that in gold when I reach Dawson."

Lily smiled at his pluck. There was a good chance he'd never reach his destination. Many turned back after seeing the Chilkoot Pass and many more drowned in the rivers. Even if he survived, he might not be one of the lucky ones that staked a profitable claim.

"Cash."

"I can't pay it, missus." His face grew pink with shame that Lily understood from personal experience.

Lily sighed. It was not the first time she'd hauled a load for nothing but a man's gratitude. Still she had enough to fill her pot, so where was the harm?

"All right. Load it on," she said.

He did so and soon they were on their way up the beach.

"I'm Amos Luritz."

Lily introduced herself and her dog.

"I was a tailor in Brooklyn."

Lily smiled.

"I made this coat."

"Very nice."

"Men's clothing, repairs and alterations, but I do make all my daughters' dresses. I have two beautiful daughters, Sasha and Cora. They're with my in-laws until I can make my fortune."

"Then we'd best get you to town."

"I could make you a dress when we get to Dawson, in exchange for your trouble."

"Oh, that's not necessary, Mr. Luritz."

"You can't make a living giving away your work."

"True. But I did quite well today."

"I'll make you the most beautiful dress in Dawson."

"I fear you'll be too busy digging for gold."

He nodded at this. "Would you take one of my nuggets?"

"That would be lovely, Mr. Luritz. But I'll likely have so many of my own, I'll not need yours." She winked at him and he chuckled.

"You're a good lady, missus."

She compared this greenhorn to Jack. Two men, both without means, only this one had a clear and useful profession instead of several hundred pounds of baggage. If she had come across Amos first, would he now be her partner? She wished he was, for she felt no inclination toward him. What was so different between this man and the one she had chosen?

She pondered that mystery as Amos trudged along beside her on the half-mile trip to Dyea, yammering all the way about the nuggets he would find and the money he needed to open his own tailor shop in Brooklyn. She stopped him from showing her a photo of his wife and daughters. Lily didn't want to have their images in her mind should something happen to this brave little tailor.

She worked until the sun hung low in the sky and all the arrivals had made their way to Dyea. Days were growing short now, adding to her anxiousness to be gone from this place.

She stopped at the log home of Yaahl, the Chilkat

Indian whose wife, Diinaan, fed Nala in exchange for Lily's accounting work. The couple and their family carried loads over the pass to the upper end of Lake Lindeman. Diinaan carried only seventy-five pounds a trip, a white man's load, she called it, but her husband could carry two hundred pounds at twenty-six cents a pound. It was Lily who had encouraged them to increase the asking fee from eighteen cents as the stampeders rushed in to Dyea.

"I found a partner," she said, sitting beside Diinaan on the bench outside the door.

Nala was busy wolfing down the mixture of rice, dried salmon and bacon grease.

"Oh, so you going now soon. Yes?"

"Yes. I'll need to pick up the sled and buy dried fish for Nala. Plus I'd like to hear anything more you can tell me about the trail."

"Yes, I tell you much trail news all the way to top lakes. I miss your good advice and account…" Her words fell off.

"Accounting."

"Yes."

Lily had taught Diinaan bookkeeping in exchange for a sled, that for a time there, she had feared she would never need.

"It's important to keep track so you aren't cheated."

They exchanged a smile. Lily would miss Diinaan

because, although they were separated by race and culture, at heart they were the same.

Nala began licking the bowl until it spun like a top, the metal bottom ringing against the rock. Lily called her off. It was time to face what she had avoided for much of the day—the man, her partner, waiting in her tent. Her insides went tense as she returned to her tent and Jack.

She reached her temporary home a few minutes later, hopeful that Mr. Snow had dried his clothing and was now wearing both a shirt and trousers. She called out and waited until he shouted a hello, then she drew a large breath of icy air and ducked inside. Lily gasped as her gaze darted about—for in a matter of mere hours the man had turned her orderly home into chaos. Every crate had been opened and the shavings scattered about. Piles of sheet metal and pipe covered her bed, tools and gadgets of unknown usefulness were strewn over her kitchen table. And there in the midst of the chaos sat Mr. Snow, on her bed beside her oil lamp, calmly polishing some kind of round gauge with a bit of white cotton, that she recognized belatedly as one of her embroidered handkerchiefs as he whistled softly to himself.

Her jaw dropped at the sight, her nerves and restless anticipation forgotten amid the anarchy. Lily narrowed her eyes upon him and he stilled. The whistling ceased as silence stretched.

Her voice was a soft exhalation bubbling with

indignation. "Isn't this exactly what comes from letting a man into your home?"

He flushed and rose, staring down at the handkerchief and then hiding it behind his back.

"The packing was all soaked. I have to dry the metal or it will rust."

"This is the most useless bundle of nonsense I've ever seen a man haul from Seattle. Even the piano that went through here had more value than this lot."

"No, it will be useful."

"For what, building a metal boat? Are you daft, man? You can't haul two tons of pig iron to Dawson."

"It weighs only 820 pounds."

She turned in a circle, dismay now rushing in to fill the void left by her shock. "And not one sled or rope or scrap of food or canvas," she muttered. She fixed him with a cold stare. "Where are your mining tools?"

"Already cleaned and dried. There." He pointed to a stack of crates. "Carpentry, mining and sheet metal."

"And what are you planning to eat, shoe leather?"

"I have dried lentils, rice, bacon and coffee."

She sighed in relief. Nala whined and Lily was grateful for the distraction of removing the dog's harness. Once finished, she turned to Jack Snow.

"When I come back, I'd best be able to sit on my bed."

She dropped the canvas flap and stepped out into

the cold night. What the devil had she been thinking to bring him into her home?

Lily snapped her fingers and Nala appeared, trotting beside her as she picked her way through the mud to the saloon, where she took her meals. The men shouted a greeting as she entered. She waved as she went to the back, where Taps had her dinner waiting. The barkeep had been a bugler in the army, thus his name.

"I'll need a second plate to go."

Taps stilled. "Did you find a partner, Lil?"

"That's so," she piped with a bravado she did not feel. Lily was used to feigning grit and a cheerful disposition, for who wanted to listen to a dour performer? But sometimes she wished she were back in her mother's kitchen making apricot preserves. *No sense in looking back at what's lost,* her mother would say. *Forward, girls, forward.*

"Fine, fine," said Taps, adjusting his greasy hat.

"And he's a strapping big one, too," she added as much to herself as to him. It wasn't all bad, was it? She'd gotten a man and could head out now. Lily tamped down her rising panic.

"But he's got only one leg?"

Her laugh sounded hollow, but no one seemed to notice but herself. She'd not let them see her anxiety over her new partner. "So far as I can see his only fault is that he's a man."

Taps nodded. "Then you'd best sleep with that revolver under your pillow."

Her smile slipped. "Don't worry about me." She glanced about and located the closest stampeder. "George! Kiss me."

George's bushy eyebrows lifted but he did not argue. He took one step toward her and wrapped his arms about her waist.

Nala leapt to her feet, bared her teeth and gave a menacing growl. George lifted his hands in surrender, backing away.

The others laughed.

"She's better at defending me than my dear old dad," said Lily, pressing a hand to her chest. In truth her father hadn't given a fig about her and had left them like the rest. What was it about her that made them all go? Her mother insisted it wasn't Lily's fault, but why then?

Taps slid her dinner onto the bar and Lily quickly finished her only meal of the day, using her bread as a sponge to capture the last of the gravy. Then she patted her middle and allowed two men to boost her up to the bar. She began with a hearty rendition of "My Darling Clementine," followed by several rousing drinking tunes that the men could sing along with, then turned to some sweet love songs and finished with "Pretty Saro." That one made many a greenhorn weep. Her hour done, she climbed down from the bar, gathered up the second plate of food and headed back to her partner.

When she reached her tent she found he'd packed up the crates and bags of gear. Only a few items of clothing still remained on the line and he sat in the single chair beside the stove with a leather journal clutched to his chest and his head thrown back as he snored softly.

He'd turned down the wick of her oil lamp. That and the glow from the small window in the potbelly stove made his skin a warm, rosy color. Lily studied him again. Asleep, Jack Snow was still handsome, but the threat was gone. Now she felt only an inexplicable tenderness and the need to brush the locks of hair from his forehead. She reached and then stopped herself by clenching her fist. No, not that way. That was the way to build attachments that would make his leaving more painful. She sealed herself against him in an effort to protect her bruised heart from further battering.

She was freezing from her walk across the tent town. It might be only October, but the temperature dropped at night like a rock tossed from a cliff.

Nala whined.

"Shh," said Lily as she moved forward to place Jack's supper on the flat round top of the stove to warm. As she straightened she caught the unfamiliar scent of him—sawdust, leather and the musty smell of the sea. The heat of the stove penetrated the frosty cold that seemed to cling to her skin, making her linger near him.

It wasn't his full open mouth or the straight line of his nose, it wasn't those feathery black eyelashes brushing his cheek that drew her. No, it was only the stove. She needed the heat, that was all, and tonight the cast iron was throwing more than usual, wasn't it?

"Damn, it's him again," she whispered.

Nala nudged Jack's hand with her big wet nose and he startled awake to find himself surrounded with Lily on the left and Nala on the right. He clutched the armrests of the chair for an instant and the book slid to his thighs. His eyes grew wide and then he relaxed, resting his hand on Nala's head and scratching her behind the ears.

Lily didn't know which shocked her more, that Nala had sought attention from this stranger or that he had given it without thought. So much for her watchdog. Lily felt Nala's betrayal like a pinprick in her heart.

She'd seen several men try to approach Nala, hands out, voices soothing, but she had snapped at them all. Lily stared at Jack Snow. What made him different?

He stretched and then cast her that beguiling smile. The man could coax cider from an apple. Lily frowned.

"Must have dozed off." He glanced about. "Got it all stowed, partner."

Partner. She liked the sound of it on his lips. Lily dropped her gaze and pointed to the stove. "I brought supper."

Jack's smile broadened. "Excellent. I'm so hungry I could eat a horse." He thumped Nala on the ribs. "Present company excluded."

Nala's tail thudded against the chair back.

What was happening here?

"Eat your supper."

He drew the plate to his lap and looked about. It was in that instant she realized she had no utensils. So she brought him the large spoon she used to measure coffee and handed it over. His fingers brushed hers and she stilled at the startling sensation running up her arm like the feet of tiny birds.

She backed away, sitting on the bed behind him. He turned his chair so that he faced her but he did not fall upon his food. He must be hungry, yet still he hesitated.

"Go on," she urged.

He pursed his lips. "You've eaten?"

It seemed hours ago. She smiled and nodded. "Yes—eat."

He waited a moment longer and then attacked the beans and rice as she poured him a cup of coffee, black. When she set it on the stove she found him laying the three strips of thick bacon into the bread, which he folded in half. He finished the sandwich in five large bites.

"Where did you find Nala?" asked Jack, resting a large hand on her dog's wide head.

Lily smiled before she answered and for a moment Jack forgot the question. Did she even know how lovely she was?

"When I first laid eyes on her, she was in the jaws of an alley cat that was big as a lion. She was a pup no bigger than this." Lily indicated a distance of six or seven inches between her palms. "But I chased that cat down and made her drop the pup. She gave me this for my trouble." Lily pointed to the little puncture below her right eye, the only flaw in her beautiful skin. "Tried to take my eye out. And Nala's still got the scars on her head where that cat bit into her." She patted the dog's ribs affectionately.

Jack scratched the dog's head feeling the bumps on her scalp.

"I feel them," he said.

Lily nodded and continued her tale. "I carried her home in the pocket of my coat. Can you imagine? She was so tiny, her eyes weren't even open. Had to feed her milk from my finger, and it was no small trouble stealing milk each morning, I can tell you."

Jack frowned at the thought of Lily having to steal milk. He found himself wondering what Lily had endured in her youth and how she had managed to come out so well. True she was guarded, but who could blame her? Likely she had seen enough of life's troubles to be streetwise and was apt to be much more astute in that regard than he was.

Nala sat beside his chair, eyes closed as she enjoyed the stove's heat.

Jack lowered his plate, still sticky with the gravy and a few stray grains of rice, to the floor. Nala needed no second invitation. Her pink tongue lapped the pewter until it seemed spotless.

Lily retrieved the plate and set it aside.

"Was that good?" said Jack to Nala in a friendly tone that made Lily's stomach flutter.

"She's not your dog." Her voice came out harsher than she'd intended.

His eyes rounded. "I'm sorry. I should have asked permission before feeding her. It's just. Well. I had a black dog once."

"What kind?"

"Teddy was a chow. When his eyes got cloudy, we just stretched a rope in the back, like a clothesline. He loved to run and knew exactly when to stop. He was a good boy." His sad, wistful expression made her sorry for her sharp words.

Lily extended her hand and Nala moved to sit beside her cot. "Do you have a tent?"

He nodded.

She tried to turn her mind to business, instead of the crisp, dark, curling hair that showed above the open two buttons of his union suit.

"We'll need to compare lists of gear to see what we still need and what can be left behind."

His brow wrinkled as if he couldn't understand leaving things. Did he even know what was involved in this journey?

"Yes, all right," he said.

They talked late into the night, her new partner taking notes and making lists of the items they had, needed or would abandon. He was educated, but lacked practicality, as she had feared. She failed to get him to agree to leave the metal behind, nor would he share the utility of this load, except to say it would be "the practical application of a working model" whatever that meant.

She liked that it was practical, at least in his eyes and since she would not be carrying it, she said no more. She shared what she had learned from the Chilkat Indians and he spoke of what he had gleaned from newspapers, maps and geography texts. But in truth, neither of them had seen the trail that would take three to six months to cross, stretching over five hundred miles, first through the narrow gap between great mountains and then down lakes and rivers that became the Yukon River, which would finally carry them to the goldfields in Dawson City.

Exhaustion took hold and they grew silent.

He gazed at the woman who only looked more beautiful by firelight. She was an astute planner, he'd give her that, but that was not why his gaze lingered on the graceful curve of her neck and the soft wisps of dark hair that caressed her skin.

"Why did you come?" she asked.

Jack snapped his gaze back to hers, shaking from his reverie. He was uncomfortable with the personal question.

"For the same reason as other men. I came to test myself and my ideas."

She laughed. The musical sound made his palms sweat. He clamped them to the arms of the chair.

"You're a strange sort, Jack, and the first I've come across wanting to test ideas. The rest of them come to get rich. I've come for that, too, but I've also come for the adventure."

He leaned forward, drawn by the energetic sparkle in her eyes. Lily's thinly veiled accent marked her as lower-class Irish. Not the sort of woman he must have to regain his social position. But he didn't rule out an affair, if she was willing.

She'd be used to hard work, at least.

Once upon a time, he would not have even spoken with someone the likes of her, yet here they were— partners. What would she say if she knew that the only labor he'd done involved rowing on crew and playing for Princeton's football team? They'd won the national championship last year against Lafayette. He wondered how they were faring this season without him. He thought of his teammates. Many would be graduating without him come spring. He'd been too ashamed to say goodbye, didn't want them to know of his family's ruin, but now that he thought of them he wondered how many others had lost everything when the bottom dropped out of the market. Still, he couldn't tell them, not even Eric, his roommate and closest friend. He was too humiliated and found it easier to wall away his sorrow. Sins of the father. His chin sank a little closer to his chest as he wished he had Eric along instead of this lovely, resolute little woman. His head nodded forward, surprising him. He snapped upright.

"You have a bedroll?" she asked.

He nodded.

"Stretch it out beside the cot."

He was wide awake now. He'd never shared a room with a woman, and just thinking of sleeping in the same tent as Lily Delacy Shanahan aroused more than his mind.

"But what will people think?"

"People? You mean the raggedy greenhorns sleeping on the beach or the swindlers in town? Here, men care only for themselves. Plus, I don't give a fig what they think or what they say. I answer to no one but myself. What you should be worried about is what I think, because if you so much as lay a finger on me in the night, I'll shoot you through the heart."

That said, she laid her hand on the grip of her revolver and eyed him. He nodded his understanding, but could not help but notice the quick rise and fall of her chest. It didn't match the cool look in her eyes. Something didn't fit, but he said no more as he retrieved his blanket roll.

"I'm off to use the necessary," she said.

"Is there one?"

"Not really." She smiled. "Come, Nala."

Jack had his bedding open and had rolled his coat for a pillow when he heard Lily screaming just beyond the canvas flaps.

"Let her go!"

Jack leapt to his feet and hurtled out of the tent.

Chapter Four

Jack skidded to a halt in the muddy street, dark now, except for the glow of lamps and candles shielded by canvas, but he saw them instantly, tussling in the narrow thoroughfare. He took in the scene in a fraction of a second. Two men—one straining to hold Nala's harness as the dog jumped and barked in a vain effort to reach her mistress, the other with Lily's wrists pinned before him, preventing her from reaching her weapon.

Something inside Jack snapped. One minute he was on guard and cognizant and the next he was a wild animal tearing and punching. He grabbed the man gripping Lily by the back of his pants and the collar of his dark coat and lifted him into the air. Her attacker writhed and kicked, for just an instant before Jack threw him onto a stack of firewood, scattering the neat pile. The man lay unmoving amid the strewn cordage. Then he turned on the one holding Nala. The ruffian had taken his eyes off the dog, his jaw dropping open as he witnessed Jack's approach. In that instant, Nala turned and sank her teeth into the man's forearm. Jack heard the bone snap. The fellow gave a shriek of pain, but the hound did not let go and began a violent shaking of her head. The man howled in agony.

The idea of forcing the dog to release him never even crossed Jack's mind. He was too deep into the all-consuming rage. He added his weight to the dog's attack, punching the man's face with all he had. The attacker dropped to the ground and fell silent. Only then did Nala unlock her jaws.

Jack turned back to the other man, still unconscious and then returned to the one lying face-down in the mud. Lily moved beside Jack. Instinctively he grasped her around the waist, dragging her tight to his body, holding her in the protection of his arms, his eyes scanning for any remaining threat.

The haze of red receded by degrees and Jack saw the circle of spectators, gawking at him as if he were a madman.

Lily spoke first. "They tried to steal my dog."

A short, stocky man stepped forward. His face bristled with gray whiskers and tobacco juice glistened on his chin. "Jonathan, get some rope to tie these two." Next he pointed to a man who stood stoop-shouldered in muddy boots. "Bobby, get that horsewhip of yours."

Jack suddenly realized what was happening. Vigilante justice—his stomach cramped at the thought. Disapproval filled him. Men could not simply take the law into their own hands. Then his mind flashed to an image of Lily struggling vainly for escape. The fury overtook him again and he decided they deserved far worse.

"Call the authorities!" someone shouted.

There was a moment's silence and then men guffawed.

"Authorities?" said the stocky man. "There ain't no law 'til you reach the Canadian border."

Lily had told him as much. But he hadn't really understood it until now. He'd never lived in a place where people made up the rules as they went along.

This tent town was an illusion. All these men were gathered only to ready themselves for the push to Dawson. Then the entire town would vanish and remake itself inland. They were like ants, scurrying in the mud.

"What will you do with them?" Jack asked, longing to bloody his fists on the men's faces again.

"Whip 'em. Then we'll run them out of Dyea."

Jack glanced down to see Lily's strained, brave little face and pulled her even closer, shaken at the realization that he would have killed for her.

Lily still clung to his middle, staring up at him in

astonishment. Was that horror or a kind of newfound respect? The need to protect her warred with the desire to claim her as his. Jack slipped one hand up to tangle in her hair, taking possession of her.

She pushed off him like a swimmer from the side of a pool and stepped back.

Her words came to him again. *We're not that kind of partners.*

"Damn," he muttered and let her go.

The two men were dragged off, feet-first. Jack looked at the distance he had thrown the first man and could not quite believe it.

Nala jumped up on Lily, muddying her fine crimson coat. But she hugged the dog, resting her head against the thick scruff of the mongrel's neck.

"Good girl, Nala. That's my girl." Her hound dropped to all fours. But Lily just followed her, squatting in the street before him. She straightened at last, coming close enough for him to breathe in her fragrance of cinnamon and musk again. She placed one hand flat on his chest, reminding him of her earlier caress.

The small action nearly stopped his heart and made it surprisingly difficult to draw a full breath.

"That was very brave," she whispered. She stepped back and laced her fingers together then wrung her hands. "Thank you."

He blinked. "You're welcome."

"Who's your man, Lil?" asked a ruddy-faced gent with a fine crop of hair sprouting from each nostril.

She lifted a hand, presenting him to the group of curiosity seekers.

"Boys, meet Jack Snow, my new partner."

Jack braced, waiting for someone to recognize his surname.

A ripple went through the crowd, but after a moment he realized it was not for the reason he feared. Perhaps he had finally found a place where he could be who he was now instead of who he had been.

Some of the male bystanders looked amused, while others simply stared, slack-jawed. A few stepped forward to shake his hand or clap him on the shoulder. He breathed again when he realized they did not know him or his family. The scandal that had blanketed the pages of the papers in New York meant nothing to these men. No one knew. No one cared—no one but him.

Lily's smile was bright and her laughter contagious. She seemed the darling of the street with many admirers already. It took a long while for the men to return to their tents.

At last, Nala had had enough and ducked between the flaps and out of sight. Lily laughed and followed her example.

"He staying in your tent?" asked a man with a gray-streaked beard.

She turned and rested a hand on her hip, looking down her nose at the man. "Your partner sleep in your tent, Bill?"

"Well, yeah, but…"

"But what?" she asked, daring him to say another word.

He rubbed the toe of his boot in the mud. "It's different."

She laughed. "Get your mind out of the gutter, boys." She aimed her finger at them. "All of you. The only female Jack will be sleeping with tonight is Nala."

Jack pressed his lips together as the others laughed. With that she sniffed and disappeared into the tent after her hound. Jack suddenly worried over his bedding and the muddy dog that preceded him into the tent. He hurried to follow.

Just as he feared, Nala had dragged his bedroll into a nice muddy mess on which she was now curled. Lily ordered her dog up and handed Jack his bedding, now streaked with dirt.

"Don't worry. If you plan on being a miner, everything you own will soon look like this."

Jack accepted the grimy blankets with dismay that lasted only until Lily's next words.

"Let's get some sleep."

Jack stood as if petrified as she sat on her cot and removed her boots with a button hook, carefully placing the worn leather beneath her bed. Then she peeled out of her coat, revealing a neat blue woolen bodice and matching skirt.

She began to brush the mud off her coat.

"Do you have a sweetheart, Mr. Snow?"

He thought he'd prefer jumping back in the icy inlet waters than tell her about his former fiancée, Nancy Tinsen.

"Never stayed with one long enough to call her that."

Lily pulled a face, and then unbuttoned her bodice. She stopped when the garment gapped, revealing the fine, soft swell of her breasts above the corset that cinched her in the middle.

"Here is what will happen. You'll excuse yourself and go for a walk. When you come back the lamp will be out and I'll be in bed. If you try to crawl under my blankets, I'll use my pistol."

"What if you try to crawl under mine?"

That stopped her. She gaped a moment and then laughed. "Well now, then I suppose you have your choice to throw me out or keep me."

"I'd keep you." He held her long stare. She looked away first.

Her voice seemed breathless when she next spoke. "I can't see that happening."

Now it was his turn to smile. "Can't you?"

He was gratified to see her flush. So he hadn't imagined the pull between them. He didn't want a full-time woman, not when he was still bruised and battered from his failed engagement. But he wasn't beyond taking what a woman offered.

"You can take that walk now."

Jack lifted the flap but she called him back.

"And Jack?"

He turned, thinking her beautiful in the lamplight. "Hmm?"

"Thank you for tonight."

He pinned her with a steady stare. "What are partners for."

Then he left her, before the temptation to stay caused him to do something he'd regret. He paused beyond the tent, waiting for his eyes to adjust. He could scarcely make out the dark silhouette of the figure across the road.

"Toss you out already?" he asked.

Jack could see little beyond the glowing tip of a cigarette, but he made his way over.

"So it seems." He walked to the man who offered his tobacco pouch. "No, thanks."

The man took another puff. "Thing about canvas is that voices carry. I guess folks know just about everything about their neighbors here, 'cept they aren't neighbors, since folks come and go by the minute. Nobody really cares for anyone but themselves—and their partners, of course. The rest is all entertainment."

"Why you telling me this?"

"Just to thank you for livening up this little corner of the swamp. I'm George Suffern."

Jack shook his hand.

"When you two pushing up the Chilkoot?"

"Sooner is better," said Jack.

"I suppose. The steamers will keep coming until the passages freeze. Father Winter hits early in the mountains. Maybe best to stay down here, then head up come spring."

Jack sat on the crate beside him. "No, you're wrong. Best to get up to Lake Bennett and spend the winter building your boat. Then you'll be in position when the ice break-up comes. From there it's all downhill to Dawson."

"Through rapids and lakes filled with more mosquito larva than fish."

Jack laughed. "That's why it's an adventure. A test of a man's metal."

"And what about Lily? She's your partner now, so it's your lookout to see she gets to Dawson. Big responsibility. I reckon that'll test your metal more than the Golden Stairs or the White Horse Rapids."

Jack winced as he chafed against their bargain. If he were a different kind of man he'd leave her behind and never look back. But, unlike his father, Jack valued his word and kept his promises. So he would attend to his responsibilities, but it annoyed him that he'd somehow fallen into the worst of all situations, giving him all of the responsibilities of keeping a woman with none of the benefits.

He glanced at the tent in time to see the light extinguish. Lily was now climbing into her narrow bed alone—such a shame. Jack stood, drawn by the perfect image of Lily's fine luminous skin glowing in the moonlight. His throat went dry as he took a step.

George cleared his throat, making Jack recall his presence.

He stopped and gave the man his attention. He didn't like the man's mocking smile.

"My daddy used to say that you should never tie an eagle to a plow horse, because the arrangement won't be good for either of them. I'm afraid, son, you've got yourself in just such a situation."

Jack wondered if he were the eagle or the horse. But he'd heard enough lectures about the folly of this venture from his mother who had advised he stay put, lower his expectations in the marriage market and seek a bride outside their former circles. It might still come to that, but first he would try and be his own man. Jack thought his mother might even admire his wish to restore them to their rightful place, if she could only see past her fears of losing him forever. He knew the risks here. The dangers were real, but they were real back there. What hope did he have, cloaked in scandal, flat broke, with no degree and no prospects? Save the one his mother had found him.

He cringed. Here, at least, he stood a chance to be his own man instead of having to marry a woman he did not even know. But if he failed he might be forced to that to provide for his mother and sister. The thought left a bitter taste in his mouth.

I'm sorry, Mother, I've got to try, he thought, placing a hand over his heart and her telegram that had found him in Seattle.

His greatest fear was dying up here and leaving his mother and younger sister dependent on the charity of his aunt and uncle.

"You two sure are a mismatched team." George blew a smoke ring. "Maybe you should…she told me that before this she'd never been more than five blocks in any direction. Don't think she's prepared for this, though she knows her own mind, I suppose."

Jack felt a chill run down his back at the realization that Lily knew nothing of the dangers of this wild place. She'd shown tonight how ill-equipped she was, nearly losing her dog to ruffians. Somehow he'd been taken in by her bravado, but now it suddenly became clear that his job would involve more than carrying her to Dawson. He'd have to defend her from other men as well. Could he do it? He had to.

Jack lifted his collar but felt no warmer as he realized he was not the eagle, but the workhorse.

"'Night," he said to George.

"See you in the morning."

Jack returned to the tent, but Lily said nothing as

he slipped inside. He found Nala on his bed again and began a wrestling match that ended in a draw, with him under his blankets and the big dog stretched out beside him, half under Lily's cot. The rest of the night involved Nala's steady encroachment onto his territory with the relentlessness of any claim jumper. Even sleeping on the deck of the steamer had been more restful than this.

Small wonder he did not hear Lily rise, but came awake to the sound of many male voices and Lily's clear soprano piping above the rest.

"Seconds are a nickel more."

Jack opened his eyes and glanced about the empty tent. The aroma of fresh-brewed coffee brought him to a sitting position and the mouthwatering fragrance of biscuits had him into his boots and out the tent flap.

There stood Lily behind a plank table which held a giant cast-iron griddle filled with fluffy brown biscuits. Beside that sat the coffeepot that looked as if it had been kicked down a long and rocky slope.

"Oh, there you are at last. Mind the table while I check the next batch. It's fifteen cents for black coffee and one biscuit. No seconds on the coffee."

With that she left him to the line of men holding empty cups and bandannas. Jack burned his fingers trying to lift out one of the golden cakes and thereafter used the spatula. He'd only two left when she reappeared with a square bake tin filled with a new supply.

"I've never seen a more industrious individual in my life," he said.

She smiled at him and then went back to pouring coffee while he stayed staring after her. He'd never met a woman like her. She was a dynamo of activity. Had it been only yesterday he had judged her worthless as a partner? It was obvious now that Lily was more than she appeared.

Chapter Five

Jack noticed that some of the men brought her a half cup of coffee beans instead of cash, which she collected in a bag on the table. The coins went into a small can. Nala spent her time scouring the ground for any crumbs left by the hungry stampeders. When the second pan was empty she called to the men still waiting in line.

"That's the lot, gents."

A groan rose from the line, but they shuffled off.

Lily collected her pot, can and tins. "The board and crates go just there."

Jack disassembled the makeshift table and followed her inside where Lily divided the remaining dough and greased the pan. She cooked two lovely fat biscuits, offering Jack one. They drank the remains of the coffee black and strong.

Nala sat without begging, which surprised Jack.

"Doesn't she like biscuits?" he asked.

"I give her all she can eat, once a day."

"What about table scraps?"

She leveled him with a cool eye that made him pause to wonder what he had said to earn such a look.

"There aren't any." As if to prove her point, Lily used her index finger to retrieve all the crumbs from her plate. "I've got to go down to collect fares from the arriving ships and you can help me today. Tonight we'll buy whatever we don't have and set off tomorrow."

"What about my gear?"

"Did you meet George?"

Jack nodded.

"I'll pay him to watch the place. He'll be happy to have a job that requires only sitting and smoking."

They were down at the beach a few minutes later. It was a long day, helping men collect their goods and carrying them to the hotel. Lily used Jack like a second pack animal, but he didn't mind, because the labor kept him from dwelling on the past.

As they took the last man up the hill, Jack caught Lily staring speculatively at him.

"What?" he asked.

"Never expected you to last 'til noon."

It amused him that as he was judging her, she had been judging him and finding him lacking. Had he improved her opinion of dandies?

"Were you? It's hard not to judge on what you see," he said, thinking of himself more than her.

She nodded her agreement at that. "It's a rare man willing to do a full day's work. That's why most of them will fail. They're better at spending money than making it."

"Perhaps I'm the exception."

She grinned and nodded. "I hope so."

That evening they purchased the foodstuffs they needed and Lily collected her sled. The tent, clothing, snowshoes and food all fitted nicely. His tools and equipment did not. That left over seven hundred pounds. Lily tried several times to get him to leave the "uselessness" behind, but failing that, she rented a pushcart that he could use to the base of the Chilkoot. From there he would have to tote his belongings. Lily sold her tent and contents to George Suffern who had sold his lot to a new arrival, and all was ready for their departure.

Jack slept better the second night, his day's labors gracing him with a weariness that kept him from both restlessness and dreaming.

Nala woke Jack by stepping on his face and he sat up in time to see Lily's lovely pale shoulders disappear beneath her shirt. It was a sight he wouldn't mind seeing each morning. He whistled a tune and rolled his bedding.

"You're in a fine mood today," she said, turning

toward him as she fastened the last button and drew on her coat.

"Departure day," he said. "Just happy to be on our way."

She lifted her eyebrows as if she were not entirely convinced that this accounted for his gaiety. "They say a light heart makes for an easy journey."

The smile faded from his face. A light heart? His was still heavy with guilt and anger and confusion. Why had his father done it?

"What is it, Jack?"

He shook his head and gave her his back, packing up the last of his gear.

They ate cold biscuits and headed out before dawn, joining the others who set their feet upon the same trail.

Lily seemed in high spirits as she steered Nala through the mud, anxious to get out of town and onto the properly snow-covered ground so the sled would glide. But, though the ground was frozen, the march of many feet kept the ice from the trail. Lily worried aloud about the runners scraping over the rock, but there was nothing to be done about it. Five miles up they reached the first ford on the swift, shallow Dyea River. Lily refused to use the precarious jumble of driftwood and logs, not so much for the shoddy construction, but because the builder, named Finnegan, demanded a toll.

"We've been together three days and I've yet to see you spend a dime," said Jack.

"Nor will you until we reach the pass. We'll need all I've made when we get there and at the lakes for boat-building."

"That's true." Jack had exhausted most of his money on the journey and on his gear.

"I've been collecting coffee beans for months so I could sell coffee on the way. I figure the snow and the timber for fires if free." Lily looked uncertain now, hesitant. "Would you like me to help haul our gear across, or will I set a fire and sell coffee to passersby?"

He doubted she could sell much. Men were anxious to be on their way and still fresh from town, but he didn't say anything that might hurt her feelings. Plus, he thought she'd be more hindrance than help, so he set her off to the opposite side to set up her stand, leaving himself to the important work. He spent the next three hours towing their gear over, one load at a time.

Lily built a little fire and brewed coffee and cooked beans, which she sold for two bits a plate to the passing greenhorns, doing a brisk business. She brought him a portion and he ate it so fast he nearly choked.

"I didn't think I was hungry."

She retrieved her plate and patted his cheek before turning back to her fire. When he finished the last load, she scattered the burning logs and they ate what was left of the beans.

The trail up the opposite side of the creek was easy, with only a gentle slope. It did, however, reveal glimpses of the looming range they must breach to attain the interior.

Nala pulled the sled effortlessly, while Jack struggled with the cart as the wheels continually bogged in the soft spots on the trail.

"Someone should throw some gravel in this patch," he grumbled.

Lily laughed. "Are you going to stay behind and fix the road?"

He shook his head.

"Nor is any man, for it would only make it easier for the next. It's a race, don't you know?"

Jack realized she was correct. He was no longer in the theoretical world of textbooks and hypotheses. He was not about to build a model; everything hung on his ability to bring his materials to the gold and put his invention to use. Lily was right. The swiftest would have the best claims. There would be no prize for those who came too late. He knew his history and bore no illusions. The best ground would have been taken before news reached the outside, just like in California. Thank goodness his machine did not depend on his securing a virgin claim, for he did not plan to surface-mine, but instead to tunnel into the frozen earth. If it worked as he intended.

For a time he walked silently, carrying his hopes and doubts. The trail grew far worse, cutting through spruce, hemlock and cottonwood. The narrow path became a tangle of roots, laid bare as skeletal arms by the army of marching feet.

They reached a stretch where Nala could not pull the sled and Jack's cart became more a hindrance than a help.

So he called a halt. "This is the easy part of the trail?"

Lily said nothing to this, her breath coming in streams of condensation in the cold air.

"We have to portage this part," he reasoned.

She nodded.

He made the first trip carrying what he estimated to be over a hundred pounds. Nala carried loads of thirty. They inched along, cutting back, retrieving goods, carrying them only as far as they could see the trail. And all the while men streamed past them, making a similar relay. Lily was happy to reach the river once more, where the cart again rolled on the coarse gravel that wound around the enormous boulders.

Glaciers, he realized. Only a massive moving mountain of ice could have set such huge rocks here.

They crossed the river twice more before reaching Pleasant Camp at sunset. Jack's shirt was soaked with sweat and both he and Lily had wet feet. Even Nala groaned as she settled at her mistress's side.

The camp was only a grove of a few trees and moss perched on the rocky ground, giving them a place to throw a rope between two spruce trees and hang a bit of canvas. Lily gathered wood and began a fire as Jack reordered their gear.

"Only seven miles today," Jack said glumly, thinking of the four hundred and ninety-three remaining as he came to sit beside the fire. "I'd hoped to reach Sheep Camp today."

"And I'd hoped to find gold in this river and save ourselves the journey."

He stared at her, knowing that he could have made that camp if he'd had a male companion to help with the portages instead of doing the job of two men.

She set about soaking dried peaches as she mixed flour, salt and lard. When she rolled out the dough on a planed plank and set it on her cast-iron skillet he recognized what she was about. Sugar went into the rehydrated peaches, as well as cinnamon. The pie was covered with a second sheet and the dough trimmed and fluted. Finally she covered the skillet and buried it in a bed of coals. Jack's mouth watered at the aroma. Soon there were thirty men gathered, looking longingly at the skillet.

"Would your wife sell a piece of that pie?" asked one.

Jack was about to correct the man's assumption and send them off when Lily piped up.

"I'll be auctioning each piece. There's eight pieces

total." She eyed the gathering men. "Not enough for all, just like the gold in Dawson."

The greenhorns began jostling to get a look as Lily scraped the coals off the lid of the Dutch oven and peeked beneath. She shook her head.

"Not yet."

Jack realized that he would have none of the pie, and he was surprised at how much that disappointed him. He had prepared for hardship and deprivation. But his imagining had not included ignoring the scent of cinnamon and bubbling-hot peaches.

The first slice sold for $6 and the last for $14. Lily had made $76 on one large pie. As the auction winners returned their forks and plates, Jack began to resent that skillet, which he had to carry, but received no benefit from.

Their agreement included her feeding him, but he had not specified what the meal might be. He watched Lily soak a large dried salmon in a pot of water, then add oats and set the whole mess over the coals.

"Nala eats better than we do," he grumbled

"And she works harder than either of us," Lily countered, patting her dog. "Now stop sulking."

Lily took the fist-sized scraps she had trimmed from the pie and pressed them into a rough circle then added a cup of peaches she had set aside. She folded the circle into a crescent and placed the covered skillet back on the coals to cook.

"How much will that go for?" he asked.

"I'm not sure. Would you rather I sell your half, partner?"

He met her gaze and found her eyes twinkling. They shared a smile.

Lily shook her head in mock admonishment. "Men are all alike."

"I just wanted a bite."

She reached out and stroked his hand. "And you shall have it and half the money from the pie, or we can pool it for supplies."

Before he could stop himself, he had grasped her fingers. She was not quick enough to escape him. The tingling awareness flared again. He leaned forward.

"They thought you were my wife," he said, finding his voice low and gruff.

"Let them. It will keep them from all manner of foolishness on the trail." She glanced at her hand, still captured by his, and then at her skillet. "The turnover will burn."

Jack didn't care. He wanted to pull her into his lap, bend her over his arm and kiss those red lips. He leaned forward.

"Jack. Let go."

He did and she went about as if nothing had happened. But her cheeks flushed and her nostrils flared as they had when they had climbed that final slope. So, the brief encounter rattled her, as well. It was both disquieting and satisfying to know that he was not alone in his kindling desire.

She lifted the turnover and carefully flipped it, then replaced the lid and coal topping. A few minutes later Jack was juggling the hot, flaky pastry, trying not to let the thick, bubbly liquid escape to the ground.

He took a bite and burned his tongue. The icy water from the stream kept him from serious harm.

"Patience," she cautioned, blowing on hers.

He stared at the sight of her, lips pursed as she exhaled and felt the desire rising in him like the boreal tide off the Taiya Inlet. And now, staring at her, patience was the very last thing on his mind.

Just watching her made his insides bubble in molten energy, like the filling he gripped in his two hands. The urge to kiss her was irresistible. Damn, he wanted her more than he wanted the pie.

"You're beautiful," he said.

She laughed. "No, but I could be."

He didn't think it polite to disagree, but Lily was lovely as a cherry blossom, pink and fresh and sweet. "What do you mean—could be?"

"In Dawson, where the women are scarce, I figure, the fewer there are, the better I'll look."

Her giggle captivated him. He stared at her, really looking, and he knew she would be beautiful anywhere in the world, but somehow she looked most alluring by firelight under a starry sky. This wilderness suited Lily, her mirth making her cheeks rosy and her eyes sparkle.

Lily finished her half of the turnover and scoured her skillet with sand, then seasoned it with grease before packing it away.

He watched the easy grace of her movements and listened to her soft humming. Somehow Lily made him feel at peace. He wondered again about her and realized he knew next to nothing.

"Did you leave anyone back there, Lily?"

She turned and peered at him.

"Family you mean? Sure, plenty. I've got three sisters. And four brothers. I'm the oldest." Lily lifted her hand to start counting her siblings from bottom to top. "Cory is next oldest and working on the docks, then Bridget, employed as a kitchen maid in a fine house on the hill. Tried to talk her into coming. She's pretty and has a passable voice, but she has a sweetheart who shovels coal on a steamer in the bay and so she'd not have it. Mary is a fine seamstress. One day she'll have a shop if I've anything to say about it. Grace is working in the same factory. She's been at it since she was fourteen. Patrick and Joseph are a year apart, but you'd never know it. Linked at the elbow, those two, and hit hard times. They're out of work and taking what comes. My sisters are looking after them and will see they don't starve. Donald is the next. Bridget's lost track of him. He was heading south for work but they haven't a word."

She barely paused to draw breath. Her crates repacked, Lily joined him at the fire.

"What about you, Jack?"

"A sister, Cassandra, and my mother. That's all."

"Your father?" she asked.

"Gone." He stared at her wide blue eyes and felt a pang of guilt at the half-truth. "Yours?"

Lily looked away. "Oh, yes, he's gone, too. I don't remember him." Her voice sounded funny, strained, tight. She stood and gave him her back. Something was definitely wrong.

"Lily?"

"Shall we put the bedrolls here or there?"

"Are you all right?"

When she turned back her face was composed and she had that businesslike manner about her. "Of course."

But she wasn't, he felt it.

He wanted to ask her again, but it was obvious that Lily was doing her best to put the matter aside. He let her, for now. After all, he had secrets of his own to protect.

He set out their bedrolls.

Jack lay down and waited for her to do the same as he considered bringing her next to him in the night. Lily squashed that plan by calling Nala to lie between them, forming a living wall. Jack smiled. The hound and he were already good friends and he did not fear losing an arm. He petted the dog to test his certainty. The dog closed her eyes to savor his touch. Lily frowned.

Jack grinned. "Nala seems to like it."

Lily narrowed her eyes, but said nothing to this as she turned from him, lying on her side and giving him her back.

Chapter Six

The following day they traveled the four gentle miles from Pleasant Camp to Sheep Camp, which they reached as the morning was only half spent. Jack had to give credit to Lily for she was a tireless worker. Despite her inexperience on the trail and inability to carry much weight, the woman had sand.

His spirits flagged as they struggled up Long Hill, shuttling their belongings a few hundred feet and then returning for more cargo. This way, Nala could make the trips with them, taking some of the load from Jack. They had sent the cart back early, for the trail was too steep and rocky to use it. Until they reached Lake Bennett, Jack would have to carry and pull like a mule.

To bolster his determination, he thought of his little sister, Cassie. When he made his fortune, he'd see she attended Wells or Vassar so that she had more than her good looks and a sizable dowry to recommend her as a wife—she'd have a fine education as well. His father had not thought it important that Cassie attend anything past finishing school, but Jack disagreed. Perhaps he would never finish his degree, but his sister would have a chance to finish hers.

Jack lifted another load, biting down with grim determination, as if he could see her there at the university. Yes, he'd get her there if he was damned trying.

Cassie's care was the job his father should have shouldered. But he was gone and so it fell to him. Jack lifted another crate full of tools and trudged along. Raising a refined, well-educated young lady, took money, lots of it.

Jack dropped the load beside the others. Lily had said she would carry only her gear, but she relented when she recognized he would not leave his "folderol" behind. She passed him with the empty sled, whizzing over the snow in the running tracks she had made, skirting around the line of lumbering men as she went.

Yard by yard they crept along the ground, like ants carrying a caterpillar, until they breeched the final hill and saw the last piece of flat ground from here to Stone Crib. Lily waited at the crest of the rise, motionless in the twilight as she stared out. He could see nothing but the men before him until he was nearly even with her and then he understood what had stopped them.

The little depression was filled to bursting with men and tents and gear. A center artery of traffic marched through the middle of the group. Beyond stood the Golden Stairs.

"Is that black line the trail?" asked Lily, her voice low and reverent.

"No, or not only the trail. Those are men, fixed in lockstep from bottom to top."

Her eyes widened at that.

"It's the Chilkoot Pass, the most devilish climb from here to hell and back. It rises a thousand feet in a half mile."

Lily continued to stare. "So that's it. My friend, Diinaan, told me that if you move from the trail to rest, you're hours getting back in line."

"Come on, let's get down before it's full dark."

The final three hundred yards took all Jack had. They set their canvas on the bare snow and Jack realized only belatedly that he had toted no firewood from Sheep Camp. He fell back into his blankets exhausted and began to doze.

Lily prodded him awake.

"What am I to cook on?"

Jack did not open his eyes. "I'm not hungry."

She sniffed. "Perhaps not, but Nala is and the food is frozen."

Jack sat up. Nala had to eat. He looked about at the fires of other camps. Lily stared down at him with eyes flashing fury. He'd not seen this look before. Her tight expression radiated discontent and he found he didn't like disappointing Lily.

"Isn't that just like a man to set off with no plan at all?"

"I'll get some," he said, already on his feet but she marched over to the closest fire and set into conversation with the stampeders gathered there.

After a few minutes she returned for her kettle and Nala's food. Jack roused himself to set the camp properly and when he had finished organizing their gear, she returned with the kettle nearly full of oats, rice and two large strips of reinvigorated dried salmon.

His mouth watered as she set the offering before Nala, who ate every single morsel and licked each stray oat from the kettle.

"I agreed to make them cornmeal biscuits," Lily informed him.

"We don't have cornmeal," Jack pointed out.

"They do. In return we'll have two strips of bacon each along with three biscuits, plus use of their fire to make our own coffee."

The woman negotiated everything and always seemed to come out ahead. Jack joined the men to watch Lily melt snow in her skillet, to which she added bacon grease and cornmeal until she had a fine dough. The aroma of biscuits cooking with the bacon drew many longing looks from weary men. Jack thought some gathered just to look at Lily.

"You'd make a fine cook in Dawson, ma'am," said the rangy one, whose name Jack could not recall. It hardly seemed useful to remember names.

"If the money's right, but I'm thinking I'll do better singing in the bars," she said, giving them a smile that stunned them speechless.

The man with the deeply lined face asked her for a sample. Lily grinned at her audience and began to sing as she tended the biscuits.

The men shut their eyes to savor her sweet voice. Yes, Lily would do well, very well, if they survived the trip. Jack felt the weight of responsibility pressing on his weary shoulders.

When she'd finished they shared what they knew of the trail. The man who they called Cincinnati leaned in, conspiratorially.

"I got it from a grave digger from Baltimore that the Mounties are at the top of that." Cincinnati motioned to the trail, shrouded in darkness but still looming before them all.

"I should think that would keep order," said the rangy one.

"That ain't all. He was turned back because he didn't have the one ton of gear they're requiring to pass."

"What?" Lily's eyes widened in disbelief. "Why?"

"And they're checking food supplies. If you ain't got a year's worth of grub, back you go."

Jack and Lily exchanged a long look.

"It's to keep men from getting up in those mountains and starving to death, I'm sure," said Jack. "It's sensible."

"Well, *we'll* not be turned back," said Lily.

Jack was growing to like that stubborn set of her chin and the fire in her eyes. The gal was full of piss and vinegar and he was starting to believe that having her as a partner might not be the worst he could do.

"How you planning on getting that grub?" asked Cincinnati.

"You said the grave digger turned back, didn't you?" asked Lily.

He nodded. "After his first trip up them Golden Stairs."

"Then others will, as well, and they won't want to haul their gear all the way home, will they?"

And damned if she wasn't right. As he set about the labors of carrying his gear to the summit one painful load at a time, Lily inventoried what they had and assembled what they lacked, a collection that nearly mirrored the list the Mounties recommended, including 150 pounds of bacon, 75 pounds of raisins and 400 pounds of flour. Then she paid a Chilkat Indian hauler to carry everything to the top, where she waited, just past the checkpoint, guarding their belongings as Jack made trip after trip with his gear.

It took Jack ten days to finish the last climb up the fifteen hundred steps cut into the ice and snow, wearily dragging himself along the guide rope with the rest of the stampeders. The line of men groaned and sighed, heaved and swore up the thirty-degree incline. Many turned back and each one that did gave Jack more determination to be among the ones to reach Dawson.

"That's the last of it," he said, sinking beside Lily on her canvas tarp. "I'd have been here sooner if I had a partner who could carry."

"If you had a partner who could carry, he'd have been dragging his own gear up the pass, not yours. I saw my gear delivered and without you lifting a finger, plus the food stores those redcoats required."

Jack looked at her gear which had returned to its original size, meaning that she no longer carried the food. "Where is it?"

"Jack, you can barely manage your working model and I don't want to overload the sled. I sold most of the food."

"Did it occur to you that you might need it at Lake Bennett?"

"It did, but money is easier to carry."

"Supplies will be more dear."

"In as short supply as women, I wouldn't wonder. Imagine all those clothes falling to ruin and all those hungry men, desperate for a hot meal and a bit of entertainment."

"You should have asked me."

She handed him a biscuit and coffee. "Yes, I should have."

Her contrition and the food melted his ill-humor.

Lily narrowed her eyes on him. "Do you want your half of the money now or at Lake Bennett?"

Jack disliked handling money. "You keep it for now."

She tilted her head. "You sure?"

He nodded and Lily shrugged, setting about the process of making their supper. After a while she handed him a plate.

Jack accepted it gratefully. He'd not had to cook a thing since he'd hit the beach. It made him feel guilty for his temper over the food supplies.

"I'm sorry I was short with you, Lily. The money's yours, not mine."

"Some of it maybe. But some I earned since we were together. That means you get a say in how we spend it."

He took a forkful of beans, chewed and swallowed, then nodded. He helped her clean the plates with snow and packed the kitchen box. She gave him a wary look at first, but allowed him to do as he liked. After supper they settled with their coffee by the fire, Lily with an arm around Nala and Jack on her other side. Lily no longer used her dog as a wall between them, allowing Jack closer at meals. He liked her company. She didn't talk drivel, but kept them on practical matters. Every so often she spoke of her plans. He liked that best, for she looked off at the horizon when she spoke, her body finally still, her hands at rest and her face holding a look of such longing, it about did him in. He admired her dreams and her drive.

They set the tent and Jack loaded his stove with wood to keep them warm at night. The next day they began the descent to Crater Lake. The trail was difficult but at least downhill. It was unfathomable that the distance between the Scales, below the Chilkoot Pass, and Crater Lake was less than five miles. They were well and truly into the mountains now. The wind bit deeper and the snow fell faster. They used Lily's sled for all the gear, making short trips and shuttling forward, bit by bit. Jack worried every step that they would not reach Lake Bennett in time to make a proper shelter before the real cold hit. It was November already and still they had not reached that last great lake. The nights were twenty hours long now, so they traveled by moonlight and by the shimmering Northern Lights. When they stopped they huddled together, the three of them, dog, man and woman, in their blankets by the fire, and still he never felt warm.

When the cold grew so deep that the coffee froze in his cup before he could drink it, Lily finally convinced him to cache some of his gear so they could move forward. And still it was January before they reached Bennett. This would be the launching point for the boats, because it was the first of the connected lakes that became the Yukon River.

As they descended the final incline, the narrow lake seemed only a bare expanse among the trees, surrounded by an odd assortment of structures, hastily erected and shoddily made. Lily signed on to help a woman run her kitchen, which did a better business feeding men than any other in the vicinity. Instead of pay, she received food and shelter for them both. That freed Jack from having to build a cabin, so he had time to retrieve the remainder of his gear, using Nala and Lily's sled. On each return trip he found more and more men building their boats on the shore so as to be ready for the break-up when they would sail to Dawson. When, at last he had all his belongings, he turned his attention to constructing their boat.

Jack planned their conveyance carefully, since it had to carry more weight than most. It needed a reinforced hull, which would make it heavy and unwieldy. He took the problem to Lily. She did not understand construction but he trusted her opinion.

"I'm afraid I won't be able to see past the gear piled in the middle."

"Make it longer, then the gear won't go as high."

"I've made it the length of the pines here. It will be sturdier that way."

She nodded at the logic of that and then considered his drawing, pointing to a spot in the bow. "If I stood here, I could see for you."

"You'd spot for snags and rocks." He nodded, liking the idea, for it kept him from having to construct a raised steering deck and extending and weakening the rudder. "Yes. That might work."

They shared a smile, which Lily ended when Jack tried to stroke her cheek.

"Off to work with you. You can't build a boat while standing in my kitchen."

He spent the next hour looking through his gear for his whipsaw and tools, finally returning to Lily.

"I think they've been stolen."

"Don't be silly, I'm a better watchdog than all that." She paused, coffeepot in hand on her way past a long table of seated men. "I rented the saw to George Murphy and his brother, Tim. Larry Kristen has your hammer, but no nails. Those he has to buy elsewhere. Martin—"

"You *rented* my tools?"

"Well, you didn't need them to haul freight. Now that you're back, I'll only rent them at night, or would you prefer to work nights? I can get more for them in the day." Lily must have read the answer in his darkening expression for she lifted a hand. "Days then. The sun is only up for two hours a day." Jack grumbled. "I'll see you have them all tomorrow, first thing."

She headed toward the kitchen and he stormed behind her, frustration boiling over. Why must he stand in line to use his own tools?

"You had no right to rent what is mine."

That stopped her in her tracks. She thumped down the heavy pot on the sideboard and pressed her fists deep into the folds of her skirt.

"And whose dog and sled are you using?"

Jack ground his teeth together at her point. The fact that her point made perfect sense only annoyed him further.

"Lily, you said we're partners and we share what's ours."

She nodded, but her expression remained uncertain. "That's so. You shared my sled. I shared your tools."

Jack scowled, finding no ready answer to this and wondering why her logic made him even madder than before.

"We've a need for money to buy the fittings and hardware for the boat," she said.

That was also true, and he should have accepted her reasoning, but he found it did nothing to assuage his annoyance. It seemed he couldn't be near her at all lately without picking a fight and most of those fights made no earthly sense afterward.

And then it struck him. He wasn't here about the

tools or hardware. His heart was not pumping and his skin was not flushed out of ire. He came back again and again to fight, because this was as close as he could come to satisfying the emotions she stirred in him. He was here looking for a fight when what he really wanted, what he really needed was—Lily.

He took her by the shoulders. Her mouth dropped open in surprise as she recognized what he was about to do an instant too late. This time he wouldn't let her slip away. This time he'd have what he came for.

Jack drew her in, slanting his mouth across hers, taking possession of her. She stiffened at the contact and then threw her arms about his neck, pressing her body tight to his.

Finally, Lily was in his arms.

Chapter Seven

Her fingers tugged in Jack's hair, demanding more as he met her soft lips. The desire he had smothered each day and every night now roared within him. He pressed down hard, feeling the heavenly softness of her lips crushed against his. He opened his mouth, silently demanding she do the same. Her lips parted and he thrust inside, savoring her wanton little moan and the slick, silken texture of her mouth. Her tongue danced with his as he cradled her against his body, pressing her back. At last, he supported her weight and still she clung to him with all the fierceness of a tigress. He'd known she would be just this way and the proof fired his blood and aroused his fantasies. Lily's surrender held the sweetness of honey and the heat of a branding iron. No matter how closely he held her it was not enough.

Somehow, he had surmounted her barricades and he basked in the delight of her soft body, full breasts and thrilling little cries of excitement. He laid her across his arm, wishing he were alone so he could take off her top and cup her lovely full breasts in his hands. How many times had he imagined holding her like this— And here was a battle he could win, a battle that made sense, perfect sense.

She'd let him. Her kiss left no doubt. He could do all the things he'd imagined as he lay beside her night after night on the frozen ground. He'd never wanted anything so much as he wanted Lily. Why hadn't he done this weeks ago instead of bickering about this or that?

Lily's hands were tugging at his shirttails. A moment later she had them up and out of his trousers, her fingernails raking over his skin, arousing him to madness. He eyed the table behind them and draped her half across it.

A pot clattered to the floor and Lily startled, then stiffened in his arms. An instant later she turned her head away, depriving him of her full mouth as she pushed against his shoulders.

"Let me up, Jack."

Somehow he'd taken her to the table beside the kitchen stove, where her employer, Sasha Cowdan, now stood staring at the two of them tangled together like newlyweds.

Lily slipped from his arms and tugged at her

blouse, her face flaming with embarrassment. Jack tucked in his shirt.

What the devil had gotten into him? He'd just wanted to speak to her about his tools. No. If he were honest, he'd admit he'd come for this, had wanted it since that day in her tent when she'd stroked his bare chest. And he would keep coming back for this as long as she'd let him. Lily was like a hunger now, something he could not control with his mind. He needed her body, her mouth, her throat.

And she needed him, too. Her kiss told him that. No wonder she'd held him off all these days and weeks. It wasn't to protect herself from his unwelcome advances. It was to keep him from learning they *were* wanted.

"I'm sorry," she said to Sasha.

He wasn't. He'd never be sorry for something that perfect. Why hadn't Nancy ever kissed him like that? Why hadn't she held him as if she were drowning and only he could save her?

Lily elbowed him and then cast her gaze from him to Sasha. Jack had forgotten the woman was there again. He couldn't seem to see anyone or anything but Lily.

She glanced at Sasha. "He's sorry, too."

But he wasn't. He'd do it again when he had the chance, was already planning their next encounter. Somewhere private—their boat! Yes, he'd have her alone then under the stars with the northern skies glowing with their shimmering light.

"Jack. I don't know what got into you," said Lily, trying and failing in pulling off the rebuke.

Into us, he wanted to say, but he couldn't seem to speak as he stared into her blue eyes. Her lips were swollen. His mouth twitched in a satisfied smile. He'd done that to her. His kisses made her cheeks and neck flush a tempting pink and her lips full with wanting.

She placed a hand on her bodice, which was rising and falling in a manner that made him take another step toward her.

But she turned away, helping Sasha mop up the hot water which now steamed from the floorboards.

"Out of my kitchen, Jack Snow," said Sasha.

"Tools," he said to Lily.

"Tomorrow," she said without looking up.

"You'll bring them?" he asked.

She hesitated, biting her lower lip between sharp white teeth. How he wanted those strong teeth to score his skin as she raked her nails over his back again.

He waited, taking in the worry in her eyes. She *should* be worried, very worried. She had been wise to hold him off, had somehow succeeded. But now he knew her secret.

She wanted him, too.

"Well?" he asked.

"Yes, yes. Now go."

His smile held the sweetness of victory. She could come to him and he'd be waiting for Lily to forget her resistance and again give him the sweetness of her kiss.

He left them, wondering why he had ever thought he wanted a sweet, compliant woman when he could have wildfire. As he walked out into the night to cool his skin, he compared her to every woman he'd ever met and found each one lacking. Lily, despite her best efforts, had roused him to near madness with just a kiss. Why were all the women back there as pale and meaningless as their poorly painted watercolors and self-indulgent poetry? Not one could do a blessed thing except order servants about and primp. None of them could have walked all the way from Dyea.

He scowled up at the sky, wondering what it would feel like, for once in his life, to take what he wanted instead of doing what was expected of him?

Lily rose even earlier than was her custom to track down Jack's tools. She hoped to have them gathered and returned to his boat before he even rose from his bed on the opposite side of the large dining room.

Nala stood when Lily left her bedding and stretched, nose down, back arched and then shook as her mistress rolled her thin pallet and blankets. Her hound walked silently behind her as she slipped out into the dark predawn. The sun had begun to rise again, peeking up above the mountains with a dim, joyless light that never seemed to penetrate the clouds before falling back below the horizon for eighteen hours at a stretch. Lily covered her face against the cold and slid her hands out of her gloves so she could maneuver her sled behind the dog. She hung the lantern first and then gathered the leather straps.

Her dog stood still as Lily strapped her into her harness and then mounted the sled. Nala began to yip and bark in excitement as she bounced straight up and down in her harness traces waiting for Lily to draw on her gloves. The instant she had her feet secure upon the boards and gripped the drive bow, Nala was off, bounding on the fresh snow and breaking a trail with her massive chest. Lily laughed in delight as the wind burned her cheeks. The cold made her eyeballs ache, but she didn't care. She loved the thrill of dog-sledding. It seemed the perfect mix of exhilaration and beauty. In a few minutes they were away from the half-buried buildings and flying over the frozen lake. Here the wind had scoured much of the snow away, making it ideal for Nala to run with all she had. They traveled in a magic golden circle of light, provided by the lantern. The only sound was the slide of the runners as they scraped over the granular snow. Lily made a circuitous route to the camps of the men who used Jack's tools, stopping to gather them like fallen apples from the half-finished boats that lined the shore. The whipsaw was last and with that aboard she turned toward home. Nala now settled into a tireless trot that Lily knew she could maintain for hours.

As she left the lake, and slipped between the tall silent sentinels of trees, Lily marveled at how the snow crystals shimmered on the dark trunks of the evergreens and how the snow-laden branches dipped to brush the ground. She spied Jack's building site and smiled. When he rose the tools would be here waiting and best of all, she would not have to face him. For the only thing more exhilarating than riding her empty sled was kissing Jack Snow.

Something moved beside the boat. Lily pulled on the brake and called for Nala to halt. A man stepped into the circle of light. Jack, she realized.

Her heartbeat tripled as she stared at him, tall and handsome. He placed a gloved hand on the upturned boat and brushed off the snow.

Lily lowered her muffler and tried to speak, but her voice was breathless, as if she had been pulling the sled.

"You're up early."

His grin was charming, but the twinkle in his eye spoke of mischief.

"Following you."

"I have your tools."

Jack unloaded them. "Ride me back for breakfast?"

She hesitated. To say no would be rude, for he'd have to wade through the snow to return to the hotel. But to say yes was to allow him to stand behind her on the foot boards, his big body pressed close behind hers.

She didn't remember nodding yes, but a moment later he was there, encircling her, his arms reaching around her to grip the drive bow. She lifted the reins and Nala glanced back.

"Ya!" said Lily and they were off.

Jack laughed, echoing her excitement in the joyful sound. After a moment she steered them away from the hotel and out onto the lake, wanting Jack to feel the thrill of riding with Nala running full-tilt.

Her dog hit the lake at a run and they whizzed along, Jack gripping the bow as she leaned back against him.

He called her name and she turned her head, tilting it back to look at him as they raced over the frozen lake. But he didn't speak again, only moved forward to kiss her.

His mouth was hot and cold all at once and his tongue slipped along her mouth. She felt a moment's resistance, but she could not hold on. The world was flying by too fast and Jack was holding on too tight. Lily surrendered to the thrill of the ride and the kiss and the man who had found her weakness in him.

In a moment he broke free and howled like a wolf

to the dark sky. Lily laughed and turned them back for home. Nala slowed to a trot as they hit the deeper snow and brought them safely to the hotel.

"I'll never forget that ride if I live to be a hundred," said Jack.

Lily smiled, wondering if her mother would be proud of her. Was this the adventure her mother had intended? Had she known what would happen by releasing Lily into the world? It was such a marvel, this territory, and she now felt it flowing in her blood, becoming a part of her.

Jack stepped down and then turned to kiss her again. But Lily was ready this time.

"Ya!" she said, sliding away from him as Nala trotted toward the kitchen, where Lily stored her sled.

"You can't run forever," he called.

Perhaps not, she thought. But she sure could try.

Over the next several weeks Lily avoided him when possible as he worked tirelessly on their flat-bottomed boat. She had a knack for visiting only when the lakeshore was filled with other builders and by being on the far side of the room when they lay down to sleep.

He cautioned himself to patience. The break-up was coming—not just for the lakes, but for them, and with it, his opportunity to have Lily alone.

He built his craft on the shore, electing not to set it up on the ice as many others did for he feared the break-up's power and unpredictability. No one could say exactly when the ice in Lake Bennett would fail, but Jack expected it would be awe-inspiring. When he could not work for exhaustion, he gathered with other men to share what they knew of the river. He borrowed a tattered copy of the December fifteenth edition of the *Dawson City News,* now four months old. Jack had read the passage concerning White Horse Rapids often and knew it by heart.

The rapids are a half mile long and dangerous. A reef of rock juts from the left shore as the river narrows and the water boils with waves running five feet in height. Here a long boat comes in handy as a short one falls mercy to the waves. The landing is to the left beyond the reef and to the right lie the graves of those who drowned in their attempt.

He had not shown Lily the article, for he saw no need to have a hysterical woman on his hands, but he did bring her to see his completed boat. She surveyed his work with a critical eye.

"You've doubled the planking on the bottom," she noted.

"To strengthen the hull," he said, noticing how her dark hair shone in the light.

"Then why not the front?"

"It's called the bow."

He tried for her hand and she stepped around the boat on the pretence of inspecting his handiwork, but actually putting the hull between them. He smiled. *Run, but you can't hide.*

"That's the part that's likely to hit the rocks at White Horse Pass."

He scowled, staring at the boat again, thinking that she might be right. "How do you know about the pass?"

"Did you think that because I'm Irish I can't read?"

He had indeed thought that. "Of course not."

She sniffed. "Men are laying wagers on the break-up. Odds say it will be on May twenty-fifth."

"Did you lay a bet?"

She laughed. "Jack, I don't lay bets, though I have occasionally taken them."

She glanced across the frozen lake. "Snow's already gone from the hillsides, but this ice is as stubborn as any Irishman, overstaying his welcome." She turned back to him. "I know it's May already, but do you think we'll see Dawson by June?"

"Possibly. July definitely."

"And the snows coming again by September. That's not long to lay your claim on the Eldorado."

"I won't be digging by a stream. Those claims will be long gone."

She sighed, the worry returning to her eyes. How he wished he could hold her and assure her that everything would be all right. But her concern was well justified. He'd been so focused on the possibility of being alone with her that he'd nearly forgotten the danger of the rest of the journey. Arriving late to Dawson would be the least of his worries.

"I hope you know what you're doing."

"Afraid you'll have to feed me all next winter, too?" He tried for a smile and failed. He wanted her so badly he ached. Did she have any idea how much?

Her composure slipped. "I promised you that I would help you all I can, Jack, and so I will."

"Lily?" He reached for her but she held up a hand to stop him.

"No, Jack. Not again. I know what you're wanting from me and now you know the way of it with me, as well. But I need you to understand. I made a promise to my ma to see more than the walls of our tenement. I'm here for an adventure and to be part of something bigger than myself. You've become very dear to me. But if you're thinking to have me, I'm asking you not to. I know a man like you doesn't choose a woman like me for long. I'm trying to be wiser than my ma. She fell to temptation a time or two. They didn't stay. Nor will you, Jack. So don't make me fall in love with you and then cast me off so you can return to New York alone."

"Lily, I never intended…" But he had intended exactly that. He'd had so little respect for his partner he was ready to do whatever she'd allow him to do and it shamed him. "You're right, Lily. You deserve better."

Lily stepped outside the restaurant to stare out at the frozen lake. It had been reported that the river beyond Bennett had already given way some eight days earlier and those with the smallest boats had dragged their crafts across the thinning ice in an act that Jack called lunacy. Perhaps, but they were already under way. Even so, she was still trapped. Stuck in this frozen purgatory between Dyea and Dawson and trapped between what she wanted and what she knew would come.

Taking Jack would be her ruination. She felt it in the marrow of her bones. Yet she wanted it so badly it pulsed inside her with each beat of her heart.

Soon the two of them would be sleeping together in a narrow boat. Lily feared what would happen then. For she did not think she still had the will to say no, and she didn't expect a man to have the will to deny his pleasure. Perhaps that was the way between man and woman, passion over common sense.

Why hadn't she chosen that little tailor for a partner instead of this big, handsome, unattainable man?

Jack had kept his distance since she'd asked him not to shame her. But the tension between them had not lessened. All that had changed was the new awkwardness they shared as they waited their release from the ice that trapped them here.

At first, the crack sounded like a rifle shot, but then it was followed by another and another. The ground under Lily's feet rumbled and one of the men shouted.

"The ice is breaking."

Lily dashed toward the lake with the others. She elbowed her way through the crowd. The lake seemed alive with slabs of ice pitching and colliding. They squeaked as they scraped across each other and exploded with sharp pops as the ice snapped under forces she could not imagine.

Lily's heart beat fast as the rumble started. Water surged through and around the thick platforms of ice, tossing them one upon the other. She scanned the shore, searching for Jack, needing to share this moment with him. She found him, eyes pinned on her as he pushed through the crowd.

"Look at it!" she called, her words lost in the rumble.

He looped his arm about her and drew her close as they turned to watch the bottleneck of ice gathering, piling upon itself over the roar.

"That won't last now that the water's flowing." His voice was a shout directly into her ear and yet she could barely make out his words.

She had not even finished nodding when the dam broke in the middle releasing a slurry of freezing water and ice down the center of the lake. Gray water foamed and frothed as it greedily snatched great slabs of ice and carried them along.

Men cheered, threw their hats and scrambled to load their boats. The break-up had come at last and the race was on again.

"Come on, Jack. We need to load the boat."

Chapter Eight

"Tomorrow," Jack declared as if he had some power of divination.

"Are you mad? We'll be the last to leave the shore and last into Dawson."

"I've counted over six thousand boats here. That and the ice will make a pretty picture. I'll not be taken down after coming this far and I won't put you on the river in this."

"But Jack—"

"Look." He pointed toward the water.

Lily took her eyes from the flowing ice to stare in the direction he indicated. There was a shabby little vessel no bigger than a bathtub.

"Do you want to watch that man drown or have to stop to fish him out of the lake?"

He had a point. Lily had been so busy working in the hotel that she had not had a chance to see much of the boat construction, though she did keep close tabs on Jack's progress.

He continued. "Plus those ice sheets could tear even a strong boat into pieces and pop holes in our hull like a child poking a finger through a paper wrapping."

Lily watched five men push a squarish boat, loaded high with gear, off the muddy bank and onto the tumble of ice now thrusting onto the shore. They heaved and strained as the weight of the thing bogged down. Then, in what seemed only a blink of the eye to Lily, the ice shifted, tumbling from beneath one of the men, casting him into the lake. His friend tried to grab him but he disappeared between the ice sheets. The men on shore shouted and danced but none ventured onto the unstable ice to try to find him. He came up again in the fast-moving slurry of ice and water. Men dashed along the shore and finally got a rope around him, but in the meantime the boat rolled, throwing all their gear into the lake.

Lily felt her stomach pitch as she pictured all they owned being lost to the bottom of Lake Bennett. She turned to Jack. He did not seem pleased to be proven right, but rather saddened by the confirmation as he sighed heavily.

"They're all mad," she said.

He stared out at the insanity unfolding before them.

"I've built a strong boat. But I don't know if

anything can withstand that." He motioned with his
head toward the rushing water. "I'd never forgive
myself if anything happened to you."

She nodded, suddenly in complete agreement.
"We'll wait until you say so, Jack. I trust you."

On impulse she reached out to hug him, thankful
that he was so wise amid the chaos. But then she
recalled the last time she had held him and hesitated,
drawing back to leave him standing with his arms
open to accept her. He let them fall to his sides and
a small line formed between his brows.

They stared at each other in awkward silence as
the water crashed behind them. She couldn't warn
him to stay clear of her and then throw herself back
into his arms. It wasn't fair to either of them. But
she yearned for the comfort and protection he could
provide and longed to listen to her heart, as it whispered words of hope, instead of doing what was wise
by keeping clear of him.

She'd seen the look of surprise on his face when
she'd asked him to leave her alone if he planned to
abandon her in Dawson. He'd confirmed her fears
without so much as a word. He had planned to do
exactly that. After all they had endured together, it
hurt that she meant so little to him. Still, she should
not be surprised. That was the way of the world.
Lily was a realist. Men like Jack did not take up with
girls like her, at least not in public and never for the
long haul. Fate had thrown them together, and all she

could do was try to prevent herself from becoming nothing more to him than some shameful little secret.

Funny that she thought her chances better with the heaving ice floes in the lake than in Jack's arms.

That afternoon Jack saw many more stampeders set off. In his mind he knew they should wait, but it was still hard to watch the others go. Huge floating blocks of ice bobbed along to the mouth of the lake where they piled up like rock candy on a stick. Jack loaded the boat and lashed everything down. He'd agreed to assist in the launching of other boats in exchange for similar help.

The following morning, Lily met him by the boat, which now rested the lakeshore. Her cheeks glowed rosily, for nothing enhanced her beauty more than being out of doors and on an adventure. She seemed made for this wild, beautiful country. He drew in the line and helped her aboard. Nala followed with a graceful bound and then set her large forepaws on the gunwales, her tongue lolling as she waited with Lily for Jack to climb aboard.

Yesterday, she'd told him that she trusted him. It was a precious thing and he knew it. He meant to be worthy of her confidence and to be certain his precious cargo reached Dawson safely. Only now the most precious thing aboard his eighteen-foot-long vessel was Lily.

He turned back to the boat, pushing off with the

help of two other men. Then they heaved the second vessel into the water. Jack's obligation complete, he waded out to his boat, climbed aboard and released the line. The current took them beyond him, the lake was alive with the skiffs, boats of balsa, barges, canoes, kayaks and one vessel that appeared to have been made of packing crates tied together with twine.

"That one looks like a coffin," Lily said, pointing to their right.

She sat fearless in his conveyance beside her mutt who sniffed the air as her ears and gums flapped in the breeze. What a novelty for the dog not to have to pull them along. The winds grew fierce at the northern end of the lake, dragging them sideways. Jack and Lily both leaned with all they had against the rudder, trying to hold them in the center of the lake.

"Glad I reinforced the thing with sheet metal," he shouted.

"You've a knack for building, Jack, and that's a fact."

He glowed at the praise of his partner.

His boat performed well, and by late afternoon they had reached the checkpoint at Marsh Lake where the Mounties confirmed that each person had 700 pounds of food.

"That man's crying," said Lily. She set her jaw and stared at the unfolding tragedy as one of the herd of stampeders was cut away from the rest.

"Hard to fail after coming this far," said Jack.

"He won't be the last." Lily's grim judgments, though accurate, were sometimes dispiriting.

Would they be among the few who completed the journey? They'd seen so many give up or be sent back. Jack swallowed back his uncertainty. He had no room for it.

The winds were good and his sail carried them across Marsh Lake, but he pulled in before they reached the mouth.

"There's still an hour left of light," she said.

"White Horse Rapids is next. We need more than an hour to get past that and we need full light. After that there's snags and sandbars and more rapids."

"You sound as if you've seen it."

"Only in my mind." But he planned to walk the cliff and see for himself. It was images of White Horse Rapids that had kept him up many nights, worrying. Tomorrow there would be more than risk, there would be danger. He wondered how the first of those who had set off had fared on the river. They'd faced the rapids with ice and water running as fast as it would at any time in the season. Tomorrow they'd take their turn.

"Jack, you're scowling like a man with a bellyache. What's wrong?"

"Wondering if the boat will hold water on the White Horse."

"It will hold."

Did Lily have any idea of what was before them? He decided to explain it to her after supper. He turned the rudder and steered them up onto the muddy shore, where the mosquitoes waited to devour them. Lily started a fire and added damp wood to the logs. The smoke drove off the worst of the blood-suckers, but the whine of their wings was persistent and maddening. As she worked, the temperature dropped and the flying menaces retreated.

Nala ceased snapping at the bugs and settled beside her mistress with a groan, as if she'd walked all the way across the lake. Other campfires sprang up along the banks. Few wanted to face the joining of river and lake in the dark.

Jack's back ached from manning the rudder and sails, but he said nothing of it as he sank onto a log. His attention turned from his sore muscles to dinner the moment he caught the aroma of the stew that Lily had apparently smuggled aboard, carrying the precious cargo all the way from the mouth of Lake Bennett without his even knowing. It was a welcome surprise and he rather enjoyed eating together from one pot. They sat side by side, dipping their spoons as they stared at the fire and beyond to the glint of ice floating past them.

His attention lifted to the ribbons of green and blue light that shimmered across the sky.

"Oh," she said, following the direction of his gaze. "The Northern Lights. So beautiful. It's one of the things I love best about the winter nights in the Yukon."

Jack looked up. The aurora borealis. The shimmering curtain of color was only visible on clear dark nights. They had seen them many times in Bennett, but this might be the last of them as winter turned to spring.

He smiled and drew her closer, keeping his arm about her shoulder as they gazed at the sky and was rewarded when Lily nestled against him. He drew a breath of complete contentment. Such moments of peace and splendor were rare on their journey.

"What else do you love?"

"Many things. The clear blue of the glacial ice and whizzing over the snow on the empty sled with Nala going full out and watching the mountain peaks at sunset when the colors change so fast you don't dare blink."

He prized those things as well, felt privileged to have experienced them with her. He didn't know when it had happened exactly, when he had fallen in love with this wild country. But he knew he'd miss it more than he ever imagined possible. The world here seemed so alive and vital and the people lived *full out,* as Lily had said. It was so different from the stale, stagnant world he had left. And to think, had he not come, he might never have known what he missed.

"I loved watching the break-up," he said at last.

"And leaning against the rudder beside you, eating your peach turnovers and listening to you barter." He sat contentedly beside his partner, feeling that this moment might be the most perfect of his life.

Lily drew a deep breath as she watched the lights shimmer and undulate across the wide sky.

"I think this is what she meant," she said at last.

"Who?"

"My mother. When she knew she was dying she waited until we were alone and then she told me to sell everything to the last tack and get out of there. She told me to fill my life with adventures so I didn't end up like her, dying with regrets for what she never did."

She lowered her head and Jack heard her sniff. He looped his other hand about her and hugged Lily. She buried her face in the lapel of his sheepskin coat for several moments. Jack held her, thinking of Lily beside her mother's bedside. If the woman hadn't told Lily to go, he would never have met her.

"You've done just as she asked," he whispered, his lips an inch from the top of her head. "Well, I'm glad to be a part of your adventures, Lily. Honored, in fact."

She drew back and wiped her eyes. "Do you think she'd approve?"

He nodded. "Most certainly."

He hadn't realized how sheltered he'd been in his private school and university, how little he had seen outside his own circles. It had caused troubles between them at first, but now he trusted her intuition and her opinion. He'd never felt that way with a woman before. But Lily was different in so many ways.

Like him, she didn't speak of her troubles, and, surely, hers were different than those of the privileged son of a successful business owner. But would she share them if he asked? He found himself needing to know her better. The last time he asked about her father she'd changed the subject. Should he try again? He decided his need to know her outweighed the risk that she might turn the tables on him.

"What does your father do?"

Lily's smile faded and she gave him a sharp look. "I don't know. He didn't stay around very long and I don't really remember him. Ma said he drank his wages mainly, and we were better off without him. But I know she missed him. I did, too, or I missed the idea of him." She shrugged, as if growing up without a father was of little consequence. But he knew better. It hurt to be abandoned, even if you were already a man when it happened.

He thought of his father and felt his mood darken as well.

He gave her a little hug and she gave a half smile, then patted his cheek. "What about you, Jack? Did you have a mother who kissed you good-night and a father who came home each evening to find his slippers and paper waiting?"

Her voice held a forced levity that tugged at his heart. Is that how she pictured his life? She wasn't far wrong, except it was all an illusion, the perfect couple and their lovely children, built on a shallow foundation that did not hold against the first flood. But he didn't let her steer the conversation away from her pain just yet.

"I'm sorry."

"Don't be. That's all said and done. And look at me now, here on a river that will carry us all the way to Dawson in your fine strong boat." Nala rolled against her leg and groaned, glancing at her mistress, who scratched her head absently. "And should I make my fortune there, I'll be able to help my family so they can see what a great, wide wonder the world is, as well. But I don't know if I'll go back myself. I'm starting to take to this territory. It seems a good place to me."

Jack didn't know why it troubled him that she should wish to stay, unless it was because he knew he had to go. He had obligations back there in the States, a mother and sister. With luck and hard work he'd make his fortune and then he could choose his own bride.

Jack glanced at Lily, knowing it was a lie, for he couldn't really choose any bride. There were rules to any game and he needed to abide by them if he were to gain reentry to that world. He couldn't, for instance, choose the daughter of an Irish immigrant without being shunned by one and all. It just wasn't done.

Jack lowered his chin and stared at the fire, smoldering with the glowing embers.

He understood the expectations and had abided by them his whole life, never feeling their constraint. He did now.

Lily still stared up at the rolling aurora dancing across the sky. Her profile was chiseled, with a pert, upturned nose and a sloping jaw that narrowed to her pointed chin. Her neck was stretched, revealing its long, lovely length. How he wanted to stroke it and feel her pulse race beneath his lips. She turned to him and smiled.

"What does *your* father think of your grand adventure, Jack? Good sport between college and a career?"

He was about to lie, as he would have done had anyone else asked a question that brushed so dangerously close to his family secrets. But this was Lily who had given him only honesty.

He braced himself and began with the truth. "I don't know what he would think. He'd be sad, I expect. Truth is, Lily, my father died before I left for the Yukon." He paused, wanting to tell her the rest of it, but years of practice at keeping up appearances stopped him again.

This half-truth grated. He wanted her to know what had happened because if he deceived everyone around him, even those closest to him, then how was he any different from his father?

She took his hand. He opened his eyes to find her staring at him with the sweetest look of sympathy upon her face.

"Well, that's a pity, Jack."

Pity—no that was something he did not need from Lily. He drew back into his protective armor, letting her see only what he was willing to reveal.

"Yes. It's why I came actually. I am his only son. He lost everything shortly before his death. So it fell to me to settle his estate. Nasty business, dealing with creditors, banks and lawyers. They left us quite destitute."

She raised her brow, but her face did not register shock or the look of distaste he'd seen so often among those he had counted as friends before his fall from grace. She didn't judge him and she didn't turn away in embarrassment. For Lily only saw whom he had become, not whom he had been. He squeezed her hand, happy he'd agreed to be her partner. Their meeting, which he'd originally counted as misfortune, had turned out to be lucky, indeed. He admitted to himself that she might just be the best thing that had ever happened to him. With her, he didn't feel sorry for himself or like the son of a failure in business. And he didn't think back nearly as often, for there was too much to look forward to.

"But you said you also have a sister?"

Jack smiled. "My little sister, Cassandra, and my mother are both staying with my mother's older sister, Aunt Laura. It has been very difficult for them, losing their home and all they ever knew. It was through no fault of theirs, you see."

"Bad things happen to good people all the time, Jack. Being good is no protection at all."

"I suppose. They are my responsibility now. They are both depending on me."

When he looked back at her, he found she gave him a steady assessing stare. What did she see?

"Now I understand why you didn't quit with the others, Jack. Your back's to the wall as well, isn't it?"

He nodded, wondering why he'd told Lily so much.

She took his hand. "Find your fortune then, for success is the best revenge."

Jack nodded at the wisdom of this. But he didn't want a fortune. He'd had that and now saw how it had insulated, softened and corrupted him. He was lucky for the chance to do something other than eat dinner at the club and attend social outings that he feared would now bore him silly. But then what else was there for him to do?

It was his job to pick up the pieces of the life shattered by the recklessness, inattention and shortsightedness of his father—wasn't it? He had thought so. Did think so. It was just that he was so far from them. It made it seem like some dream, instead of his reality—a life he barely recalled now. He looked about him at the dark trees silhouetted against the glimmering sky. Would all this become a dream as well?

He hoped not, because he wanted to remember each moment of this journey. He wanted to remember Lily standing at the bow of his boat, nose to the wind and hair flying out behind her.

Lily stifled a yawn.

Jack thought of his earlier plans to have her alone, to lure her to the boat and have his way with her. The impulsiveness and sheer recklessness of his thinking now embarrassed him. Lily was not a toy.

"Would you like to bed down here or in the boat?" he asked.

"Let's sleep in the boat, beneath a piece of canvas. It should keep most of the bugs off and block the wind," she said.

Lily had said let's, as in *let us.* Jack found he could not suppress the rush of heat that flooded him as his noble thoughts battled with his carnal desires.

"Cold will keep the bugs off and we'll be away before they're about." Did she notice the catch in his voice?

They stowed her pots and crawled back into the boat, lying on the flat wooden platform he'd hewn from logs. Nala jumped in and curled at their feet. Jack removed his boots and draped a piece of canvas across the gunwales. It was a far cry from the slim, fleet boat he used to row in the Delaware Canal at Princeton, but he was proud of his little vessel. It carried all their gear and still had ten solid inches above the water line. He prayed to God that would be enough.

It was the end of May now, he realized, and his classmates would have already graduated and would soon be setting about beginning promising futures. Jack found that his musings did not precipitate the familiar pangs of regret any longer. Time and distance made them seem less significant, or was it that he had prospects of his own?

Lily snuggled beneath the blankets beside him, the heat of her body warming him.

He pulled the canvas up, but she stopped him by placing a hand on his.

"Leave it back for a bit. I'd love to watch the lights."

He lay beside her, hands folded behind his head, staring up at the heavens at the miracle above them.

Lily settled her head on his chest, at the juncture of his shoulder and he curled his arm about her, determined to ignore the slow pulsing desire that beat with his heart.

"What's before us tomorrow, Jack?"

He admired that about her. She focused her energy

only on immediate obstacles. Should he tell her the truth?

"Don't be sugarcoating it for me. I can take it."

He chuckled, wondering what she'd do if he petted her head. He had spent much time thinking on what her hair would feel like. He rested his palm on her crown and she nestled closer allowing him to caress her hair. The rhythmic stroke and her gentle breathing calmed him.

"Marsh Lake is shallow. We may have to pole through parts and hope the winds don't ground us on a sandbar or snag us on logs."

"I'll watch ahead and spot for them," she promised.

"After that it's Big Windy Arm. Treacherous winds. Some say it's more dangerous than the rapids."

"White Horse?" she whispered, as if to say it aloud was to bring bad luck.

"Yes, and then Miles Canyon. The trick, I'm told, is to ride the hogback."

"What's that?"

"The ridge of white water coming together in the center of the rough water."

He felt her nod and continued.

"We try to ride it about half the distance, then swing right to avoid the rocks dead center. They look like spears, I'm told."

"Well, they'll be hard to miss seeing."

"And even harder to miss hitting as the water

Send For
2 FREE BOOKS
Today!

I accept your offer!

Please send me two free Harlequin® Historical novels and two mystery gifts (gifts worth about $10). I understand that these books are completely free—even the shipping and handling will be paid—and I am under no obligation to purchase anything, ever, as explained on the back of this card.

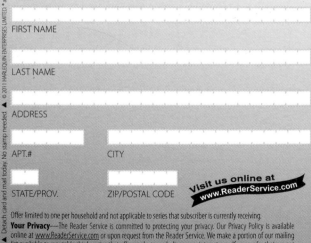

246/349 HDL FEGY

Please Print

FIRST NAME

LAST NAME

ADDRESS

APT.#   CITY

STATE/PROV.   ZIP/POSTAL CODE

Visit us online at
www.ReaderService.com

Offer limited to one per household and not applicable to series that subscriber is currently receiving.

Your Privacy—The Reader Service is committed to protecting your privacy. Our Privacy Policy is available online at www.ReaderService.com or upon request from the Reader Service. We make a portion of our mailing list available to reputable third parties that offer products we believe may interest you. If you prefer that we not exchange your name with third parties, or if you wish to clarify or modify your communication preferences, please visit us at www.ReaderService.com/consumerschoice or write to us at Reader Service Preference Service, P.O. Box 9062, Buffalo, NY 14269. Include your complete name and address.

(side text) H-H-09/11 ▲ Detach card and mail today! No stamp needed ▲ © 2011 HARLEQUIN ENTERPRISES LIMITED. ® and ™ are trademarks owned and used by the trademark owner and/or its licensee. Printed in the U.S.A.

rushes at them, then splits into two streams. They've got pilots for hire at the checkpoint."

"We'll not need one, Jack. You'll be pilot enough, I'm thinking."

"I've never shot rapids, Lily."

"And I've never been first mate, but we'll do it together as partners."

Jack didn't tell her that she'd not be along for either White Horse Rapids or Miles Canyon, for he meant to set her ashore to portage the rapids to keep her safe. If he was lucky and survived the passage, he'd pick her up below.

"What are you not telling me, Jack?"

Damn. How did she know him so well?

Chapter Nine

Jack woke to find Lily curled snug against him. Her breathing had left a fine dusting of frost on his coat, but her body had kept him warm. He'd never slept beside a woman like this, in quiet tenderness, and he liked it more than he had any right to. It was a joy he'd never expected.

A shout came from close by and he realized the voice came from the river. The sun had not even crested the trees and already the parade of boats had begun. He sat up and Lily groaned in protest.

He glanced about at the dark outline of boats gliding along. The lake was crowded with vessels already.

Lily took Nala ashore and Jack prepared to cast off. She didn't keep him waiting. He pushed off and hoisted the canvas wave catcher. He'd learned of the triangular sheet from his discussion with a man called Cap'n Hegg. This sail helped stabilize his vessel and kept the wind from dragging them across the lake. Next Lily raised the square center sail, which she had stitched with an awl as nimbly as any New England whaler. And they were off, wind whistling past him as he turned the rudder. His blood rushed with the water that pulsed beneath the hull.

"Look out, Jack," called Lily, pointing at a low-riding skiff that cut before them and seemed without rudder.

The skiff careened sideways. Jack pulled hard to the right, sending Nala thumping to her side and then scrambling to her feet with much clicking of toenails on the deck. Lily clutched the gunwales as the wind left their sails.

Jack swore as the boat shot before them, nearly brushing their side. The men on board had perhaps three inches of freeboard above the water line, and Jack thought they had no chance once they hit the chop farther out, for though Marsh Lake was shallow, the winds tossed the water into three-foot swells.

"Jack! Look."

He followed the direction of her gaze and saw two boats collide. The one struck broadside floundered and filled, sending the men out into the lake. It sank out from under the occupants so fast there was no time to save a thing. The men were hauled aboard the craft that had scuttled them, and the swearing carried over the water. All about them men fought the wind and the water, the worthiness of their crafts and each other.

The farther north they traveled the bigger were the ice floes. He had hoped the largest pieces would have cleared this portion of the water, but it was not so. As the sky brightened to a steel-gray, they moved along with the heavy, dangerous bludgeons. Jack's stomach churned as they struck one and then another. The dull thump vibrated through the beams below his feet, like rolling thunder. His hull was double-thick, but would that be enough?

Lily moved to the bow and leaned out. Jack wanted to call her back, but he realized that with the sail and the center load he could not see well enough to steer them clear.

"There's another. Right, Jack."

He turned them and was horrified to see a slab of ice the size of a riverboat bob past.

"Slight left," she called.

This was a large tree, roots sticking up six feet above the water's surface. Not having a line of sight proved more disconcerting than he'd imagined and he wondered if his need to carry his gear would jeopardize Lily's life. Nothing aboard was worth that. He gripped the rudder with sweaty hands and looked to Lily who charted their course. He'd need a man to do the job when he set Lily ashore.

"Lake's ending!" Lily pointed to the passage.

Jack leaned out to see the white water. Nala seemed to sense what was to come, because she dropped to all fours and sank to the bottom of the boat. Lily gave her a reassuring pat and then resumed her place at the front, clutching the gunwales and bracing.

Swift water was what he had been told, but that did not prepare him for the flume or the pulsing thrum of water rushing through the narrow channel. Before him the bow lifted and Lily was momentarily two feet above him. In the time it took his heart to beat, the boat rose and then fell, thumping the river that now seemed solid as stone.

They no longer needed the sail and it hindered his sight, but how to lower it now that they were speeding along? Lily left her place and crept aft, hand over hand, like a baby learning to walk. She was making her way to the mast.

"Go back," he called and then thought better of it. If they were hit by ice she'd tumble off into the river, but the bow was not safe, either. Jack could barely swallow past the dread over her safety for he knew he'd have no chance to rescue her before he shot past. "Get down!"

But she either could not hear him or would not listen for she continued. Jack clutched the rudder and braced, trying to hold their course to the center of the white water as Lily reached the mast. A moment later, the canvas flapped madly. She gathered the flaccid sail and had one side secured when they pitched to the left and she sprawled over the boxes, sliding off and onto the deck. He released the rudder to rescue her and the boat immediately turned sideways, tilting dangerously. He glimpsed the water and the catastrophe that loomed as he dove back for the rudder to bring them about.

"Stay there!" she shouted, pointing a finger at him as if he were her second hound.

Jack gritted his teeth and pulled, bringing them around. Lily regained her feet and managed to tie down the rest of the sail.

He could see more clearly now, though the blind spot directly before him was troublesome. He compensated by searching far ahead and steering accordingly. That was how he noticed the red flag tied to a pole on the left bank. Below it was a sign, black paint on a wood slab. It read: Cannon.

Did the writer mean *canyon?* Could they have journeyed twenty-three miles from Lake Marsh already? Jack thought back to the blur of water and rushing shore, feeling certain they *had* reached Miles Canyon, the stretch of rapids second only to White Horse. Already he heard the dull roar of water.

He grounded them. There was a portage here, but the half-mile of skids, a kind of wooden railroad track, complete with cart and mule team, would have many other vessels waiting before them and it would take several days before their turn. The rapids themselves would take no more than ten minutes to cross or to finish them entirely.

Lily stared at him. Confusion wrinkled her brow.

"What are you doing? We've the rapids next."

"Not we," he said.

Lily gaped at him a moment and then her mouth snapped shut as her eyes narrowed. Jack braced for a different kind of rough water.

"If you're thinking of leaving me behind, I'll not have it."

"We have to stop at the checkpoint." Jack indicated the large tent beside the Canadian flag. Nala jumped overboard before they'd even grounded, but Lily did not leave the boat.

"I'll wait here," she said, then folded her arms and glared as if daring him to try to drag her out.

He didn't, but instead lined up with the others. The officer asked the man before him for the address of his next of kin. That gave Jack a momentary pause as he imagined his mother receiving a letter from the North-West Mounted Police and winced. But when it was his turn, he gave the address and in return received a serial number and instructions to paint it on both sides toward the bow.

"We've checkpoints along the way. Expedites searches for the missing." The Mountie held the pencil over the ledger and glanced up at Jack. "Any others aboard?" asked the Mountie.

He hesitated then said, "My partner."

"His name?"

Jack swallowed. "L. Shanahan."

"His next of kin?"

"None," said Jack, feeling the sweat pop out on his brow. Lying was one of the traits he hated, for hadn't his father's whole life been a lie? Yet he'd done it to keep Lily with him.

"Women and children are required to walk the rapids. Any others?"

Jack stared. "Just the dog."

The officer dismissed him with a nod.

The seriousness of what he was about to do struck home, by not listing Lily, he'd prevented her family from ever knowing what became of her, should something happen. Jack turned back to the Mountie.

"How many lost so far?" Jack asked.

"Ten the first day and fifty-six boats. Though at least twelve sank before they even reached the center of Lake Bennett. Lucky for them as they didn't drown. Safe passage." He turned to the man in line behind Jack. "Next."

Jack headed back to the boat in a daze, wondering what he would do if anything happened to Lily.

Lily straightened as she saw Jack's odd expression. Anxiety pushed away some of her anger. His pale face and haunted eyes did not bode well. What had he learned?

"Nothing good, I'll wager," she whispered and pulled Nala close to her side.

Jack laid it out for her. Women were not permitted to ride the rapids, but he'd listed her as L. Shanahan and had not listed her next of kin.

"Rather go missing than have them know I drowned," she said.

"You should walk," he said.

"So should you. Be better than trying to pilot the boat alone."

"I'll take on another passenger."

"Their gear will weigh you down and experienced pilots charge $200 per boat. I checked."

"It's worth the money not to lose the lot."

She pictured the boat capsizing and Jack spilling into the river. "If we spend it on a pilot, we'll have nothing when we get to Dawson. What will you do with all your gear and no claim?"

"We might not make it if we don't."

"I can swim. Can you?" She didn't mention that her swimming experience involved being thrown into the bay and nearly draining it dry before someone pulled her out.

He nodded. "But no one can swim in that."

Lily looked into Jack's eyes and saw the worry.

"Jack, I'll pay for a pilot if you say so. But I'll not leave you alone on that boat with a stranger."

"A pilot won't take a woman. And the wait is four days."

"Four! It's too long. We could be halfway to Dawson by then."

He held her gaze and she knew that they could also be buried at the side of the river in the same amount of time.

Some of the fight went out of her. "What do we do, Jack?"

"I designed the boat to the weight of our equipment, so I can't take on more gear. I need to find a spotter, but I don't want to risk your life, Lily."

"But I'm your partner, Jack. If you're going, then so am I."

"Don't ask me, Lily. I couldn't live with myself if something happened to you."

Lily clasped his hand and stepped close. "Then steer us safely through."

Jack gathered her into his arms and rested his chin upon the top of her head.

"I never imagined I'd grow so attached to you, Lily."

She smiled at this and drew back. "And I'd be hard-pressed to pick between you and Nala."

"I don't snore or shed," he offered and she laughed again.

The laughter died as she watched him paint the serial number on both sides of the hull. Then she climbed aboard and hid beneath the blankets as he recruited four men to push them off the bank. Once they were beyond the reach of the Mounties, Lily emerged to see the steep gray walls of Miles Canyon rising beside them, constricting the river to one-third its breadth. The water sloshed against the cliffs and spilled back into the white water.

"Beyond the curve lies a whirlpool," called Jack, his voice losing the battle with the increasing roar of the water.

Lily swallowed hard, but did not regret her decision. They were partners and they'd see it through together.

The canyon seemed to rush at them. Jack leaned on the rudder, sending them first right and then left, weaving through the waves that burst up against the hull, splashing Lily from one side and then the next and then both at once. The boat pitched down, then bobbed up, sending Nala into Lily and taking both their feet out from under them. They rolled about, unable to gain their footing as water poured in over the sides. Above them, the gray menacing cliffs closed in.

Lily dragged herself up as they burst from the limits of the canyon to the rocky bank beyond. Freed from the constriction of solid vertical rock, the water swept out, filling the space. And then she saw it, dead ahead.

"Whirlpool!" she shouted and pointed to the right, looking back to see Jack staring at her, but he did not change course.

He couldn't see it, nor could he hear her. She motioned madly to the left.

Jack swung the rudder right, sending them careening away, but the boat now leaned dangerously, the load making them top-heavy on the sharp turn. The portside gunwales dipped and water spilled into the boat.

Jack stared in horror, first at the whirlpool, then at his listing boat as ice water poured into the hull. He straightened the rudder, heaving against the force of water and held as the whirlpool skittered them sideways. The boat righted with six inches of water sloshing in the bottom. It would stay afloat, he was certain.

His frantic heartbeat marked the seconds the whirlpool held them and then with a swiftness that seemed impossible they were cast back into calm waters and wide even banks. They had navigated their first rapids, but they had come within a hair's-breadth of capsizing and his confidence had been shaken badly.

Jack sagged against the stern as Lily clapped and danced her way back to him.

"We did it!"

"Because of you." He hugged her, closing his eyes to enjoy the feel of her arms about him and her body pressed to his side. Suddenly it wasn't enough.

He drew her before him, staring down, letting her know what he wanted. But this time she didn't run so he pulled her in. Her soft curves molded to his hard planes. She was wet as a seal and cold as the northern river. Her eyelids fluttered closed as she lifted her chin, offering her sweet lips to him again.

His mouth slanted over hers, taking her in a sweeping kiss. His tongue plunged into her mouth, caressing and claiming her.

She clung to his shoulders, her strong fingers digging into his flesh. He wanted to lay her on the deck, strip her bare and make her his.

They thudded into the gunwales. Lily gave a cry of surprise as Jack pressed damp kisses along the cool skin of her neck. Her head fell back and she moaned as he swept her into his arms, his teeth scoring her neck. It was always like this between them, wild and exciting as the rapids.

Some part of Jack's brain registered a scream and shouting. Lily pushed at his shoulders, but it only made him more determined to hold on.

She turned her head, twisting away.

"Jack. Look!"

Chapter Ten

‎~~~~~~

Jack lifted his gaze and followed the direction she indicated. Another boat bobbed out of the canyon. But this one was in more trouble than they had been. The men on board bailed and shrieked. Lily straightened and Jack released her as they both leaned out to watch the unfolding catastrophe.

"They're sinking!"

Jack stared at the half-filled skiff. The men now used their hats to bail, but the vessel continued to dip into the water, sinking by agonizing degrees. Jack took out his oar, making for them against the current in the calm water.

He judged the distance and the speed the skiff sank and knew he would not reach them before they lost the lot.

From behind them came a floating barge, complete

with piles of gear and a fully erected tent. Somehow that craft had shot the rapids unscathed. Jack realized that such a flat conveyance could not take on water or sink. But it could break apart in rough water and it could split into pieces on rocks. The men on the barge steered for the struggling men.

Jack heard a cry and saw the skiff drop below the surface, taken down by a ton of supplies. The men flailed in the icy water as Jack drew beside them. His vessel was stout and he had no fear of them overturning her as they came aboard.

He offered his hand and dragged both passengers in.

One was crying. "Everything. We've lost it all, Cameron."

The other passenger cradled his head in his hands, so at first Jack did not recognize the man who had helped him launch his boat. His heart ached for them as he turned them toward the shore. The two defeated greenhorns would have to hike to the Mounties' outpost at the mouth of the rapids and seek help there, for they had not really lost everything. They still had their lives.

Jack deposited the wet and weeping stampeders on the shore by the portage. Lily and Jack exchanged a look and he knew Lily understood. This could just as easily have been them.

She lingered by the men, patting their shoulders and hovering. Jack noted the Mounties approaching.

"Let's go, Lily."

She glanced up and saw the lawmen and quickly climbed aboard, calling Nala in.

He used the long pole and pushed them back into the gentle current.

They were well in the center before she spoke.

"You built us a strong boat."

"Don't congratulate us just yet. We still have White Horse Rapids."

"Yes, but that's tomorrow's trouble. We are safe and whole today and on our way to Dawson."

Jack rested a hand on the gunwales. "I hope she'll last."

She came to sit beside him at the rudder, nestling close.

"I've watched the building, Jack. Many of those men have no business wielding a hammer much less trying to run rapids. Those two were luckier than most. Because of you, they survived."

"I didn't do anything."

"You turned back."

"Anyone would have."

She sighed and patted his hand as if he were a boy. "No, some would not. It's still a race, Jack. When I imagined this adventure, I recognized the danger, but I never considered seeing so many men fail. It's heartbreaking."

Her teeth chattered and he knew they must get her dry before she got frostbite. He draped the blanket around her and rubbed her shoulders, but she began to shiver, so Jack turned toward shore. He found a nice flat place and was halfway to the landing when he realized the spot was occupied by two men digging.

He and Lily stared as the stampeders heaved a stiff body into a shallow grave. Jack changed the angle of the rudder and with a slow surreal motion, usually reserved for dreams, they drifted by the tableau.

"The river will flood that bank and take them back," said Lily.

Jack made for deeper water, sending them out into the river's gentle flow. How could this be the same river they had battled only minutes ago? He just couldn't get his mind around the change.

"I'll bring us in at the next likely spot and we'll have a fire to warm you up."

"I'll last 'til sunset."

He gave her a hard look and used her words against her.

"And leave a toe or two here? I'll be damned if I'll let your toes turn black, either."

She gave him an approving smile and then disappeared around the front of their gear. Jack thought she meant to spot for hazards, but when several minutes passed, and she didn't appear, he grew worried. He called but received no answer, so he tied the rudder and went forward to check on her.

He rounded the boxes to find her in the bow, her wet clothing stripped off and cast about her. She was naked and crouched, so that he could see her long pale back, narrow waist and lovely pear-shaped bottom. Lily, not yet seeing him, rummaged in her bag, drawing out a white chemise. Jack was so shocked he staggered back against the side with a thud. She turned, giving him a clear view of the full swell of one breast before she clasped the garment to her chest. Her eyes widened and she rose, pressing the chemise tight, but managing only to cover her breasts and sex. She was lovely as a Rubens painting, pink and curvy, with slim arms and tapering legs. Her knees were rosy as her cheeks.

"Who's steering the boat!" she cried.

Jack tried to answer but succeeded only in stammering.

Lily's eyes narrowed and she straightened, looking just as indignant as a woman could. She lifted a slim arm and pointed to the stern. "You get back there."

He retreated, Nala trotting beside him, but the image of Lily, naked, her wet hair curling about her shoulders, stayed fixed in his mind like a beacon. He'd never forget that sight as long as he lived. Her body managed to be earthy and ethereal at the same time as it was sensual and divine. How would he ever look at her again without seeing beneath her clothing?

Jack untied the rudder and kept his eyes on the river while his mind dwelled on her body and all its lush curves and tempting hollows. What lovely contradictions. Slim, yet plump, short yet lithe. The palms of his hands sweated and twitched as he clenched the handle he'd sanded smooth, but not as smooth as her skin.

Lily appeared in his sight shortly thereafter, fully dressed, with a blanket shawl. Her wet clothing was either stowed or hanging aft.

"Don't look at me like that, Jack. I'm not some morsel to be devoured."

He tore his gaze from her, casting it down river and somehow he held it there for several more miles, as Lily hoisted the sails. He did want to devour her— every luscious mouthful.

Jack recognized Squaw Rapids from the white water, but decided that he had better have full light to run them. That would mean they'd take the first tomorrow as a warm-up to the more treacherous White Horse Rapids.

He gazed up at the clear sky, knowing the lack of clouds would bring a cold night. Would she nestle against him again and would he be able to resist her? He knew the temptation would be worse, now that he knew exactly what lay beneath her clothing. He dreaded and anticipated the night in equal measures.

Lily waited until they grounded to slip from the bow and then tied a line about the sturdy trunk of a pine. She secured a second line before joining him. He could tell from the tension in her body that she was struggling as well.

"Are you planning to stare at me all the way to Dawson?" she asked.

He decided to grab the bull by the horns. "Hard not to."

"Well, who asked you to come sneaking around like a peeping Tom?"

"I called. You didn't answer. I was worried."

"A gentleman would have averted his eyes."

"I doubt that."

Lily shoulders sank a little as her pretence of indignation slipped. "You'll not convince me you never saw a woman in the buff before, Jack."

"Never saw one like you, Lil."

She straightened and faced him. Her eyes were wide and glittering. The expression reminded him of grief, but that made no sense. She must still be angry and that was well and good. As long as she was spitting nails, she'd keep her distance and he'd have a fair chance of not following the impulse that was filling his mind even now. But then he recalled their kisses and how she had melted against him. At Lake Bennett she'd asked him not to shame her and he'd tried to do as she asked.

"I've ruined it, haven't I?"

He didn't pretend not to understand her. For it was true. Everything felt different now.

"I can't think of you as just a partner, Lily. Not for a long time now."

"But I'm still your partner."

Jack shook his head. "I want more."

She stared at him with wide troubled eyes.

"You sleep in the boat," he said. "I'll bed down on the bank."

He bailed the boat and then gathered a pile of wood three times what they'd need just to keep away from her as she set out the cooking pan, beans and bacon, just so he could work off some of the steam that now seemed to flow through his veins instead of blood. He was aflame with need and stuck here in the wilderness with a woman who tempted him to distraction, but whom he respected too much to seduce.

He stomped a branch and it splintered, flying in two directions.

He retrieved one and threw it with all his might. It contacted the trunk of a pine and fell to earth, none the worse for his fit of temper. When he finally deemed it safe for him to approach her, he stomped back to camp and dumped the gathered sticks with the rest.

Lily eyed the mountain of fuel and then studied him, but wisely said nothing. Instead, she offered him a full plate of supper. Jack took it and sat apart, staring at the water.

When he finished she took the plate and washed

it with the rest. He watched her arm move in a rhythmic sweep and noted the gentle sway of her hips as she leaned over the water. He gritted his teeth and forced himself to look away as she set everything back to rights. Then she hesitated, standing beside the fire between the boat and where he sat surly as a bear with an infected claw.

"I'm sorry, Jack." Lily didn't move from where she stood, just out of reach, yet near enough that he could smell her fragrant skin. He wanted to roll in that scent until it covered him.

"Go to bed, Lily." *Please go to bed or I'll not be responsible.* He'd never felt the blood-lust so strongly, not even when he was a green lad or when he'd thought himself in love with Nancy. Lily was different, her pull powerful as the moon changing the tides. His instincts told him that bedding her wouldn't solve his dilemma, for he wanted more from her than a tumble. He tried to imagine a life with her—Lily in New York at a dinner party with the Sniders and winced. They wouldn't accept her and he doubted she would accept them.

It wouldn't work, no matter what he wanted. No matter how he pitched it in his mind, he knew that she wouldn't fit in his world, which meant he needed to get her to Dawson and then say goodbye.

Lily stared at him, his arms bunched as he clasped his hands like a man striving to keep from taking what he wanted. The thought of him holding her filled Lily with a simmering desire. She stared at his hands, imagining them cupping her breasts, kneading and stroking. Her body trembled as a sheen of moisture covered her skin. The breeze blew and the temperature dropped with the sun, but she did not feel the cold, for she was warm in the heat of her wanting.

It had been easier back at Lake Bennett, surrounded by thousands of men. The close quarters and complete lack of privacy acted to keep them apart. Jack had his work and she had hers. Now nothing separated them but her certainty that she could have Jack for a day, a week or a season, but never for a lifetime. But she feared that knowing this was not going to stop her from doing something that she would regret. She understood that he would leave her for some fancy white-gloved, New York debutante who had elegant speech and who could run his home in a way that would bring him comfort and pride. Lily's stomach pitched as she imagined the welcome he'd receive if he were foolish enough to bring her home from the Yukon.

It was impossible for her to live a life with no regrets because no matter what she did with Jack, there would be regrets. The only question was which ones? Would she regret loving him and then saying goodbye, or would she regret missing the most memorable adventure of all by turning him away? Despite all her misgivings she wanted him.

A life worth living involved taking chances—did that include risking her heart?

They'd shoot White Horse Rapids tomorrow and there was more than a passing chance they'd drown and be buried in shallow nameless graves with the others. If she knew ahead of time that this would be her last night on earth, what would she do? Her eyes fell on Jack.

She didn't know how it would all end, but she knew she would have him, at least once, for this was an adventure she could not miss, regardless of the danger.

"We've the rapids tomorrow," she said.

He met her steady gaze and nodded, wondering where she was going with this.

"I want to be with you."

"I'll not put you ashore, Lily. You're my partner for good and all."

"That's not what I mean. Tonight, I want to be more than your partner."

He stood in a fluid motion that showed his grace and power. She followed him and met his stern stare with the slightest incline of her head.

He was beside her in an instant and holding her in his arms.

"Are you sure, Lily?"

In answer she lifted her chin and kissed him with

all the passion she had held hostage in her heart. How could she have ever thought that loving this man could shame her? It wouldn't, not ever.

A rain of gentle kisses dropped along her neck, each one sending a shudder through her. His tongue caressed the outer shell of her ear, her knees grew weak and she swayed in his arms. She tilted her head to give him full access to her neck. He traveled its length until he found her willing mouth. Questing lips sought the soft comfort of her own. His mouth slanted across hers, rousing her until her skin burned with inner heat. He held her head, tilting her to accept his kisses as she pressed forward her hips, finding evidence of his need.

His nimble fingers danced over her coat, unfastening her buttons and then his own. He laid the garments on the ground for a bed and then waited for her there. She followed him as she had always followed him, coming to him there upon the wide grassy bank, allowing him to peel away her wrapping until she shivered in her chemise and drawers. His garments followed with none of the slow kisses. She had just a moment to look at him, naked and virile in the fire's glow, his muscles taut, his skin golden and his male member jutting from a nest of dark curls. The sight sent a thrill of excitement through her middle. He retrieved the blanket and lay beside her, bringing the heavy robe up and over them both.

His dark head descended to her bare shoulder,

kissing a trail along the edge of her chemise and releasing the ribbon ties with his teeth. Jack's warm knuckles brushed the swell of her breast and she gasped at the roughness of his skin and the tenderness of his touch.

When his lips touched to one of her nipples, it budded with a pulling tightness that rippled through her middle. His drawing kiss and questing tongue sent pulsating waves rolling to the juncture of her legs. Warmth and wetness spilled from her as she quivered in his caress. The insistent throbbing brought a cry to her lips and she reached instinctively for his hips, splaying her fingers over the taunt muscles of his buttock. His hands left her breasts, stroking her belly with feathery kisses that sent her head spinning. She arched against him, trying to press his big, male body to hers.

She wiggled and strained, wanting him to touch her everywhere at once. His thigh lifted, pinning her legs and then pressing between her thighs. She opened her legs to him, needing him now as much as he needed her. His fingers danced lower, tangling in her tight curls and opening her soft folds.

She tensed at the intimate contact.

"Trust me, Lily. Trust me as you have all this long journey we've taken together."

She closed her eyes and lay back into the warm sheepskin that lined his coat. Jack would take care of her as he always had. His fingers dipped inside her, the slow friction was heaven. On the next stroke, she lifted her hips to meet him.

He kissed her as she rocked gently against his fingers, penetrating her secret places, bringing her a new pleasure. When his thumb began a wonderful circular dance about her swollen flesh, she could not contain the gasps of excitement.

"I can't resist you. You're too sweet."

He shifted, lifting to his forearms as he positioned himself over her. She spread her thighs to make room for him as his hips lowered to meet her own. His fingers withdrew and his male flesh replaced them. He slid into her slowly. Her body was slick, but he was big and the sensation of fullness frightened her. She stopped moving, but he did not, slowly slipping forward, invading her body, taking what she had offered.

As he reached the delicate barrier of her virgin skin her body resisted.

"Lily?" His voice trembled and his body poised, shivering half-sheathed within her. He left the decision to her. Her body pulsed with the need he had roused. She lifted her arms to circle him, clasping his shoulders and sliding the full length of his back, now slick with sweat, until she came to his hips. He held his weight from her, resting on his elbows.

"It will only hurt for a moment."

She nodded and tugged at his hips. He gave a sharp thrust and the fine tissue tore away. His gaze never left hers. Her eyes widened as she felt the barrier release with a tiny tug. An instant later he was fully joined with her.

Was that all—just that little twinge? Lily smiled up at him.

"I'm fine, Jack."

He lowered his head into the hollow of her neck, muffling his words. "Thank God."

Her body needed to move. She rocked tentatively against him. He lifted his head, his expression one she had never seen. He looked wild, excited and possessive all at once. He stared down at her as if she belonged to him.

His hands slipped down and captured her knees, drawing them up until her ankles rested at his shoulders.

"You're mine now."

"Yes," she whispered. "I'm yours."

He clasped her hands, drawing them high above her head. Squeezing her fingers he lifted his hips and then drove forcefully into her body. She locked her ankles about his neck unable to keep herself from lifting to meet the frenzied thrusts that pressed her deep into the folds of his thick coat.

"Wild as the Yukon, just as I imagined," he whispered.

His strokes were velvet, each one building upon the next. Something was happening deep inside her. It started in the place he had first touched her; the pressure of his body in hers and the friction made her ache for more. She threw her head back and spread her thighs wide to bring him deeper as the tension broke, surging through her like white water. She cried out like the wild animal he accused her of being, panting and gasping as her body bubbled with a pleasure that wrung from her a long moan of delight.

"Ah, yes, Lily, that's my girl." He thrust once more and then held them joined together. Deep inside her body, she felt him move, though his body was still and then came a rush of liquid from his body to hers. He groaned and fell upon her, collapsing with a completeness that would have frightened her had she not felt the same lethargy. They had energy only to lie together, slick with sweat and panting from their exertions.

He enfolded her in his arms, carrying her with him as he rolled from her and onto his side with his face pressed tightly in the lea of her neck.

Within her body she felt his flesh slipping from hers and sighed with frustration at losing the connection between them. She stroked his head, listening to his soft breathing as he fell asleep in her arms. Sometime in the night, he roused to place more wood on the fire, slipping into his clothing. The night was cold, so she did the same, lacing her chemise and drawing on her bloomers, finding a tightness in her legs. She gave a little groan.

"Did I hurt you?" he asked.

"No. My muscles are sore, is all."

He stroked his big hand over her hair and smiled down at her. "Only natural."

Lily returned his smile as he gathered her up in his arms, warming her again. She stared up at the sky, but the gray clouds kept her from seeing the stars. She felt herself falling asleep, wishing she could sleep beside Jack every day for the rest of her life. She didn't regret what they had done. It was beautiful and right.

Chapter Eleven

The whine of mosquitoes woke Lily. She opened her eyes to find Jack standing far down the bank at the water's edge with Nala who was fetching a stick he threw out into the river.

She smiled at the picture they made, as if he were a boy with his dog instead of a man about to fight the river once more. She stretched and felt a twinge of sore muscles at her thighs. A glance showed a small smear of dried blood there. It was not time for her monthly courses, so she wrinkled her brow a moment as she stared. Had he torn something inside her?

The blood had ceased so whatever it was had passed. Lily washed herself with a wet rag and icy river water and then dressed.

As she slipped into her woolen stockings, and added layer upon layer to her outer garments, she remembered the sweetness of their joining and the words he'd whispered. *You're mine now, Lily.* But what did that mean?

She wasn't. Couldn't be if he was to have his dream. And he wasn't fool enough to bring home a poor Irish wife. Choosing her would make him an outcast, hold him back in his aim to return triumphant to New York. And even if he did ask her to come with him, her dreams of adventure did not include living in a city known for its hatred of the Irish or being snubbed by all Jack's high-class friends.

There was the rub. If she let him go, he could live his dream and she could live hers. But if they stayed together, they'd face a mean choice; to have each other, they'd have to forego all they had fought and struggled for. They would have to give up their dreams.

Lily thought of her mother, as she buttoned her coat. "I understand now, Ma, why you took those men to your bed. But you made me promise the impossible. You can't live a life without regrets, though sometimes you get to choose which ones to live with."

This morning she was brimming with remorse, because she'd tasted what it could be like between them and now she must let him go. Once was a risk. More than that was foolishness. She'd wind up like her mother, pregnant and alone. She doubted the saloons in Dawson would hire her then. Her entire grim future stretched out before her. Repeating her mother's mistakes, walking the same tired treadmill.

No. It had to stop. He was a man, so he'd want more of her. That meant she needed to remind Jack of his dreams and responsibilities. He had obligations to his family and they came before her.

She couldn't cost him everything that he'd fought and struggled for. Lily closed her eyes against the pain of what she must do.

A life worth living, her mother had said. A life without regret. Lily hung her head and wept.

Jack walked back along the shore toward the curling fire of their camp. Lily was up. He smiled as memories of last night mingled with anticipation of seeing her again.

"Find Lily," he said to her hound and pointed.

Nala trotted off, head high, stick clamped in her mouth. Jack watched Nala drop the stick upon the ground beside her mistress. Jack wished he had something to give Lily, as well.

Lily grabbed Nala around the neck and hugged her tight, burying her face in the big dog's neck.

Jack slowed. Something was wrong. He set off again now with greater speed. When he reached her, she did not look up, keeping her eyes fixed on the frying bacon, worrying the thick strips unnecessarily with a fork.

"Lily?"

She waved at the mosquitoes but did not look at him. He dropped to his knees beside her and waited, hands pressed to his thighs. He had a sick feeling in his stomach. Had he hurt her?

"What's wrong?"

She lifted her free hand and pressed it to her mouth as if to keep from crying. Blue eyes shone from within red-rimmed lids. A knife blade of anxiety sliced across his middle. Why wouldn't she speak to him?

"It was a mistake, Jack."

"No. It wasn't. We're perfect together."

She shook her head, covering her eyes with the palms of both hands. "We have to stop. It's not right, what we're doing."

Was this about sin, then? She was Catholic and such things prayed heavy on the spirit. After all they weren't married.

He opened his mouth to reassure her and then stopped. He wanted Lily, more than he'd ever wanted a woman. But how could he have her? How could he bring her back to New York and make her a laughingstock?

She met his gaze now, her expression hard and her eyes wise. She waited and then he recognized that she understood all this already, had worked it all out, while it was only just hitting him. He couldn't marry her, not if he was to return to the life he left. Not if he was going to do as he promised and return his mother to society and see his sister educated and well wed, to give them back the life they had lost. Was he a cad to still want those things?

And what about Lily? What did she want?

He'd taken a virgin. He had a duty to her now as well.

"I'll marry you," he said, his voice no more than a whisper as if that was all the breath he could muster.

Her eyes widened, but the lines about her mouth remained hard.

"What about your sister and your ma?"

"I'll send them what money I can."

"No, Jack. It's a generous offer. But I'll not cost you everything."

He couldn't meet her eyes.

"They'll never accept me."

"I know that."

"It won't work. We're too different you and I. And we want different things."

He swallowed the lump that seemed to be rising like bread dough in his throat. His eyes began to sting.

"You're smart, Jack. I don't have to explain how the world works to you. Right now it's only about you and me. If we go on, there'll be a baby to reckon with."

He nodded his understanding, taking a moment before he spoke. "I'm sorry Lily. I never meant to hurt you."

"I know that." She turned back to the fire, serving out his breakfast and handing it to him. He accepted the plate certain that he would not be able to swallow.

His heart ached with the grief over what he had done. Until Lily, he'd never had a female friend, one he could confide in. And now he had destroyed the trust and very likely their friendship. Lily should have been wedded and bedded by a husband who loved her, instead of being taken on a wild river by a man half crazed by lust.

If he had known it was her first time he never would have… It was a lie.

Jack felt his heart bleed with guilt and shame. He was a fool.

Lily packed up the camp while Jack set the sail. When she finally climbed aboard with Nala, she moved to the bow without looking at him.

He was about to push off, but instead he stood on the muddy beach, eyes on Lily, where she stood gazing out like the figurehead of a ship.

"Will we still be friends?" he asked.

Lily filled with a deep, welling sadness as she looked at him. Regret, she realized, for what she still wanted and could not have. "We're partners until Dawson, Jack. Just as we promised. Now cast us off."

He did, releasing the lines and pushing the boat off the bank, then climbing aboard.

If she had known that her choice to lay with Jack would include this hollow, dry ache, would she still have done it? Lily stared out at the river scanning for obstacles. Here it was all so plain. She could see the dangers and move to avoid them. But with Jack, it was different.

It was not until they were sucked into Squaw Rapids, that Lily came from her musings. The surging white water forced her to focus on what was before her. Perhaps if she could just keep looking ahead, just as far as she could see, she could get through this.

She found the speed more exhilarating than terrifying. But the rush of water and blur of the shore did not make her forget Jack's words. *You're mine, now.* And afterward, *I'm sorry, Lily.* They played over and over in her mind. She had other regrets as well, among them she regretted her own stupidity at bringing such a wedge between them now when they needed to pull together more than ever.

Lily stared at the cliffs rising up from the rocky bank, her stomach churning like the water at its base. This was the passage that everyone feared and word was that there were many new graves on the banks beyond the canyon.

She looked back to see Jack turn the rudder, making for the bank. He'd said he would study the water from the cliffs and watch some others try to shoot the rapids before they took their turn.

It showed wisdom. Jack was a cautious man, usually, but not where she was concerned. Had she made a mistake loving him? Her head said yes, but her heart longed to hold him again. If they didn't reach Dawson soon she might fall back into the same trap.

They scraped the rocky bank. Jack left her to watch their belongings so he could hike to the portage on his scouting mission. While he was gone a smooth-cheeked Mountie came poking about.

He copied down the number they'd painted on the bow.

"You two planning to portage, ma'am?"

"No, we'll run them."

"No, ma'am. You'll walk around. The boat can go through with the others."

She'd said they had four men aboard, including her husband.

"But you're required by law to portage."

"Oh, well then, that's what I'll be doing, of course. I'd not want to break the law."

"They can hire a pilot. We've a list of qualified men."

"Hire? Oh, I'll ask them to do so. Worth the money, I'm sure."

"Better safe than sorry." He tipped his wide-brimmed hat and marched off like a police officer. Most of her encounters with such men involved being told she couldn't sleep here or rest there or dawdle on this corner—and here they were, still ordering her about. *Move along, move along.*

Lily settled down to watch the river knowing she'd

do as she liked and no man, uniformed or otherwise, would tell her different, for this was her adventure for good or bad.

She understood the risks, but she'd not leave Jack blind on the most dangerous stretch of water from here to Dawson.

Lily turned her gaze to the river. All the men that passed looked exactly the same, grim and wide-eyed. She noticed one man, small, with a dark hat and full beard. Her Brooklyn tailor.

"Mr. Luritz!" She waved frantically and called again.

He turned and spotted her.

"Miss Shanahan!" He waved back. "I haven't forgotten your dresses!"

She cupped her hands over her mouth. "Good luck!"

He waved again and then held on to his hat as the boat picked up speed. Lily whispered a prayer for him.

She watched until his flat barge disappeared, dropping from sight as if it had fallen off the edge of the earth. Lily wondered at the drop, for he had vanished, mast and all. The parade of crafts continued through the afternoon. Jack came back before dark. He was uncharacteristically quiet.

"It's that bad?" she asked.

He nodded his head.

"Jack, I don't like secrets so you'd best tell me."

"I saw three boats go down."

"A flat barge?"

Jack wrinkled his brow. "Yes. One like that hit the rocks and broke apart. But Lil, I saw two other barges make it through."

Had Luritz crossed safely?

"Another craft capsized. They were all drowned. Seven men." He shook his head. "Another took on too much water and sank. I hope we're not over-loaded. I've calculated the height of the sides, but I never saw water boil like that."

"Mounties came by and took our number."

Jack looked somber. "They told you that you needed to walk."

She nodded.

"They're checking all passengers, Lily, and they're checking the boats."

"Then I'll need a pair of pants and a good hat."

Jack stared a moment and then spoke in a low, scratchy voice. "If anything should happen to you, I'll never forgive myself."

"Jack, you need me. I'm your eyes."

"I don't want you aboard."

She glared. "I'm your partner to Dawson. You agreed."

He tried unsuccessfully to stare her down and then nodded once. "All right. But if they stop you, you'll walk."

Lily had a horrible image of watching from above

as Jack struck a rock he did not see. But she accepted his hand and shook.

"Deal."

He didn't let her go. She didn't pull away. The heat between them blazed anew.

"Jack?"

"It's bad water, Lily. Real bad."

She nodded and squeezed tight to his hand. "We'll make it through. You've built the best boat on the river."

His grin was lopsided, but his eyes remained troubled. She released his hand and hugged him. His arms came about her hard and fast, clasping her tight. She felt the tension in him and the strength. What would she give to be a New York debutante?

"We'll make it, Jack. I just know it."

She thought she felt him kiss the top of her head before he set her aside.

"'Course we will." His eyes glittered.

Lily wondered at the horrors he'd seen this day and was glad she did not have those pictures bobbing about in her mind.

Lily washed and packed her gear as Jack scattered the coals on the rocks. Then he waited on the bank as she changed into a pair of dungarees that fitted her round bottom a little too snugly. The old work shirt was torn at the hem, but covered her curves. She tugged on a battered old hat and regarded him from beneath the brim.

"Well?"

Her skin was too fair and flawless to fool anyone at close quarters. But from a distance she might pass for a boy.

"Where did you get those?" he asked.

"Traded for them."

He cast a disparaging look at her attire. "I think you were robbed."

She stared up at him. "Ready?"

The Mounties checked them in a little farther down river. Lily stayed with the boat and kept her head down. Afterward they waited on the bank for their turn behind two canoes, an overloaded skiff and a barge complete with tent and stove.

"My, they'd never have to go ashore," said Lily admiring the practicality of the craft.

"Unless the lashing fails and they break apart."

They proved prophetic words, for the barge operator was clumsy and as Lily and Jack watched them from the bank they failed to make the turn after the landings, crashing immediately into the boulders before the 300-foot bluff of black basalt now directly before them. Lily gasped as the barge lifted, spilling the men into the water, their tent crumpling as the stove dragged it into the river. She could not hear the logs break, but she could see them separating like the stays of a fan as the goods fell through the cracks.

Two men scrambled to the shore, but the others were swept along.

Lily turned her worried eyes on Jack.

"Improper rudder," he said.

The skiff went next, turning neatly round the bend to the left and out of sight. The canoes went together and then it was their turn.

Chapter Twelve

A whistle brought Nala into the boat and a few moments later they joined the other vessels pulled downriver by an ever-increasing current.

The river began gently enough. Jack spotted the red flag on the pole and the sign announcing they were in the canyon. He knew before he reached the looming cliffs that the river would be forced to a hard left. Jack also knew from his scouting that there was a reef on the left bank, a mad tangle of logs and rocks, but the cliffs lay to the right with the faster water. Where he placed them was all. He had decided to hug close to the reef to put them in a better central position as they took the next right angle through the canyon. Lily had worked out sign language that mainly involved her pointing to hazards and then waving to clear water. She spied the reef, as sure as any springer spaniel spotting game, and waved him right, but he took them close then turned the rudder with all he had. The water roared like a maelstrom and pulsed like the heart of a great serpent. He hugged the horse's mane of white water, shooting out into the canyon. Lily noticed the reef a quarter mile downriver and pointed. The most dangerous part of their journey rushed at him with inhuman speed. The reef further pinched the churning water into five-foot waves.

She motioned to the right and he leaned, fighting the rush of water that tried to snatch the rudder away. The waves beat against the sides and splashed over the deck, knocking Lily down. She righted herself as he held them in position. Just then the boat pitched as if some sea monster had hit them from below. Not a rock, he knew, but the waves, tossing them up and then leaving them airborne an instant before they crashed back to the river.

Lily's feet left the deck. Jack stared in horror as she seemed to move in slow motion, flying up into the air as if catapulted. She sailed over the side and into the white water.

"Lily," he howled, but the roar ate his words. He searched the water, but saw nothing.

Nala leapt over the side, disappearing after her mistress.

Jack shot past the reef, hitting the widening river and the slowing water. He leaned over the gunwale, looking for Lily. Her hat bobbed along, but he could not see her.

"Lily!" He could hear his voice now and the splashing.

He ran to the bow. There they were.

Nala swam nose in the air, thrashing her forelegs at the water. Lily clutched her dog round her thick neck and Jack found he could breathe again.

"I got you."

Nala changed direction, making for the boat instead of the shore. He reached for an oar and extended it to Lily. She clasped hold of the pole and he dragged her to the side. Jack hauled Lily up first and then the two of them tugged her dog out of the water.

With his girls safe, Jack staggered back. Lily sank down beside him and Jack grasped her, dragging her into his arms.

"I nearly lost you," he whispered, pressing his cheek to the top of her wet head.

"No, I'm here."

He closed his eyes at the joy of it. The shock of her fall brought home just how much he needed Lily. She was more than his partner. More than the object of his desire.

"Thank God."

"And thank my hound." Lily patted Nala who had already shaken off and lay at her mistress's feet.

Jack squeezed her tight and kissed her wet, cold

lips, warming them with his own. There was a whooping cry from close beside them.

She drew back and stroked his cheek, pride beaming from her over what they had accomplished together.

Jack pushed his hat back on his head.

"We did it," he said, grinning at her.

"We sure did." She held her smile until it became brittle.

He stood and offered his hand, she let him pull her to her feet, then she stepped away. The moment was gone and he'd lost her again.

"Damn, boys, we've shot them rapids!"

Lily popped her head over the edge of the hull. He followed her example to see a skiff with two men, one at each oar, drift past them toward the many sandbars to the left of the widening river.

"We made it, Jack. Dawson's only a hop and skip from here."

Actually they were yet to reach the halfway mark. But they would be on the river for all of it and the Chilkoot Pass, their first winter and now the White Horse Rapids all lay behind them.

"Damned if we didn't," he said.

"I've got to change. Go to the back again and don't come forward unless I call for you."

He nodded and did as she bid him, knowing what would happen if he didn't. Since their night together, he had kept his hands off her, but not his mind. He watched her at the bow, taking in every nuance and each gesture. He watched her by the firelight when she slept. And now, as he knew she was changing, he remembered that day he had seen her there, savoring the memories as a starving man recalls a feast. He had not stopped wanting Lily, had accepted long ago and many miles back that he'd never stop.

Lily did not forget the sight of the fresh graves beyond the White Horse Canyon or the icy bite of the river after she had been pitched in. So she stayed well back as they took Five Fingers Rapids, named for the fingerlike rocks that jutted up from the river. Lily thought the black humps of rock looked like the body of the whale that ate Jonah.

They made it past Big Salmon and Little Salmon, through the community of Sixty Mile, so named for its distance from Fort Yukon. They camped on the river when possible to discourage the mosquitoes that now flew in black clouds on the shore. Jack had rigged a metal-and-brick floor in the boat as a platform for cooking. She set their fires in a metal basin that Jack would use for a wheelbarrow once in Dawson. As daylight stretched to eighteen hours a day and the river grew calm, she suggested they work in shifts, each sailing the boat for six hours and then resting. This brought them to Dawson City on July 4, 1898.

Lily stood beside Jack at the stern as they sailed

the last two miles along the wide river, flanked by green pine on one side and the white-capped mountains of The Dome on the other.

"It's a fine way to celebrate Independence Day," said Lily.

"But we're in Canadian territory," Jack reminded her.

Lily waved off his observation as she studied the shore. There were many cabins, each with nice piles of dirt just waiting to be sorted.

"What are those? They look like wooden gutters in the stream." She asked pointing at a series of wooden troughs set beside the tributaries leading out to the river.

"That's a Long Tom. It's kind of an extended rocker box. You feed the dirt into the top and then rock it like a cradle. The stream water running through and the rocking washes away the dirt and gravel leaving the heavier material, including the gold, to be trapped in the riffles."

She stared in wonder at the filthy man who threw shovelful after shovelful into the top of the contraption.

Jack pointed. "At the bottom are small slats of wood that trap the heaviest material and gold is heavier than any other thing out here."

Lily craned her neck as they sailed on, wishing she could see to the bottom of that trough. Next came a little inlet which held hundreds of logs, just waiting for the sawmill. Two horses ate hay from a trough made from a canoe and everywhere freshly sawn planks covered half-constructed buildings.

"That's it. Dawson City," said Jack as he turned the rudder.

Lily studied the rough collection of structures, looking for the biggest and grandest of them all, for that was where she planned to work.

"We should stay on the boat a few nights," said Jack, who had become more and more sullen as they neared their destination.

"We'll see," she said, not wanting to be alone in the boat with him, knowing they would separate afterward, knowing their parting would make her more apt to forget all the reasons that sleeping with him was such a bad idea.

As it happened, Lily was offered a job the day she set foot in Dawson, singing at the Pavilion, an arrangement that included a shared room at a boarding house and board at one of the hotels. She also rented a five-by-five piece of warehouse space, so Jack could search for a claim on which to try his invention without worrying about his supplies.

She came to the boat when the last of his gear was stowed in the guarded warehouse and handed him a billfold.

"What's this?" he asked.

"It's $428.00, your half of what we earned since we partnered up." She extended the money, waiting.

"Thank you, partner."

She held on to the wallet a moment too long.

"You won't go spending it in the gambling halls, will you?"

"I'm a Baptist, Lily."

"What has that to do with squandering money?"

"We don't drink and we don't gamble."

"Are you funning me?"

He shook his head. "No, ma'am."

"I never heard of a man not drinking or gambling." She glanced about. "I hope there aren't too many other Baptists around here."

"I wouldn't worry."

She returned her attention to him. "Will you come see my first show? Just for luck?"

Jack shook his head, feeling the ache already gripping his heart. Their parting had come.

"I'm heading up Bonanza Creek. I hear there is a claim or two for sale there that's played out. Might be able to buy it now." He held up the wallet.

Lily toyed with the lace collar of her best blouse. "The owner of the Pavilion says all the good claims were gone before the fall and all that's left is grubstakes, working for those that own the claims."

He patted her cheek. "Don't worry, Lily. I'll not starve."

She clasped his hand and held it to her cheek, closing her eyes for a moment. When she opened them, they glistened. At first he thought it was her frequent temper, but then he realized it was tears. Lily was close to crying.

Her voice broke and she tried a second time to speak. "Well, if you do come back, come to the Pavilion. I haven't forgotten my promise to look out for you all I can."

She released his hand and they stood suddenly awkward in the street. They had been through so much and he had grown to care for her.

"A hauler offered me five hundred dollars for Nala. I turned him down." She looked worried. "I've a favor to ask, Jack. I don't want her stolen while I'm working. Will you take her for a while? They won't let me keep her at the boarding house and she likes you."

"I'd be glad to have her."

"Don't sell her."

"Never. And I'll bring her to see you when I'm in town for supplies."

He felt the time between them slipping away.

Had she given him Nala to protect her dog or to insure she would see him again? He stared at her lovely face and wondered why he could not think of anything important to say.

"You were a good partner, Lily."

She smiled, but then her chin trembled and he thought he'd said the wrong thing again.

"I never had much luck with men, Jack. Hard to trust them, you know. But you kept your word. And

I thank you. And I'll not say goodbye, for you're coming to see me with Nala. Promise."

He nodded, finding a lump in his throat prevented him speaking. Once he had wanted to be rid of her and now that he was, he found he was not ready to let her go. He hoped she'd kiss him, but she didn't.

Lily hugged him, pressing her lovely face into his dirty coat. He stroked her hair and lowered his chin to breathe in her fragrance once more. Then she pulled back and called Nala. The hound came, but her tail was down and she looked to her mistress.

"Go on, Nala." Lily motioned her away.

Jack turned and headed for the river. He couldn't look back, because if he did he'd do something foolish. Nala somehow sensed that Lily would not be coming with them and she whined anxiously.

Jack felt his shoulders sag. The weight of the journey, the sorrow of their parting and the uncertainty of his future all preyed upon him.

Would his invention even work?

Chapter Thirteen

Lily could not have asked for a better start. Before the week was up she was the object of a war between the Pavilion and the Forks. The Forks had a piano, but the Pavilion offered her a better wage. After hearing her sing, the owner of the Pavilion, Donald Trost, was determined not to lose her. He was stocky, with a ruddy complexion and a nose for business. They were much alike in that and she enjoyed negotiating with a man who knew how it was done. He managed to get her exclusively and for six nights a week, with a second show on Saturday nights. In return she arranged to receive a small percentage of the house, plus she did not have to drink with the customers or dance with them. The large hall had a stage where she performed nightly, with the exception of Sundays, when the Mounties shut down all such establishments. They also forbade the carrying of firearms and kept the stampeders in tight check. Because of them, Dawson City was far safer and more orderly than San Francisco had been.

The Pavilion was just a sawboard hall, rough-hewn and still smelling of sawdust, but the stage was wide with kerosene lamps all along the edge and a real curtain. She had high hopes that there would be a grand hotel next year with painted walls and a fine chandelier. Goods would be arriving soon by ferry.

Lily planned to stay as long as the gold, longer perhaps, for she loved it here. The men and women she met all shared her thirst for adventure and impressed her daily with their toughness. And if that were not enough to recommend this territory, the scenery was like none she'd ever imagined, and it was populated by such wondrous creatures. She'd seen a moose with two calves on the bank at Forty Mile.

Wouldn't it be wonderful to make a life in the north and grow with the territory? There was hope here and people willing to work hard to succeed—all kinds of people from all over the country and the world. It baffled and thrilled her.

Her first Saturday night was standing-room only. When the Mounties threatened to shut them down, Trost limited the number of entrants, which allowed the barmaids to get through the mob to bring them beer.

It was on the second Saturday that the first green-horn threw a small sack of gold dust at her feet. For that she blew him a kiss. It was not the first bag or the first kiss.

Her only regret was that Jack did not come. Three weeks already and she had not seen him or her dog. She wanted him to hear her sing and see how the men cheered and stomped their feet. Somehow it mattered to her that he witnessed her success.

Lily had to admit that she had entertained worries that Jack would become like the men her mother had brought home as soon as they reached Dawson, using her for the warm bed, free food and pocket money she could provide. But it seemed the opposite was true. He didn't need her for anything and that troubled her more than she had thought possible, for she still needed him.

The little tailor had arrived, hat in hand, but he reported having had to hock his scissors in order to eat. Lily went with him to retrieve them and then buy fabric. She allowed him to use her room when she was on the stage. Within the week, Luritz had made her two new dresses. One was pale pink with a tight bodice of satin and a frothy full skirt. The color complemented her pale skin and made her cheeks look rosy. The second was a heavy black velvet gown that matched her hair. During the final fitting, her tailor's stomach gave a loud growl.

She eyed him suspiciously. "When did you last eat, Mr. Luritz?"

He hung his head. "I can't find a mine owner to take me. Too little and too old, they say. But I wasn't too little to climb those mountains."

Jack had been right—all profitable claims were staked, leaving the newcomers without hope of mining their own land. Mine owners had their pick of the thousands that poured in from the lakes. Here, as back there, men had no work.

She'd never been in a situation where she had plenty while others went without, and she found she didn't like it. She might not be able to feed them all, but she could feed this man. Lily went to her dresser, brought back the remains of her unfinished breakfast that held thinly sliced toast and strawberry jam and offered it to her tailor.

"Here, Mr. Luritz."

His face colored, but he took it and ate it with a frightening speed. She remembered what it was to be that hungry. It devoured a person's pride.

"Mr. Luritz, I have need of another outfit." Two was actually more than she'd ever had or needed, but she had the gold and he needed it. "Not for the stage. A skirt with matching jacket. Are you up to the task?"

"Yes, yes."

"You're hired. Come back tomorrow morning at

nine. We'll have breakfast together and then go get the fabric."

He tipped his hat, showing the second strange circular hat beneath. "You're a good lady, Miss Lily."

Then he left her. She watched him out the window as he crossed the street, wearing no gloves. Had he lost them on the journey or sold them?

That afternoon she went to buy men's gloves. While she was out she spoke to every woman she could find about what a job Luritz had done on her gowns. Dolly Isles and Felicity Volmer, who both boarded at the same hotel, asked her to have him come round to see them, for the women in Dawson found no shortage of opportunities to earn a living.

Just before showtime, she tracked down Donald Trost, finding him in his office and asked him for the use of the smaller storeroom behind the stage.

He didn't even glance up from his ledger. "For what?"

"A tailor shop."

"I'm using it."

"The tailor will pay you eight percent of his profits for rent. You'll make money, Donny."

"I like when you call me Donny." He was on his feet now, smiling at her. It seemed an expression he had not much experience with. "All right, then."

Lately she'd found him staring at her more and more, and not in the way a man looks at his cash cow. It made her wary.

He dropped the pencil and slapped the account book closed, then stood and tugged on his vest. He stepped out from around his desk, leaning back against the edge and held out a hand. She didn't want to take it. He was too damned big and experience had told her to stay clear of a man's reach. But he'd never threatened her, so she pushed back her uncertainty and accepted his hand.

"You know I'm fond of you, Lily. Very fond." He lifted her hand to his lips. His mouth was dry and his cheek as coarse as sandpaper.

She resisted the urge to tug free. Out in the hall, the fiddler began tuning with a familiar plucking. Trost couldn't keep her long. It would be bad for business.

"I've been thinking about you. We'd make a good team, you and I. I'd like to start seeing you, Lily. What say you to that?"

She knew this game. You didn't need to pay a wife a salary, for she had to work for free and she could not quit. Lily was certain Trost would like that situation, while she would not. Now, how to stall him indefinitely and still keep her job?

She retrieved her hand. "I think that if I'm not on that stage for the opening number my boss will fire me."

He laughed at that and she made it to the door.

"Running won't help, Lily. I'm a determined man."

That last comment sounded more threat than promise.

The fiddler began and she stepped to the center stage, waiting for the workmen to draw back the curtain. Her performance went on without a hitch. The curtain was drawn and she stooped to collect the two small bags of gold dust thrown by admirers, tucking them in her bodice.

A frantic barking caused her to turn toward the stairs. Her dog pushed through the curtain, nose down as she followed Lily's scent.

"Nala!"

Her dog lifted her head and spotted Lily, then began a wild yipping and twisting.

Lily stooped to rub the dog's belly and stroke her head. Nala righted herself and rested her head on Lily's shoulder.

"Oh, Nala, I've missed you," she whispered as she hugged her dog.

"Still feed her once a day, all she can eat."

She glanced up at the familiar voice to see Jack, now clean-shaven and looking tall and handsome with a new confidence that seemed to surround him like a halo. Her heart rate surged and before she knew it she was lunging toward him. He scooped her up in his arms and turned her in a wide, sweeping circle.

"Oh, Jack, you terrible man. Where have you been?"

He laughed and set her down.

"Working—though I'll say you seem to be better at extracting gold than I am." He laughed and the sound warmed her inside and out.

"Did you hear me sing?" She could not keep the excitement from her voice.

"You're like an angel. They're all in love with you."

All but him, she thought, and was unsettled at the pang of regret.

She took a good long look at him, filling herself with the pleasure of being beside him again, then taking in the changes. He looked thin and tired.

"Have you eaten?"

"You going to make me some of your biscuits and bacon?"

"I can do better than that." She drew out one of the bags of dust and dangled it before him like a watch on a chain. "I'll buy us both a steak."

He grinned. "Sharing supper, just like old times."

"It was less than a month ago, Jack."

He nodded. "Seems longer."

She felt a tugging at her heart. It was that way for her, too. Had he missed her? She prayed so, for it would be such agony to be alone in her torment.

She linked arms with him and led him out, stopping for the wolf skin cloak she'd purchased. At the restaurant she paid for three dinners, so Nala could have salmon and rice. Nala finished first, of course.

Over dinner Lily learned Jack had a claim that had panned out for the last miner, but that he was digging in, following what he thought was a promising old stream bed. The deal included a rough cabin, but he'd had little time to make improvements.

"My machine's up and running and it works, Lily. I only need to engage investors and then I can produce and sell the machines to the mine owners."

"It works?"

"Better than I had hoped. I'd love to show it to you, Lily. I want you to see what I've done."

The excitement in his voice warmed her heart nearly as much as the knowledge that her opinion still mattered to him.

She reached across the table to lay her hand upon his. "I'm so proud of you."

A moment later he had hers captured between both of his hands. "You haven't even seen it yet."

"I know you, Jack. If anyone can build a gold-digging machine, it's you."

His thumb stroked over the skin on the back of her hand. Her reaction to the tiny caress struck her with a force that caused her to inhale sharply. She felt her stomach tighten and her skin flush. Lily drew her hand away before she did something or said something that would embarrass them both. His absence had been hard on her, so hard that she'd nearly forgotten his plans to make his fortune and leave her behind.

"I have a canoe," he said. "We can make it in less than an hour."

Say no, Lily. Tell him you have plans. Tell him that you've moved on. But what she heard herself say was, "I'm off tomorrow."

He grinned. "I'll pick you up for breakfast. Dress in your old clothes."

"I still have them."

He walked her to her door and waited. She wondered what he'd do if she kissed him goodbye? The possibility started her heart on a mad thumping that made her positively dizzy. Try as she might, she could not keep from casting glances at his mouth as she recalled their night together.

There were men everywhere here and yet she could think of only one, one that didn't want her. And *that* made her a damn fool.

He paused before a door that led up the back stairs to her room.

"I can't wait for you to see my system. I don't think I'll sleep tonight. Of all the stampeders in Dawson, you're the one whose opinion I value. If you think I've got something, I know I do."

Was her opinion all he wanted from her? She had so much more she could give him. But no matter what she did or how successful she was here, she couldn't turn herself into the kind of woman he sought.

"I swear if you'd been at my father's side you'd never have let him invest in those railroad stocks."

She wanted to be by Jack's side. She lowered her head, plucking aimlessly at the rabbit fur of her muff.

He clasped her chin between his thumb and index finger, lifting her gaze to meet his. "Thank you for the meal."

She held her breath, hoping he would kiss her again. She knew she was a fool, but she didn't care. She wanted to feel his lips again, inhale the fragrance of wood shavings and smoke and tangle her fingers in his thick hair.

She leaned in, kissing his cheek as he did the same. She closed her eyes against the bitter disappointment. Didn't he want to kiss her?

"Lily?" The voice came from behind her.

She broke away from Jack and turned to see Don Trost scowling at the two of them.

Her boss stood in the evening sunshine, his posture erect, his fists clenched. Jack, by contrast, leaned casually against the door frame, scratching Nala behind the ears.

"Jack Snow, this is Don Trost, owner of the Pavilion."

Jack wisely decided to nod rather than shake. Don continued to scowl. Lily's caution turned to annoyance.

"Was there something you wanted?" she asked Don.

"I couldn't find you after the show. Alexander said you stepped out with a greenhorn."

Lily tapped her foot. "And?"

Don glared at Jack then turned his attention back to Lily. "You never accept invitations from the men. I was worried."

Some of her ire melted, until she began to question his motives.

"Jack's my old partner. We were just…catching up."

Don had seen them kiss, but he had no claim on her. She hadn't even agreed to see him. Still he had a murderous glint in his eye. Lily had witnessed enough street fights to recognize when one was brewing.

She waited for him to decide if he would fight Jack. The two were evenly matched in size, and she knew that despite the ban on firearms, Don carried a small pistol in his pocket. She'd seen him in action and knew he didn't fight fair. Jack likely would follow some Princeton code of sportsmanship and get himself shot.

"Well if you're done reminiscing, I'll take you in."

Ah, now that was a problem. If she accepted, Don would think he had some claim on her and if she didn't she'd leave them to themselves, which was a bad idea. Two tomcats should never be left alone in an alley.

Jack conceded his claim with an ease that nearly broke her heart. "See you tomorrow, Lily."

Didn't he care what she did or who she did it with? That realization struck her like a punch to her middle. She watched him go with a mixture of despair and longing.

Jack held a pleasant smile and replaced his hat before calling to Nala, who left her side to trot off with Jack. That second betrayal brought enough water to her eyes to blur her vision.

Don did not wait for Jack to disappear before confronting her. "Just what kind of a partnership was this exactly?"

"What's that supposed to mean?"

"Lily, I'm not blind. I saw the way you looked at him."

Had Jack seen?

Don clasped Lily's upper arm and tugged her forward, causing her to stumble against him.

Lily saw Jack retrace his steps toward her. His smile was gone and his gaze was fixed on the place where Don clenched her forearm.

Nala was quicker. The dog shot forward, teeth bared, and leapt on Don, taking him to the ground.

Lily swiftly grabbed her dog's collar and pulled her off. Don aimed his pistol at Nala. She stepped between them and glared.

"You'd best go, Don."

Trost stood, mud now clinging to his back and

fine trousers. His face was pink as the inside of a prize-winning watermelon and his expression had turned murderous. He kept his eyes on Jack as he lowered the pistol.

Lily placed a hand on his wrist. "Take yourself off or tomorrow you will find yourself a new singer."

That seemed to break his concentration.

His eyes flicked to her for an instant and then back to Jack.

She squeezed his wrist. "I mean it."

He shook her off and her hand came away muddy.

"We've a contract."

"That says I leave when I want."

He spun and stormed down the boardwalk, his heels pounding an angry rhythm on the planking.

Lily's shoulders sagged and she turned back to Jack to find him glaring at her.

"Does he have some claim on you?"

"No."

Jack nodded, but his expression stormed like a rain cloud.

"If he bothers you, you let me know."

Lily smiled. He cared enough to defend her and that counted for something.

Lily smiled. "He's just protecting his investment."

"And what is he to you?"

"My boss, of course."

"Is that all?"

"For now." Oh, he didn't like that answer, not

judging from the lowering of his brows and the thinning of his lips. Lily felt happier than she had in days. "I'll see you at breakfast, Jack."

Chapter Fourteen

Lily met Luritz in the parlor of the boardinghouse to deliver instructions to eat at the hotel without her, then buy the yardage for her garments and meet her tomorrow morning at the Pavilion. She was excited to show him the little storeroom in which he could set up shop and knew there was much potential business here repairing clothing and producing new garments. With luck, he'd be headed home to his beautiful daughters before the snow began to fly.

Jack arrived shortly thereafter and they set out, reaching his claim at mid-morning. The day had a crispness to it that she liked. It felt good to be out of town again and back on the river. Her high spirits fell when they reached his property.

Lily did not like the rough, windowless cabin Jack inhabited. If this was how the men lived when they were not in the bars, it was no wonder they were willing to throw bags of gold at her.

Next he took her to his digging site and together they entered the tunnel he had somehow carved from the permanently frozen ground. She knew from listening to the miners that only the top few inches ever thawed this far north. So the ground had to be melted by setting fires, waiting for them to burn down and then scraping off a few inches of thawed gravel before beginning the process again. Permafrost, they called it.

Jack's tunnel looked larger than the others she had seen from the river, large enough to use a wheelbarrow instead of a bucket to clear the material and high enough to stand in. Lily had feared she'd have to crawl.

"You must have been lighting fires day and night."

Jack smiled. "Not exactly."

He led her by lantern into his mine shaft.

"Is it safe?" she asked.

"The walls are frozen solid. See the ice?" He brought the light close to the side of the tunnel, pointing out the white crystals scattered through the gravel. "Can't collapse," he assured, pounding on the solid wall.

As they descended, Jack indicated different layers of sand and gravel, rock and strata, whatever that was. It all looked like dirt to her, but he seemed greatly excited by the tiny differences in color and consistency. He'd kept a record of how many dollars per pan he'd extracted from the various levels and the numbers kept going up as they went down. They were up to sixteen dollars a pan when they hit the end of his tunnel.

"How much farther down can you go?" she asked.

"All the way to bedrock and then I'll continue along, heading under the river. No matter where the gold came from or how long ago the ancient rivers deposited it, the placer gold can go no lower than bedrock. Might find some large nuggets down there."

Jack hung the lantern from a spike he'd driven into the wall of the tunnel. As he lifted the light she saw what he'd made out of the collection of metal and parts.

"Is it a steam engine?" she asked, stepping closer to touch the round boiler he had riveted together. *Impressive* did not begin to cover it. She'd seen the boat he'd made, but this was truly marvelous. "But why have it down here? And where are the wheels?"

Jack laughed. "No wheels. I place it, then fill it then use it."

"For digging?"

"That I still have to do."

"Well don't keep me guessing. What does it do, Jack?"

"It's a steam engine, as you said, but I use the steam to melt the ice and loosen the gravel. Then I only have to gather up the load and haul it up to my Long Tom and let the stream wash away the gravel."

Lily's eyes widened. "That's genius! All the mine owners will want one."

"I hope so. My next step is to gather investors and make more from this prototype. Then I'll sell the engine with instruction on how to use it to best effect." Jack waved his hands. "I patented it before leaving."

"You could sell them outright or take a percentage of all the mines that use your machine."

Jack cocked his head.

"That's a thought. But I'm still testing it. Perhaps, after I work out all the bugs. So you like it?"

She hugged him in answer, gratified to feel his strong arms wrap around her once more.

He didn't release her, so she smiled up at him, basking in the close familiarity of his embrace. His grin made him look boyish. She wanted to kiss him, but she reined herself in.

"I'm proud of you."

"Thanks, partner." He let her go and she had to stop herself from stepping back toward him as he moved to the machine.

"You'll make a fortune." Her smile faltered as she realized that the faster he succeeded in regaining his wealth, the more quickly he would leave her behind. The realization took all the joy from her. Her shoulders sagged.

"Come on." He drew out a match. "Let me show you how it works."

Lily spent the next hour waiting for the water to boil and then for the steam pressure to build, but once he had the engine up to heat, it melted the ice from the gravel like hot water through cold butter. Jack manned a rubber hose, fixed with a nozzle that helped him control the steam flowing from the end.

It was truly a wonder.

Jack extracted a wheelbarrow full of material in a matter of minutes, then released the steam and doused the fire in the boiler. He wheeled the material up to the surface and then sent it through his Long Tom, concentrating the gravel to just the heaviest matter, while the rest washed through the riffles and back into the river. She kept a sharp eye out for nuggets as he tossed away the larger pieces of waste rock.

After he had shoveled the last of the material into the box and let the water diverted from the stream wash over it, he slid a plank down across the top opening, shutting off the water. Lily helped him collect the sand and gravel that had survived the rush of water. The total barely filled his gold pan and she was disappointed to see no nuggets. He took the pan inside where he kept his washtub, right in the center of the ten-by-ten foot room. Nala appeared and then wandered out again, as he washed the concentrates free of sand. The gold seemed to grow before her eyes as the gravel fell into the catch basin. She plucked out the largest nugget, the size of an almond, and held it up toward the only light which streamed weakly through the open cabin door. The days were more and more overcast and she feared, though it was only September, that it might soon snow.

Jack extracted and measured the nuggets that were coarse and ranged from the size of a grain of rice to one as large as her thumbnail. When he finished weighing the haul, the single pan came to $2.50 worth of gold. Lily beamed with pride.

"Not folderol?" he asked.

She giggled and shook her head. "Seems I am wrong on some infrequent occasions."

His hands were wet, his face streaked with dirt and he still made butterflies quiver in her belly. She needed to touch him so she removed her handkerchief, using it to wipe away the grit from his cheek.

"If you'd have told me what it was, Jack, I'd have seen the point of it."

He captured her hand, staying it in midair. "Didn't trust you then."

"And now?"

"With my life."

He pressed his cheek to her hand, closing his eyes briefly as he rubbed his whiskered face over her palm, and then released her.

Why did he hold her and then set her aside? Was it because he still wanted her, but cared just enough not to use her when his intentions had not changed? That thought stole all the joy from his touch.

"Oh, Jack. It's not been the same without you. Why don't you come to my shows?"

He stared in silence as she waited, hoping to hear what it was that made him look so grieved.

"Once a week, Jack. It's only a few hours. Come for Saturday night. Do promise you'll come."

"I don't think that's wise." He hesitated, opened his mouth to speak and then clamped it shut again. Finally he spoke. "Is everything all right with you—since we parted?"

She nodded slowly, not understanding his odd expression, which looked like concern except for the tension in his jaw and the speculative lift of one brow.

"Never thought to find Dawson to my liking, but it's rugged and new, full of hope and promise. You needn't worry about me. I'm fit and flourishing. I love it here."

"But that's not what I meant. Is everything all right with you, since we…"

And suddenly she understood. Heat flooded her face and neck as she realized he was asking her if she was with child. So that was what this was about, his guilty conscience. She wasn't here to see his machine or give advice. That recognition hurt her more than his absence for she hated to be reduced to an obligation. No, she couldn't stand that.

She straightened, trying and failing to maintain a grip on her dignity. "You needn't worry on that account."

In fact, she'd had her monthly courses already, they'd come with a pang of regret that confused her. Had she really wanted to carry a child that he would see as nothing but an obstacle, an unwelcome tether to a woman he wanted to leave behind?

"There's nothing holding you here. When you're ready to go, I mean."

"I'm happy to hear it." But he didn't look happy, for he did not smile and his body remained taut with a palpable tension.

She turned away to stare out the door of his cabin to the yard where Nala gnawed on the end of a branch that was nearly as long as she was. How she wished she could love Jack as Nala did, without regret or shame.

Lily wanted to curl in a ball, wrap herself inward and rock like a child in her mother's arms.

She heard him approach, but could not bear to turn about. It hurt too much to look at him and see the remorse in his eyes.

Jack would hold her if she asked him to. He would comfort her and kiss her. He could take her up in those arms and she realized she'd let him, but she did not ask and he stopped before reaching her. She knew he still wanted her and she longed for him, but she had just enough pride not to ask and he had enough scruples not to use her as he had done.

Lily should be grateful, instead of resenting his restraint. She glanced back again, finding him standing, torn between his needs and his aspirations.

Well, she'd not make it easy for him.

"Take me back to town, Jack." She knew she had to go now or make an utter fool of herself.

She stepped out into the open air, glad for the chill that cooled her heated cheeks.

"Lily?" He rested a hand upon her shoulder.

She glanced back, then slipped from beneath his gentle restraint. "I'll be at the canoe with Nala." Lily patted her thigh and called to her dog. "Come on, girl."

Her hound left her stick and trotted along as Lily made her way down the bank.

Jack appeared a few moments later, holding the canoe as she climbed in. Nala leapt to the center and Jack pushed them clear of the bank. He paddled her home in silence.

After an eternity, he drew up to the riverbank in Dawson, but did not get out. Lily stepped ashore and Nala leapt clear with her, but Jack called the dog back. It was the first word he'd uttered.

She patted Nala. "Go on, girl."

Nala hopped back into the canoe's center section and whined.

Lily tried to keep the tears from betraying her, but was not certain she succeeded.

"Lily?" Jack's brows were lifted as if he did not know just what to make of her. At last he said, "I'll come see you on Saturday night." He waited and she made no reply. "If that's all right with you."

Which would be worse, seeing him or not seeing him? She nodded her consent and left him, hurrying up the grassy incline to the muddy road, away from the man who tore her insides up like glass through soft clay.

Chapter Fifteen

The following Saturday, Lily peeked through the curtain again, looking for Jack. She could not keep herself from checking every few minutes. As her music started and the curtain was pulled, he still was not there. The crowd erupted in cheers as Lily scanned the corners for sight of him, desperate as a castaway searching for land. She forced a smile and began her songs, performing the dance steps she had added, feeling low-down and blue. The audience did not seem to notice her false face as she held out hope until the very last number.

Still he didn't appear.

She called herself a fool as she gathered up her wrap and muff. But by slow degrees Lily's hurt feelings dissolved into concern until she couldn't shake the worry. He'd said he'd come and he hadn't. Jack might have done her a bad turn, but he'd kept his word on every occasion but this one. She knew she should go back to her room and go to bed, instead of contemplating a trip upstream in the middle of the night. But she found herself gathering up her sacks of gold and offering one to Bill Connor, a stagehand and bouncer. He had a lazy eye and wide shoulders, perfect for digging, but on reaching Dawson, he'd found he had a morbid fear of closed spaces and so was unable to hire on with any of the mining operations.

Bill was married to a pretty laundress named Babe, who Bill said made a fine living running her dirty water over a greased board to catch the gold dust that clung to their duds. Bill was smitten and Lily knew she'd not have to worry about any shenanigans when she was with him.

She held up one of the pouches of gold she'd collected from the stage. "This is yours if you take me downriver to Bonanza Creek."

Bill asked no questions, but pocketed the bag. "I've got to tell Babe. She'll be expecting me."

"Meet me at my place afterward."

He nodded.

"I'll walk you home, then go tell her."

Lily could not push down the feeling that something was wrong as they headed to Jack's claim. The timing was bad and they had to make their way in darkness, as the sun now disappeared for twelve hours and would not be up until after seven the next morning. The miners who had not come to town were all asleep, so Bill paddled undetected past the claims that lined the narrow creek.

Nala greeted Lily when she was still half a mile out. That she had wandered so far afield did nothing to ease Lily's growing concern.

Nala barked as Bill grounded the canoe and then hopped aboard before they continued on their way. Lily now urged Bill to greater speed as her worry turned to panic. It seemed to take hours to reach Jack's claim. At last the bottom scraped mud. Nala leapt from the boat, barking and cutting back and forth. The minute Lily had her feet, her dog was pushing her along. Lily did not need the urging. She lifted her skirts and ran.

"Jack!"

She arrived at his empty cabin, breathless and with a burning stitch in her side.

"Jack!"

She called again, to no avail. Nala barked from the mouth of the tunnel and then disappeared into the darkness. Lily's stomach dropped.

"Bring the lantern," she called to Bill.

Together they entered the tunnel, but as Lily continued, the light did not. She turned back.

"Bill?"

"I can't go down there, Lily. I'm sorry."

Why had she brought a man who was good for

nothing belowground? She dashed back to snatch the lantern from him.

"Wait here." Lily left him, hurrying into the cold earth, holding Nala's collar, pressing her fingers into the solid reassurance of her thick coat and warm skin. "Jack!"

Her voice echoed off the icy corridor. *Please let him be alive.*

Lily came to the steam engine and pressed a hand to the boiler. It was cold as the grave. Before her lay a pile of uncollected gravel. She fingered the dirt, finding it had not yet frozen solid. Hoisting the light she searched the ground, seeing the wall before her that marked the end of his work. Where was he, still back in town, at some other saloon or with some whore at the edge of town? Lily cursed herself for a fool.

"Jack?" she whispered.

Nala whined and began to dig as if in a rabbit hole. Lily stepped forward onto the pile of gravel. Something moved beneath her feet. Lily shrieked as she stumbled back. She lowered the lantern and saw that what she first thought to be a rock was Jack's boot heel.

Lily cried out, laying the lantern aside as she fell to her knees and began digging with Nala. After a moment she had exposed his leg. Her brain began to work now, the panic lifting.

"Find his head, you fool," she muttered.

Lily recovered the lantern and climbed the pile of debris. From here she could see that by some miracle his shoulders and head were not buried.

"Jack!" She ran to him, laying the lantern beside him and brushing back the gravel that covered his hair and neck.

"Lil?" he whispered. "Knew you'd come."

She stroked his cheek. "What have you done to yourself?"

"Pinned. Can't move."

Sweet Mother of God, was he paralyzed? Her heart hammered as she called her dog and together they dug.

"Bill! Get down here now!"

He didn't. She kept digging.

"Go to the next claim," she hollered. "Get help. There's a man buried here."

"I'm going!" came the reply.

Lily dug with her bare hands, scratching and clawing.

The digging caused more gravel from the top of the pile to slide into the place of what Lily had removed. Gradually she gained ground. She had part of Jack's back exposed when she heard the voices. Nala left her and a moment later two lights bobbed down the tunnel.

"What in the name of heaven?" said one, pausing at Jack's machine.

"Help me!" cried Lily.

They set to work with shovels and cleared the gravel from on top then hauled Jack roughly from his self-made tomb.

"Careful. He might have broken bones," said Lily, but they already had him up.

Jack's clothing and body were caked with mud and grime, but he was free. His eyes fluttered shut as he went limp between the two rescuers, who each held one arm about their own shoulders. Lily shrieked and wrapped her arms about his middle. He didn't rouse and his body was cold as ice, but the steady beat of his heart caused a wave of such relief she thought her own knees might give way.

"We need to get him out, ma'am."

Lily released Jack and followed the men up the tunnel. Jack's legs dragged along the ground. Lily broke out in a cold sweat, fearful he'd broken his spine. By the time they'd reached the mouth of the tunnel, his legs were working, but he still sagged heavily on his human crutches.

Lily now preceded the men, directing them into the cabin, where they lay Jack out on his bed. Lily took charge. "Bill, get a doctor. Don't come back without one." She pointed at the men. "Clean water, you." She pointed at the final man. "You, lift him up a bit, so I can strip him out of his clothing."

Jack groaned as she carefully peeled off the filthy attire. His skin was pale beneath his clothing and thankfully completely devoid of any blood, though his back and thighs showed large purple bruises. The first miner returned with a full pail, just as she finished wrapping Jack in her fur-lined cloak and his wool blanket.

"I need a good fire to heat the water and warm him. Does he have a pot?"

"He's got a gold pan," said the second. "That's what I use for washing and vittles."

Jack opened his eyes and smiled up at her, then winced. "Knew you'd come."

"Oh, Jack." The tears she'd contained spilled out.

"Saturday night then?"

She nodded. "Lie still, Jack. The doctor's coming."

Lily could barely breathe past the panic. What if his ribs were broken or he'd crushed something inside? What if he were bleeding inside right at this very moment? She swallowed hard as her vision blurred and tears splashed onto Jack's face.

His eyes opened. "Don't cry."

"I'm not." She dashed away the evidence and pressed her palm to his forehead. He was so dreadfully cold.

She glanced behind her to see the men both working over the stove, trying to get a fire started. Lily lay over Jack, pressing herself to him as she vigorously rubbed his arms.

After a few minutes his shivering began. The tremors were terrifying, spastic contractions that wracked him until he shook like a dead squirrel in the mouth of a hound. Throughout, Lily clung to him, waiting for the fire or for her skin to warm him. When the fire was good and hot, the men carried Jack to his only chair, setting him close to the heat.

Lily sat on an overturned bucket beside Jack to be sure he wasn't burned.

She heated water in a metal basin and when it steamed she added sugar and held it to his lips, tipping the cup as he drank thirstily.

His hands stopped shaking and he managed to hold the second cup himself.

"How long, Jack?"

"Ceiling came down Wednesday morning."

"Should have froze, I expect," said the first miner.

Jack looked up. "Hello, Nate. Likely would have, if Nala hadn't lain on top of me. Never left me." Lily recalled Nala coming to meet their canoe and wondered over it. Jack nodded at the other miner. "Daniel. Thanks for coming."

"What's that thing in your mine?" asked Nate.

"Something I'm working on," he said.

Lily's eyes narrowed on the man, her protective instinct engaging as she rose.

"He needs rest now. Thank you both." She hustled them back toward their claims.

"Call if you need us," said Daniel, doffing his hat. "You're even prettier close up, Miss Lily."

She gave him a smile and shooed him off, returning to Jack as quickly as possible. When they were gone, she hurried back to his side. He offered his hand and she clasped it, pressing his palm to her cheek. Her eyes drifted closed. He was here. He was safe and that was all that really mattered.

Lily stayed by his side, pouring hot coffee into him and keeping the fire going, until the doctor arrived. He checked Jack over and announced that his ribs were bruised, not broken and his body battered, but intact. The doc said the worst of his troubles came from lack of food and four days without water.

When he said that Jack should have died from dehydration, Lily cried again.

Before the man was even out the door, Lily was cooking. She made biscuits with gravy and Jack ate nearly a pan full. She helped him to bed and watched over him while he slept. When evening found him still sleeping, she crawled under the blanket and lay beside him. He roused enough to draw her into his arms, press his nose to her hair, inhale deeply, sigh and begin to snore for the first time. Lily felt herself relax. He would be all right. But what about the next time?

Chapter Sixteen

Jack woke to the aroma of frying bacon. For a moment he feared it was another hallucination, but when he opened his eyes he saw Lily by the stove in his little cabin.

It all came back to him in a rush: the collapse, realizing he was trapped and then Lily. Once again she was there when he needed her and she'd stayed through the night. He remembered waking long enough to weave a lovely thick strand of her hair through his fingers before dozing again.

"That smells like heaven," he said, trying to sit up and being momentarily arrested by the pain that shot through his ribs and down his back.

Lily was at his side in an instant.

"Are you aching? The doctor left some laudanum."

"That will just make me sleep again." Jack pushed himself to a sitting position, wincing despite his efforts not to do so.

"Coffee?" she asked.

He nodded, his head spinning with the pain of sitting up. Her arm was around him now, gently supporting him as she held the bitter and sweet coffee to his lips.

The heat filled his stomach and bolstered his spirits. Lily had not forsaken him. If she had treated him as he had her, would he have come? Her actions proved to him again how dauntless she was.

"Jack, what happened?"

"Stupid. I didn't consider the steam would not dissipate. It collected on the ceiling and then a section thawed. It all came down at once. The gravel hit me from behind, pinned my legs first and then my arms. When I came to, it had all frozen solid again, like a crypt. Just dumb luck it didn't suffocate me."

"It's too dangerous, the steam."

"No. It's not, but I learned something. The ceiling has to be braced until it has a chance to freeze up again."

"I don't want you going down there anymore. You can come live with me in town."

He frowned. Did she have so little faith in him? He'd learned a valuable lesson and knew the machine could be viable with just the addition of braces.

He shook his head. "I need to stay here and finish my testing."

"Testing? You were nearly killed, Jack. It's not worth your life, is it?"

He didn't answer.

"I promised to help you, Jack. You can stay with me until you're feeling better. No need to go back down in that tunnel."

"But I will go back."

Her eyes went wide and her expression fell. She started crying again and he wiped away the tears. It hurt like a son of a bitch to lift his arms, but he gritted his teeth and caressed her damp face.

"I was so frightened, Jack," she admitted. "I couldn't bear it if anything happened to you."

He rocked her gently back and forth, gritting his teeth against the ache in his ribs.

"Nothing happened. I'm all right now. When I got pinned down there, all I could think was that if I died your last memory would be of me hurting you again. Now, at least, I have a chance to ask your forgiveness."

She recalled him asking her if she was with child without coming right out and saying so. Lily could not bear to revisit that topic, so she gathered up his empty coffee cup and threw the dregs out in the open front door. Nala rose to investigate this new addition to her yard and Lily returned to Jack, perching on the edge of his bed.

"We made a mistake, Jack. Both of us. You don't have to worry about me. I understand the way things work and I'll land on my feet. Besides, I'm here for an adventure. I just got more than I expected, is all. Plus, if I were with child and needed a man to help raise it, I wouldn't have far to look, now would I? Dawson is crawling with candidates."

Jack made an involuntary growling sound. Did the idea of her foisting his child off on some stranger fill him with fury or just catch him off guard? She'd never seen such a black expression on the man.

His breathing increased and he went pale again. He fell back to the pillow, his eyes still fixed on her.

Lily studied Jack from beneath her lowered lashes. His frown and glowering expression pleased her far more than it should have. If any of her pretty speech were true she'd be past caring what he thought or felt for her. So why did she keep coming back to the well, knowing it was dry?

Jack forced himself up on one elbow, exhaling sharply as the pain took the color from his cheeks. "I don't want that."

She nodded her acknowledgment.

"And I didn't mean for it to happen."

She gave a mirthless laugh. "That's usually the way of it."

"I'd take responsibility for a child, Lily."

She pressed her lips together to keep from shouting that she didn't want to be a responsibility to him. She didn't want to be another obligation like his mother or his sister.

Instead she said, "I know, Jack."

He wasn't the sort to turn his back on her for he could have done that a hundred times along the journey.

His eyelids drooped.

She sighed. "Rest a bit."

She pressed a hand against his shoulder and he eased back into the narrow bed.

He closed his eyes, taking shallow breaths. Lily could not resist brushing the soft locks of hair from his forehead. He lifted his hand and captured hers, lacing their fingers, before rubbing her knuckle over his soft, dry lips. He kissed her there and then lowered their hands to the bedding as if the intimacy was nothing more than a brief thank-you.

But the soft caress and brush of his mouth made her stiffen as the rippling excitement gripped her insides and set off a shiver of hopeless longing. She stared down at him in hungry anticipation to find his eyes closed and his expression at peace.

Damn the man!

She tried to tug her hand free, but he resisted, holding her fast.

"Stay a little." He raised his lids as if bone-weary, looking up at her with his soulful whiskey-colored eyes, warm and welcoming as the autumn sun.

His eyes closed again. "Steamers are running.

That means there'll be goods. I can buy what I need to build more engines, just as soon as I scratch up the venture capital."

Lily wondered who would be fool enough to invest in a machine that caused cave-ins, but kept her doubts to herself.

"The steamers brought something else," said Lily. "A letter from my sister, Bridget. She gave me a rundown of all I've missed. They're struggling, of course, but all hale and healthy, thank the Lord."

"Younger sister?"

"They're all younger, remember, Jack? I hope they've received my letters. Won't they be surprised to hear what I've been up to?"

Jack grimaced as if ashamed of what they'd been up to.

"You needn't worry, Jack. I mentioned you only by your first name. Far as they know you're just another one of the men, out of work and desperate enough to come and try your luck."

He flushed and she knew she'd hit the nail on the head. Was it so humiliating to be associated with her?

"I didn't tell you not to mention me."

She pressed her lips together to keep from telling him that he didn't have to. His expression said it all.

Jack reached for her hand, there beside his on the bedding, but she lifted it and clasped hers together in her lap.

He changed course and lifted himself up, with a groan, leaning back against the wall behind his head. The pain squeezed through him and then was gone. He'd been lucky—very lucky.

"My sister, Cassie, will be ten in March. She should be in school now." A public school, he imagined. Quite a shock after attending a fine private school. She'd been on track to attend Wells College, like Mother, when their fortunes turned. "My mother's family owned a pharmacy in Rochester. It's how she met father. My grandfather wanted him to learn the ropes, so he sent him off on the road. When he brought mother home there was a row, but they came around. My mother is beautiful and accomplished and it wasn't as if she came from nothing. Her father owned his business, after all. The funny part was that *her* family did not approve of dad. Can you imagine? They wanted a professional man, not a salesman, and had no idea who he really was. Well, that turned the matter and my grandparents went to see Mother's parents. After that it was all smooth sailing."

He finished his story and smiled at her. His smile faded by slow degrees as he realized too late that he'd insulted her again. He cleared his throat and fell silent.

Lily picked at her fingernail, head lowered. "It's a pity you lost your pa, Jack. It's a hard thing."

He clenched his jaw. His father didn't deserve

Lily's concern. His father had abandoned them in every sense of the word, and Jack was tired of keeping up appearances.

That half-truth, told by instinct to protect the family name, now became intolerable. It didn't sit right to lie to Lily. He wanted her to know everything, even something this dark, for it was as much a part of him as his skin. So he straightened, preparing himself to tell her that his perfect little world was as cracked as an eggshell dropped on a stone floor.

"He wasn't lost, Lil."

Lily's eyes fixed on him, cautious now, for she knew him well enough to recognize his change in mood. Lily folded her arms protectively about her middle and lowered her chin before speaking. "He wasn't?"

"He left in the most cowardly way possible."

Jack wondered what she'd think after he told her. At home the news had spread like a breaking tidal wave, washing through the community. Jack had learned during that dark time that there was nothing so unforgivable as losing one's money, unless, perhaps, it was losing one's fortune and then putting a bullet in one's forehead.

In the end, the only visitors were the creditors who appeared with a speed of buzzards smelling a corpse.

"Jack?"

He lifted his chin from his chest and met her worried gaze.

"When my father learned we were ruined, that he'd lost everything, he…he killed himself, Lil."

She gasped, holding her hands over her mouth in shock, but he forged on, needing to get it all in before he watched her walk away like the others.

"He went into his study, used a revolver. I heard the shot and found his body."

Lily pressed her fists to her cheeks. "Oh, Jack, that's a terrible thing."

"Yes. Terrible." He looked up at her, holding her gaze. "Do you know what was worse? No one came to the house to pay their respects. Not one of my mother's close friends or a single member of any of the societies to which she belonged. It was as if we were contagious. I wonder if he knew what would happen, if he understood just what his actions would bring. He was a coward, taking the easy way out and leaving us to face the consequences."

He waited for her condemnation at speaking so frankly about his father or for her to remind him that his father burned in hell. She did neither. Instead, Lily slid her hand along the blanket until it rested on his.

"What about *your* friends?"

"I left school without telling them. Too ashamed to face them." He drew a breath, steadying himself to tell her the rest. "I was engaged back then, Lil.

She was the daughter of one of my father's business associates. I went to see her just after I returned from college to tell her the news. She cried, of course. So I tried to reassure her, comfort her. It wasn't until later that I realized she wasn't crying for me but for what *she* had lost. She waited until after the funeral to return the ring."

Lily blew out a long breath. After a moment she said, "She's a fool."

"She knew enough not to wed a penniless man."

Lily's smile seemed sad and wise all at once. "There's worse things. Like not having the decency to give your sympathies when a man has lost his father."

She was right again. He shouldn't care what they thought. He was lucky to learn so early just what kind of people they were. Unlike his poor mother who was still devastated by their swift rejection.

It was on her account, mainly, that he plotted his revenge.

"I still want to prove to them that my family doesn't need them. If I can make this work, my mother and sister won't have to suffer for something that was none of their doing."

"I would think there would still be talk."

"Don't fool yourself. Money is all that's needed for them to reenter society and those bastards will pretend that Mother was just in Newport for the season, instead of returning from exile."

The thirst for a triumphant homecoming still burned his throat. But now it was tempered by the knowledge that he didn't like them. He'd be well rid of the lot.

She squeezed his hand. "If you're needing to spit in their eye, Jack, well then, I'll help you all I can."

He should have expected it from her. She didn't turn her back on trouble, wouldn't judge him or think less of him for his need to set things right. Jack wondered if Lily had any idea how precious she was becoming to him.

Jack thought of his mother's telegram and frowned. When he'd come north, he had wanted to make good so they could reenter Society. He'd fought and struggled, determined not to give up. Now he didn't even know if he wanted to go back to New York. But he had to, because he'd not abandon his sister and mother as his father had done.

Now he dreamed of Lily at his side. But each time he tried to imagine her there, presiding over his household, overseeing dinner parties with business partners, he felt queasy. There must be a way to have her.

Chapter Seventeen

∽∾∾◈∾∾∾

Lily stayed at his side while his body healed. Jack had been damned lucky. Cuts and bruises were all he had suffered. That evening Lily snuffed out the light and lay beside him, fully dressed, keeping him warm through the long night. He relished holding her, inhaling her sweet scent with each breath and snuggling safe and warm beneath the blankets.

He'd missed this intimacy.

Thursday morning he'd managed to get up on his own two feet and make it outside to relieve himself. The food and drink that Lily had been forcing down his throat had bolstered him more than he could have imagined, and he no longer seemed weak or confused. He had some spectacular bruises blossoming like purple roses on the backs of his legs and his torso. He guessed the fact that the collapse had been mostly loose gravel had saved him. Had there been a good-sized rock among the load he'd be dead, or worse—paralyzed.

By the afternoon he was well enough to sit at the table and share a meal. He loved playing house with her; Lily brought life even to this crowded, tiny cabin. No, he thought, she brought life back to him. He hadn't realized that part of him had died with his father. Jack had been so focused on his own mission that he'd had no time left to enjoy living. He'd built his machine and set it to use on his claim, working like a demon, going days without even seeing the sun rise or set. But all that had changed with Lily.

He knew she had to go back to town, but he wanted to keep her here. As he grew stronger and no longer needed her, he felt her restlessness and recognized she was preparing to go.

He knew he should let her.

Lily cleaned up after supper and poured the remains of the coffee into two battered tin cups. It had become their habit in the evenings to take turns washing up and then sit together by the stove with the last cup of coffee before bed. He coveted the time with her, talking about nothing and everything.

Lily went out first, leaving Jack with a gold pan full of warm water. The steam curled up into the dry air as he stripped and scrubbed himself with a rag and soap. He tried to ignore the hitch and tug of his stiff muscles as he forced them to move. Afterward he set his union suit aside, opting for only his jeans and soft blue flannel shirt.

Lily returned and he stepped out into the night.

The nights were growing longer now but the sun only receded for six hours, dropping from sight and then reemerging in the Northeastern sky.

He finished his business and retraced his steps, returning to her.

She handed him the wash basin, smelling of soap, her cheeks glowing bright from scrubbing. He tossed it out in the yard and entered, finding Lily now in the chair near the stove.

"It's getting darker again. Soon we'll be able to see the Northern Lights again," she said.

Jack nodded and then added more logs to the fire, in preparation for the night.

"We don't have anything like that back home. Can you see the lights in New York?"

"No, but I understand they do see them on occasion in the Adirondacks."

"I love them. I love everything here, and I've decided to stay."

He paused, crouching beside her. Did she mean here in his cabin? His heart accelerated at the thought of having her here.

"After all, what better life could I hope for? There are so many opportunities in the north for me and the land is so beautiful. I've never seen a prettier place on earth than here in Dawson. And I love the people. They're from everywhere and all with the same desire to make something for themselves and their kin. Self-made men—it's thrilling."

Jack frowned. He didn't like that plan; it would separate them. He stared at her bright smile and the vitality twinkling in her eyes. Why did she have to be Irish? Why couldn't he stay?

He hedged. "It's an interesting place. Likely change when the gold runs out, though. Might not be so easy to make a living."

Lily nodded. "I don't need much and there'll still be trappers and the lumber is good while it lasts. I just wish I could make everything stop and be the way it is right now."

Jack nodded and then retrieved his cup, not wanting to say anything that might break the quiet harmony.

"I think I'll be heading back to town tomorrow," she said.

Jack winced. Of course, her job was there and she was doing well with her singing. If his machine paid off and he could provide for everything she'd ever need, would she move in with him? His stomach knotted as he stared at her, wondering how to broach the subject that plagued him.

As silence stretched, Lily's eyes grew worried.

"I'll stay if you need me."

He did need her, but not in the way she meant.

It wasn't right to keep her here now that he could get by without help.

"I can manage."

She dropped her gaze and nodded. Had he said the wrong thing?

"All right, then," she said.

"I'll take you tomorrow."

"You don't need to."

"I need supplies and I've got to see about investors, then get about building my engines. Sooner is better for me."

She held her cup in her hands, not looking at him as she spoke. "Well, if you think you're strong enough."

"I'm strong enough."

Lily stilled at that, the cup poised halfway to her lips. She lowered the coffee as she wondered if he had meant to imply what she thought.

She pushed the cup across the rough-hewn table as her desire for him gurgled up from inside. *Don't you do it, Lily.*

But she knew she would, knew from the intent possession of his gaze and the slow steady pulse down low in her body.

She'd do it again and consequences be damned.

Jack held his breath as she sat still as ice waiting for the kiss of the sun. When she lifted her gaze he saw the desire flash, but she remained motionless, her fists flanking her coffee, her knuckles white from clenching the cup. He watched the battle between body and mind as she looked at his hands cradling his cup, his mouth and finally his eyes.

"You're black and blue from your shoulders to your knees."

That was her mind talking now. Her body spoke as well, her chest rising and falling with the increased speed of her breathing and the lovely flush of desire spreading up her neck and into her face. Her pupils dilated until they were dark circles ringed with brilliant blue.

He gave her a half grin. "Only on the one side. The other didn't get a scratch."

She captured her lower lip between her teeth and his breath caught. Now his fists were clenched as well. He could almost hear the debate in her mind. Should she come to him or not? He stared at her mouth and prayed.

At last she stood, crossed the room and set the lantern beside the bed. Then she turned to him.

"But you want me to stay?"

He nodded slowly, afraid to go to her. Like a hunter sighting a deer in a meadow, he made no quick movements.

"More than anything."

Her smile lit up her beautiful face. She'd come here and saved him, stayed to nurse him and here he was planning to be a cad by taking advantage of her the minute he was well enough. That was no way to repay her kindness.

But he didn't want to let her go. If he could just think of a way to have her, just find some means to make her stay, not just for the night, but forever.

"The night then," she said and snuffed the light.

Jack settled back upon the mattress, taking nothing for granted. She'd slept with him since his rescue and he'd done no more than hold her. But he was stronger now and his body pulsed with blood and desire. He prepared himself to resist her enticing fragrance, soft skin and warm body.

She lay half against him as she had the first two nights. The mattress was too small for them both to lie on their backs and so Lily had spent the first two nights on one side or the other. When she faced him, her arm went about his middle in a relaxed hold that felt just right. But when she turned away, she pressed her back against him. Even on that first night, the contact of his hip with her soft, round fanny was a nearly irresistible temptation.

He lay still and stiff as a chunk of wood, waiting for Lily to settle. Listening for the soft breathing that would tell him she slept.

Instead, he felt her fingers unbuttoning his shirt.

"Oh, thank God," he breathed as he took her in his arms and kissed her. She accepted him, letting him explore her sweet mouth before pulling away. Next came the soft rustling of fabric and in a moment she was beside him, naked, her skin already beginning to grow chilled.

Jack stripped out of his clothing and slid in beside her.

"I've been dreaming of this every night," he growled, drawing her in.

Her throaty laugh was arousing as hell.

"I've missed you, too, Jack."

Tomorrow she'd leave him again, but tonight she was all his.

He held one hand on the center of her back, guiding her until she came to rest on top of him, stretched out from his chin to his ankle.

Lily settled her hips against him and made a sound of satisfaction in her throat as the soft curve of her belly pressed to his erection.

He leaned close and whispered in her ear. "You're driving me mad."

With exquisite slowness she trailed one finger over his chest and down his belly.

"Do you remember the first time I touched you?"

He did—that first day he'd arrived in Dyea, wet, cold, after Lily had rescued his dreams with his gear. He nodded, his chin brushing the top of her head. Lily's finger continued its maddeningly slow descent from his chest.

"You asked me why I did it. And the answer is, because I can't bear not to."

Chapter Eighteen

Her finger continued its torturous descent down his abdomen sending flames of desire licking down his belly to his groin. His hand stole up the warm velvet of her thigh.

She used her toes to shift her body upward until her lips were beside his head and her tongue caressed his ear. Jack groaned in delight.

He breathed in the spicy scent of her as she shifted to his side, giving herself access to all of him. Her fingers played along his skin, stroking his belly, teasing the fine hairs and following them south. He gritted his teeth at the sweet torture she wrought. Her hand moved to the base of his erection and his breath caught. He longed for her to wrap her fingers tight about his shaft.

But she did not grip him. Instead she used her

thumb to run the length of him, making his whole body twitch and jerk with the small spasms of delight.

"Do you like that?" she asked.

"Heaven," he breathed.

"And this?" Her fingers danced over his swollen flesh without mercy, arousing him even more.

His need grew large as the appetite of a grizzly waking from hibernation. He was insatiable, needing to feast only on her.

If he didn't stop her, he'd come right here in her hand. He grasped her wrist and lifted her fingers, taking each one into his mouth in turn and sucking the throaty morsels. He was rewarded with a series of tiny moans. In her delight, she arched toward him. It was too much to resist and he moved from her fingers to her throat, rolling her to her back so he could suckle the nipples of her lovely full breasts. He lapped and lathed one as he gently kneaded the other. She gasped and rubbed herself against him, offering what he most desired by pressing her nipple to his lips. He took the tiny bud into his mouth, using his teeth to tease the tender flesh. Lily bucked her hips.

He clasped her taut bottom and tugged her forward, lifting one leg to his waist. Then he slid his hand to her cleft, finding her slippery and hot with need.

He rubbed his thumb over her swollen nub of flesh and she shivered and gasped, tiny whimpers of delight encouraging him. His thumb continued to stroke and rub, exploring her body. She rolled to her back as he came to his side, grasping her leg and tugging her beneath him. Her hips moved in a rocking invitation against his hand.

Blood engorged him. He forced one leg between hers, bringing his knee up to the juncture of her legs. She moaned and lifted herself to rub against him.

Oh, sweet mother of mercy, he could wait no longer.

He moved into place above her and she spread her legs wide as he entered, lifting her hips to meet his. He stilled then, savoring the sweetness of this joining, wanting it to last all night. But Lily bucked, bringing him deeper into her body as her fingers raked his back, urging him on. The twinge of pain did not stop him but instead added to his pleasure.

He dropped one hand on each side of her head, holding his weight off her as he prepared to ride her as fast and as hard as she wanted.

With each stroke he sank farther into her sweet flesh. Lily threw her head back and her hands fell away, gripping each of his wrists for support as she writhed against him. Familiar cries told him she was close as she lifted and opened to savor each thrust. He gritted his teeth, trying to last, praying she would reach her pleasure before he found his. The race would be a close one. He'd never known a woman so full of life and so eager to take her pleasure.

It thrilled him and excited him far too much. He felt the battle lost as the sweeping surge of pleasure started deep within him. He plunged, arching as he pressed fully into her, his body quivering inside hers.

She cried out as he came in a hot rush of pleasure. And then he felt it, the rippling, rolling contractions of Lily's orgasm, squeezing him, pulsing about him, prolonging his own pleasure as he enjoyed hers.

So sweet.

If he lived a hundred years, he knew that nothing would ever be as good as this. What they shared was special. He knew it.

No New York socialite would ever hold a candle to Lily's passion, her beauty, her heart. It seemed suddenly very obvious that it was he who did not deserve her and not the other way around.

Reluctantly he shifted his weight from her, so as to allow her to breathe. She made a growling sound of disapproval in her throat and clung to him as he rolled to his back. He stroked her hair and wondered what he had ever done in his life to deserve spending even one night with her.

Lily startled and blinked. She lay half on Jack's chest wrapped around him like a monkey. How could she have fallen asleep like this? And then she remembered and blushed. She knew better than to do such a thing again, and yet, when she'd realized he was well enough to lie with her, she could not resist him.

She had considered for only a moment and dismissed all consequences and the realities of their situations.

No, those were best faced in the cold morning light. She blinked at the soft gray light that filtered through the cracks around the door. Her nose and cheeks tingled from the cold and she could see her breath. It seemed that the bedding and their bodies had kept them warm enough as the fire died.

She slipped from the bed, stifling a curse as the icy air attacked her from all sides. Lily hopped into her clothing with as much speed as possible and roused the fire. She glanced back at the temptation of the bed and Jack, but she knew what would happen if she ventured there again.

She gave a heavy sigh and headed out to find Nala. When she returned she found Jack dressed. He took her up in his arms and hugged her.

"Last night was wonderful," he whispered and then dropped a kiss upon her temple.

"Yes."

"Are you still going?" His breath heated her cheek and fanned down her neck.

She didn't want to. But if she stayed here she'd be no better than his... Lily nodded her head.

He pulled back and stared down at her with an expression she couldn't read. Disapproval? Regret? She wasn't sure.

"Shall I make breakfast?"

Jack stepped away, releasing her and taking up the coffeepot. "I can get something in town."

She nodded, feeling bereft that she had to leave this tiny little cabin and that he no longer needed her. Even if she stayed, it would change nothing; sooner or later he would leave, while she had decided to stay in the Yukon. There was no better place for the likes of her. Here she had a chance to be judged on her merit instead of her accent.

Jack set his cabin to rights and collected some of his belongings, including a nice cache of gold to take to the bank. A few more like that and he'd be on his way down river, she thought glumly.

Lily tied her cloak beneath her chin and raised the hood. "I'll wait by the water."

He nodded. As she walked away she could hear him muttering. Jack appeared a few minutes later, joining her and her hound in the canoe, and pushed off, pointing them downstream toward the sawboard metropolis of Dawson City.

Once in town she walked him to the bank and waited while he made his deposit. The bags of dust were guarded by Mounties who would escort the gold to the steamers that carried it to San Francisco. Jack's gold was in very good hands.

He let her pick the place for lunch and ordered eggs for them both as if they were not selling for eighteen dollars a dozen.

When she protested, he waved off her concerns.

"Have you ever thought of visiting New York, Lily?" he asked.

The rush of hope hit her with unexpected force, constricting her throat. But his guarded expression and furrowed brow made her pause, as she tried to understand what, exactly, he was proposing.

She tried not to let herself hope that things had changed between them, for she knew that no matter how much money Jack made, it would not be enough to gain her entry into society. So why did she hold her breath?

"There's nothing for me there," she said.

"I'd be there."

She cocked her head, confused by this sudden turnabout.

When Jack flushed and dropped his gaze, Lily's stomach flipped. What was he asking her that made it impossible to meet her eyes? She stared at him in confusion, for she would have imagined that New York would be the very last place on earth that he would wish to be seen with her...unless.

She set her shoulders as if readying herself to take a blow. "Say it plain, Jack."

"Always taking the direct route, up the trail, down those rapids and now here. All right, then. I'll say it plain." Jack rubbed his cheeks with both hands as he did when preparing to launch into something new. "Would you come with me, Lily?"

She bit her lower lip to keep from interrupting him

by shouting yes, held back by the dark suspicion that reared its ugly little head.

"If I sell my machines and I do well, I'm sure I could afford to buy you a town house. Somewhere fashionable. Twelfth Street even, only two blocks from Union Square."

"Buy me a…" The confusion cleared as her suspicion solidified like mortar, understanding now exactly what he was offering. He'd have to buy her a house, because she couldn't live in his. Not when he married another woman.

She stood, clutching her napkin in her fist as flames lapped at her face. "Jack, are you proposing to make me your mistress?"

He flushed as he glanced about at the other diners who had ceased eating in favor of taking in the free entertainment they provided.

He stood opposite her, reaching out to clasp her elbow. "Lily, please."

She twisted away, avoiding his grasp.

The waitress, who was scrawny as a stray cat, arrived carrying their plates, oblivious to the excitement.

"Eggs over easy?" she asked.

Lily never took her eyes off Jack as she spoke. "Give mine to the dog."

Lily's departure marked the beginning of a dreadful week for Jack. She would not see him, except from the stage and her friend Bill kept him from venturing any closer. She was clearly livid with him, and the more he thought about it, the more he came to the conclusion that she was right. He'd been out of line to ask her, especially when she'd only just finished telling him that she loved it here. What business did he have dragging her to New York and shutting her up in what amounted to an elegant cage? Lily needed to be free, to live a life of excitement, as her mother had wanted, not to exist in a half life as his mistress.

To make matters worse, word had spread about his cave-in and, as a result, he had no success getting potential investors to even consider laying down their hard-won capital on his invention.

He feared his only option was to mine his claim, take what he could manage to extract and then make his way home, tail between his legs. The thought of leaving Lily troubled him more than the recognition that he had failed. How was that possible?

He was sitting alone, nursing a beer at a dirty table in the Blue Wolf, a small saloon which sat on the corner of Harper and Third, when someone took the opposite seat.

He glanced up to find Lily staring at him with those intense blue eyes.

"No luck with the investors, I see."

His shoulders sank under the weight of his failure. Word had reached her of his failings. It reminded him of how he'd felt back there, after his father had died and before he could find the money to leave.

"No."

"How much does it cost to make one of those things?"

"Two hundred and sixteen dollars in materials each."

"And how many were you wanting to make?"

"Six to ten to start."

Lily stood, reached into her purse and withdrew a sack. The weight of it when it contacted the table and the way it remained upright and immobile, told him exactly what lay within.

"There's two thousand, Jack. See if you can talk the supplier down sixteen dollars a piece for buying in volume."

He stared up at her, astonishment rendering him dumb. There was no doubting from her expression she was still furious with him, yet here she was, offering him what must amount to all she had in the world.

"Why?"

"Because I promised I'd help you all I could. Now take it and do what you came to do, so you can go back there and reclaim what you've lost."

Chapter Nineteen

Lily called herself every kind of fool, for why else would she give him the means to pursue his dream instead of stamping it beneath her boot heel?

August had flown and September brought the first snow flurries. Since she'd handed over her fortune to Jack five weeks ago he had moved to town and now she faced the possibility of running into him on a daily basis. And though she knew she'd earn another bagful in the coming months, it didn't assuage the hurt. The night that had changed her life had not changed his.

When he'd asked her about New York she had actually thought she meant something more to him. Her own feelings for him had clouded her thinking to the point that she didn't understand that he meant to set her up in some shoddy room as his mistress.

Had he heard anything she'd said about what she wanted, about how much she loved it here?

Lily burned with shame at not being the kind of woman he could be proud of.

Word was that he'd managed to construct several machines and convinced some of the larger outfits to try them out. That meant Jack would be here through the fall and winter.

Lily knew where that would lead. Her only hope to salvage her dignity was to leave. That meant she needed to make enough gold to carry herself safely away, and to that intention she dedicated herself.

Word from the new arrivals was that the next big strike had been made by three lucky Swedes. Rumor was that gold was washing up on the beaches in Nome and although she didn't believe such talk, the men who had failed to secure a claim did and they were leaving in droves. Nome was over a thousand miles down the Yukon River. But now that the river flowed, ferries came and went with regularity, carrying goods and passengers, and would do so until the freeze-up, after which only the dogsleds used the river as frozen highway. It was best for her to follow them and quickly, before the need to be with Jack overcame her last shred of dignity.

Jack's business was well under way. By early October he'd built eleven machines and sold four already. They were up and running in the mines and the initial reports were so favorable he had appointments with three other mine owners.

As part of each agreement, he trained the operators in the use of the engine and taught them precautions so as not to be scalded by the steam. The contract stipulated bracing the ceilings, for he did not want a repeat of his accident. He believed firmly that his own mishap was the reason that it had taken so long to get his operation rolling. Word had spread that his machine caused cave-ins and that was bad for business. But now the results spoke for themselves.

Business was good. It was his personal life that was a tangle. He'd received four more letters from his mother begging him to come home. She was certain they could find a likely match if he were willing to look in circles outside New York.

Jack found himself making opportunities to run into Lily on the street. She always reacted in the same way. Her eyes went wide and then she plastered a false smile upon her face that would have done the women back home proud. She'd ask about his health or the business, but before he could tell her anything she'd excuse herself for some appointment or another.

He was a fool and he knew it. But he didn't know how to fix it. He hadn't meant to insult her, had only been trying to find a way for them. But Lily was a proud woman and it pained him that he'd hurt her so deeply.

Jack left town for his appointment craning his neck as he always did for a glimpse of Lily. He did not see her as he headed up the Eldorado to Claim #16, owned and operated by Fred Anderson.

The day was cold and cloudy, the tiny ice crystals stinging his cheek as he reached Anderson's mine earlier than expected. He found the miners working the end of an overnight shift. The foreman was covered in grime except for a band across his broad forehead where his hat must have been.

"Oh, so you're the inventor. Nice to meet you. We're running four times our regular tonnage and now that we've got the second steamer up, it'll go even faster."

Jack frowned. "What second steamer?"

"The boss bought a boiler from Kentucky Jim and rigged a nozzle—a bigger one—from a fire hose and he ordered another boiler that will arrive before the freeze-up. That'll give us three."

Jack felt a prickling unease crawling up his neck like an army of ants.

"You've braced the ceiling?"

"Yup. From the nozzle to a good twenty feet back."

"That's not enough!"

Next thing he knew he was running with the foreman at his heels. He reached the first group of miners on the steamer he'd constructed, but they couldn't hear him shouting over the sound of the nozzle blasting the gravel. The air was so wet it scared Jack to the core. He glanced up and saw only the operator stood under the bracing he had insisted run the length of the mineshafts. Jack turned a lever, releasing the steam. All the men turned toward him.

"Out!" he cried, grabbing one man after another and shoving them toward the main tunnel.

They stumbled back into the main shaft and stared at him as if he'd lost his mind. But when the crew foreman recognized Jack, he ordered them out and the men scrambled up the shaft toward safety as he reached the operator and sent him up as well.

"How many more?" he called to the fleeing man.

"Nine down below," he called back, still scrambling toward the surface.

Jack grabbed the lantern and headed down the main shaft. He could hear the other engine farther down. He lifted the lantern and looked at the ceiling, noting that water dripped from the passage. This was bad—really bad.

He reached the men, standing below the braced portion of the tunnel and turned off the steam.

"You're weakening the ceiling. Out! Everybody out!"

The men did as he ordered, but the tunnel was wide enough for only one at a time. Jack watched the lights retreating with the men as he waited his turn to flee. There was no sound with the first collapse, just a light that was there and then gone. Three more lights winked out as the men closest to him turned and ran back. He could see the lanterns bobbing before their terrified faces as they ran hunched over. There was a horrible scream cut short as more of the ceiling broke loose.

Only three men made it to the braced location to join him and the operator of the nozzle. Four of the nine now stood with Jack in the shelter of the timbers.

The men dug frantically through the loose gravel. The first man they unearthed was already dead. They dug no farther.

"They're all gone," cried one miner.

"Calvin was first. He might have made it out," said another.

"I saw him fall," said the last. "He's dead."

The first miner began to weep.

"Douse the fire in the boiler," ordered Jack.

"But it's light," argued the second.

"The fire will eat up all our oxygen."

One of the men snatched up the cask of water. Jack grabbed his arm.

"No. We may need that. Just scatter the coals on the ground."

They did. The embers glowed an eerie orange. Two lanterns remained. They doused one and turned the wick low on the other.

"They'll start digging us out as soon as the tunnel is safe," assured Jack.

But how much of the steam-soaked tunnel had come down? Would help reach them before their air ran out?

Lily dressed, stopped at the bank and then headed for the steamer offices. She had finally earned a tidy amount, enough to carry her to Nome and allow her to set up in a new boomtown. The threatening skies gave her the push she needed and by the time she reached the docks it was snowing in earnest. She watched the flakes vanish into the river. Soon it would be ice once more, the steamers would cease and the only way out would be by dog team — and Jack had her dog.

She picked a steamer leaving on Friday. That gave her six days to get her affairs in order and to retrieve Nala. Lily poured gold from her pouch into the scales to the correct measure and bought a one-way ticket to Nome. As soon as she lifted the ticket she felt ill at the thought of leaving Jack.

She headed up Front Street clutching her ticket with grim determination, knowing that Nala was just the excuse she needed to see him. If she thought about the reality of never seeing Jack again she'd lose her nerve. She was just going to get her dog. She put one more foot before the other.

"You're a fool over that man, Lily, and he'll be your ruination."

"Miss Lily?"

Had she spoken aloud? She turned to see Amos Luritz, the tailor, standing before her.

"Good morning," she said.

"Miss Lily, wait until you hear. Such news, I have. My business is so good, mending and sewing all day that I can't keep up. I had to hire an assistant!" he said, beaming. "Such a blessing and who would have guessed my fortune is coming from thread instead of gold? And it's all because of you. You gave me a business here."

"No, no. It's because you work hard and you are a very good tailor."

"Come spring I'll have enough to buy a ticket down the Yukon on one of these fine ferries. Sure will beat walking all the way from Dyea. And in Seattle, I'll find a steamer to take me all the way home to New York." His smile changed into a look of surprise when he noticed that she held a ferry ticket in her hand. "Are you leaving, too, Miss Lily?"

"I might be." No, she was. Why did she say *might?*

"What about your singing? What about your partner, the inventor?"

Was she really ready to sail to a new camp without him?

Lily squeezed the ticket, indecision twisting her insides. She should go, but she longed to stay.

"Mr. Luritz, I won this at cards and the company won't exchange it for cash. It's only to Nome and it leaves on Friday. Would you like it?"

She held out the ticket.

"No, no, Miss Lily, you've given me too much already."

She smiled. "But what about your beautiful daughters? Are you really going to spend another winter without them?"

He hesitated, eyeing the ticket. "I can't take it."

"You'll be home by Christmas."

He accepted the gift.

"Chanukah," he corrected. "Would you like to see their pictures now?"

Lily nodded. "Yes, I would."

He took a creased studio portrait from his pocket and extended it. Lily looked at the bright-eyed daughters surrounding a smiling woman and knew that she wanted to be as happy as this tailor's wife. She wanted it with Jack.

"You need to get home to them," she whispered, her throat now constricted.

He nodded, taking the picture and looking down, brushing a finger over his wife's face. "I do." When he looked up his eyes were swimming in tears. "How can I thank you?"

"By getting back to your children, of course."

The shouting in the street brought both Lily and the tailor about.

A red-faced man with a sunken stomach and a full mustache shouted again.

"Cave-in!"

Lily's heart stopped. Where was Jack? Her knees went to water and the tailor caught her before she hit the boardwalk. Terrible possibilities arrested her, making it hard to breathe.

"Miss Lily?"

"Where?" she whispered.

"Anderson's claim," shouted the stampeder. "All men to the site for digging."

She found she could breathe again, until she remembered that Anderson was using Jack's invention.

She headed out with the others.

She was nearly to the claim when Nala greeted her. Jack was here.

Lily sank to her knees, hugged her dog and prayed.

"Please, heavenly Father, let him be aboveground."

But he wasn't. The information was confusing and she had to speak to many men to learn that fifteen had been down in the mine on two steam engines. Jack had cleared six from the first machine and was heading to the next when the shaft gave way.

Lily found one of the survivors, a pale Welshman named Bobby Durham. A dirty, lopsided black hat sat low over his eyes that darted about in a frantic sort of way. He was smeared with mud and still shaking.

"Where's Jack Snow?" she asked.

"Dunno."

"You were with the second crew?"

He nodded, wiping the sweat from his face and smearing the mud onto his cheek. "I'd be dead if not for him. Brian was right behind me. Then the others."

"Where's Brian, then?" she asked.

He put his head in his hands and wept.

Lily clasped his shoulder.

Durham began a steady rocking to accompany his sobs.

"The others?" she demanded.

His voice was muffled by his hands pressed over his mouth, but she made it out.

"Behind me when the ceiling fell." He looked at her, his eyes crazed with grief. "The whole thing slipped loose and fell."

"Wasn't the tunnel braced?"

"Over the engine."

Lily's stomach churned as she realized what might have happened. She swept the area for Anderson. She found him, ordering men about.

"Mr. Anderson."

He turned to her, his face registering surprise at finding her here. "Miss Lily!"

"Was the tunnel braced?"

"I got no time for this now."

"Jack told me that the entire tunnel had to be braced so the steam wouldn't weaken the earth."

Anderson looked around at the men who had gone still and silent.

"He never said so."

Now she understood. Wood was expensive and Anderson had not done as he was told. Jack had come to check on operations, found the oversight and ordered the miners out. Her eyes narrowed on him, but she reined in her fury. This was not the time.

"How many men are trapped in there?"

Anderson cleared his throat. "Nine unaccounted for."

"And Jack?"

Anderson motioned with his head. "Among them."

Durham was on his feet now and facing Anderson. "He came to warn us. Told us to get out. Saved my life." Durham stepped up to Anderson. "You knew?"

Obviously, the miner had figured out who was responsible, and much as Lily would have liked to let Durham strike Anderson, she needed information.

"Was any of it braced?"

Anderson nodded. "Yes, over the engines, where the ceiling is wettest. I never knew that this could happen. I swear to God."

Lily knew it was a lie. Soon the others would know as well, for though she had not spoken to Jack, she'd heard from her regular customers who worked for grubstakes that Jack came to the mines to teach them how to use the engine. But she'd gain nothing by arguing.

Four or more hours had passed and they had achieved nothing. How much air would there be in the small chamber in the frozen earth? Had any of them even reached the braced portion?

Lily went to the mine entrance, now buzzing with men hauling out dirt in a bucket brigade. The buckets traveled hand to hand like a centipede moving its legs. Lily stared at the pile of earth they had moved and tried not to let the tiny flame of hope within her die.

She sat helpless beside Nala as the pile of earth grew. Shouts came from inside the tunnel.

"They found a body," came the call repeated from one to the next.

Lily's heart stopped as she waited. Another hour passed before the earth released the man. Durham's partner, Brian, just two yards back of him, was carried out on a plank. Dirt clung to his clothing. Someone had covered his face with a red handkerchief. But the bruising on his hands and the unnatural concavity of his chest deformed the corpse. Lily held her breath at the horror while the procession passed before her.

Durham howled like a frightened child as his friend was laid on the cold ground. Lily knelt beside him and prayed for the Lord to save the man she loved.

She sat back on her heels as the realization settled over her like a shroud. She loved Jack and she might never get the chance to tell him. What if she had lost him for good?

Grief, black as poison, welled within her. Inside, she screamed out her pain and horror. Outwardly, she could not even lift her hand to wipe her face.

Durham had recovered himself somewhat and swept an arm about her.

She turned to him. "Jack's gone, isn't he?"

He blinked at her, his eyes red-rimmed and watery.

"He was shouting and pushing us. Last I saw him he was headed deeper to the second team."

Lily pressed her hands to her face and sobbed.

The miner continued. "But that means he was well back and closest to the section they braced. He might have made it under the timbers before all hell broke loose."

Lily lifted her head. Jack would have placed himself behind the others as he ushered them out and that act of heroism might just have saved him from the falling rock. They needed to get to him quickly.

She clasped Durham's forearm. "How long would the air last?"

The weary miner pushed his dirty fingers beneath the crown of his hat and scratched his head. "I don't rightly know."

Dark came early now and the icy snowfall added to the misery. The men in the bucket brigade stood, cold and wet, passing the gravel from one to the next as twilight closed in and lanterns were set every few feet along the line.

It was full dark when they dragged out the mangled body of Calvin Toddy. Hope flagged as the men acknowledged that the chances of saving anyone was dropping with the temperature. Anderson's men stayed, but some of the volunteers abandoned the line. Men who had come to the aid of the victims were not going to waste precious days and hours digging dead men from the earth, not when the breath of winter was already on them and the smallest streams showing thin coatings of ice at night.

The pace slowed as a skeleton crew continued grimly through the night, sure that their rescue mission had changed to one of recovery.

Lily stood in grim silence as a pall settled over them all. The black shroud of grief threatened to take her again. Even if the men had survived the collapse, she recognized now that they wouldn't reach them in time.

That meant she had seen Jack for the last time, heard the final utterance from his lips and received her last kiss.

What had she said to him on the street yesterday? She could not recall, but realized that she should have followed her heart and thrown herself into his arms, instead of cloaking herself in her foolish dignity. Now it was too late.

Chapter Twenty

Lily's ears rang as she stumbled along the path that led back toward Dawson. Someone clasped her elbow, supporting her, keeping her moving.

"No!" She dropped to her knees in the dirt.

Jack was back there. Alive or dead, he was there and she would stay until he was found.

Against the blackness that threatened to consume her, she fixed on the pinprick of light. Jack had been last in line to leave. He might be under a small section of the tunnel that had been braced…waiting in the darkness. At this second, he might still live.

Lily found her feet and retraced her steps.

She found Anderson sitting at the mine entrance, directing men to send the dirt from the bucket brigade through the Long Tom to extract any gold.

Lily fumed. He had the manpower to search for

gold but not to dig out his men. It took a moment to realize that the men on the line were no longer passing the buckets from hand to hand, but carrying them several yards each.

"Where are all the others?"

Anderson shifted the cigar to the opposite side of his mouth. "Gone, like you should be."

"But they may be alive."

Anderson said nothing to this. Instead he brushed off the snow that clung to his coat and shifted the soggy cigar from one side of his mouth to the other.

"I'm sorry, Miss Lily. Men aren't going to leave their own diggings to muck about after men that's clearly passed. Winter's coming. They got to get the gold out while the water's flowing."

Lily felt the darkness creeping stealthily forward, threatening to take her to that place where she could not fight again. She pushed against it. Jack needed her.

"We could hire more men."

"What about if you do the singing and I do the mining?"

It was all she could do not to point out his short-comings to date.

"What if *I* paid for a team of miners to dig?"

He blew a frustrated breath past the cigar which had long ago gone out. "I'm already digging. Tunnel's only wide enough for one man. And I'll have them run twenty-four hours."

"I could tunnel alongside you or…" Lily paused as the idea sprang at her all at once. Could it work? "How deep is the tunnel?"

"Hit bedrock at eighteen feet and been tunneling along it for some time."

"Why don't we tunnel straight down from the top?"

Anderson sat back and thought. "It's less earth, but the chances of hitting the steam engine right dead on, well it's twenty to one."

"What are their chances if you go in the main tunnel?"

He'd run out of excuses and so just stared at her a moment.

"It's a waste of time and money," he said at last.

"But what if it's my time and my money?" she countered.

"The dirt you dig is mine."

She nodded her acceptance of his terms.

"I'll get you the wood to set the fires and thaw the ground, and, hell…" He rubbed his neck. "I'll need to hire new miners anyhow. Might as well do it sooner as later. You'll have a crew soon as I can raise one."

"Thank you."

He removed his cigar and fixed her with a steady stare. "Snow was a lucky man."

Jack closed his eyes and prayed that the other steam engine had not been crushed in the tunnel collapse, for they'd need it if there was any hope of moving all the earth between them and the outside. Then he prayed for the souls of the men he'd tried to send to safety, only to see them fall.

When he opened his eyes he noticed the lantern flame flickering. He knew the lantern ate their oxygen, but he could not bring himself to snuff it. Somehow to sit in icy darkness was too much to bear. The effort of digging or using the steam engine would burn up too much air. None of the men had a watch and time did funny things when there was no daylight. Had it been twenty-four hours or two days? He listened for the sound of digging, praying that help would come.

He needed to see her again, needed to tell Lily that he'd been a fool. How could he ever have thought of his partner as anything less than what she was—the object of his desire, the reason to go on living and the equal partner he did not deserve? He didn't need to return to New York, and it pained him that he had set himself such a vengeful ambition. The one person whose opinion really mattered and the only one who believed he could succeed was Lily.

If he lived, he'd tell her what a fool he was. He'd beg her forgiveness and pray she would take him back.

Lily looked out over the chaos of the rescue. The first steam engine had been recovered. But they had found no survivors. In twenty-four hours she had the wood hauled up the mountain to the digging site and erected tents for the workers to rest when they were not digging.

She had set up a kitchen on-site, brought in food and men to prepare it. But they had made only twelve feet in the first twenty-four hours. Now at the thirty-sixth hour they were down eighteen feet and had hit neither tunnel nor bedrock.

What if they missed the men by a few yards?

Anderson's first team continued to dig slowly through the collapsed tunnel, finding no more dead, although five men remained missing.

The shift ended and the workers, tired and dirty, lined up to be fed.

That afternoon the Mounties arrived to begin an investigation of the collapse. They interviewed Lily and several of the miners, while Lily chaffed at the delay.

The new foreman, Doug Donaldson, a thin man with a knobby nose and a knot on his forehead, came to her at the kitchen tent. The snow had changed to rain, hampering their efforts to burn the earth enough to melt the ever-present ice.

"Are the fires going out again?" she asked wearily. Her bones ached now from the tension. "I told you to build them under the cover of the roof of the shelter and just transfer them."

"Coals won't do no good. We've done struck bedrock."

Lily's stomach flipped. Had they missed the tunnel or was there was no tunnel to strike?

She rushed to the hole that more resembled a well than a mine shaft. Had they dug too far forward or too far back, a little right or a foot left? She didn't know.

From down below the clang of steel on rock reverberated through the soles of her boots.

Lily tried to think which way the tunnel had been. No, that wasn't right. She meant which way the tunnel *was*.

The tunnel lay on bedrock and the men were not above or below that. That left a full circle of choices to try. She had often thought, when creeping down an alley in San Francisco or a dark hallway in the tenements, that distances seemed longer in the blackness. With that slim knowledge base, she made her decision. The clanging ceased and from down below came the shout of one of the men.

"It's solid, Miss Lily," the digger cried. "Now what?"

"Dig back toward the tunnel entrance." She pointed, trying to force a calm confidence into her voice. "That way. We've just missed it."

A moment later she heard the sound of a pick striking frozen ground.

Lily thought of her mother and the last act of love

she had performed for her, preparing her body for burial, and she wondered how much longer she could pretend that she had some meaningful reason to continue, that there was a shred of hope.

Jack straightened. His chest rose and fell with rapid, increasingly useless breaths. The lantern flickered dangerously and he knew they were reaching the end. He couldn't tell if the light was dimming or if it was his vision.

"What was that?" croaked Henderson.

"A vibration. Did you feel it?" said McKinsky.

"I don't feel nothing."

The men sat still and silent in the darkness. Seconds ticked with the rapid beating of his starving heart. Then it came again.

"There!" cried Henderson.

"I felt it," whispered McKinsky.

"Coming from that way," said Jack, inching toward the front of the tunnel. "Grab your picks. Hit the bedrock so they know we're here."

Just as the men snatched up their tools, the lantern sputtered and snuffed out.

Lily sat at the opening of the hole, watching the bucket of dirt slowly rising from the earth on the pulley system the men had rigged. They might just as well be digging with a pair of tweezers for all the earth they moved. It was too far down to start a fire. By the time they set it and let it die out the shift would pass, so she had ordered them to use their picks.

Down below her in the hole the men stood to wipe their foreheads, stilling for the time it took to draw the damp handkerchief across their faces, and she resented the delay.

"Damn, I've a powerful thirst," said one. "Think she'd lower down some water?"

"Would you want the man digging you out to stop for water? No rest until the shift is done."

"What's that?" said the first.

"What's what?"

"That shaking in my feet."

They stilled, both worrying that the twenty feet of frozen earth might somehow break loose and bury them as well.

"Feel it?"

"Yeah, like someone tapping," whispered the other, and then let out a shout. "Miss Lily! There's somebody banging on the bedrock!"

Her head and shoulders appeared over the opening, placing her in silhouette, like an angel coming from heaven above.

"Which direction?" she shouted, excitement ringing in her voice.

The men put their ears to the frozen ground and listened. They shared a knowing look and one nodded.

"This way," said one.

"Then dig, boys! Dig like it was you trapped in that pit," she called.

The picks rang against the soil, chipping the frozen earth as if it were baked clay. A niche appeared and then a foothold and then a divot. The earth would not yield easily, but the men were strong and determined.

"Stop, stop!" shouted one. "Listen."

They did, but heard nothing in response.

"The tapping's stopped," they shouted in unison.

Lily lay on her belly, peering down.

"Then dig faster!"

They scrambled to do her bidding. The picks whistled and clanged and then came a hollow sound a moment before they punched a hole.

They thrust the lantern into the gap and peered inside.

One got his head and shoulders into the tunnel.

"They're not moving," he called. "I think they're dead!"

Chapter Twenty-One

The words pierced Lily's heart like shards of broken glass. But Lily did not let her heart break, not yet. Not until she'd seen Jack herself. Instead she did what she always did when her back was to the wall—she fought. She shouted from her place at ground level, her voice now authoritative and shrill as any commanding officer.

"Don't think! Drag them out. Hurry!"

The miner reached a tentative hand forward and clasped the arm of the nearest man. He gave a groan.

"Alive! This one's alive."

Lily turned from the hole. "Get a rope and some men to haul these miners up."

The first body was yanked from the shaft dirty and still. She could not tell who the miner might be. She paced at ground level like a caged animal, waiting, praying as the man was hauled up.

He crested the rim.

"Dan Slater," cried one of the miners. He knelt beside the inert form. "Breathing."

They carried him to the tarp and laid him on a blanket, wetting his face with water on a rag. His eyes fluttered open.

"Am I dead, then?" he whispered.

Lily stroked his cheek. "Alive, Mr. Slater, as I pray are your fellows. How many still down there?"

She knew eight were unaccounted for and she held her breath for his answer.

"Four."

She tried not to let that crush her hopes.

"Their names?"

"Henderson, McKinsky, and the damned engineer who made that hell machine."

Lily left him in the care of the tailor, Amos Luritz, who had followed her to the mine and had refused to leave with the rest of them. She hurried back to the hole where another man was lifted, limp as a rag doll. This was Henderson, the operator of the engine, and he did not revive so quickly. In fact, he did not rouse at all, but his breathing was regular so Lily returned to her place. The next man crawled out on his own: McKinsky, his shoulders so broad he could barely fit through the opening. It took four men to haul him to the lip of the crater where he kicked and clawed his way back to the surface. When she looked back down she saw another still figure with the two diggers.

"Cummings," called one and motioned for the rope.

Where was Jack?

And then she saw him, crawling weakly from his prison.

"Snow," called the miner.

"Jack!" she cried, lying on her belly in the mud to be closer to him, reaching both hands down into the pit.

He lifted his dirty face and held a hand up as a visor as if the dim light from the cloudy day was too bright for him to see.

"Lily?"

They looped the rope beneath his arms.

"What are you doing here?"

One of the diggers slapped him on the shoulder. "She'll be real glad to see *you*."

Jack's feet left the ground and he dangled between heaven and hell, ascending like an angel to the pearly gates. Lily was here. He blinked against the bright light that nearly blinded him after so much blackness. The last he remembered was the hammering and then…then he could not breathe and then, nothing.

He looked at Lily's sweet, stern face, staring at him as a mother would at a wayward child, happy at his return and angry that he'd ever left. He raised a hand in recognition at his fierce little partner.

How brilliant to dig straight down. They never would have reached them in time otherwise.

From below came the call. "That's all. Beyond this pocket, the tunnel's collapsed."

"Haul them up," Lily said to the men working the pulley system. "Take my hand, Jack," Lily said.

She grasped hold and would not let go, even as the men dragged him back to the surface. His legs gave way, but they pulled him back from the chasm. The sweet fresh air filled his lungs and snow melted on his cheek. What a miracle!

She fell to her knees beside him and he looked up into the face that he had longed to see.

He grinned at her. "Howdy, partner," he said.

"Oh, Jack!" Lily cried, and threw herself at him, clasping her two small arms around him and squeezing so tight that she pressed the very air from his lungs. "I thought I'd lost you forever. I thought…"

Was she crying? He drew back, holding her face between his hands.

"Lily, I'm all right now."

"I was afraid I'd never get a chance to tell you…to say…oh, Jack." She kissed him hard and then drew back to assure herself that he was really here in her arms.

He stared at her. "I must have died after all then."

She clung tighter. "Don't joke about that. Jack, I was wrong about everything. I love you, and all I want in the world is to be by your side. If you still want me to be your mistress, I'll go with you to New York or anywhere you say."

Jack stilled, but Lily clung, afraid that she'd lose him again, afraid that he'd changed his mind and no longer wanted her.

"You love me?" He stared, his expression so serious it frightened her.

She nodded.

Her eyes rounded and the lump in her throat seemed to grow. She could barely breathe past it.

"Please, Jack, say something."

"I was wrong about us, wrong to ask you to come with me."

Her heart, already battered as an old tin pail, now twisted in dread. After all this, had she lost him anyway?

She interrupted him before he forced her to go. "Please, Jack, give me a chance to prove how much I love you."

He stroked her cheek. "You already have, time and time again. But I don't want you to be my mistress, Lily. I'm ashamed I ever asked you."

Ashamed. Yes, it had been the trouble from the start.

"I understand, Jack. I know the way of it."

He placed his hands on hers, holding each one as if she were precious to him instead of an obligation he must discharge. Well, she'd not stand in his way. She loved him too much to be a shameful little secret or worse an open scandal. His thumb swept in circles over the back of her hands.

"I don't think you do."

How she would miss the deep rich timbre of his voice.

"When I was trapped, it was your face I saw and your voice I longed to hear again. I can't get on without you. I've fallen in love with you, Lily Delacy Shanahan, and I want us to be together—always."

"What?"

"I love you, too, Lily. Madly and with my whole heart."

Her head snapped up and she looked into his whiskey eyes as the shock of his words washed through her.

"Love me?" She gaped.

He nodded, one corner of his mouth quirking as he continued to hold her gaze. "Desperately."

The cresting wave of joy broke over her and then reality returned, stealing her elation. "But, oh, Jack, what should we do?" His family wouldn't accept her, his friends, his associates.

"Marry, I hope."

The astonishment of his proposal brought her scrambling in an effort to stand, but he held her.

"Lily, I love you and I don't want a mistress. I want a wife—I want *you* as my wife."

She was shaking her head madly from side to side. "But I'll ruin everything. You *can't* marry me."

"I can, if I can convince you to forgive me for my colossal arrogance and agree to accept me."

Lily's legs went rubbery and her head began to spin. The ringing in her ears made her own voice sound tinny and strange. "But what about New York, your mother and…everything?"

"Funny about that, I don't really think I belong there anymore. Not when everything I have come to love is here."

"What do you mean? You're not going back?"

He drew her into the shelter of his arms.

"I realized something down in that hole. I'm not the man I was when I came here. I feel sorry for those fools back there, jostling for social position and spending all they have to impress people they don't like to begin with. That's not for me anymore."

He stroked her cheek and she felt her heart stop. What was he talking about?

"You want to stay in the Yukon."

He nodded. "There's nothing I want or need that I can't find right here."

It was her fondest desire to remain in the northern territory, and to have Jack at her side would make the adventure so much sweeter.

"We could make a life here, Lil. You and me. What do you say?"

"I say yes!" She hugged him.

He cradled Lily against his strong body, leaning

her back, taking her lips with his in a kiss filled with love and promise.

Nala barked, startling them both. Lily drew back as her black Newfoundland licked Jack across the muddy dark stubble of his cheek.

Lily laughed. "I think she approves."

Jack grabbed Nala and hugged her, too. The three of them sat in the mud together and Lily thought she had never been so happy.

Jack made an attempt to stand, but swayed. Lily was there helping him as she had been from the start. He looped a hand about her shoulders and stretched, drawing a breath of air and then grinned down at her.

"We'll have a grand life, Lily, one full of adventure just like your mother wanted for you. And one that will make us both proud, because it will be ours."

"But Jack, what about your mother and sister?"

"We'll see they get what they need, help them all we can, just the same as we will your family. Soon as we get on our feet again."

"I'll help you, Jack."

He nodded, then swallowed, as if something blocked his throat. "Yes, I know you will, just as you always have. I should have seen that a long time ago. That day I met you on the beach was the luckiest of my life."

She patted his chest with her open hand. "You didn't think so at the time."

"Because I didn't understand then that you were the only partner for me."

"You're sure?"

"Yes, Lily. Partners forever and always."

Epilogue

One month after the collapse, Commissioner Ogilvie of the North-West Mounted Police completed his investigation, finding Jack blameless and commending him on the rescue of the miners. Anderson was cited and agreed to pay damages for the deaths at his claim.

The mine owners using Jack's engine were allowed to recommence operations and the general consensus was that the steam greatly aided the miners and was less dangerous than setting fires in the shafts.

Lily had left the stage to prepare for her wedding and on a cold November day she stood on a crate in the back of St. Mary's Church as Amos Luritz finished the hem of her wedding dress.

The tailor had missed the last ferry out to help

with the rescue. Lily meant to see he was aboard the first boat come spring.

She fussed with the scalloped lace trim at her throat, admiring the sheen of ivory satin bodice as Mr. Luritz finished attaching the last of the pearl buttons that lay straight as her spine.

A knock sounded at the door. "They're ready, Miss Lily."

"Yes, coming."

Amos bit the thread and stepped back, clasping his hands and smiling with delight.

"You remind me of my Tessa. Such a beauty. May you have all the happiness we've shared."

He offered his hand and Lily stepped down. "Thank you, Amos."

"You'll excuse me for being a nosy yenta, but who is walking you down the aisle?"

Lily lowered her head a moment, then gathered herself up, not wanting to spoil her happiness with even a moment's thought of the father who had never been there.

"I'm afraid I am walking alone."

"Well, I've never been in a church before, Miss Lily, but if you'd grant a man his wish, I'd be honored to escort you to your husband. Such a blessing."

Her heart twisted and she was afraid she might cry.

She extended her hand. "Oh, Amos, I'd be very grateful."

He lifted his elbow and she clasped it. When they reached the door she turned and snapped her fingers. Nala, sleeping beside the stove, startled awake, stretched and trotted to her side.

Mr. Luritz reached in his pocket, retrieving the remnant of lace and the tiny blue satin pillow which held two perfect golden rings cast from nuggets from Jack's claim.

He stooped and tied the lace about Nala's neck. "Such a ring bearer I've never seen."

Lily scratched behind her dog's velvety ears. "It wouldn't feel right not to have her here with us."

Amos patted Nala's wide black head and stood, opened the door and offered his elbow once more.

She nodded to Bat Samuelson, who cracked his knuckles and began to play a fast, upbeat version of "Ta-Ra-Ra Boom-De-Ay." The tinny chords drowned out the sound of ice hitting the windows behind her. It had been a struggle to get the piano across the street from the Forks with the ice and snow now freezing the ruts in place until the thaw, but Lily had managed it. Everyone stood and turned to look as she paused in the entrance. The assemblage, mostly men, removed their hats and pressed them to their best clothing, smiling at her.

"Go on, girl," Lily said to Nala.

Her dog glanced back and then preceded them, stopping only once to sniff one of the pews. Amos clasped Lily's hand at his elbow and lifted his chin, setting them in motion. As she began her journey down the aisle, the piano player switched to "Oh, Promise Me."

The miners, obviously unaccustomed to weddings, whistled and applauded as she passed. Two men even waved. She blew them a kiss.

The little church glowed with candlelight, shining bright as a new penny. Pine boughs tied with white ribbon decorated the altar before which the minister waited, Bible in hand.

There to her right, stood Jack. He wore a black suit and a gleaming white shirt, a thin black tie with a gold nugget tie tack big enough to choke a cat. His thick hair was combed, parted and slicked back; she imagined he might have looked like this back in that world he had left for her.

Amos took Lily's hand and placed it in Jack's.

"You be good to this one," he said. "She's got a golden heart."

Jack nodded and guided her to his side.

"Dearly beloved," began the priest.

Lily knew that she would remember this day for the rest of her life.

"May I have the rings?" asked the priest.

"Nala," said Lily.

Her dog stood still and elegant as a greyhound as the priest untied the ribbon and freed the rings.

Jack accepted hers and took her hand in his. Lily held her breath as he slipped it onto her finger.

Then it was her turn to glide the golden circle onto Jack's hand.

The priest finished with the words that joined them together and said, "You may kiss your bride."

The congregation roared their approval, hats flew into the air and Nala began to howl. But Lily did not hear it, for she was in Jack's arms, right where she belonged and she was certain that their adventures together had only just begun.

* * * * *

COMING NEXT MONTH FROM

HARLEQUIN®
HISTORICAL

Available September 27, 2011

- **SNOWFLAKES AND STETSONS**
  by **Jillian Hart, Carol Finch, Cheryl St.John**
  (Western Anthology)

- **INNOCENT COURTESAN TO ADVENTURER'S BRIDE**
  by **Louise Allen**
  (Regency)
  Third in *The Transformation of the Shelley Sisters* trilogy

- **THE CAPTAIN'S FORBIDDEN MISS**
  by **Margaret McPhee**
  (Regency)

- **THE DRAGON AND THE PEARL**
  by **Jeannie Lin**
  (Chinese Tang Dynasty)

You can find more information on upcoming
Harlequin® titles, free excerpts and more at
www.HarlequinInsideRomance.com.

REQUEST YOUR FREE BOOKS!

HARLEQUIN® HISTORICAL:
Where love is timeless

2 FREE NOVELS PLUS 2 **FREE GIFTS!**

YES! Please send me 2 FREE Harlequin® Historical novels and my 2 FREE gifts (gifts are worth about $10). After receiving them, if I don't wish to receive any more books, I can return the shipping statement marked "cancel." If I don't cancel, I will receive 6 brand-new novels every month and be billed just $5.19 per book in the U.S. or $5.74 per book in Canada. That's a savings of at least 17% off the cover price! It's quite a bargain! Shipping and handling is just 50¢ per book in the U.S. and 75¢ per book in Canada.* I understand that accepting the 2 free books and gifts places me under no obligation to buy anything. I can always return a shipment and cancel at any time. Even if I never buy another book, the two free books and gifts are mine to keep forever.

246/349 HDN FEQQ

Name   (PLEASE PRINT)

Address   Apt. #

City   State/Prov.   Zip/Postal Code

Signature (if under 18, a parent or guardian must sign)

Mail to the **Reader Service:**
IN U.S.A.: P.O. Box 1867, Buffalo, NY 14240-1867
IN CANADA: P.O. Box 609, Fort Erie, Ontario L2A 5X3

Not valid for current subscribers to Harlequin Historical books.

Want to try two free books from another line?
Call 1-800-873-8635 or visit www.ReaderService.com.

* Terms and prices subject to change without notice. Prices do not include applicable taxes. Sales tax applicable in N.Y. Canadian residents will be charged applicable taxes. Offer not valid in Quebec. This offer is limited to one order per household. All orders subject to credit approval. Credit or debit balances in a customer's account(s) may be offset by any other outstanding balance owed by or to the customer. Please allow 4 to 6 weeks for delivery. Offer available while quantities last.

Your Privacy—The Reader Service is committed to protecting your privacy. Our Privacy Policy is available online at www.ReaderService.com or upon request from the Reader Service.

We make a portion of our mailing list available to reputable third parties that offer products we believe may interest you. If you prefer that we not exchange your name with third parties, or if you wish to clarify or modify your communication preferences, please visit us at www.ReaderService.com/consumerschoice or write to us at Reader Service Preference Service, P.O. Box 9062, Buffalo, NY 14269. Include your complete name and address.

HH11B

*Harlequin Romantic Suspense presents the latest book
in the scorching new* KELLEY LEGACY *miniseries
from best-loved veteran series author Carla Cassidy*

*Scandal is the name of the game as the Kelley family fights
to preserve their legacy, their hearts…and their lives.*

Read on for an excerpt from the fourth title
RANCHER UNDER COVER

*Available October 2011
from Harlequin Romantic Suspense*

"Would you like a drink?" Caitlin asked as she walked to the minibar in the corner of the room. She felt as if she needed to chug a beer or two for courage.

"No, thanks. I'm not much of a drinking man," he replied.

She raised an eyebrow and looked at him curiously as she poured herself a glass of wine. "A ranch hand who doesn't enjoy a drink? I think maybe that's a first."

He smiled easily. "There was a six-month period in my life when I drank too much. I pulled myself out of the bottom of a bottle a little over seven years ago and I've never looked back."

"That's admirable, to know you have a problem and then fix it."

Those broad shoulders of his moved up and down in an easy shrug. "I don't know how admirable it was, all I knew at the time was that I had a choice to make between living and dying and I decided living was definitely more appealing."

She wanted to ask him what had happened preceding that six-month period that had plunged him into the bottom of the bottle, but she didn't want to know too much about him. Personal information might produce a false sense of intimacy that she didn't need, didn't want in her life.

"Please, sit down," she said, and gestured him to the table. She had never felt so on edge, so awkward in her life.

"After you," he replied.

She was aware of his gaze intensely focused on her as she rounded the table and sat in the chair, and she wanted to tell him to stop looking at her as if she were a delectable dessert he intended to savor later.

Watch Caitlin and Rhett's sensual saga unfold amidst the shocking, ripped-from-the-headlines drama of the Kelley Legacy miniseries in

RANCHER UNDER COVER

*Available October 2011
only from Harlequin Romantic Suspense,
wherever books are sold.*

HARLEQUIN® HISTORICAL:
Where love is timeless

Make sure to pick up this Western Christmas anthology, featuring three delicious helpings of festive cheer!

Snowflakes and Stetsons

The Cowboy's Christmas Miracle
by Jillian Hart

Unfairly imprisoned, Caleb McGraw thinks nothing can touch him again. Until he sees his lost son and the caring woman who's given him a home.

Christmas at Cahill Crossing
by Carol Finch

A growing love for Rosalie Greer persuades ex-Texas Ranger and loner, Lucas Burnett, to become involved in a special Cahill Crossing Christmas.

A Magical Gift at Christmas
by Cheryl St.John

Meredith has always dreamed of a grand life but, stranded on a train, she finds she has everything she needs with just one strong man to protect her....

Available October 2011.

www.Harlequin.com

HH29659

Carol Marinelli

brings you her new romance

HEART OF THE DESERT

One searing kiss is all it takes for Georgie to know
Sheikh Prince Ibrahim is trouble....

But, trapped in the swirling sands, Georgie finally
surrenders to the brooding rebel prince—yet the
law of his land decrees that she can never
really be his....

Available October 2011.

Available only from Harlequin Presents®.